The Kick

Praise for *The Kick*

'A fine, considered and fascinating memoir of a life lived as close to the full as possible.'

John Banville, *New York Review of Books*

'A superb insight into the social transformation of post-imperial England and post-colonial Ireland in the middle of the last century – amusing and haunting.'

Declan Kiberd, *Irish Times*

'By turns funny, quirky and lyrical.'

Ciaran Carson, *Guardian*

'Murphy writes with dignity and candour.'

Karl Miller, *Spectator*

'His wonderful eye for fabric shines out especially when he quotes fragments from his notebooks.'

Ruth Padel, *Literary Review*

'A lively and even brave account of a rich and complicated life.'

John Montague, *Irish Times*

The Kick

A Memoir of the
Poet Richard Murphy

RICHARD MURPHY

CORK UNIVERSITY PRESS

Published in 2017 by
Cork University Press
Youngline Industrial Estate
Pouladuff Road, Togher
Cork, Ireland

British Library Cataloguing in Publication Data

A CIP catalogue record for this book is available from the British Library

ISBN: 978-1-78205-234-0

Typeset by Dominic Carroll, Ardfield, County Cork
Printed by Hussar Books, Poland

www.corkuniversitypress.com

To my beloved older sister, Mary Cookson,
a painter of talent, whose lifelong kindness
and generosity enabled me to write

Contents

List of Photographs

continued overleaf

Review of *The Kick* by John Banville

If an Irishman's home is his castle – or his coffin, in Leopold Bloom's mordant variation on the old saw – then certainly the poet Richard Murphy has seen more crenelations rise and fall than most of his fellow countrymen. Murphy comes from the Anglo-Irish upper middle class, those Protestants 'planted' in Ireland in Cromwellian times and earlier, a people for whom the house, and especially the Big House, was less a place of shelter, comfort and privacy than a symbol in stone and brick of a separate and stubbornly enduring culture.

He spent his early childhood among the mansions of the west of Ireland, with repeated long intervals in Ceylon, where his father was the colonial Mayor of Colombo, and where his mother did good works among the sick and saved the lives of thousands during a malaria epidemic. In adulthood he returned to the west, living in an isolated cottage, making himself into a poet, and earning his living from the sea; later he set out on restless wanderings in Ireland and abroad, building or renovating a series of houses, large and small, which in succession he left or lost, one of them to fire.

The place that dominates the earlier sections of *The Kick*, his elegant if inelegantly titled memoir, is the place of his birth, Milford, his maternal grandfather's house on the Mayo–Galway border, built in 1625:

> We were surrounded at Milford by dark mysterious old woods, where none of us dared to walk alone at night, full of hair-raising creatures that made weird sounds. Beyond the garden wall, too high to climb, an immense bog stretched as far as we could see, from the upstairs study window through the branches of a yew tree, to the pale blue hill of Castlehacket on the horizon.

Instead of building a house for his wife and children in Ireland, Murphy père had converted the former servants' quarters and kitchens at Milford to make a self-contained home, known rather grandly as the East Wing; there was no electricity, gas or telephone, and scant running water, but the five seasons that Murphy spent there with his mother and siblings and grandparents, which he describes without romantic frills, were an idyll, despite 'our predicament as an Anglo-Irish family, isolated under the aegis of a Protestant clergyman on a remote demesne in neutral Éire, dominated by Roman Catholic priests and threatened by German invasion.' It is a predicament from which Murphy, like so many of his Anglo-Irish brethren, has never quite escaped. He retains that ambivalent attitude toward his ancestry which is the subject of many of the finest essays of Hubert Butler. Here is Murphy describing his mother's antecedents:

> Her parents may not have had two pennies to rub together, as they used to say, but both had Anglo-Irish pedigrees, going back on her father's side to King Charles II and his mistress, Lucy Walters, through the brother of Patrick Sarsfield; while on her mother's family tree there dangled a French marquis, the poet Geoffrey Chaucer, and at the tip top – could you believe it? – William the Conqueror!

The ping! of that exclamation mark is the uncertain note that sounds repeatedly throughout these pages.

The figure of his mother commands the opening and the closing of the book. The early pages, in which Murphy, preparing to write his memoir, probes this formidable ninety-four-year-old's still sharp memory a year before her death, are a sort of overture weaving together in subtle and deliberately blurred fashion many of the themes that will be elaborated upon later. In a tea chest full of family papers, collected by his mother 'in seven countries and preserved through two world wars', he had found a diary which she had begun in 1914, at the age of sixteen.

She was born in Galway in 1898, and after she had married, ceasing to be Betty Ormsby and becoming Mrs W. Lindsay Murphy, she would sign her nationality on official forms as 'British and Irish', thus neatly attesting to a duality not only of nationality but of tribal allegiance. 'She was proud and ashamed of being Irish. Proud of the Irishmen, especially her relations, who had given their lives in Britain's wars; ashamed of Ireland's neutrality, and the bombing of Britain by the IRA before the Second World War.' One thinks of the novelist Elizabeth Bowen, another tough-hided Anglo-Irish lady whose deep and enduring love of Ireland did not prevent her doing a bit of low-level spying on the country for Britain during the Hitler war, and who always insisted that she belonged most authentically somewhere in the middle of the Irish Sea, halfway between her two beloved shores.

Murphy laboured – that seems the word – under another kind of duality, signalled early on when he recounts a dispute at his Church of Ireland christening in the Mayo village of Kilmaine between his grandfather, Reverend Thomas Ormsby, and the officiating clergyman, over whether the child was a boy or a girl; his grandmother put an end to the argument by asking, 'Why don't you look?' He was to be no sissy, however, and was always able to stand up for himself. At the end of a tea party given by his Aunt Bella – Dr Isabella Mulvany, bluestocking and educator, known to friends in her youth as 'the Chief' and bearing in Murphy's memory of her a strong physical resemblance to her Anglo-Irish contemporary Oscar Wilde – the child Richard, urged to say thank you, crossed the room instead and delivered the grande dame a smart kick, just for devilment.

Like so many boys who have difficulty locating their true sexuality – he refers to himself in adulthood as 'androgynous' – Murphy was in his earliest years extremely close to his mother, displaying so much affection toward her that she called him her 'kissing son', and addressed him in her letters to him at his first boarding school, at Baymount in Dublin, as 'My own K.S.'. When the eight-year-old Murphy revealed the secret of the code to a boy whom he considered a friend, he was immediately made a target of ridicule. He found a truer friend in Bernard Dobbs, in later years to be British ambassador to Laos, who in bed after lights out 'used to whisper to me about women's breasts'. These late-night anatomy lessons were about the extent of the instructions the prepubertal Murphy received in what used to be called the facts of life. 'The worst fault of Baymount was that women didn't add up to much in our masculine equations, with the result that my mind was poorly prepared for the later equations of sex.'

From Baymount he went with his brother Chris to the Canterbury Cathedral Choir School, where he was happy, but where one of his schoolfellows, catching a glimpse of Mrs Murphy on a visit, insisted she looked too young and beautiful to be the boys' mother, and 'spread a hurtful rumour that Chris and I were adopted'. The war and its dangers brought them back for a time to Milford, and the care of private tutors, one of whom, Miss Sarah Stokes, stirred young Richard's interest in poetry – 'It was enough for her to say that Milton was a great poet for me to want to capture the greatness of Milton.' But life in and around the East Wing had its practical side also. With a loan from his mother, Richard went into the poultry business, rearing a flock of Rhode Island Reds and selling the eggs, while Chris bought a herd of wild goats in Connemara and herded them by road and ferry to Milford, 'where he milked them and made some good cheese but little profit'. Richard, it seemed, was the more successful entrepreneur: 'My poultry were so profitable that the family expected me to become a businessman, in contrast to Chris.'

Back at school in wartime England, now at King's School in Cornwall, Murphy continued to undergo his never more than mournful sexual awakening. Here at night in the dormitory an older boy 'attacked me with fists before lights out and seduced me with whispers when five other boys who shared the room had fallen asleep', and climbed into his bed in the dark 'for the sake of a spasm of manual relief'. The boy was a monitor's 'kick', meaning one whom the monitor romantically fancied. At King's, the word could be applied to anything that produced excitement or pleasure, not necessarily sexual. 'The guilty kick I got at night made me hunger for purification through history, literature and music during the day.' The scene was set for – yes, you guessed it – Oxford.

Murphy applied for a scholarship to Magdalen College, along with Kenneth Tynan – 'He played with his fingers and sniffed like a horse nosing a trough' – and, again along with Tynan, was awarded what was known as a Demyship, after undergoing a viva voce conducted by C.S. Lewis, 'a short plump man who was sitting on a sofa smoking a pipe'. Lewis was to become both Murphy's and Tynan's tutor, and both have written of him in tones of unashamed adulation.

'My Oxford', Murphy admits, 'was a better preparation for a memoirist than a poet.' He gathered the usual quota of famous, colourful or eccentric acquaintances, including some, such as the future Faber editor Charles Monteith, who were to remain friends for life. On the day that he won his scholarship he was accosted in the street by John Simopoulos, the son of a former Greek ambassador to England, who was to be to Murphy what Anthony Blanche was to Charles Ryder in Waugh's *Brideshead Revisited*, inviting him to his rooms to listen to Bach and smoke Balkan Sobranie cigarettes, after which they lay down together and 'I let him unbutton my trousers while he unbuttoned his …'. Almost at once, however, Murphy flees, and next day in terror consults a doctor in the fear that he has contracted syphilis. 'Thereafter I went to chapel every day and read the lesson so well that I won an award.'

In the summer of 1946 Murphy returned to Milford suffering from depression. If 'mad Ireland' had, as Auden suggested in his great memorial poem, hurt Yeats into poetry, the country had an opposite effect on Murphy the nascent poet. 'Going to school and university in England', he writes, 'had allowed the west of Ireland, that mournful, impoverished, tempestuous country, to remain in my imagination as the most beautiful place in the world. Ireland would be my cure.' He did some serious reading that summer, finding in Yeats a favourite to displace Wordsworth, and before long had returned to full health. By now his parents had moved from Ceylon to Nassau, where his father succeeded the Duke of Windsor as governor of the Bahamas, and he went out to join them for an extended holiday. Suddenly, as it seems, the great world began to open before him:

> The news that I had passed my degree with second-class honours reached me in New York on the eve of my twenty-first birthday. That night Peter Hoguet, a playboy whose parents were friends of mine in Nassau, took me to a party at a nightclub on the roof of the St Regis given by the daughters of Joseph Kennedy. I was on my way to the Bahamas.

Ireland, however, was to call him back from the glitter of café society, via a stint as an unlikely insurance clerk in London, where after office hours he began to write poetry reviews for the *Spectator*. He was continuing to work hard at his own verse, and in 1951 he won the Æ Memorial Award, which brought with it a £100 prize, in those days a not inconsiderable sum.

Almost immediately he moved to a remote cottage in Rosroe near the mouth of Killary Harbour in County Mayo, one of the most beautiful sea-scapes in all Ireland. A former tenant of the house he was renting had been 'a German translator of sorts', according to neighbours, who had fed the birds roundabout until they were so tame the cats could catch them without effort. Lying in bed one day, Murphy spotted a wad of paper wedged between the rafters and the corrugated iron roof to stop the roof from rattling, and taking down the paper discovered two letters, one addressing 'My dear Ludwig' and the second 'Dear Professor Wittgenstein'.

The first of a number of fairly menial jobs that Murphy took was that of water bailiff for a neighbour who had been in Ceylon and whom he had known there; his job was to guard the salmon from night poachers along an eight-mile stretch of river that the neighbour was renting from Lord Sligo. It was at this time, too, that he fell in love with the pookaun, or *púcán* in Irish, a type of small fishing boat, nimble and quick, but hard to handle and dangerously unstable in bad weather. Later, Murphy was to purchase another kind of boat, a forty-year-old Galway hooker, in which he was for some years to earn his living, ferrying tourists on fishing trips in the often treacherous waters around the shores and islands of Mayo and Connemara. Murphy writes about the sea with the passion of a natural sailor, although he is painfully, and sometimes comically, honest about the many mishaps and near disasters that he experienced.

On the island of Inishbofin at the end of the 1950s Murphy met the man who, as one can read between the lines of *The Kick*, was to be the unrequited love of his life. Tony White was a highly talented but unsuccessful actor on the London stage who had thrown up the theatrical life to live on Ireland's west coast, a place that he loved with an almost violent and jealous passion – the friendship between the two men nearly foundered over Murphy's venture into ferrying tourists, which White believed would destroy the purity of this stretch of wild, unsullied coast. A tinge of real tragedy inflects the otherwise highly measured tone of the book, in the account of White's premature and avoidable death from an embolism following an accident in which he broke his leg badly in an amateur football match. Although he does not say so, it is possible that White's death soured the west for Murphy, and led to his leaving there for the more tranquil Wicklow and Dublin.

In 1955, surprisingly, perhaps, Murphy married. His wife was Patricia Strang née Avis, whom he first met in Paris in 1954, when they were both staying at the Cité Universitaire, and Avis pushed a note under his door announcing herself as a fellow poetry-lover, asking if he would like to meet her, and signing herself 'George Sand'. The daughter of an eccentric, domineering South African businessman, Avis already had the start of a brilliant career behind her. At seventeen she had got into Oxford when it was ten times harder for a woman to do so than a man, and had read medicine so as to have an excuse not to return to South Africa and her impossible father for seven years. Before she could qualify she had married a high-born Englishman, Colin Strang, had suffered seven miscarriages, and had found her way into a fast literary circle that included Kingsley Amis and Philip Larkin, with the latter of whom she had a brief affair. She and Murphy were married in London in 1955, and a year later they had a daughter, Emily. The following year Patricia suffered a late miscarriage. Murphy's account of burying his stillborn son is a fine example of the quiet power that he can bring to his writing, which is not at all a 'poet's prose', but is prosaic in the best and most solid sense, and all the more effective for that:

As clouds are dimming the moonlight, I shine a torch. He looks
like me. Yet also like a figurine moulded from clay and fired thousands of years ago. Having dug deep enough, I tip the body from
the bowl, gently, and look at him as he lies in the earth: head
with a high forehead, full of intelligence; nose and chin, mouth
and ears like mine in a photograph my mother has kept from my
infancy; the eyes closed. After touching my tongue, I inscribe on his
forehead with my forefinger the sign of the tree, and recite in the
name of the Father and of the Son and of the Holy Ghost, though
I do not believe in them. I bless him in his grave as I was blessed in
childhood; then bury my unborn son.

The marriage was an open one, which inevitably led to tensions and
recriminations. One of Patricia's lovers was a civil servant in the perhaps aptly
named Irish Department of External Affairs, who was also the author of a
book on French Catholic writers. This was Conor Cruise O'Brien. The three
met first for dinner at the Red Bank restaurant near the offices of the *Irish
Times*. The account of the evening and O'Brien's subsequent behaviour is a
fine example of Murphy's quiet ferocity in the skewering of those who have
wronged him:

> Conor sat facing us, often breaking into French to impress Patricia.
> I thought he was showing off but she was awed by his brilliance …
> Then he seemed to recognise and smile at a friend at the far end
> of the bar. Again and again he did this, usually after a witticism in
> French. I wondered whether we might ask the friend to join us,
> another sophisticate who might have amused Patricia. But in a
> quick glance over my shoulder I caught sight of Conor in a mirror
> on the far wall of the bar, smiling at himself.

According to Murphy, his wife never recovered from the stillbirth of her
son. They were living at one of Murphy's many houses, Lake Park, a Regency
fishing lodge in County Wicklow, which they had bought, with money
grudgingly donated by Patricia's father, from Ernest Gébler, who had lived
there with his wife, Edna O'Brien – in the way of most literary memoirists,
Murphy seems never to have encountered anyone who was not someone –
but now Patricia, bored and unhappy, wanted to move back to London. She
travelled to South Africa to get her father's permission to sell Lake Park, but

almost immediately wrote to Murphy from Johannesburg asking for a divorce. Murphy sought, and got, custody of his daughter, but his attitude toward his wife was, and is, stark: 'I hated her for wanting a divorce.' Much later in her sad life, far gone in drink and despair, Patricia was to commit suicide.

Indeed, suicide is a recurring theme in *The Kick*. Patricia's brother had already done away with himself, as had one of Murphy's school friends. And then there was Sylvia Plath. Murphy had met Plath and her husband, Ted Hughes, in the early 1960s, and it was when the couple were staying with him at his house in Cleggan in 1962 that Sylvia delivered that by now well-known 'gentle kick' to Murphy's leg under the table. 'This alarmed me because I didn't want to have an affair with her, or break up her marriage, or be used to make Ted jealous …'. Plath, however, was already on the downward spiral that would end with her taking her own life the following year, and was desperately searching for help in all the wrong places. A few days later, Hughes went off on his own to County Clare, leaving Sylvia with Murphy, who panicked, he tells us, and asked her to leave the next day by taking a lift to Dublin with the poet Thomas Kinsella, whom Murphy had invited to come and help him entertain his fascinating but unpredictable guests. Murphy seems to harbour a residual sense of guilt for his inability to help Plath in her desperation, but surely she was even then beyond saving. Years later, Hughes admitted to Murphy that he had been cruel to leave Plath alone in Cleggan, and wondered if he had acted more quickly in the final week of her life would her suicide have been avoided. A bleak admission, an unanswerable question.

The Kick is more an account of a life in the busy world than the chronicle of the making of a poet. Murphy is unassuming in the matter of poetry in general – a description of a verse-reading 'contest' with James Dickey is comic and mercilessly accurate; he is disparaging of his early work, and admits to the difficulty he has always found in the making of verse. One has the impression from these pages that he does not consider himself a 'born' poet, and certainly he is no celebrant of life's happinesses, as he considers his colleague, Seamus Heaney, to be, although he does wonder, somewhat slyly, whether Heaney is really as happy as he seems. At the end, after giving an account of his mother's death – her last words to her nurse were, 'Well, it's dark outside. Can't you come part of the way?' – Murphy hands on the metaphorical baton to a new generation. At the old lady's funeral, his daughter Emily reports, her own daughter, three-year-old Theodora, was overheard remarking to a younger cousin, 'Aren't we lucky, Isabella, that we're not old: it'll be a long time before we have to die.'

The book is a fine, considered and fascinating memoir of a life lived as close to the full as possible. If in places it is a little self-serving, well, the self that is served is not undeserving of the attention. Murphy treats warmly those whom he loved, and fairly those he did not, while yet missing no opportunity to settle scores that he considers in need of settlement. Sorely missing are an index and photographs;* surely in that tea chest of papers kept by his mother there must be a cache of family snapshots, a selection of which could be included in subsequent editions.

John Banville
New York Review of Books, 15 May 2003

---

* The present edition includes an index and a photographic section.

Acknowledgements

I thank Dr Barbara Browning Brown, emeritus professor of English literature at Marshall University, Huntington, West Virginia, for devoting seven years of her life in Dublin, from 1996–2002, to giving me unstinting editorial and inspirational advice, mostly by email and phone, while I was abroad. With more than a hundred notebooks covering four decades to be sourced for this memoir, I could never have managed without Barbara's help.

Also, I thank Mike Collins of Cork University Press, Dominic Carroll, and the cover designer, Alison Burns, for celebrating my ninetieth birthday with a beautiful new edition of this memoir.

I continue to be grateful to the Arts Council of Ireland for long, generous support of my writing.

Richard Murphy
Sri Lanka, April 2017

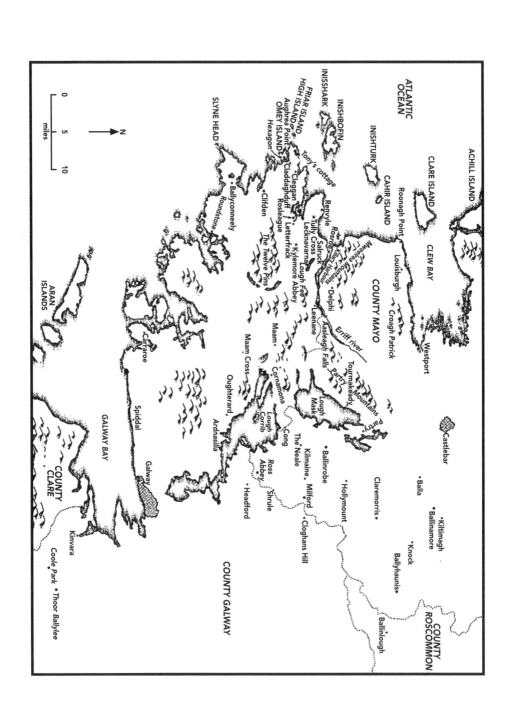

As artificiality is natural to men, so are variety and deviation on all sides of the norm; and this constitutes the principal interest of the species, alongside the power to play with this happy fact in imagination.
Stuart Hampshire

A year before my mother died on 28 January 1995, at the age of ninety-six, my older sister Mary was driving her across the moors in Northumberland to enjoy the view, when our mother turned to her and said, 'Darling, I'm afraid you'll have to get me put down, because I'm never going to die naturally – the trouble is I don't want to miss anything.'

'You're utterly selfish! You always were!'

My mother scowls at me across a tea tray in her sunroom at Highfield, where Mary and her husband, Gerry Cookson, have provided her with a cottage on their estate. A minute ago she was telling me to read aloud from a little black diary begun by her in London on 21 September 1914. This morning I found it in a tea chest of family papers she had gathered in seven countries and preserved through two world wars. She was thrilled to see it again, as I was to look into her heart as a girl of sixteen. But now she is angry because I have not moved my chair in response to her complaint, 'Your shoulder is touching one of my plants.'

'Can't we forget about your plants?' I ask irritably.

'But I love my plants, and I don't want them to get damaged.'

Well she knows that my shoulder could do no harm to a sturdy rubber plant from a garden centre near Hadrian's Wall. At ninety-five, she still loves giving an order in the form of a courteous question that demands an active response. But at this moment her coercive tone of voice makes me determined not to obey.

'Nanny spoilt you,' she taunts. 'It was my fault for keeping her on till you went to school. I should have got rid of her. Well, if you're not going to move your chair, I'll have to move the plant myself.'

So the blame will be mine if she falls and breaks her pelvis. Naturally, I rise to catch hold of her arm as she totters and sways across the sunroom. Too late!

1

She shakes off my hand, jerking her arm to her bosom, as if to say she needs no help from a son who isn't gentleman enough to stand in response to his dying mother's possibly last request. Defying pain and extreme decrepitude, she moves the large clay pot a few inches, and returns in triumph to her rattan throne. There, she casts on me the fury of her far-apart pale blue eyes and says, in a voice of martyred unselfishness: 'Do have another of these delicious scones that Mary baked.'

'No thanks, I've had more than enough.'

'Darling, why do you have to be so difficult?'

Her question reminds me of a Sri Lankan proverb: one crab says to another: 'My son, why do you have to walk sideways?' Quoting this now would prolong the row, and defeat my purpose of hearing, and writing down, things she remembers about her childhood and ours, before all her memories are lost. So I ask in a tone of contrition: 'Was I always a problem?'

'Quite often.'

'How, for example?'

'Well, you surely remember the time I took you to tea with Aunt Bella when you were three years old?'

'Tell me about Aunt Bella,' I reply, putting away the diary until we are both in a better mood.

'She was Daddy's aunt, his mother's sister, a very important old lady, Dr Isabella Mulvany. She was headmistress of Alexandra School for forty-seven years and the first woman to get an honorary degree in Ireland, from Trinity College. He was Aunt Bella's favourite. She was devoted to him, took him to England and France during his school holidays, and educated him. Aunt Bella never really liked me.'

'Why?'

'Because she wanted you to marry one of her intellectual pupils.'

'Me? Don't you mean William, my father?'

'Of course. My brain's gone completely.'

'No, it's remarkably clear, but sometimes you confuse the generations when we're talking about the past.'

'I know. I often think that Mary is my mother, because they are so alike.'

At seventy-one, Mary is her oldest child. Our mother still regards the five of us as children. So young she looked in our childhood that people after church would say, 'You could be their sister.'

'Who was that pupil Aunt Bella wanted William to marry instead of you?' I ask.

'I can't remember, but I think the man she may have married was a planter in Ceylon who lost all his money after the war, and drowned himself in a rainwater tank in Devon. No, it can't have been. Wasn't there someone in the colonial service who did rather well, becoming governor of Hong Kong, until he was put in prison by the Japs? Are you writing all this down? I do wish you'd stop. Do have another cup of tea.'

'What did *you* think of Aunt Bella?' I ask, when there's a pause in her picking up and putting down pieces of the Ormsby silver inherited from her five maiden aunts, including a jug in the form of a cow that gives milk out of its mouth.

'I was deeply in awe of her, everyone was. She was rather terrifying, but she had a heart of gold. Put that notebook down, or I can't go on. Let me see what you've written.'

'Sorry. I'm taking notes because I want your own words to survive. Don't you want me to write about you?'

'I'm not sure. I'd like to read what you're going to publish before I die. Don't write anything nasty about us! Can't you hurry up and finish the book?'

'If it were to contain only things you consider nice, who would believe it?'

'No one, I suppose. Finish up these scones!'

'I'm full, thank you very much. Was Aunt Bella a martinet, as one of her pupils, nearly as old as you, recently said?'

'She was good to me, but *awesome*. Of course, Aunt Bella never forgave you for what you did to her at the Royal Hibernian Hotel, where she lived rather grandly in her retirement. Surely you remember.'

'No, I was too young. I was often teased about it by Mary and Chris. Tell me what really happened.'

'I can't remember. You're wearing me out with your questions. My brain's gone. Have some more tea.'

'No, thank you.'

The back door opens, and triggers an alarm that sounds like the high-pitched yelp of a dog. It makes us jump, but they say it's good for security; not that it would stop an intruder or prevent a robbery or save our mother from an assault. Mary joins us, having placed in our mother's kitchen some dishes for supper she has cooked in her own house across the garden.

'Mary, tell him about Aunt Bella's tea party!'

'Do we have to keep raking up the past for Richard?'

'He's doing a wonderful job on my papers.'

'I know. He's the only member of the family who's exactly like you. He won't throw anything away, and he's a writer; so he can write about you if you let him have your papers. Nobody else is going to do so.'

'I suppose not,' our mother says, rather sadly, as if she would like to think we'd all spend the rest of our lives writing about her.

'Will you tell me,' I ask Mary, 'what *you* remember of Aunt Bella on that occasion?'

'I remember sitting in a rattan chair on a green carpet under a broad conservatory roof, looking around, and thinking how lucky Aunt Bella was to be living in a grand hotel. I wished we could all live in a hotel and order whatever we wanted at any time. She was the centre of attention, a very big woman, very plump, in a long black dress down to her shoes, with a high collar. That's all. Mummy will tell you the rest.'

'We were standing up, just about to leave. Aunt Bella remained in her chair. You see, she was almost eighty, and everyone respected her. Christopher, aged five, had said goodbye like an angel. You both were dressed to match in embroidered smocks with brown leather gaiters buttoned on hooks over your walking shoes. Nanny must have been off duty that afternoon. I whispered to you to go up nicely and say *Thank you very much Aunt Bella for the lovely tea party*, but you ran across the room and kicked her.'

'Why?'

'Just because you liked to be naughty.'

'How did Aunt Bella react?'

'She told you to say you were sorry, and you yelled "I won't!" So she caught you by the arm, and said she wasn't used to children yelling "I won't!" and you kicked her again. She never forgot it. I felt quite dreadful.'

'And she cut you out of her will,' Mary remembers, laughing.

'She's an absolute communist,' my mother says in a tone of angry disapproval of my brother Chris's daughter, Fiona Murphy, who writes for the *Guardian*.

'Why do you say that?' I ask.

'Because she picked up the newspaper and wouldn't look at the Queen.'

The Queen was giving her speech at the opening of Parliament, on television.

This reminds me of a warm dry afternoon in the summer of 1940 after the evacuation of the remnants of the British Expeditionary Force from Dunkirk.

All five of us children were at home with our mother at Milford, prepared to face a German parachute invasion of the west of Ireland and defend our grandfather's old demesne on the Mayo–Galway border to the last of his twelve-bore cartridges. We were ashamed of de Valera's neutrality. But that was no reason not to go riding, I felt, except that George VI was to speak to the empire on the wireless and we had all been told to listen.

A few minutes late I rode into the Pleasure Ground, ducking my head through the doorway, and dismounted, as a sign of respect, at the drawing-room window. A slow voice with a suppressed stammer was coming from our Pye wireless, powered by large wet and dry batteries, on a table by the window. My mother was biting her lower lip and looking at me as if she were striving as a good Christian not to let sorrow at having such an undutiful son turn into rage. As soon as the broadcast ended, she said I was a disgrace to the family: England was standing alone, thousands were being killed in air raids, Daddy was far away in Ceylon serving the empire, and I had shown no respect to the king by arriving late to listen to his speech in my shirt sleeves and with a dirty face.

'The oldest woman in England was 113 when she died yesterday,' I read out from *The Times* to my mother in her sunroom at Highfield.

She replies: 'How miserable she must have been.'

'She drank a glass of port every day,' I continue and my mother responds wearily: 'I won't buy a bottle of port. It's not much fun being alive when you're very old.'

'Then let's talk about when you were young.'

'Oh, I can't remember a thing.'

'Would you like me to read from your diary?'

'I'd love that. Where did you find it?'

'With all your papers.'

'You're not taking it to Ireland, I hope. It might get lost.'

'I promise you, nothing will be lost. We'll make copies of your papers there and give a copy to each of the family.'

'That's a good idea. Have they all agreed that you can have the papers?'

'Yes, all four have agreed – Mary, Christopher, Elizabeth and Edward.'

'Well, then, I've nothing to worry about. Read to me now, if you like.'

So I begin again to read from the little notebook bound in shiny black boards, with lined pages measuring six inches by four, filled at first in the delicately firm left hand of Betty M. Ormsby, her name signed at the top of the first right-hand page, above the words 'Diary – Begun Sept. 21, 1914'.

> This diary is chiefly written to keep an account of our doings during the War. When the war started between Austria and Servia partly owing to the murder of Austria's Crown Prince by a Servian, Mums, my brother Jack and I were staying in Thistle Cottage at Luss on Loch Lomond. This was during the month of July. Then on the first of August the three of us went over to stay with Aunt Kitty and Aunt Edith at Ballinamore, County Mayo, Ireland. Soon after we got there the news got worse and then on Tuesday the 4th of August England declared War on Germany. Britain had to come to the aid of Belgium a smaller and weaker country.
>
> On Thursday 20th August Jack got a printed letter from Major Cowper head of the G.A.O.T.C. stating that all boys of the Corps in or anywhere near Glasgow were to return and report themselves immediately at the Academy. So we returned to Glasgow.

'What do the letters GAOTC stand for?' I ask.

'Glasgow Academy Officers' Training Corps,' my mother recalls with no hesitation. 'Surely you know that. Go on.'

> On Thursday Mums and I left Glasgow for Brampton (Hunts) to stay with the 2 Great-Aunts on the way to Fards in London. We left Jack in Glasgow. He started School the day before we left.

Fards, I know, was my mother's father, a major in the Army Pay Department at the War Office. 'The two great-aunts,' she tells me, 'were Granny-Aunt Kate Bowen-Miller of Milford, who gave me £50 as a wedding present, and her sister Croasdailla, called "Cogie" Bowen-Miller, a clergyman's widow. They lived in two little houses, side by side, in Brampton. They had painted all the windows in the house black to save the expense of putting up blackout curtains during the war.'

'After this,' I prompt, 'you were in London, staying with your parents at the Linden Hall Hotel in Cromwell Road, and attending classes at the London School of Art in Kensington. Shall I go on?'

'Go on now.'

Monday, Sept. 21st

Found in Times of Thursday last Capt. Duckworth's name among those wounded. Saw an aeroplane pass in the morning. Had tooth-ache all day.

In afternoon a Mrs. Fortescue came to tea. Her nephew has joined the army as a private with 8 other gentlemen & likes it very much.

Neither of the Thursby-Pelham boys have joined the army yet. Their father won't allow them to because they are both at University training for the Royal Army Medical Corps & he considers it would ruin their careers as doctors. He does not think there is any neces-sity for them to join. Practised piano in afternoon.

'Those boys had an awful time from me. I thought it was terrible of them not joining the army, so I sent them red, white and blue cards with captions like, "Have you done your duty? Join up!" I was in love with Kenneth, and thrilled when my cousin Anthony Ormsby from Canada kissed me goodbye when he was going to the front – where he was killed.'

'Did it never occur to you,' I ask, 'while you were painting or playing the piano in London and later in Scotland, after those young men had been sent to the front, that you should have gone there yourself as a nurse?'

'I had typhoid and nearly died; it left me very weak. I was in such pain that with my heels I wore holes in the sheet, rubbing my feet up and down. My brother Jack put up a ladder to my window and spoke to me. He wasn't allowed in the room in case he caught typhoid. My mother hung a wet sheet over the door. She was nursing me and didn't wear a mask. She cut off my hair believing it would bring down the fever. My hair used to be so long I could sit on it. Mums made all the decisions and wanted to keep me as a perpetual child.'

Pinned into her diary I find a letter from Captain Ralph Duckworth, who was being nursed in the house of the Empress Eugénie, the eighty-eight-year-old widow of Napoleon III, at Farnborough in Hampshire. 'He was my hero when I was small,' she says.

5th Oct. 1914.

My Betty dear

How very sweet and nice of you to write to me and send me sym-pathies. They hit me on the 9th. Only a bullet through the thigh, but as the wretched thing did not heal up they kept me on my back in bed till yesterday …

This is where the Empress Eugenie lives and She with the Princess Clementine of Belgium and Lady Douglas Haig and 5 nurses are looking after 4 of us. They are extremely kind Betty dear but one does feel dreadfully wild beasty with grapes instead of buns and flowers instead of biscuits don't you know, so many are the friends they bring to see us. One day when Elvira was taking tea with me the Empress brought the Queen and King with the Princess Mary and the Prince of Wales and many folks in waiting. They were very affable and kind but stayed so long our tea was cold …

This war, Betty dear, is going to be a long one, it has hardly yet begun, so hurry up and get your Red Cross certificate as soon as maybe. With my salaams to your Father and Mother and ever much Love to yourself,

Bonne chance de votre ami fidèle, R.D.

At this point my mother's attention is diverted. 'Will you let Sooty out, she wants to go into the garden.'

I open and shut the door for the cat, and continue reading.

Sunday, November 15th
Knitted bedsocks in morning. Fards went to see Col. Ovens at Guys Hospital. Colonel Ovens told Fards that Captain Loder Simmonds has been killed. He said he was blown to pieces a few minutes after he had tied up Colonel Ovens' wound.

In the paper today was the death of Lord Roberts. It was very nice Lord Roberts dying when among his troops.

The response of Kenneth and Brian Thursby-Pelham to the 'patriotic post-cards' they had received from Betty reached her two days before Christmas.

This evening I had an Xmas card from Kenneth Thursby Pelham on which he said that he & Brian have applied for Commissions in the Army. We are all very pleased.

'What happened to Kenneth and Brian?' I ask.

'I'm afraid they both got badly wounded,' she replies, adding, 'We'll have to let Sooty in, it's raining, and she hates being left out in the rain.' I hate having to jump up and down to please my mother in pleasing her cat.

'Go on reading now, I'm listening,' she says, when the cat is restored to her lap. I continue:

In future I am going to write this diary with my right hand.

'It looked the same to me,' she says, 'whether I wrote backwards or forwards. I used to have to ask someone on which side of a blank paper I ought to begin, because I was never sure. Sometimes, when I turned over a page in writing a letter, I wrote backwards, but didn't notice that I was doing this, because both ways looked the same. It wasn't that I wanted to be different by using my left hand, it was natural. I used to fight against the teacher if she tried to make me use my right hand, and I said to her, if you make me write with my right hand, you should make all the others write with their left, to be fair. Dr Laurence Levy in Rhodesia asked me to leave him my brain so that he could examine it after my death. He was professor of surgery at the University of Rhodesia.'

This remark, which our mother has often repeated, upsets Mary, who once replied: 'If you think I'm going to take your head in a plastic bag on a train and go round London looking for a hospital willing to accept it, and fetch it later to bring to Ireland for your funeral, Mummy, you must be mad. Perhaps one of the boys will do it. Why don't you ask them?'

'You could have been a writer,' I tell my mother.

'If I'd gone to a university. I always wanted to go to a university, but my father and mother wouldn't hear of their precious little darling going away from home.'

It wasn't done, not by ladies who were expected to make themselves pleasing enough for gentlemen to want to marry by pretending to be more ignorant and less clever than their suitors.

Our mother was born in Galway on 16 September 1898, a year of famine in the west of Ireland, when nationalists were celebrating the 1798 Rebellion. Her parents may not have had two pennies to rub together, as they used to say, but both had Anglo-Irish pedigrees, going back on her father's side to King Charles II and his mistress, Lucy Walters, through the brother of Patrick

Sarsfield; while on her mother's family tree there dangled a French marquis, the poet Geoffrey Chaucer, and at the tip top – could you believe it? – William the Conqueror!

When asked to state her nationality on forms in Ireland during the Second World War, our mother used to write 'British and Irish'. As Ireland was neutral, this declaration of her divided loyalty was brave, but embarrassing to my brother Chris and to me. We felt that people might condemn or mock us for being two-faced; and wasn't it rather a sickening reminder of the British and Irish Steampacket Company's ships in peril of U-boats on the long night crossing between Dublin and Liverpool, on our way to and from our school in England? With similar duality, our mother liked to be addressed as Mrs W. Lindsay Murphy MBE, suggesting Scottish blood and service to the empire. Having saved thousands of lives in the last great malaria epidemic in Ceylon, she had received the honour from King George V at Buckingham Palace in 1935. She was proud and ashamed of being Irish. Proud of the Irishmen, especially her relations, who had given their lives in Britain's wars; ashamed of Ireland's neutrality, and the bombing of Britain by the IRA before the Second World War.

Keeping our mother alive when we were children was a responsibility that Mary, her eldest child, turned into a passion. A mild illness suffered by our mother would cause Mary to suffer even more. Her love had been fortified by abhorrence of the 'selfishness' of 'you boys'. Chris and I often provoked our mother to accuse us of being 'irresponsible' and 'horribly aggressive'. Mary would echo these accusations. It was worse when 'Mummy's' temper snapped. She'd bite her lower lip, drop her tearful eyes to the floor, and say in a pitiful voice what she wanted us to think she felt: 'You're killing your poor mother!' Then Mary would fly to her rescue, and make us feel thoroughly ashamed.

After lunch nearly every day at Highfield, Mary used to drive our mother over the moors between Whittonstall and Blanchland to give her a breath of fresh air. I went on one of those drives. While Mary was speaking, our mother kept staring out of her own window, missing nothing in the bare brown landscape undulating to the horizon under dismal clouds.

Suddenly she interrupted Mary, and said: 'Do look over there, darling! Isn't that perfectly beautiful? Not a person or a house to spoil the view.' This was the ideal of beauty, nature untainted by humanity, that she pursued by painting watercolours of Loch Lomond during the Great War.

'You ought to do a painting of this,' she added, reminding me of rare treats at Milford before the war, when she would send the gardener on a bicycle three miles to Kilmaine to hire Martin Walsh to drive us in his Ford V8 to Connemara. On the long and lonely road through the Forest of Cong to Cornamona, as the car turned a dangerous corner, suddenly a great stretch of Lough Corrib and its islands would appear, causing her to gasp and say, 'What a wonderful surprise! Do stop the car, and let's enjoy the view!' Our teasing and squabbles in the back seat would be silenced for a moment as we watched in awe. Then she would turn and sigh, 'Oh Mary, what a pity you didn't bring your painting things!'

It was always a 'surprise' turning that corner on journeys we made to Connemara, and Mary's painting things were often forgotten in the excitement of packing a picnic lunch, bathing togs and fishing gear. If only Mary had remembered to bring them, we believed, she might have become as famous as Paul Henry.

At every meal at the round table in our dining room in the East Wing of Milford, Mary and our mother acted a little drama. Mary would put more food on 'Mummy's' plate than 'Mummy' thought she could manage.

'I can't possibly eat all that,' she would say, while transferring one of two slithers of boiled leg of mutton from her willow-pattern plate to Mary's. They always sat next to each other to perform this rite. As soon as our mother's head was turned towards 'one of you boys' on her right, Mary would slip the meat back onto her plate, and then the argument would begin.

'You can't force me to eat it.'

'Mummy you'll die if you don't put on some weight. You need it to build up your strength.'

But Mummy would not give in, and the meat would return to Mary's plate. Back and forth it went. The victor would be the one who could most convincingly say, 'You must be unselfish and do this to please me.'

Mary had learnt this from our mother and would insist, adding, 'We don't want you to die.'

There was a legend as to how our mother's mother, Lucy Thomson, eldest of the seven good-looking daughters of Captain Colin Thomson and his wife, Maria Louisa Augusta West, had become engaged in 1893 to Tom Ormsby.

Lucy was helping her mother to run Salruck House on the Little Killary Bay in the centre of an extremely remote and almost bankrupt estate of barren mountains and lakes. Her days were filled with painting watercolour landscapes devoid of people, and giving first aid to her father's miserably poor tenants, especially their children.

Tom was twenty-two, a subaltern in the South Staffordshire Regiment, on leave at the seat of his family, Ballinamore. The austere Protestant house had a frown on its dismal grey face, as if it disapproved of the country it had occupied for one hundred and fifty years. A trout stream ran through an oak wood stocked with pheasants in the walled demesne. There were three long avenues, each with a gate lodge occupied by a loyal though Catholic family: one to Claremorris, another to Balla, and the most impressive to Kiltimagh. Poor children used to run out in bare feet to open the gates for carriages of the gentry to pass through. Tom was the fifth and youngest boy, known to his family as 'good Tom'. His five maiden sisters lived at home, looking after their widowed invalid mother, who at sixteen had married her cousin, aged twenty-nine, and had borne fifteen children, ten of whom survived. Tom's oldest brother, Anthony, had inherited Ballinamore in 1888.

Tom had met and fallen in love with Lucy on a visit she had made with her mother to his grandmother, Mrs Bowen-Miller, at Milford. In order to propose to her, and ask her father's permission for them to marry, he rode from Ballinamore fifty miles through the mountains to Salruck.

Soon after he arrived, Lucy's sisters Emily and Louise thought of a plan to put the courage of this nice young eligible man to the test. They told him a secret. All her life Lucy had longed to possess a heron's egg. She would love him if he could give her one. It was springtime, and the birds had a nest at the top of a pine tree, which of course Tom did his best to climb. Halfway up, he was attacked by the herons with their long beaks and claws. The girls kept egging him on and screaming with laughter, but the herons won. He had to come down, bleeding and without an egg. The girls covered his hands and face with sticking plaster, and sent him into the drawing room where Lucy was expecting him to propose. She burst out laughing, but, with her father's consent, agreed to marry him. He had proved his courage and satisfied her mischievous sense of humour.

Tom Ormsby and Lucy Thomson were married three years later on 18 May 1896 at Ootacamund (known as Ooti), a hill station preferred for its coolness by army officers and their wives in the south of India.

In old age at Milford, my grandmother confided to Mary that she had never enjoyed sex, especially not when she was first married, when it was a shock to her romantic innocence.

As a bachelor obliged to 'set an example' in the Ceylon Civil Service for eleven years before his marriage, our father could not be described as happy. His regular weekly letters home to his mother in Dublin are weighed down by the drudgery and boredom he overcame by moral rectitude, willpower and the satisfaction of a well-paid job that commanded more respect than was given to the military or the planters. Since his own father's death in 1916 he had supplemented his mother's pension as a clergyman's widow who devoted herself to voluntary work for the Mother's Union and the Soldiers' and Sailors' Benevolent Society.

What he felt free to enjoy was the slaying of wildlife, big and small, with rifle or shotgun. Years later, when I was seven, he taught me to shoot crows with an airgun from our back verandah in Colombo. He never liked talking about himself, and thought poorly of men who did, a trait that helped him to rise in the Civil Service. But he did tell us, and we listened with awe, how he was nearly killed by a dangerous rogue elephant that jungle villagers had begged him to shoot to save their crops and lives. The elephant, after being shot in the ear, had charged him, and our father, trying to escape, had tripped on a thorn bush. Trumpeting with fury, the wounded elephant had stood with hind legs on one side of our father and forelegs on the other, just long enough for him to creep away. A moment later the elephant fell, so close to him that it broke his rifle at the stock.

Uncle Kipher, our father's younger brother, in response to a challenge in his boyhood, had lain down in a hole he had dug between two sleepers on the Galway to Clifden railway track while a train ran over him. When war was declared in 1914 he went as quickly as possible to the front, where he led his platoon through a gap in a hedge covered by German machine-gun fire at Languemarck near Ypres. Wounded, he was rescued and put sitting with his back to a haystack, where he took out a tiny copy of the Psalms, bound in green leather, his mother's parting gift, and marked Psalm 92 verse 12 with an indelible pencil – *Such as are planted in the house of the Lord shall flourish in the courts of the house of our God* – shortly before a sniper shot him through the head. That his death on 21 October 1914 was not a futile waste of a young life, but a glorious martyrdom in the cause of freedom and justice, all the black-bordered letters of sympathy received, answered and preserved by our grandmother in Dublin conspired to affirm.

A pale complexion runs in our family on our mother's side, but knowledge of this never deterred her from saying to me, when I would be feeling as well as usual, 'Darling, you do look frightfully pale. Hadn't you better see a doctor?'

It was she who told me that her brother Jack, at the age of seventeen, in the third year of the war to end all wars, was riding in a group of officer cadets around the arena at Woolwich, when the riding master, who had forgotten his name, yelled out an order addressing him as 'that man who looks like death'. After a pause she added, 'We both looked like death.'

'Death' became Jack's nickname in the army from that moment. He enjoyed excellent health, except for a spot of trouble with his digestion brought on by his own courage. Out in India with the Royal Horse Artillery a few years later, he accepted a challenge from his brother officers, after dinner in the mess, to chew up the wine glass from which he had drunk a toast to the king-emperor. He swallowed every fragment.

Once, on a pig-sticking expedition, Jack was warned by the yelling and shouting of coolies that a panther was hiding in a clump of *jhow*. Instead of standing back, he rode his horse into the clump, beating the bushes with his spear. The panther, with a loud roar, sprang at his horse's head, clawing it, while the horse reared and struck out hard with its forefeet, before leaping out of the bushes and throwing Uncle Jack high into the air. In his account to our mother, the panther ran off, but two brother officers hunted it down until one of them ran it clean through the body with a spear.

Our father proposed to our mother on his knees. We had been told this by our grandmother at Milford. Betty was twenty-four and William eleven years older. A tall man, his face would have been not much lower than hers when he knelt. It would be wrong to describe her as little or small or low in height, as the strength of her feelings livened her face, commanding everyone's attention. All their lives together they looked up to each other.

I think she looks beautiful in a touched-up miniature sepia photograph, oval-mounted in a gold frame, hanging in my bedroom now. Taken when she was sixteen, it shows her profuse brown hair in two long plaits tied by satin bows on her breast.

On her visits to me in Ireland, or mine to her in England, after my father's death in 1965, from time to time she told me how they had met on her brief passage through Dublin with her mother in April 1922, between the signing of the Treaty and the outbreak of civil war. Each time she spoke, she'd remember a different detail of their romance. Her words are pieces in a jigsaw puzzle that has taken me years to put together, with many gaps.

'Did you know it was in Holy Week that I met Daddy, and it was in Holy Week that he died? He was staying with his mother, a clergyman's widow, in Dublin while on sick leave after malaria in Ceylon; and giving up the colonial service because he'd got fed up through being alone. His only brother, Kipher, had been killed in the war. He himself had volunteered three times for the army, but each time had been rejected as he had very short sight …

'My mother and I were staying in quite respectable lodgings at Ranelagh, having rushed over from Scotland, because Uncle Anthony, my father's oldest brother, had died. Fards had gone ahead to the funeral in the family church on the Ballinamore estate. Mummy and I didn't want to go down to the death house too soon because the aunts were in such deep mourning, always deeper in Ireland than anywhere else. They adored Uncle Anthony. He was head of the family, never married, and his five maiden sisters treated him as a god.

'I was walking outside the railings of St Stephen's Green with my mother, and my mother's Aunt Wilhelmina West. Everyone teased Aunt Willie because she was a bit mad and bizarre. She wore a white coat and white stockings because, she said, "the Queen always wears white". Her hat was broad-brimmed and vividly green velvet. Of course I was wearing black. We were on the pavement near the Shelbourne Hotel, when suddenly Aunt Willie screamed and rushed out into the middle of the street – I don't know how she wasn't killed – and held up her hand in front of a huge man who was crossing and said "Halt! I want you to meet my grand-niece." She dragged him over and introduced him as William Murphy.

'I was worried because there were holes in his gloves – you mustn't publish this – he was wearing a blue thick stuffed woolly reefer jacket, too small for him, so it made him look fat. I noticed there were buttons missing and the sleeves were too short. That's why I fell in love.

'He seemed so old that I called him Uncle Willie, and teased him by pretending he was interested in my grand-aunt. He took us all to a cinema, one of those silent films to which I paid absolutely no attention. We saw the last picture before everything closed down for Easter. Do you want to know if we held hands? I expect we did.

'This was a lively diversion, because my mother and I had been sitting in rather dull lodgings. And he gave me a bunch of white carnations. When I was quite young in Scotland we used the language of flowers for sending messages. A white flower meant innocence.

'Billy's family, his sisters Kay and Eileen, had always called him Willie, but because that was the name of my poor aunt, I changed his name to Billy. We soon discovered that my Granny Thomson at Salruck and Billy's mother at the Rectory in Clifden had been the greatest friends. My mother knew of him, but I don't think she'd ever seen him. Before the war his brother Kipher had been in love with my Aunt Violet, a much younger sister of my mother; but my Granny, although she was ever so holy, was anxious that her seven daughters should make good marriages. Kipher was very charming but had no money, so he and Violet were sent for a walk up the mountain behind the house, where she broke it off. Kipher was still in love with her when he died in battle.

'Where were we? I remember: it was Easter 1922. The picture houses were closed on Good Friday, so Billy took me to St Patrick's Cathedral where they sang parts of the *St Matthew Passion* beautifully. There were torrents of rain and we heard shooting every night. That was when the IRA under Rory O'Connor seized the Four Courts, and on Easter Monday we went to Handel's *Messiah*.

'Then Billy called at our lodgings one day bringing more carnations. My mother made some excuse to leave the room. As you know, she was all for romance, and for me to have the joy denied to herself of marrying a man purely for love. Anyway, as I've often told you, Daddy went down on his knees and proposed.'

'Can you remember what he said?'

'No, but what does it matter? When Mummy came back and heard that he'd asked me to marry him, she said he must go down to Ballinamore and ask for my father's permission. He was supposed to catch an early train from Broadstone Station, but, being Irish, missed the morning train, and arrived at Claremorris after dark. All he could find to drive him out to Ballinamore, about four or five miles, was a horse-drawn sidecar, with seats on each side of a box for luggage, and no protection whatever from the wind and the rain. At the gate lodge the jarvey was given directions to the back door, because only carriages drove up to the front.

'Mummy had sent Fards a telegram with as few words as possible, to save money: it simply said MURPHY ARRIVING. The family at Ballinamore knew nobody called Murphy, so they thought it must be a coded warning of the imminent arrival of the IRA, who were still burning Big Houses and shooting RIC policemen, who had been disbanded. After Billy explained who he was to the servants, they told the jarvey to bring him to the front door, where he went up those big stone steps and pulled the old brass knob of the bell.

'The aunts were terrified. They had just sat down to dinner with Uncle Charlie, the new head of the family. The servants weren't allowed to answer the door because they couldn't be trusted. So Uncle Charlie got up and with a great effort, because the door was double locked, opened it on the chain. Not until Billy had handed in a letter from Mummy to Fards was he allowed to come in.

'Fards was sick upstairs in bed with flu, and the aunts were scandalised at this intrusion on their sorrow. The only one who was nice to him was my Granny-Aunt Kate, one of the Bowen-Millers of Milford, my Ormsby grandmother's sister. She had enjoyed a romance in her youth which the whole family had crushed.

'William went upstairs to see my father, who was furious and said he didn't know what my mother was thinking about, except that she wanted to pay him back for his having ridden fifty miles on a horse from Ballinamore to her bad-tempered father in Salruck to ask permission to marry her. He was all the more furious because I had got engaged once before to a junior officer in the navy in Scotland. He believed a promise should never be broken. He told William to go back to Dublin and put his request for permission to marry me in writing.'

So Betty went down with her mother to Ballinamore to persuade the family to give their consent for her to become engaged, defiantly wearing a ring that Billy had given her. 'We had to go in the back door of West's, the jewellers in Grafton Street, because the front had been bombed.' Her father and Uncle Charlie were kind, but the aunts (except Granny Aunt Kate) had been 'frozen with shock since the arrival of Murphy'. From Ballinamore, in Betty's first letter to 'Billy dearest', she wrote: 'This house is so lonely and full of sadness, and I do feel so sorry for the Aunts: they can have had so little real happiness & life must be dreadfully empty for them.'

The aunts wore black silk chokers fastened with diamond clasps on their necks. When expressing disapproval they would finish their sentences on an indrawn breath. One by one, in five separate interviews, they required her to tell them why she wanted to get married. Aunt Kitty, who bossed all the others, is said to have regarded marriage as 'unladylike'. None of the sisters was ever allowed to remain alone in a room with an eligible bachelor; therefore none had received a proposal.

So they put their heads together, said prayers as usual in the drawing room after breakfast, and decided to invite their good friend Archdeacon Treanor to tea, and delicately sound him out about Betty's suitor. Treanor came to tea and thawed their hearts by saying: 'Young Murphy is a gentleman. His brother gave his life for king and country and their father, Canon Richard Murphy, was a saint.'

Permission to announce the engagement came from Ballinamore to Darroch, on a green hill above Luss, in the form of a letter from Uncle Charlie, as head of the family, to his brother Tom at the end of May. Billy was already staying at Darroch.

When I got the photographs in my mother's wedding album enlarged and bound as a present for her ninety-fifth birthday, I asked her for some notes to go with the pictures. She told me:

'My wedding day was sad because my father was very ill. I was married in the Church of Scotland at Luss on Loch Lomond on 5 July 1922. An Anglican padre conducted the service in the presence of a Church of Scotland clergyman, who didn't interfere. One of my bridesmaids was Church of Ireland – that was my sister-in-law, Eileen Murphy. The other, Phyllis Jordan, was a Roman Catholic from a family who lived at Thornhill near Ballinamore. They believed the Ormsbys had taken their land from them hundreds of years ago, but we were good friends. At the end of this ecumenical service, long before such a thing had been heard of, a Wee Free Presbyterian minister called Mr Jubb said a very long prayer.

'We had only nine days for a honeymoon in Scotland before my poor husband had to return to Ceylon. When I went out to join him three months later – it took me that long to get my trousseau and everything ready – I was accompanied by my mother *and* by Phyllis, my bridesmaid. Daddy was very good about this. My mother stayed until after Mary was born in a creeper's bungalow on a tea estate in the hills, almost exactly a year after our wedding. I had a Sinhalese doctor and a Sinhalese midwife and my mother to help, but I got an abscess on the breast which was very painful and it had to be lanced.'

What marriage did for my father is conveyed in letters he wrote from Ceylon to his mother during the month after the wedding: 'You will be interested to hear that a man named Hughes thinks I look about fifteen years younger than when he last saw me! I am greatly resigned to Ceylon once more and feel extraordinarily fit!'

Among the family documents preserved by my mother, I found a letter dated 10 June 1925 from my father's Aunt Bella, Dr Isabella Mulvany, then head-mistress of Alexandra College, written to him on essay paper, two years before I was born. In her large, forceful script, which crosses the faint red line of the left-hand margin, she describes her nephew's wife and child as 'both your precious possessions', and comments, 'Betty is a very charming young woman, with such easy unaffected manners, and she is very attractive in looks.' But by the third page, Betty has become 'your little G.O.C.' who 'will not allow the answers to the Cross Word Puzzles to go to you until the next mail!! She says you look at the answers before you try hard. So I am obeying her this time but if you prefer it, I'm old, may say No.'

What did Aunt Bella look like in her youth and in her prime? My brother Chris possesses a photograph on glass, an ambrotype, showing three handsome girls, two of them standing behind and on either side of one who is seated, all dressed in black crinoline, with the hooped skirts of the late 1860s. The youngest, on the left, is our tall-for-her-age and handsome grandmother, Mary Louisa, born in 1856. On the right, recognisable by the strength of will in her androgynous face, stands Isabella Marion Jane, two years older. On the chair sits the eldest, most musically talented sister, Margerie Kate, born in 1851. At the age of twenty-six she died of cancer, and I never knew of her existence until not long ago I saw her name on a tombstone in Mount Jerome cemetery. The images have been touched up, with a suggestion of rouge that puts life into the faces and dots of gold on the necklaces that give the young ladies distinction.

I wish I'd asked my father to tell me about his life before he was married, and about the lives of his parents and grandparents. To find out more about his family, I searched through public records, and had some luck in being given by the librarian of Alexandra College two images that have fixed Aunt Bella in my mind, not as the old and awesome monument I kicked at a tea party when I was three, but on the day of her triumph as one of the first nine women to obtain university degrees in Ireland, 22 October 1884, when she was thirty. These were pioneer achievers in the cause of women's rights to equal education.

Instead of preparing themselves at home for domestic duties in a ladylike manner, these Dublin girls had gone out bravely to study in college. Now they were getting their reward, wearing long black dresses with gowns and hoods, instead of white satin with bridal wreaths. Miss Mulvany has put on her mortarboard and turned her face in modesty to avoid the camera's eye. Her profile has the dignity of an emperor on a Roman coin or tomb.

In the first view, she is standing tall in the back row of the group, outside the Royal University of Ireland in St Stephen's Green, posing for a photograph that will appear in the *Irish Times*. The Bachelor of Arts degrees have just been conferred on them by the old Duke of Abercorn, chancellor of the Royal University of Ireland. They have suffered him quoting Tennyson's line about 'sweet girl graduates in their shining gowns'. Isabella has the strong face of a man who looks as if he might go far in the empire. In time to come she would encourage my father to achieve that ambition.

The next day they would find themselves headlined as the 'Nine Graces', with a hint of patronising mockery. Casting them as worshipful figures of Greek mythology was perhaps a rearguard male reaction to defend the system that allowed boys, the empire builders and destroyers of the future, a better education than their sisters. The intellectual triumph of these women – Aunt Bella excelled in teaching Latin and mathematics – would frighten men off, proving those men, who would rather die than be accused of cowardice, too cowardly to propose. The future historian Mary Hayden, one of the nine, remarked in her diary three years later: 'It was a blessed relief to meet a man who didn't know I was a BA, and didn't begin by saying he was quite afraid of me. To which I often felt inclined to reply "the more fool you".'

In the second image, from a photograph taken on the same day as the first, Miss Mulvany stands alone in her shiny black gown. She seems to be clad from neck to ankles in polished steel, with a dazzling breastplate. The academic hood shows a little white fur slung over her left shoulder. In contrast to the severity of her costume, her arms are adorned with lace cuffs. Only her thumbs on top of her mortarboard are visible. Her fingers, which never stopped writing letters, reports, minutes of meetings, exams and accounts, are concealed, because she holds this male academic trophy like a black shield centred upon her womb, its long tassel hanging down, catching no glimmer of light. Her straight black hair is combed and brushed tightly to her scalp behind her prominent left ear, and knotted into a bun on the back of her neck. She has turned her head to the right, revealing the dark lines of her eyebrows, her nose and her jaw. No wonder her friends call her The Chief. But the big surprise of this photograph is her physical resemblance to her exact Anglo-Irish contemporary, Oscar Wilde. Morally she was Wilde's antithesis, admired for 'her keen and flashing sword of wit' but feared as 'a fortress of Victorian rectitude'.

One last private glimpse of her was given to me on the phone by the actor Richard Leech, my second cousin on the Mulvany side: 'As a very small boy

I used to see Aunt Bella at Alexandra College. She'd have a bright red apple on her desk, and a little metal elephant rearing his trunk up, and the trunk was broken. I loved her. She liked boys much better than girls. In 1934 she suffered a stroke and my mother was with her when she was taken to Dr Steeven's Hospital in a coma. While they were carrying her on a stretcher across the quad from one part of the hospital to another, Aunt Bella came out of her coma and said "God's good air!'"

A Japanese professor of physiology at a college for rich girls on the outskirts of Tokyo in 1992 told me that on my next visit to Japan he would invite me to his house and show me the caves in his garden where his ancestors had for the past eight hundred years been entombed. Such piety towards the dead, continuously sustained by a family through forty generations, impresses me, in spite of a suspicion that the pedigree of bones extending so far back can only be mythical.

Shortly before my second cousin, Betty Robb, who inherited the Mulvany 'heart of gold' from her mother and grandmother, died of cancer of the oesophagus in 1989, she went out of her way in bitterly cold weather to drive from Roundstone to Renvyle to hear me read my poetry at the hotel that Lutyens had designed for Oliver St John Gogarty. As almost nobody else came but Leo Hallisey, who was saving a bog from being turned into an airport, we sat by a log fire talking afterwards about our forebears. These are her legends merged with my research.

Our great-grandfather on my father's mother's side, Christopher Mulvany, was a civil engineer who in his early twenties was associated with preparing parliamentary plans for the principal railways in Ireland. Nobody knew where he came from, because men did not talk about their families. It was whispered that he was a Catholic, the son of a poor but respectable tenant farmer. In the third year of the Great Famine, at the age of twenty-six, he was put in charge of the Grand Canal, consisting of one hundred and eighty miles of inland waterways.

One afternoon he was travelling in a hansom cab along the road beside the canal, passing the Portobello Barracks in Dublin, when he saw a beautiful young lady, dressed in black, fainting on the towpath. He told the driver to halt, stepped down from the cab and gallantly helped her to her feet. She gave her name as Isabella Fowler. He offered to escort her in his cab to her lodgings and asked if he might call the next day.

He then discovered that she was an orphan of good family, reduced to embroidering waistcoats for a firm of military tailors called Switzer's. Her father, she said, was an army captain, John Hely Hutchinson Fowler, killed in battle before she was born. Her mother had reared her in a 'grace and favour' house in Exeter, where she had nursed her mother through a terminal illness. Finding herself without two pennies to rub together, she had come to Dublin, believing she had some rich relations among the aristocracy. She was too proud to beg, and none of those who knew of her fate offered to help. Her only heirlooms were a small mahogany escritoire and a portrait of her mother, Judith Lindsay. She had brought these from Exeter, carried by her loyal and affectionate Irish maid called Mary Moore, who refused to leave her service in spite of not being paid. 'Four generations of her family worked for five of ours,' Betty told me.

Miss Fowler must have told Mr Mulvany, as she later told her daughters, that her mother was a relative of the Right Reverend the Hon. Charles Dalrymple Lindsay DD, third son of James, 5th Earl of Balcarres, bishop of Kildare and dean of Christ Church Cathedral, Dublin. This munificent patron of music had been buried in a marble mausoleum in the crypt of his cathedral in 1846, shortly before Isabella reached Ireland.

Christopher Mulvany had a mind far ahead of his time, a good income, the manners of a gentleman, though not the status (which he would soon achieve) and a noble heart. Isabella Fowler was a lady of pure mind, perfect manners and noble breeding, who had fallen through misfortune into distress. Lucky for her no cavalry officer of pedigree better than hers had picked her up only to discard her the next day. Mulvany loved her from the moment he lifted her from the ground where he had found her lying like a waif.

One day he brought a bunch of white carnations to her lodgings on Richmond Street, a few doors down from the Portobello lock and the Home for Blind Women. There he announced: 'I have to go to London on parliamentary business, and when I return we will get married.' To this she simply replied, 'Yes, dear.'

Looking for facts to confirm this legend in 1993, I found that their marriage was 'solemnized at the Registrar's Office in the City of Dublin in the District of Dublin South' on the 'Fifteenth day of February 1849'. This was not long after civil marriages had been instituted in Ireland, in order to allow members of different Churches to marry. Both were of 'full age'. She was twenty-two and he was five years older. For him, as a Catholic, marrying a Protestant had put his soul in jeopardy. For the grand-niece of a Protestant bishop descended from Scottish earls, marriage to a Catholic in a newfangled registry office was a disgrace. Not for another one hundred and six years, when I married a Catholic who had lapsed and been divorced, did a member of our family have a wedding in a registry office.

The Lindsays never entered her mother Judith's name among the numerous descendants of the Earls of Balcarres listed in Debrett's. Unmarried daughters of the gentry who became pregnant were not stoned to death in early nineteenth-century Ireland, but sometimes they were disowned and had their names obliterated from family records. The Army Lists record a John Hely Hutchinson, later Earl of Donoughmore, a man of the right age to have been her father, but no Captain Fowler called John.

Judith's telling her daughter that her father had been killed in battle before she was born was a falsehood that the Church of England's reasonable God might forgive. Mulvany, the lapsed Catholic, encouraged Isabella to have her seven children baptised in the Church of Ireland at St Peter's, Aungier Street, and helped to bring them up as devout Protestants. He eventually joined her Church as he could not accept the dogmas of the Immaculate Conception, promulgated in 1854, or papal infallibility, proclaimed in 1870.

Genealogical speculation may prove nothing more than the inclinations of the speculator, but the legends that arise out of speculation often influence our minds and actions. The legend of Fowler, dying like a hero in a battle at a time when no battles took place, affected all of Isabella Fowler's descendants for the next three generations. Most of all it steered my father's younger brother, Kipher, who was given Fowler as his middle name, towards a career in the army in peacetime and death on his first day in battle on the Western Front. I grew up feeling guilty that I might never have his courage.

And the legend of our descent from the Earls of Crawford and Balcarres had a curious sequel if not consequence. My father was given his middle name Lindsay and my mother passed the name on to four of her five children. Closing a gap in the circle of our legend legitimately, my niece Grania Caulfeild was to marry a man whose aunt was the Countess of Crawford and Balcarres.

Christopher Mulvany wanted the documentary evidence of his life's work as an engineer to outlive him and his critics. My grandmother preserved eleven of his letters written to her between 1871, when she was almost fifteen, and 1895. Alas, those documents went from father to son, instead of from mother to daughter, and after the death of the childless, last male heir, Brigadier Christopher Mulvany (my father's first cousin Kit), all trace of them disappeared.

But my great-grandfather left a wonderful legacy in the banks and locks of the Grand Canal, which he maintained for forty-five years. During and after the Famine, some unemployed labourers caused major breaches, which Mulvany repaired so well that his work has lasted till the twenty-first century. But he angered the shareholders and directors of the Grand Canal Company by employing a thousand men for longer than was necessary, to help their starving families. One can almost see how he looked, and feel how likeable he was, in these words from his obituary in the *Irish Times*:

> All along the Canal, from Ballinasloe to Dublin, and from Dublin to Athy, Mr. Mulvany's upright form and elastic step, even to the very last, were as well known as that of the daily postman, and there is many a lonely labourer's house and lockhouse in the Bog of Allen where the name of Mulvany will long remain associated with generous help and sympathy.

Family legend is like a balloon attached by invisible thread to a tiny fact on the ground of history. Once the anchorage is secure, you can inflate the balloon and ascend with it as high on hot air as the thread will stretch before it breaks. But things get the better of us in the long run. Isabella Fowler's escritoire, at one time the vital evidence of her fallen gentility, after passing from mother to daughter through five generations survives in the house of her great-great-granddaughter Isabella, Betty's daughter, who held it as proof of our legendary origins.

'A robin always comes into the house when a Mulvany is going to die,' Betty told me in 1989, when she knew her life was ending. 'My mother's brother died when he was an infant, and they couldn't get the robin off the cot. When Uncle Chris died, they couldn't get the robin out of the house.'

In the roof over the room where I was born at Milford, my Ormsby cousins, who inherited Milford, tell me there is still a nest of wild bees. They come and go through a gap in the eaves above a sash window that faces south across a bog to the hill of Castlehacket on the horizon. Their humming can only be heard in the room if no one is talking and the wind isn't making a sound in the chimney.

There were two clergymen at my Church of Ireland christening in the village of Kilmaine, County Mayo, and they almost came to blows in an argument about my sex. Mr Matthews, the deaf rector, insisted that I was a girl, and my grandfather, Lieutenant Colonel the Reverend Thomas Ormsby DSO, became what my mother calls 'peppery'. After the hymn 'Fight the Good Fight', which my grandmother accompanied on her portable harmonium, she put an end to the dispute by asking the rector, 'Why don't you look?'

At the age of six weeks I was taken out to Ceylon on a Bibby liner from Liverpool, with separate decks for adults and children with nurses. A well-qualified nanny, Miss Maud Alice Wallace, had been engaged before I was born, so I was *her* baby. She preferred boys, and in years to come would tell me I was so quiet that nobody knew there was a baby on board till we reached Colombo. After two and a half years in Ceylon, we returned to Ireland in 1930. During the next two years we sometimes stayed in Dublin with our father's mother at 42 Eaton Square, Terenure; but more often lived in an old bungalow called Ardnasilla Lodge close to the shore of Lough Corrib. My Ormsby grandparents were then at the Rectory, Oughterard, where my younger sister Elizabeth was born on 16 May 1930.

More than once my mother told me of the worst thing I did before the age of three. 'You were all very excited at seeing your baby sister Elizabeth for the first time. Nanny brought you over with Mary and Christopher, walking from Ardnasilla. After everyone had admired the baby in the nursery, we went down to the drawing room, and while we were chatting, nobody noticed that you had slipped away upstairs to have another look. When you came back you announced in a loud voice: "That's a very strong baby. I leant on her and she didn't break."'

In those days the devil was blamed for the wickedness of a child, and the recognised way of curing the child's wickedness was to give the devil a 'sound thrashing'.

My memories begin at the age of three in the operating theatre of a Dublin nursing home, when I was about to be circumcised. A doctor told me to blow up a ball, and when I woke up there was a bandage on what Nanny called my tail. The operation was meant to stop me playing with it, and did so for about eleven years.

I can't remember being nearly drowned in a well soon after Elizabeth was born. My brother Chris says: 'We were prohibited from going near the well at Ardnasilla, and I wanted to see someone swimming. So I threw a ball into the well and told you to fetch it. When you were standing on the brink, unable to reach the ball, I pushed you into the water and told you to swim, demonstrating with my arms. After going under and surfacing, you clung to a pipe overhead and began crying. I kept telling you to let go and try to swim ashore, which you could not do. Our gardener, Roger Joyce, pulled you out.'

Our mother remembers that she was bathing the baby at the time. 'I ran out hearing the shouts, and you toddled towards me saying "I'm velly velly vet." Chris wanted to be a good boy and do what he was told, which was not to go near the well, so he tried to make you fetch his ball and get into trouble instead.'

All I can remember of the incident is a dream superimposed on a memory. It seems as if I was learning to swim in a tank, sinking now and then out of my depth, and at last catching hold of a pipe above my head, holding on to it for a long time. The pipe was a few inches over the water, and horizontal. My loved and hated brother does not appear in the dream, nor am I shoved in the back, and the terror has been washed away.

We loved Ardnasilla, where we could run wild in our bare feet in a big garden surrounded by a high wall of limestone, with a bog on one side and Lough Corrib on the other. Chris had a drake that was run over by Daddy when he came on leave with a car. My duck had disappeared just before this, eaten by a fox we assumed, so Chris and I were equally inconsolable. But we were Christian soldiers, believing in martyrdom, miracles and resurrection, so I thanked God with immense relief and joy the day my duck appeared in the yard with seven ducklings.

Under Nanny's vigilance, we lived in fear of doing or saying, touching or eating or seeing anything that was wrong or wrong for us, for which we could be punished by her with a shaking that made us see stars, or, by God, with death. On our walks along the gravel lane to Miss Welby's cottage near Aughnanure Castle, where we went every day to fetch a pail of milk that we took turns to carry, I was scared of eating a strawberry or a blackberry in case it might be poisonous. When I bit a mouthful of glass out of the rim of a tumbler of water during a meal, though I spat out all the pieces as quickly as possible, I was terrified of dying there and then. Birth and death were fearfully close to each other in Connemara at that age. Many children of large families less protected than we were died of tuberculosis, diphtheria, typhoid, measles, scarlet fever and whooping cough.

We kept white rabbits in cages, and I was over the moon when my beautiful, gentle white rabbit had five babies. But then she did the most horrible thing a mother could do: one by one she ate them. There was a swallow hole we passed on our walks, and Nanny always pointed out the danger of falling in. 'You'd be sucked underground and never seen again.' We threw primroses into the stream and watched them disappear.

My earliest memory of Milford is of a ruin seen from a car at the end of a dark tunnel of lime trees; men walking around with shotguns held in the crooks of their arms; my father asleep on a chaise longue after shooting rabbits; a kitchen as big as a barn with raw stone walls blackened by soot from a great open hearth; pots hanging on hooks from a crane and boiling over on to a roaring log fire. We had come for a day's outing from Ardnasilla. Nanny took me upstairs to what they called the guest room. All the furniture had gone to the Rectory. She told me, 'This is where you came into the world from God knows where.'

My mother remembers: 'After a meal at 42 Eaton Square, Grandmother gave you a dustpan and a brush and told you to sweep up the crumbs off the floor. When you'd done what you'd been told to do obediently, you said to her: "At our house in Ceylon we have servants to do these things." You were four years old.'

Mary remembers: 'I was dressed to match Elizabeth. You and Christopher were dressed in little blue shorts to match each other …'

I never saw Grandmother wearing anything but a long black dress that almost reached the floor. She was in perpetual mourning for her brave younger son who had sacrificed his life soon after the Great War started, and for her husband who had suffered like a saint and finally succumbed to an incurable illness less than two years later.

My father's younger sister Kay, influenced by Aunt Bella, had become headmistress of the junior branch of Liverpool College for Girls. In the absence of Nanny one afternoon, Aunty Kay, on holiday in Dublin, took me for a walk in Eaton Square. Many years later she told me that when I fell and cut my hand, she had picked out of my coat pocket to use as a bandage the handkerchief that Nanny had taught me to fold into a diamond shape to look smart. I had begged her to use something else so as not to spoil my clean pocket handkerchief.

Chris remembers Grandmother, who was Aunt Bella's younger sister, as 'very intense and religious'. She was always generous to 'down-and-out ex-servicemen in tatty coats and caps' who used to appear in front of the house and sing songs accompanied by an accordion, a hurdy-gurdy or a trumpet. 'Grandmother would take me to the window, and say, "Those are brave soldiers, and they fought for their country, and now they are destitute." She was still deeply upset about Kipher's heroic death in 1914. Then she'd throw out some silver coins.

'One day we were walking from the dining room to the parlour, and as we were crossing the hall, just in front of us, the gaslight chandelier broke loose from the ceiling and fell at our feet, smashing to pieces. Grandmother promptly took me down on my knees to give thanks for our deliverance. The Lord had prevented us being right underneath this flaming gas lamp when it fell, and had made it fall just a fraction of a second before we got there. But I thought God was trying to kill us and had missed.'

Number 42 Eaton Square filled my mind with the fear of death. It was there that all three of us children – our baby sister was kept away in Oughterard for her own safety – nearly died of whooping cough. It was from there that I was taken to Aunt Bella's tea party at the Royal Hibernian Hotel, which ended with me kicking her instead of saying thank you. Dingy, respectable, mahogany gloom. The bogeyman in the cupboard.

Mary remembers – but she says these childhood memories are of no importance – lying on her trunk in the cabin of the Bibby boat as it was coming into Port Said, and thinking, as she sucked a lemon drop, that as soon as the boat had entered the harbour and the sweet had dissolved in her mouth, this moment of time would have passed and could never again return, but that she would recall the passing of this moment, the acid taste of the lemon drop, as the ship moved into Port Said, and remember this thought about time for the rest of her life.

According to Mary, Nanny was fond of me because she preferred boys to girls and she was hired at the time of my birth, when Mary was four years old and close to Mummy. 'Nanny was very strict,' Mary said, 'but even when she slapped us, she made us feel secure. Nanny told me, "Your eyes are too small and your hair is frizzy. You've no reason to be vain and looking at yourself in the mirror. The boys have the good eyes in the family."'

While Nanny did her utmost to prevent us being injured, infected or poisoned, her discipline was as punitive as custom required it to be at that time. When she lost her temper, she would say to Chris, more likely than to me, 'Come here and let me give you a good shaking.' Grasping him by the shoulders and scolding him as if he were a dog, she would shake him backwards and forwards like a rag doll until he could see nothing but stars.

When I was four and a half, we returned to Ceylon on the SS *Oxfordshire* in April 1932. As this was the hottest month of the year, Mary, Chris and I, with Liz almost two years old, were taken by Nanny upcountry on the train with two engines – 'push-you-beggar-pull-you-beggar' – climbing through tea estates to Diyetalawa. Our father was now the Mayor of Colombo, and our mother remained with him in Colombo while waiting for the new baby to arrive.

At Greystones, a bungalow lent to us by a rich planter, six men and two women served us in the house and the garden. 'I don't like the cook,' Nanny wrote, 'he is extravagant and doesn't help in trying to make things do, but I just *sit on him* now.' The night before Edward's birth on 24 April 1932, Nanny advised me to pray that God would give me a baby brother. 'The thunder rolled and crashed and rumbled over our heads and the lightning was very vivid,' she noted in her next letter. 'We have had "visitors galore", and "galore" is Richard's favourite word this morning. He has just been in to ask if angels could live with people. He said he would like one to live with him and that he would be kind to it!'

I spent most of the next three years in Colombo. Tilton, in Ward Place, was an old Dutch colonial bungalow set in a large garden or compound, a short walk from the town hall. More things frightened me in Ceylon than in Ireland: snakes most of all and the danger of a coconut falling on my head or of a scorpion stinging my foot if I were to forget to shake my shoes before putting them on in the morning. A glass of water might have killed me had it not been boiled and filtered. Nanny would often add a drop of Milton or permanganate of potash for extra purification. To prevent malaria she used to make me swallow daily a teaspoonful of bittersweet cinnamon essence, because she thought quinine was bad for young children. Perhaps this was why I wanted to become a doctor.

Polecats in the roof caused yellow wet stains to appear on our nursery ceiling. Mary can remember the eyes of a polecat peering through a ventilator grille in the wall of her bedroom, and caravanserais of ants crossing the polished red concrete floor. The legs of our beds stood in little bowls of disinfectant to prevent insects climbing up. Believing a tiger lived under my bed, I used to take a running jump into bed and lie in the centre, where the tiger could not reach me with his claws. A Milky Way of fireflies entering the room and swarming around the mosquito net lightened our darkness at night. During the south-west monsoon that began in May, I loved the drip, gurgle and patter of rain, each drop of water striking a different note in a tin or a bucket or a china bowl on the floor of the verandah.

Nanny's grey hair was plaited and coiled in a bun. Her jade necklace used to tickle my throat as she leaned under the mosquito net to hug me, calling me her pet and giving me kisses that smelt of Pond's Cold Cream. She had a wart on her forehead and her breasts were very big. 'Keep your hands up over the sheets,' she often told me, 'and never play with your tail because it's filthy.' I promised to marry her when I grew up, but when I imagined what this would be like – the 'Wedding March' in church, no possibility of escape – it made me feel sick.

Green was Nanny's favourite colour, and mine because it was hers and Ireland's. She wore a green cloche hat pulled down in front almost to her eyes, which were small and brown, whereas my right eye was hazel and my left greeny grey. A very long pin, piercing the bun, kept her hat from blowing off her head when we walked as far as the lighthouse at the end of the breakwater. We could never reach the lighthouse during the monsoon, but on a rough day, Nanny, holding my hand, once took me near enough to watch, as wave after wave of the Indian Ocean rose and spilled across the unwalled surface of the breakwater into the harbour.

Nobody knew where she came from – that was her secret. She said her father was a soldier who had died before she was born. We knew she was joking when she told us she was born in Timbuktu, as Timbuktu was not in the British Empire. She had refused to marry James Joyce, Grandfather's steward at Milford, because he had wanted a wedding in the Catholic church. Nanny had thought this would have been 'as bad as marrying a Hindu'. She inclined us to believe that the fearful loud rattle of tom-toms and the screech of pipes in Buddhist or Hindu processions along Ward Place had more to do with the devil than with God.

Every morning at six o'clock, when it was cool, Nanny made Mary and Chris do a hundred skips with a skipping rope, but she allowed me to ride around the compound on the bicycle that she had given me as a sixth birthday present. Then she would order our Tamil chauffeur to drive us in the Crossley to the officer's beach below Admiralty House on the Galle Face Green. After eight o'clock we were forbidden to go out of doors, at home or in kindergarten, without wearing heavy white topees – pith helmets – in case of sunstroke.

After lunch Nanny made us all have an afternoon rest for an hour, lying in bed but without a pillow. 'A pillow is bad for your neck,' she explained, 'it will make you stoop, and you must stand straight.' Once, but never again, I borrowed a pillow from her bed without asking her, and fell asleep. She woke me by snatching the pillow from under my head, giving me a shock. 'It serves you right.' Before I went to bed she stuck my ears to my skull with sticking plaster, and tore it off, hurting me, when I got up. 'It will stop you looking like a monkey.'

On the nursery gramophone, Strauss's *Blue Danube*, Gilbert and Sullivan's *The Gondoliers* and Elgar's *Pomp and Circumstance* were Nanny's favourite records, therefore mine. I started piano lessons at five, and Nanny took me to a concert of Beethoven and Chopin given by the pianist Mark Hambourg on 7 February 1933. As a result of being vaccinated against smallpox on the ship in Colombo Harbour before he disembarked, his left leg had swollen so badly that it had to be propped up, swathed in bandages, on a long stool beside him. Now when I hear the *Moonlight Sonata* or the *Grande Polonaise*, I remember Mark Hambourg and the spotlight on his bandaged left leg.

Nanny taught me to read and write at six. The stories she told best combined heroism with disaster, such as the disappearance of Mallory in a snowstorm within reach of the summit of Mount Everest. The books she read to herself were detective novels by Edgar Wallace.

When I knocked over the stuffed head of a buffalo that my father had shot, breaking one of its horns, Nanny advised me to own up to him like a gentleman, not to my mother. I confessed my guilt as soon as he came home from the town hall. Sitting, he made me lie across his knees while he smacked me with a slipper. That was over quickly, but worse was to follow. Instead of letting me sleep as usual in my bed in Nanny's room, he made me lie alone in his study, awake for much of the night, facing a tree occupied by a demon in the form of a snake and thousands of crows.

Chris and I, in Mary's eyes, were cruel to our younger sister Liz. When Liz was three years old, we swung her so high in a hammock attached to two temple trees in the garden that she fell out and broke her collarbone. When she was four and I was seven, I persuaded her to let me set fire to her celluloid doll on the nursery floor. She was deeply upset, and thereafter terrified of her brothers playing with matches.

Nanny had given me a cat called Marmalade, which I loved, and of which Chris had reason to be jealous. He told me one day, when I was playing with Marmalade on the upstairs verandah of the Chief Secretary's Lodge in Kandy, that cats can fall from a great height without hurting themselves because they are not like us – they have four feet to land on. He dared me, on pain of being called a spoilsport or a crybaby, to prove this by dropping Marmalade off the verandah into the garden. So I dropped Marmalade, whose legs splayed out like an *X* as he fell and landed on all fours. When I saw him lying motionless on the grass, I feared he was dead, but soon he crept across the lawn into the jungle and disappeared. Nanny said a leopard or a monkey would be sure to kill him if he didn't die of his injuries. My father beat me, but worse was the pain of losing my beloved cat.

A few days later, Marmalade came back, uninjured, and purred in my arms.

Nanny pitied the rickshaw coolies, who died young because they had to run like horses between the shafts all day barefoot on the hot red laterite roads in the sweltering heat. But when she was in a hurry, and the man pulling the rickshaw slowed to a walk, she would call him a lazy devil.

I sometimes wondered how I had been born as a boy in our family rather than as the son or the less fortunate daughter of a Sinhalese or Tamil coolie. The key to it all seemed to be that we spoke English, through which we had direct access to God through our prayers. We used to hear our father reading aloud from the Bible at St Peter's Church in the Fort every Sunday morning. I assumed that our language was God's and that He had chosen me to be the person I was because my parents had prayed for me to be born, as I had prayed for Edward. It seemed obvious that praying in Sinhala or Tamil achieved poorer results. On a little globe that Nanny had given me, she pointed out that we ruled a third of the world. In return for our privilege, God expected us to behave well, work hard, do our duty and set a good example.

The natives of Ceylon, we were assured by our parents as well as by Nanny, ought to have been grateful to us for having brought them the benefit of our language and civilisation. We had saved them from the cruelty they had previously suffered for hundreds of years under the Dutch and the Portuguese and their own despotic kings. Though my father was able to speak and read both Sinhala and Tamil, we children were taught nothing about the resplendent island's ancient Buddhist culture.

Among those who spoke English, my family believed, none spoke it as well as the Anglo-Irish, who provided Britain with her best army officers and civil servants. Though the English might laugh at us for being Irish, and the Irish resent us for being English, England needed us to win her wars through our courage and to rule her colonies with our sense of justice.

Merely by virtue of the rank my father had earned – since we had no wealth, not even a house of our own – we lived at the top of society in one of the richest Crown colonies of the greatest empire on earth. We deluded ourselves into thinking our empire might last longer than the Roman's because it was founded on better moral principles. Ceylon had one of the highest rates of literacy in Asia. My father had advanced the cause of education, particularly of women, in all the outstations where he had served, and he approved of the ultimate aim of leading the colony towards independence.

When Mary was ten and Christopher less than eight years old, custom in the colonial service required that they be brought home, to avoid growing up too fast in Ceylon and becoming decadent, corrupt and unreliable. The English missionaries who lived next door to us in Ward Place were frowned upon for letting their daughter, Mary's age, stay on and attend a school full of Sinhala and Tamil girls. The families of those girls may have been richer than ours, and some had royal pedigrees a thousand years more ancient and legitimate than our mother's, but this didn't make them 'better' in our eyes: it made them more suspect.

So Mary and Christopher sailed home with our mother on a Bibby liner in August 1933, to spend the next two years with Granny and Grandfather at the Rectory, Oughterard. Until March 1935 I enjoyed my father's attention. Every night I said my prayers kneeling, because it hurt, on the coconut mat at his feet as he lay back in a long wooden armchair on the verandah, smoking his pipe. After church on Sundays, he gave me swimming lessons in the pool at the Galle Face Hotel; and when I could swim, he took me to the beach at Mount Lavinia.

At his side on official occasions, my neck was hung with garlands of jasmine and temple flowers, and my picture appeared in the paper because I was a son of the mayor.

Nanny woke me up one night to tell me there was bad news from Ireland. Our grandmother at Eaton Square in Dublin had died on 8 July 1934. I have a memory of my mother lying on her bed weeping, still holding the telegram. My father was standing on the far side of the bed looking miserable, hardly able to speak because he was so upset. I knew that they expected me to cry, but I didn't feel sad. Was there something wrong with me? To please them, I rubbed my eyes to produce tears, and sobbed a little. Going back to bed, I felt ashamed.

Susan was my age, or a little older, my best friend at the kindergarten when I was seven. Sometimes I played at her house, and once in a cavern among the boulders protecting the road from the sea at the Officer's Beach, we touched tongues. In the bathroom at her house one day, she decided to examine my 'tail', holding it stiff in her hand. Then she plucked a bristle from the brush used to clean the WC and inserted it like a catheter, causing intense pain, 'to see how far up it would go'. Nanny used to say girls were spiteful, and after this I was inclined to agree.

I did worse when I showed my 'tail' to the poorest of our poor Tamil servants, known as the 'bathroom coolie', who once appeared in a loincloth at our bathroom's back door when I was doing what we called a 'big job'. As my 'tail' grew hard, I stood up and pointed it at him with a thrust. He retreated without a word, and I was aware that what I had done was unspeakable and the guilt would remain for the rest of my life.

When the island was struck by a great epidemic of malaria a few months before we were to leave Ceylon, my mother took me to one of the convalescent hospitals she had helped to set up in a cattle shed that the Municipality of Colombo had built but not yet used for livestock. My father had made the order to hand it over to the Ceylon Social Service League.

Looking through a doorway, I could see the floor extending a long way into darkness, covered with people who were very sick, lying under sheets on coconut mats. It confirmed my ambition to become a doctor, but meanwhile made me redouble my effort to convince God in my prayers that He should keep me alive through the days that had to be endured before we could climb the gangway at the side of the SS *Worcestershire* in the harbour, and disembark at Port Said to visit Jerusalem and the birthplace of Jesus on our way home to Ireland for good.

In March 1935 the Municipal Council gave a farewell lunch for my father and mother at the Grand Oriental Hotel. Mr C.H.Z. Fernando, a councillor, was reported to have said: 'Mrs Murphy has done wonderful work among the poor in Colombo which no other lady, European or Ceylonese, had ever done before. It seemed a wonder to everybody how so frail a lady could exhibit such indefatigable energy.'

In May 1935, aged seven, when staying with our grandparents at the Rectory, Oughterard, I found that Chris had acquired a brogue and the ability to walk on gravel in bare feet, like many children around Oughterard who had no shoes. He took delight in teaching me all he had learnt about Ireland, such as how to light a turf fire by carrying a red-hot coal in tongs from the kitchen range to the small stone hut he had built for himself in the garden. A fireside in Ireland, he said, is a place where people tell stories. We sat on three-legged milking stools and he expected me to listen, not to interrupt.

'You must be careful out of doors,' he warned me, holding up a hand with the fingers and thumb wide apart, 'never to cut your hand in the joint between your thumb and your first finger, because if you do, you may get lockjaw. Your spine will bend further and further back until your head touches your feet. You won't be able to talk or eat or drink and the pain will go on getting worse until you die because there is no cure for lockjaw.'

After this I tried to remember to keep the gap between my thumb and forefinger closed when playing in the yard or the garden. A few days later, as we were standing beside a bed of nasturtiums, he warned me that the leaves were deadly poisonous, and immediately picked a large leaf and saying, 'I want to die,' stuffed it into his mouth and began chewing. I tried to force my fingers between his tight-shut lips to grab the leaf before it had gone down his throat, but Chris went on chewing and swallowing – until he burst out laughing and called me a 'bloody fool'.

We were all a little afraid of Grandfather because he looked severe in a black suit with a broad Church dog collar and a monocle dangling on a thread. He parted his short grey hair in the centre and closed his pale blue eyes while saying grace. Little things made him cross. His habit of coming in late for meals at the Rectory annoyed Granny, while she annoyed him by letting her favourite black Labrador, Annie Snipe, jump up behind her and sit with her head resting on Granny's left shoulder, waiting for titbits to be popped into her mouth. Granny had taught her a trick to demonstrate her faithfulness. 'This is from Hitler,' she would say, offering a bit of meat, which the dog would refuse. 'This is from Mussolini,' she would tempt, but Annie Snipe would not open her mouth until she could hear Granny say: 'This is from your mistress.'

Granny was as small as our mother and just as thin, overfeeding everybody while eating little herself. She suffered greatly from rheumatism, and often in the middle of a meal would choke so badly that she had to leave the dining room to recover from a fit of coughing in the bathroom. But she never lost her sense of fun or her tolerance of our misbehaviour.

My love of the north-west corner of Connemara goes back to the summer of my eighth birthday at Rosleague, a big ivy-clad house standing high among trees with a view of Diamond Mountain and the rotting hulks of trawlers at the quay of Letterfrack. Mrs Browne, a Twining of Twining's Tea, had let the house to my father for his long leave from Ceylon in 1935. It was the last time and place in which all five of us children were to live at home with both parents and Nanny. They allowed us to run a bit wild before the school gates of Baymount Castle in Dublin would close behind us in September.

Meanwhile, for lessons Mary, Chris and I cycled to school at Kylemore Abbey, passing the unfortunate orphans, felons and homeless boys imprisoned in the Letterfrack Industrial School. The Benedictine nuns taught Chris and me in a separate class, where we learnt to say the Lord's Prayer in Irish and to sing a few Irish songs.

On Sundays our mother dressed Chris and me in Eton collars, hoping we might win Eton scholarships. The stiffness of the collars choked me. Wearing them with a black suit and singing 'Onward, Christian Soldiers' at Moyard church made me feel sick, and when at lunch I found a pellet in a mouthful of rabbit that my father had shot, I thought I would die.

Chris and I loved exploring three old fishing boats that lay at the Letterfrack pier, their planks sprouting seaweed, their engines seized with rust, under water at every high tide. Their past was a mystery. Everyone had a different story as to why these trawlers that had never caught a fish had been abandoned there to rot. Our father said they were typical of Connemara, an example of the idleness we would have to be sent off to boarding school to avoid.

Here Nanny's changeable moods of rain and sunshine governing our lives came to an end. I would miss her weather and care, the iodine sting of the sea she applied on the tip of a feather down my sore throat to make it better.

The strictness of those we loved, their ambition to improve us, the *vox humana* organ sound of their appeals for us to try harder to be good and do something useful with our lives, clashed with the rebel spirit that Chris and I found in Connemara, where those who were born and lived in thatched cottages on a few acres of poor rocky land let us ride their donkeys as much as we wished. Our kick against the pricks of our family, the maternal cleaning of string and seashells out of our pockets, the picking of spots on our faces, was to filthy ourselves in the rotting boats, and chase off through the dark woods riding donkeys bareback and back to front without bridles, making asses of ourselves.

I kissed my mother so often as a child that she called me her 'kissing son', and when at the age of eight I was placed with Chris at Baymount Preparatory School on the north shore of Dublin Bay, she began her letters to him 'My own Eldest Son', and to me 'My own K.S.'. The joy of this secret identity in a crowd of thirty-one strange and mostly bigger boys was confounded when I revealed the code to one I thought was a friend. He made me a target of ridicule.

Chris resented my being a 'K.S.', but bravely stood up for me and took the pummelling I had incurred by some cheeky retort to a mocking senior. We could no longer call each other Chris or Rick in the hearing of other boys. We were Murphy major or Murphy minor, the suffix shortened to its first syllable, ma- or mi-. Our Christian names were reduced to initials on Cash's name tapes sewn on to every article required by the school 'clothes list', from grey herringbone tweed coats and short trousers down to face flannels.

We lived in a battleship-grey three-storey baronial castle with twin turrets, dated over the hall door 1838, surrounded by woods and playing fields in grounds of twenty-four acres. The avenue was lined with beeches where rooks perched at sunset, making a raucous din. There were tall dark evergreen oaks and silver birches with witch knots growing on their branches. The only boy we knew was our much older cousin, Dick McClelland.

As soon as our parents had driven away through the spiked iron gates of the lodge, leaving us terribly homesick for the next ninety days, I started to keep an end-of term calendar, ticking off each day as it passed and reducing the number that remained to the holidays. Both Chris and I broke all the petty rules at first, and the headmaster, Mr W. Lucas Scott, complained to my father that we were having a bad effect on school discipline: 'Christopher was overheard lecturing his brother on his behaviour who retorted "Shut up, you are not my nurse."'

My letters home suggest that I was happier than I remember, but we wrote on Sundays knowing that Mr or Mrs Scott would read our letters before they were posted. 'It is great fun' and 'the boys are very nice' I wrote in my first letter to 'My darling Dad' and likewise to 'My dear Mum'; 'it is great fun / the boys are very niece / espesly Dobbs Ma / today we will be playing / football / the boys are all / fighting … / Please / give / Nan / my / love / good / bye'. There is no mention of anxieties, fears and ordeals.

My hero was Dobbs major, who invented such good stories to entertain us that Mr Scott caned him six strokes on the backside for telling lies. We counted them from the dark tiled hallway outside the headmaster's study door. I was to meet Kildare Dobbs in Canada in 1976, by which time he had won a Governor General's Award for his memoirs. He told me, 'The boys at Baymount were cruel to you because your mother was beautiful and she called you her kissing son.' I was able to remind him that he had won a five-shilling bet by eating a live earthworm and swallowing a bottle of ink.

My best friend was Dobbs minor, a year older than I was, with straight blond hair like his brother's. In the bed next to mine after lights out, he used to whisper to me about women's breasts. He called these our 'pap talks'. His mother's father, Dr John Henry Bernard, archbishop of Dublin, provost of Trinity College and friend of my father's Aunt Bella, had christened him Bernard.

The Dobbs boys had been brought up in India. Their father, a judge in the India Civil Service, and ours, the Mayor of Colombo, were equally important persons who would seldom see their sons. Both parents believed that Baymount, with no more than five or six boys in each class, and a ratio of one teacher to four or five boys, would prepare us to win scholarships to a famous public school, while training our characters. They wanted to give their sons a good start on the high road to positions as responsible as theirs in the quarter of the world still dominated by Britain.

They were proved right, in that Bernard Dobbs would become the last resident British ambassador to Laos, but wrong in the case of Kildare, who began a career in the colonial service that ended in a Tanganyikan prison on a trumped-up charge connected with licences to shoot elephants for ivory.

Baymount was run on the principle of sweet rewards to be won by punishing ordeals, and the principle was embedded in our minds by a symbolic rite of passage imposed on the youngest boy in the school at Halloween. I was the youngest in 1935. Tall gaunt Mrs Scott, who always had a drop at the end of her nose, baked a castle of a cake, and during the five weeks between our arrival at Baymount and the party on 31 October, older boys tormented me with descriptions of what I would have to undergo. 'There'll only be one big candle on the cake,' I was told, 'and you'll have to stand on a chair in the assembly hall in front of the whole school and take a big bite out of the candle while it is burning. If you blow it out before you bite, you'll be branded a coward.'

My fear was dissolved in pride at being granted this privilege. As the nephew of Uncle Kipher, who let a train run over him, and Uncle Jack, who accepted the challenge of his regiment to eat a wine glass, when the time came, I didn't flinch. At the last moment, my courage having passed the test, Mr Scott blew through his tobacco-stained moustache and put out the candle before I bit. Since then I have never cared for the sweetness of marzipan. More to my taste was the applause.

Why did I have to do this? To honour and ingest a school tradition dating from 1904, proving that I could stomach the cruelty of separation from everyone that I loved except my brother, whom I sometimes hated, for the sake of a great plan kept secret by God for my future. Now I could only see

Nanny and my family when I knelt to say my prayers on the hard linoleum, my face buried in my hands and my elbows on the bed in the dormitory. When I wrote to my mother, I dared not add a cross for a kiss or a nought for a hug, but I could speak to her and my father in the process of writing letters. Therefore I wrote a lot, far more than Chris, and came to love writing for its own sake.

Mr Scott encouraged at Baymount the production of a magazine containing stories, poems and pictures written, drawn and painted by the boys on single sheets that we stitched together to bind into a single volume. As we had neither time nor means to make copies, the magazine was distributed by mail from one home to another during the Christmas holidays. By the end of our first term, I was telling 'my darling Daddy' in a letter to Ceylon, 'I have allready got a poem into the Magazine, and I am making up a story. This term our Mag will be terribly small because every one is so lazy and in about a fortnights time it will have to be bound.' When the magazine reached the Rectory, Oughterard, it was torn to bits by Granny's dogs.

Our normal games were soccer in the autumn, hockey in the spring, and cricket in the summer terms. I was keen on all these games, my sight not requiring me then to wear glasses. We never played a match against a Catholic school. On rare occasions we fought a rough and thrilling 'war game' between Cavaliers and Roundheads, the captains choosing turn by turn the boys they wanted in their armies. Our front line was in a wood surrounding a sunken muddy lane smelling of leaf mould and garlic, where it was easy to find chestnuts and sloes as ammunition for our catapults to snipe at each other from behind trees. The enemy's banner had to be captured with bare hands. As a loyal Cavalier serving gallant Dobbs ma-, I was less afraid of being cut down by a sword in the form of a sharpened stick or being hit in the eye than of falling where a plant such as deadly nightshade might touch my lips.

On a fine Sunday afternoon, if the tide was out, we went for a long walk across the Clontarf Road and tramline to play in the sand dunes and look for shells on the shore of Bull Island. There we were warned to watch out for quicksand that might swallow us, or a rapidly rising tide like the one that drowned the Danes at the Battle of Clontarf. One dismal wet Sunday, after a reading by Mr Scott about the Slough of Despond from *The Pilgrim's Progress*, I watched two boys taking turns to thrash or be thrashed by each other, each running the length of a long room to inflict more and more powerful blows with a leather belt, until one was forced to cry 'Pax!'

Perhaps because it was unthinkable, I have no recollection of Nanny coming to Baymount in our second term to say goodbye because she was leaving us forever. But Chris remembers that she took us into the sickroom, unoccupied on that day, and when she said she would be going to India with another family, 'You rushed into her arms and cried, "Oh Nanny! Oh Nanny! No Nanny! Don't go!" while I sat there feeling, "She's leaving, so what?" I didn't think it was the end of the world, at least not as much as you thought it was, and I felt guilty that I hadn't more desperate grief.'

My prayers at Baymount included asking God to stave off disasters; to prevent a poisonous seed from the green pod of a yellow laburnum falling into my mouth; and prevent me catching diphtheria and having to breathe through a hole in my neck, with Grandfather kneeling at my bedside reciting 'A Prayer for a Sick Person, when there appeareth but small hope of Recovery'; and prevent Mussolini bombing the poor Abyssinians in order to create a new unholy Roman Empire; and never to allow a fast bodyline bowler like Larwood to aim a ball at my heart; nor let the world collide with a giant star as predicted by a sage in the *Daily Sketch*.

What was I going to be, to save the world and myself? A doctor, I thought, with bedside manners modelled on the Wykehamist motto that Mummy wanted me to live up to: 'Manners Makyth Man'. Better still, a missionary doctor in Ceylon, fighting malaria and demons, where 'every prospect pleases and only man is vile', as we sang in the choir of All Saints', Raheny. On Sundays we walked to church two by two in a crocodile through the woods of St Anne's.

We were well instructed at Baymount in small classes by good teachers, some of whom had wicked tempers. We had piano, drawing and singing lessons, but no Irish. The first twenty minutes of school after prayers every day was devoted to divinity, which meant reading and learning the Bible so well that we absorbed its style. I loved the Old Testament stories and the parables of Jesus. Mr Patterson, who had flaming red hair and a temper to match, never got cross in divinity, and gave me prizes of holy pictures.

Only in mathematics did he go berserk. He taught geometry and algebra brilliantly to boys who responded to terror, as I did, by taking extra care to understand the figures he scrawled on the blackboard, and to get our answers right. But Bernard Dobbs, looking back almost sixty years, thought he was a bad teacher, who alternately screamed at the boys in his maths class and fondled them while talking about the love of God.

He would get so excited, explaining a beautiful theorem of Euclid to those he called idiots, that he would knock on the board with his knuckles till they bled. Mistakes caused by inattention struck him as discords in the divine mathematical harmony of the universe. The result could be chaos. He often flung a piece of chalk at a confused boy, confusing him more, and sometimes the blackboard duster with a wooden back at one who seemed obtuse. In a senior class, we heard, he had lifted the blackboard off its easel and flung it at the boys.

This seemed to me more funny than fearful, as no one got seriously injured. Once I wrote home, 'Mr. Patterson really is very nice only he gets rather cross and thats what made me not like him much. But today he told me he really didn't mean it.' I respected his rage for accuracy as it was meant to help me win a scholarship in the future. The two weeks he would spend over Easter 1941 coaching me privately at Milford did in fact help me to win two. He was calmer there, and when he put a hand on my knee – never higher – I took it as a sign of his passion for me to succeed.

The worst fault of Baymount was that women didn't add up to much in our masculine equations, with the result that my mind was poorly prepared for the later equations of sex. Another bad result of Mr Patterson's method of teaching maths is that I cannot help a child to do sums for more than five minutes without being in danger of losing my temper.

Memories of Baymount by other old boys have confirmed my own. The hare leading our paperchase through the woods and fields of St Anne's was Alan Browne, who in 1956, as master of the Rotunda Hospital in Dublin, would deliver my daughter Emily. He told me in 1993 that when he first went to Baymount, three years before I did, he went through agonies of homesickness.

Chris and Bernard both recall a boy who was shamefully punished for wetting his bed almost every night. He was made to wash his own pyjamas and hang them to dry where the whole school could see them.

My cousin Dick McClelland, who transformed himself into the London stage, television and film actor Richard Leech, summed up his feelings about Baymount at the Garrick Club, where he invited me to dine in 1993: 'I cried a lot at Baymount,' he said. 'It wasn't done to cry, we had to learn to hide our tears.'

When I went back to Baymount for the first time, forty-five years after I had left, the castle had been turned into a Jesuit seminary called Manresa Lodge. The old dormitory in which the headmaster reported that I had 'raised Cain' had become a chapel in which the Blessed Sacrament was kept in a tabernacle.

Now the Jesuits have gone, and the grounds are entirely covered by houses.

In a dream I hear the voice of a railway porter crying out the name of a station where our train has halted – 'Mullingar! Mullingar!' – the first stop on the line that used to run beside the Royal Canal out of Dublin, taking Chris and me, sometimes me alone, from Baymount to Milford for the holidays, beginning at Easter 1936. I enter Mullingar through the liquids of its name, linked with a view of a golden cupola and a dog track and the Irish sound of a porter's voice borne on the wind in rain that could never dampen my joy on those homeward journeys.

What other stations excited me? 'Athlone!' because by now we have crossed the Shannon heading west, and the Ireland where we belong begins, recognised by the limestone walls and the smell of turf smoke from all the open fires in the kitchens of Connaught. From Roscommon down the line, porters, guards and people meeting friends off the train on the platforms speak with accents that I love to hear.

'Castlerea!' 'Ballinlough!' I lean out of the window looking for the rectory where Daddy was born, but cannot see it from the train. At Ballyhaunis we lift our suitcases off the rack and move them into the corridor, to be ready to jump when the train reaches Claremorris. This takes for ever, my head out of the window and soot in my eyes from the smoke of the engine.

Then there is a half-hour delay in a cold wet breeze on another platform while a very old engine with a tall funnel, standing beside a water tower, raises enough steam to reach the all-but-abandoned station of Hollymount. When Bob the guard blows his whistle till he is red in the face, I climb into a compartment with seats upholstered in the reign of Queen Victoria, smelling of dust.

The little train wobbles on the rusty tracks, not daring to go as fast as I wish it would across the bogs of south Mayo, until just before it comes to a halt, I jump down and rush into Mummy's arms. Big Martin Walsh, crippled with rheumatism, sits at the wheel of his black Ford V8 hackney and drives us, far too slowly for my liking, over six miles of muddy byroads, passing Sonny Joyce at the door of his forge and three barrel-top caravans of Tinkers in Rathgranagher, to the gates of Milford.

'Do you remember,' my mother asked in her last year, 'you arrived on the train at Hollymount, having come all the way from Canterbury, bringing me a bunch of pink tulips? Christopher had missed the boat train at Euston because he was watching *Gulliver's Travels* in a cinema for the second time.'

In the old days, Mrs Davin, followed by two or three of her seven children in bare feet, would run from the front door of the gate lodge to open the Milford gates on our return by car or sidecar drawn by a horse. She would shake hands with each of us, long clasping our hands, her large eyes, which Mary remembers as yellow with brown spots in a face of aristocratic beauty, full of affection. Sometimes she would ask us to wait while she ran inside to bring out a score of eggs her hens had just laid.

Then we would proceed slowly between the Deer Park and the Sand Park, splashing through potholes that should have been filled with gravel, to the cross-gate. Beyond this, turning a corner, we would enter a dark green nave of lime trees that stretched a long way ahead to a small bright lawn and a pair of erect Irish yews in front of the house. We would hear the dogs barking before we had reached the last gate, and Granny would be waving from her front steps to welcome us home.

The farmyard at Milford stood on a rise where the house should have been, while the house sat below the terraced Pleasure Ground on the edge of a bog. That edge of rich limestone land was a natural fort in the wars of the seventeenth century, long before bogs were drained. The original house was built in 1625 by a family called French, who were Catholics of Norman descent. They were no relation of ours; but after Aughrim's great disaster for the Irish, they yielded the house and land, with its lost names, to our grandfather's mother's ancestor, Robert Miller. To feel at home, and aggrandise his family, he called the place Milford, so that they would be known as the Millers of Milford.

He had come to Ireland as a penniless young cornet, the lowest rank of officer, in Cromwell's army, but had risen rapidly in wealth. Under the policy of settling staunchly loyal Protestants in wild and remote parts of Connaught, he had acquired a castle called Ballycushen, with a large estate lying beyond the bog to the south of Milford. His son, Robert Miller the Second, became high sheriff of County Mayo and built a mansion on a commanding site with a view of mountains to the west. A carved stone lintel bearing the date 1718 stood over the hall door until an act of God a few years later struck the mansion with fire. After this the doorway became an entrance to a stable.

Martin Joyce, the Milford herd, brother of James the steward, told us why the good Lord had punished our ancestors. 'The young Millers,' he said, 'kept a pack of bloodhounds in a place called the Fort, and to make the dogs keener to kill, they used to leave them a little bit hungry. A poor man went into the kennel to feed them, and all that was ever found of him afterwards was his boots. Before the year was out, the Big House had gone up in flames, and the Millers had to move back into the old place, because all their money was spent.'

We were surrounded at Milford by dark mysterious old woods, where none of us dared to walk alone at night, full of hair-raising creatures that made weird sounds. Beyond the garden wall, too high to climb, an immense bog stretched as far as we could see, from the upstairs study window through the branches of a yew tree, to the pale blue hill of Castlehacket on the horizon.

There were two great parks of forty acres each, good limestone land; three round raths with hawthorn-fenced ramparts; and regimental platoons of pines planted where stones had been gathered from the soil by hand long ago. The avenue, measured by the stride of Grandfather, who had been an accountant in the army, was three-quarters of a mile. The Land Commission had taken more than a hundred acres of his best land to settle poor farmers from the mountains beyond Lough Mask, which we could see only if we cycled to Kilmaine. Tall trees and high walls enclosed us in the Milford demesne.

The sun rose and set three-quarters of an hour later than at Greenwich. In summer, at the long day's end, columns of rooks a mile long would return from the cornfields of Ballycushen, Rathgranagher, Kilshanvy, Dalgan and Shrule to roost in our woods. When the columns clashed, the conglomerated cries of these raucous birds, fighting for *Lebensraum* on the branches, became as loud as ocean waves dashing on a pebbly beach.

We had no electricity, gas or telephone, and we lacked water, except for a trickle that John Hughes had to pump every day from the well; and a broad drain that we called the canal; and some bottomless pools on the bog, which we were forbidden to go near.

Instead of buying a house for us in Ireland, my father had been persuaded by our mother to spend as much money on converting the old servants' quarters and kitchens at Milford into a house we called the East Wing. Our wing was divided from the main house, where our grandparents lived, by a long dark corridor, with a door we were told to keep shut. There were twenty-one rooms altogether, not counting larders and sculleries, but only one bathroom in each wing. Grandfather's study, where he kept his guns standing in a glass-fronted case, was at the far end, under the guest room where I had been born. Our new front door faced north towards the lime trees on the avenue.

Most of our windows looked east across the Pleasure Ground, at the top of which was a place called the Lovers' Walk; but during the family's absence it had become a dense jungle of laurels, briars and snowberries, too frightening for us to go near. A yew hedge, unclipped for half a century, had grown into a dark row of trees, at the end of which were the graves of the family's most faithful dogs. We greatly enjoyed climbing and swinging on the branches of a broad solitary yew as high and old as the house, though my pleasure was marred by knowing that its small prickly leaves were poisonous. If a branch with red berries brushed my face, I would run to the bathroom and gargle with TCP, and be laughed at by Mary and Chris.

We had two young maids, who wore white uniforms with frilly lace caps and worked on and off from six in the morning until we went to bed at night. They slept in a box room approached by its own stairs at the back of our kitchen, where they kept a tiny Sacred Heart lamp burning on top of a trunk labelled NOT WANTED ON THE VOYAGE. Each was paid half a crown a week. They had to use a primitive earth closet in a garden shed instead of our bathroom. To prevent them becoming 'familiar', our mother insisted that they use a prefix, Master or Miss, before our names – Miss Mary or Master Christopher. When one occasionally forgot, it gave me a pleasant shock of forbidden equality.

'The bog is a dangerous place for boys,' Chris and I were warned by one of many workmen building a new kitchen for our grandparents in the backyard – a warning that made us want to go there right away. Chris led, and I was eager to follow, climbing bolted and padlocked gates by the well, running along a green lane rutted by cartwheels, passing an alder grove tangled with briars, where Aunty Kay had taken me bird-nesting and taught me to recognise a golden-crested wren, and entering a pine forest, till we came to a bridge across the canal and out into the sunlight on the soft ground of the bog.

Here we intruded on a mystery world of midges and horseflies, sedge warblers, green finches, magpies and scald crows. Surrounding us on all sides were stands of gorse with butter-coloured scented flowers, tall as the tallest of men, though not as high as the silver birches. Pushing through branches, we came out into a big circle of coarse dry sedge. Standing in the centre, with not a breath of air to keep the midges from biting, Chris took from his pocket a magnifying glass, saying he wanted to show me a trick that Roger Joyce, who had pulled me out of the well at Ardnasilla, had taught him. He would start a fire that we would stamp out before it became too big – perfectly safe on such a calm day, he reckoned.

Focusing the sun's rays on a long blade of sedge, he started a little fire that spread in a circle that grew slowly bigger, much to our delight. No sooner had he said 'Now it's time we stamped it out' than a gust of wind blew the flames and smoke sideways. Hard and close to the fire as we dared to stamp, we were too late. Scourged by the rising wind, the flames quickly spread through the sedge to the gorse. All we could do was wait and watch, appalled by our handiwork, until the workmen on the new kitchen roof, alarmed by the smoke, came armed with shovels. Led by Johnny Joyce the carpenter, with a hatchet and a saw, they were followed by his brother James the steward, who took longer to reach us because of his lameness, and who gave us the worst telling-off. He wagged an accusing finger and said in a tone of respectful contempt, 'Look what you've done, boys! The bogwood is entirely lost. You'll be lucky if we can hold the fire at the canal and save the house.'

It was worse when Aunty Kay arrived, who wept at the destruction of the birds she had taught me to name. Badgers were burnt in their sets; a fox was seen escaping with its brush on fire; pheasants flew away, abandoning their nests. As the fire advanced towards the canal, it left nothing alive.

Gone were the gorse, the blackthorn and whitethorn, the elder and alder, the holly, the oak and the silver birch; all gone with the wild and beautiful birds and creatures they had housed. To our shame, standing on the cinders and ashes we had caused, we could see all the way to the hill of Castlehacket, a Druid mound of blue on the southern horizon.

In the spring of 1937, our grandfather at Milford read an advertisement in the London *Times* for a voice trial to select twelve boys between eight and eleven to enter Canterbury Cathedral Choir School as boarders. The school had existed for day boys since the year 597; now boarders were to be accommodated under new staff appointed by the dean and chapter.

As our mother was then in Ceylon with our father, our grandfather wrote to them urging that he be allowed to bring Chris and me to Canterbury for the trial. Placing two of his grandsons as choristers in the mother church appealed to him. The year before our parents met and married, he believed that a miracle had saved his life as he lay dying – as the doctors thought – after a motor accident in Scotland. He had seen a vision of a Hindu *munshi* offering him nirvana – 'blessed and eternal rest and oblivion' – and of a man robed in white like an Egyptian fellah, whom he believed was Christ, offering him 'The peace of God which passeth all understanding'. Having chosen Christ, he had recovered, retired from the army and taken holy orders.

He won our parents' consent and took Chris and me by boat to England, a happy escape from Baymount in midterm. We passed the voice trial, singing in turn 'Glorious Things of Thee are Spoken' to the tune of Haydn's *Austria*, and humming the middle note of several three-note chords played by the choirmaster, Gerald Knight. The headmaster, the Reverend Hugo Charles, wrote to Ceylon, 'Their voices are very true, and they will need only a little training to make really good singers.'

The innkeeper of a medieval guest house where we spent the night puzzled me when he remarked, 'You don't sound as if you come from Ireland and have lived in Ceylon. I'm surprised that a boy from Ireland can speak English without an accent.' Did my voice have no connection with any place on earth, I wondered, and was that a good thing or a bad?

I loved Canterbury, above all the practice and performance of choral music with sixteenth-century words from *The Book of Common Prayer* in the great Gothic cathedral. Our school could claim to be the oldest in England, yet as boarders we belonged to a group of musically talented boys not much larger than our family.

We slept in two dormitories at the top of a spiral staircase in the attic of 18 The Precincts, an old flint building midway between the deanery and the cathedral. The headmaster and the matron occupied the floor below, and we could hear Mr Charles playing Bach chorales on his piano after lights out. The day boys joined us for lessons in classrooms on the ground floor. We studied English, Latin, French, history, geography and mathematics, but no science, with an average of one teacher for every nine students. Forgetting about medicine, I thought of becoming a priest or an organist composing anthems and Magnificats.

One sacrifice was required: we had to spend half our school holidays in Canterbury in order to sing the services in the cathedral, especially at Christmas and Easter; but sometimes our mother came to Canterbury for these festivals. Then I would show my devotion by attending five services a day, two more than required for singing. We used to bow at the mention of Jesus Christ in the Creed, but she would curtsy. Very soon she got to know our teachers and the boys, one of whom thought she looked too young and beautiful to have been our mother. He spread a hurtful rumour that Chris and I were adopted.

A younger man, the Reverend Clive Pare, popular with all the boys, replaced Mr Charles as headmaster in September 1938. As a minor canon of the cathedral, Mr Pare intoned at the services on a steady tenor note and added his alto voice to the choir for the psalms and anthems. He had been a choral scholar at King's College, Cambridge. Short in height and boyish in expression, with only one vice – chain-smoking – he was ardent in his desire for us to remain pure and free from the sin of lust. As far as I know he succeeded. His love of boys with unbroken voices, sublimated by his love of God, made him a good headmaster. He drove a Morgan three-wheeler sports car with a canvas roof at high speeds, and read aloud to us, chapter by chapter, books by Conan Doyle, John Buchan and Dorothy Sayers. During the half of the holidays we had to spend in Canterbury, he entertained us so well and with such good humour that he made us feel at home.

To counteract our long separations from our family at Milford, I often wrote letters of ten or twenty pages in spare moments, the words tumbling over one another in excitement, letting my mother know what I was thinking and doing. That was how I grew to love writing. One of my thoughts was to write a book about the duel fought by her ancestor in 1747. Our grandfather had shown Chris and me angry letters from John Browne of the Neale, a great landowner of papist descent, challenging the third Robert Miller of Milford, of Cromwellian settler stock, to fight him in the 'Musick Field' at Kilmaine. After both contestants had missed, when Miller was climbing on to his horse, Browne had wounded him with a 'foul shot'. Jumping walls and gates, the horse had carried Miller home to die in the drawing room. The head of the horse was buried in Miller's grave in Kilmaine, and one of its hooves, bearing a silver plaque, was kept polished in our grandfather's study.

We revelled in connections with the past, the more remote the better. The Choir School had a good library and, encouraged by my friend John Dalrymple, who was a year older, I read *Coral Island*, *Tom Brown's Schooldays*, *Mutiny on the Bounty*, *A Tale of Two Cities* and *David Copperfield* before I was twelve. We were allowed to read books during sermons. After Chris acquired a pair of glasses to correct his near-sightedness, I was glad when the oculist prescribed a pair for me.

My mother, writing a letter in her drawing room at Milford, could concentrate so strongly that she would not even look up if I shouted at her. Her power angered but impressed me. At the Choir School I learnt how to exercise that power myself, telling her, among other things I wanted her to do, to be sure to think of me at nine o'clock every night, when I would be in bed thinking of her. I would know the time because the ten-minute curfew rung from Bell Harry Tower would end on the stroke of nine, and shortly afterwards I would hear the night watchman's voice chanting on a single tenor note, with a dying fall, 'Nine o'clock on a fine night and all's well.'

Once, she confiscated a trashy magazine for boys called *Hotspur*, which she found in my luggage on my return home from school. 'You should never waste time reading rubbish,' she said, 'because so many good books have been written that even if you were to spend your whole life reading, you could never get through them all.' It was proper advice, because I have always read slowly, as if I were reading aloud, listening to the sound of the words.

Early every morning in the holidays I used to go to my mother's room, facing the Pleasure Ground, and get into her bed. A time came when she discouraged me, saying she wanted to read, and keeping her eyes on the text. I was longing to know what book could be so interesting that she preferred to give it all her attention at that hour, rather than receive my kisses and hugs with joy. It was called *Kenilworth*; I liked the sound of it, and asked could I read it, too. There was no time in our short holidays, but when she came to see me the next term at the Choir School, she brought me a new pocket edition of Sir Walter Scott's novel, with 498 pages of tiny print. Because the book had taken her attention away from me in her bed at home, at school I felt I could keep in touch with her by giving my attention to the book, making her enjoyment of it mine.

The Bible was the most important book in my early life. I handled it with reverence, never placing another book on top of it, no more than I would have stepped on a grave. The awe with which I read it obscured my mind with the dense illumination of stained glass.

The dean, Dr Hewlett Johnson, was an outspoken advocate of communism in Russia under Stalin, who, he believed, was putting into practice, albeit as an atheist, what Christ had preached. As proof that Christianity was flourishing in the Soviet Union, he wore a pectoral cross given to him by a patriarch of the Russian Orthodox Church in Moscow. The dean was a tall man of immense dignity and charm, with a shiny bald head and curly grey side locks, his legs buttoned up in black gaiters. In the holidays he let us play in his garden, where the mulberry tree was seven hundred years old and the flint wall was Roman. I remember him telling us that if we were at school in Russia we would be learning to jump with parachutes off a high tower. 'Propaganda,' Mr Pare warned us.

Canon Crum deplored the dean, and we preferred Canon Crum. He used to unlock a door at the foot of a spiral staircase and take us up to the cathedral roof, telling us the history of the building, stone by stone. His stories let us imagine every moment in the martyrdom of Thomas à Becket on the floor of a chapel near the cloisters. Gathered around him in our blue coats and shorts, we were like pigeons picking up grains of history and myth. When he preached about Christ on the Lake of Galilee, his voice sounded like an oar lifting spray in the wind, and his words would carry in a stage whisper to the farthest apse.

The dean acted and spoke so well that the masses flocked to hear him preach at what were called the Red Dean's services every Sunday evening. In the pulpit he would clear his throat three times on a bass note into the microphone before beginning to speak. Only popular hymns were sung, volume and heartiness were all that mattered, and a man who played the electric organ at the Odeon cinema during the week replaced Mr Knight in the organ loft. Fred Harvey's voluntaries ended with thunder that rolled around the cathedral stonework, causing vibrations in the glass.

Mr Knight was a tall young Cornish bachelor, rather spinsterish, with straight auburn hair, neatly parted, and thick lenses in a tortoiseshell frame. As he wanted our singing not to obscure the words of the prayer book but enrich their meaning, he had pointed the psalms so that the music would stress the syllables that are normally stressed in speech. In all our psalters he had scraped off the old pointing with a razor blade, and inserted the new in red ink. He trained us to sound the *D* at the end of an 'and' so that a deaf person could hear it at the far end of the quire, with the organ playing. Except at weekends and festivals, we sang to tiny congregations of old people. Mr Knight placed me in the choir beside the head chorister, a day boy, to learn from his golden voice to sing better, and to help him improve his accent by hearing my standardised vowel sounds. Some of the day boys pronounced 'day' as 'die' and the *G* at the end of 'beginning' as an audible *K*.

He liked us to produce a pure boy-soprano sound with no *vibrato*, which he derided as 'wobbling like a woman'. Gifted with perfect pitch, he would flush if we sang a fraction of a tone out of tune, and he could tell which boy it was if only one had sung a sharp or a flat note. Once at an evensong, unaccompanied by the organ, with no lay clerks to keep us in tune, while we were singing a canticle by Thomas Tallis, he got redder and redder in the face, glared at us and clicked his tongue. We didn't know why, until he told us in the vestry after the service that, by the end of the canticle, we had dropped a third from the note he had hummed at the beginning. To make us ashamed of ourselves, he said, 'That would never have happened in King's College, Cambridge.'

I hero-worshipped him and strove to earn his favour, as a Boy Scout in his troop and as a musician. Though my voice never won his approval, I scored on technique, studying a textbook on harmony by C.H. Kitson, and asking Mr Knight to help me compose an anthem that we might sing in our church at Kilmaine. Chris had a better voice but was apt to come in half a beat late. Mr Knight shamed me once at choir practice. Because I had poked fun at a verse in the psalms, 'I am a worm and no man', he made me sing it alone so that everyone would poke fun at me. He punished us with wounding sarcasm.

We sang no Mozart Masses – too operatic and sensual for Canterbury. Thomas Tallis, William Byrd and Orlando Gibbons were Mr Knight's favourites. I tried to make them mine, but preferred the Bell Anthem of Henry Purcell, 'Rejoice in the Lord Always', and Haydn's 'The Heavens are Telling the Glory of God' from *The Creation*. Among the settings of morning and evening services, I most enjoyed singing Stanford in B flat and Stanford in A. Mr Knight pleased me by saying that Charles Villiers Stanford was Irish.

In 1939 he appointed Alfred Deller as a lay clerk. Mr Deller had a black moustache, the temperament of a prima donna and the best countertenor voice in England. I stood in front of him in the choir and noticed that he would often begin to sing a fraction of a beat ahead of the choir, so that his voice could be heard above ours, resounding in the cathedral vaults. When the quire was seated during the lessons, he would suck lozenges and rustle the wrapping, which we were forbidden to do.

Mr Knight wanted our choir to become the best in England, as Canterbury was the mother church, but by pouring scorn on our mistakes he shook our confidence. At a rehearsal in the chapter house for an opera called *The Children of the Chapel* by Sidney Nicholson, when I was playing a piece of William Turner's music on the harpsichord from memory, I broke down. Mr Knight dismissed me from the keyboard, which convinced me that I should give up trying to be a musician.

The precentor, the Reverend Joseph Poole, having designed our purple cassocks with white Elizabethan ruffs and long white surplices, choreographed our ceremony in the cathedral with dramatic skill. He was a tall, elegant, dark young man with black-rimmed glasses, devoted to the Anglican liturgy, with a good voice for intoning at matins and evensong, and for reading *Jungle Stories* at tea parties in the house where he lived with his mother in the Precincts. My mother had invited him to stay for two weeks in the summer of 1939, and he came back saying that Milford was the only private house he had ever been in where they had morning prayers.

Instructing us in the art of walking in choral procession, he appealed to our imaginations rather than our fears of making fools of ourselves. We had to keep the same distance behind the boy in front of us as we were from our opposite number across the aisle. He suggested that we might imagine we were walking through a forest, moving with a sense of wonder under a high canopy; slowly enough to take it all in, but not dawdling; not turning our heads to look at this and that, but proceeding with reverence for the beauty of the cathedral. We should not march in step like soldiers in a platoon, he said, nor stumble, nor fall out of line. Each step should be even and digni-fied, neither rigid nor sloppy. He would show us how to walk naturally, with footfall as varied as the stresses in a line of poetry.

We were on holiday at Milford when the German army invaded Poland. Britain and France declared war on 3 September 1939. I remember the next day, sitting on a wall behind the pump house at the well, looking across a field of yellow flags and a great bog to Castlehacket hill, and counting the years the war would have to last – I reckoned five – before I would be morally compelled to volunteer and get killed. Since the previous war had ended in four years, I was hoping to escape, but knew that such a hope, in our family, was shameful.

At the end of the month we returned to Canterbury, where we acquired gas masks, identity cards and rations books. Chris had won a scholarship to the King's School and was housed at Meister Omers near the Choir School in the Precincts. The medieval stained glass was removed from the cathedral to a safe place in the country, and on the dean's orders the choir was filled with sand so that the crypt could be used as an air-raid shelter. Down there, on the grave of Thomas à Becket, we continued to sing the liturgy accompanied by a piano, and sang better with no organ to muffle our mistakes. When the air-raid siren sounded in the night, we had to wrap up and take our gas masks and our blankets to the crypt, where we would sleep on inflated mattresses.

On our wall map of Europe the little flags along the Maginot and Siegfried lines had to be moved in May 1940 when the German panzer divisions tore through Belgium and the Ardennes into France. We boarders at the Choir School were then evacuated by car to St Blazey on the south coast of Cornwall. Mr Knight came with us because he was Cornish; and Mr Poole took charge of a choir composed of day boys, who would sing better and better under his inspiring direction from a piano in the crypt throughout the war and in spite of the Blitz.

Our mother panicked at Milford, thinking we might never see each other again if the Germans were to invade England or Ireland. She sent telegrams summoning Chris and me home, separately. On the long train journey through Bristol to Liverpool to board the B&I boat to Dublin, I knitted mittens on steel needles for the RAF, earning the praise of old ladies for my war work. I hoped that by doing this while praying silently I might prevent a train crash. The Irish Sea excited more than it scared me. Our Uncle Jack had reassured our mother about the dangers: 'The risk is *very* slight and if the ship did go down the boys would always find a lifebelt or a boat and it would be a big thrill for them.'

Did the Choir School give us a good education? The best, in my case.

Of the original twelve boarders, in order of age, Chris would become a stockbroker and hedge-fund manager, Robert Tayler a doctor, Mervyn Middleton-Evans a successful florist, John Dalrymple a banker in South America, John Richardson a barrister, John Slimming a novelist, Desmond Franks a circuit-court judge, and William Mayne a famous writer of children's books.

John Dalrymple has remained a friend. He can remember Chris and me being so anxious to wear shamrock on St Patrick's Day that we brought a plant in a pot from Milford, which we kept and watered on a windowsill. And John remembers us arriving back at school with peat, which we called sods of turf, in our luggage. 'Christopher would heat up a poker in a coke-burning stove until it was red hot, then stick it into the peat and sit savouring the smoke. You must have missed home and loved Ireland more than we realised or could understand.'

Thomas Tackaberry, aged seventy, became our classics and maths tutor at Milford for a year after the fall of France. With magenta pencils he underlined or accented words as we plodded through the first book of the *Aeneid* and Xenophon's *Anabasis*. While he was marking a line, his long nails, yellowed by nicotine, would click, scratching the page, his nose dribbling a little into his grey Viking moustache.

'I come of an old Norman stock resident in County Wexford since 1169,' he wrote to our father in Ceylon. He had taught classics, English and history at Portora, Dungannon, Coleraine, and our father's alma mater, Tipperary Grammar School. But his failure to keep discipline in class had reduced him to 'eking out a somewhat precarious existence as a Grinder in Trinity College for various Arts and Divinity Exams'. At lessons in his little study, with a turf-burning stove and a large window through which we could climb to or from the Pleasure Ground, he wore a look of abject cheerfulness.

'My wife and children have been taken from me by death, and for years past I have lived a lonely life in Dublin,' he wrote, adding how happy he was at Milford, where the children 'vie with one another in making me feel at home; and amid their smiles, their laughter and their many useful and engrossing activities among goats and hens and chickens and ducks and ducklings, asses, ass-carts, ponies, querngrinding, cheese-making and what not – "I find my lost youth again".'

Chris was studying for the Oxford and Cambridge School Certificate, and I was hoping to match his success and Mary's in winning a scholarship; but too often we made fun of Mr Tackaberry and fools of ourselves. 'This is a golden rule,' our tutor would say, and Chris, laying a ruler in front of me would echo, 'This is a golden rule, Richard.' Mr Tackaberry would sigh and plead with us, too kind to criticise, too weak to control. To stop us distracting him with idle chatter, which he enjoyed, he would whisper, 'Quick, boys, Mother's coming!' and then, at the top of his voice, start conjugating a Greek verb. When two cats took half an hour to copulate on the windowsill of the study, he tried to persuade us to continue with Caesar's *Gallic Wars*. It never occurred to him to disturb the cats.

He taught, as he had learnt, by rote, scanning or parsing a text line by line, unable to impart his love of the Latin and Greek poetry that he would recite. In teaching Kennedy's *Latin Primer*, he could be sidetracked into telling us about Hebrew or Sanskrit, anything we could think of to avoid learning grammar by heart. When goaded to tears by our playfulness, he would rise up from the table, sobbing, and go out into the Pleasure Ground to light a cigarette. Our mother didn't allow him to smoke indoors. There we would see him stooped and sauntering up and down beyond her bed of lupins, killing time till the evening, when he could escape, by pleading that he had a letter to post, three miles on his bicycle with acetylene light ablaze to Martin Walsh's pub in Kilmaine.

Miss Sarah Stokes, known to my mother and later to all of us as Sally, had the strength of character that Thomas Tackaberry lacked. Born and reared in Belfast, she had played as a child with C.S. Lewis, whose books, including *The Allegory of Love*, she brought to Milford. Multiple sclerosis, though now in remission, had interrupted a brilliant academic career, forcing her to retire from the post of deputy head and English mistress of Heathfield at Ascot.

She came to us for the love of teaching children. Our lost connection with Canterbury and our predicament as an Anglo-Irish family, isolated under the aegis of a Protestant clergyman on a remote demesne in neutral Éire dominated by Roman Catholic priests and threatened by German invasion, appealed to her sense of mission. As a result, for nine months we had the benefit of being taught, one to one, by a woman who was a great teacher, moralist and lover of English literature.

Sally had to wear boots with iron braces to support her legs, but was never late for a meal or a class. She wore oval spectacles with thin black rims that gave the kindness of her blue eyes a strict frame. Her dark straight hair, beginning to turn grey, was parted in the centre and tied in a small bun on the nape of her neck. We ceased playing the fool in her presence, her reprimands were not sarcastic, and her teaching evoked our best work. Her force of character, intellect and integrity resembled Aunt Bella's, but Sally was not awesome. An ironical smile would suggest that she knew more than she cared to say, and when she wanted to punish she frowned.

My interest in music, with little practice or performance at Milford, turned under her influence to poetry. She helped me to read passages of Shakespeare that stirred me to read more. With her guidance I was not repelled by Chaucer. It was enough for her to say that Milton was a great poet for me to want to capture the greatness of Milton. In the old way of teaching, she made me learn by heart poems that I would be glad to remember, yet her mind was not fixed on the past: she admired the poetry of T.S. Eliot, and gave a copy of his most recent poem, 'East Coker', in a wartime pamphlet edition, to our grandfather. It was not his kind of poetry.

Riding was the sport that all five of us enjoyed. Edward had a little Welsh pony that he let me ride, though my legs were too long; more often I borrowed Mary's bay mare, on which she sometimes allowed me to hunt with the South Mayo Harriers. I loved hacking six or eight miles to a meet on a frosty morning, but my favourite sport was showjumping. Liz, who wore her dark hair in long plaits, was the keenest rider on her black pony Kit, and agile enough to stand on Kit's rump while trotting. I had been jealous of Liz and Edward having their own ponies and being able to hunt and spend all their time at home while we were at school in Canterbury. Sometimes Chris or I would pull Liz's plaits, but more often we teased her and Ted with mental cruelty causing them to fly in tears and screams of rage to our mother for their own protection and our chastisement.

News reached us from the BBC. Churchill's war speeches thrilled us during the Battle of Britain, but on Raidió Éireann we listened to de Valera with dismay for his neutrality, which seemed to us pro-German; and we scoffed at the Nazi propaganda of Lord Haw-Haw from Hamburg. In the morning at 7.20, an hour before our winter sunrise, we exercised, obeying instructions from a BBC programme of music and physical training called *Up in the Morning Early* – ten minutes for men, followed by ten for women.

Breakfast was at eight. Kathleen Joyce, our cook, would have got up at six to stoke the Aga and stir the pinhead oatmeal to prevent lumps in our porridge. One morning she killed a rat with a poker on the kitchen floor. After porridge with salt – our sugar was saved for making jam – we had boiled or fried eggs and rashers, followed by brown soda bread with our mother's pre-war marmalade that had crystallised during the winter. James Joyce, who killed a pig in the yard every three months, cured our bacon and provided all the milk, cream, butter and buttermilk we could consume. As we had no refrigerator, he salted the summer surplus of butter in large crocks for our use in winter. Oats for the porridge had been harvested at Milford and conveyed on a horse cart to a watermill at Kilshanvy, where it was ground.

After breakfast all of us in the East Wing, except the maids, used to attend prayers in the drawing room. Our mother was following the custom of her aunts at Ballinamore. She played a grand piano that badly needed to be tuned and we sang a hymn. The piano lid was never opened because she preferred it to support a vase of flowers that she and Mary would arrange artistically. A cat would sometimes sit on the piano and a kid goat belonging to Chris, attracted by the music, would jump through the window to lie on the floor at our mother's feet.

Our mother tried to make us self-sufficient on a modest income at a time of scarcity caused by the sinking of merchant ships by German submarines. She abhorred the black market, which impoverished old people who depended on tea with sugar. All the vegetables we needed for lunch and supper were grown in the garden, where each of us children had a plot to cultivate and the incentive of winning a prize in the Kilmaine Show. We bought mutton or beef and medical supplies in Ballinrobe. To augment the minuscule ration of half an ounce of tea per person per week, our grandmother made a herbal tea by curing flowers that we picked off the lime trees on the avenue. To supplement the sugar shortage, Mary invested in six hives of bees to collect honey from heather on the bog.

As I had learnt about poultry in order to win a Boy Scout badge at Canterbury, I chose to start poultry farming. My mother supported this by giving me a loan and a ledger in which she taught me how to keep accounts. In June I cycled to a small farm near the forge in Rathgranagher where Mrs Mary Hession, appointed by the Department of Agriculture as poultry instructor to improve the stock in our neighbourhood, supplied pure-bred Rhode Island Red day-old chickens from an incubator.

I bought twelve for a start, reared them under a lamp, and fed them on pinhead oatmeal. When the pullets began to lay, I sold the eggs to my mother at the price paid to farmers' wives by Mr Hennelly, a grocer from Claremorris. Every Monday afternoon Hennelly would arrive at our front door with his shop on the back of a lorry under a canvas roof. He supplied the bran and pollard that I mixed with our own crushed oats. During the winter my hands swelled with chilblains that split from the mixing of wet mash in frosty weather. My grandmother cured the chilblains by soaking my hands in hot water from a pot in which potatoes had been boiled to pulp.

My poultry were housed in a stone-walled paddock in a field I had to run across to avoid being charged by a vicious ram. When our mother required chickens, she would order them from me, and I would bring a hatchet to the paddock, catch a cockerel and take him away from the other fowl to the block of a fallen tree and cut off his head. My poultry were so profitable that the family expected me to become a businessman, in contrast to Chris.

Chris had bought a flock of wild goats in Connemara and herded them by road and ferry across Lough Corrib to Milford, where he milked them and made some good cheese but little profit. His goats used to roam in the woods, be hard to find and impossible to prevent from trespassing. The family regarded Chris as a dreamer who might be successful in the arts rather than in finance. We would seem, upon reaching adulthood, to have switched roles.

Chris had, and still has, a dreamer's inventive mind. Now in his nineties, every day he fine-tunes a software system he devised that makes money on the Stock Exchange when the market crashes. I remember a system he invented at Milford for waking himself up at any hour of the night without an alarm. Before falling asleep he would imagine a clock of golden hours with the hands revolving from midnight on. When the hands would reach the time at which he wanted to wake, he would stop them and will the clock to wake him at that hour. One night when he had to go with our grandfather to sing at a church far away in Tobercurry, his imaginary alarm clock woke him exactly at 4 a.m.

He led me on a search from house to house in the neighbourhood to obtain two old spinning wheels on which we spun our own wool; and he learnt how to dye thread, with lichen off rocks for a golden brown or with onion peel for canary yellow. I followed him to learn from the seventh son of the seventh son of a weaver at work on his loom how to weave on a much smaller loom at home. It may sound arty-crafty now, but during the war we practised these crafts by necessity, knitting our socks and weaving our scarves.

As paraffin oil was rationed to one gallon per house per month, and as shopkeepers ran out of candles, Chris found some candle moulds in a tool shed in the yard and a rushlight holder in a glory hole under our grandparents' stairs, then set about discovering from very old people how to make candles and rushlights. He bought tallow from the butcher in Ballinrobe, we cut rushes on the bog, peeled and dried them, and dipped them in melted tallow. Rushlights cast a ghostly glimmer in our bedrooms, and once, when Chris used a book as a rushlight holder, nearly set the house on fire. The candles, though brighter, produced a foul smell of burning animal fat.

We had baths together, and they lasted a long time because Chris told stories in the bath, one leading into another without a full stop. I sat behind him because he liked to control the taps. Mr Tackaberry kept knocking on the bathroom door and saying, 'Hurry up boys, it's bedtime! Mother's coming!' Chris claimed, as Granny did, to have seen more than one ghost. Regrettably I lacked their second sight, though for fear of meeting a ghost I would never dare to walk down the avenue alone in the dark.

I had an advantage in being a younger brother, capable of listening, ambitious to overtake. From Chris I learnt about and came to revere the rath, an earth-ringed fort with whitethorn on its ramparts, near our gate lodge, where he had found a flint arrowhead and a skin scraper, but where I had merely shot rabbits. Having heard stories at the fireside of old James Cunnane, our nearest neighbour, Chris was hoping to dig up a crock of gold; and he warned me never to cut or break a branch on the rath, as people believed the consequences would be fatal.

A brother of Mrs Cunnane had been a brigadier in the IRA during the

Troubles, and James told us that Milford had not been burnt because our family had always been kind to their tenants and neighbours. But when Chris obtained a book by Dan Breen called *My Fight for Ireland's Freedom*, we had no time to read it before our mother, having read the title, burnt the book on the drawing-room fire.

However, she encouraged us to read the myths and stories of Pat Mullen, an Aran Islander, a book that Chris obtained during our summer visit to a friend's chalet on Gurteen Bay near Roundstone. While I was trying to paint a watercolour as good as one of Mary's, Chris was picking up Irish phrases from Paddy Bolton, who claimed to have burnt down the Railway Hotel at Recess on behalf of the IRA and to have taught de Valera's children to speak Irish. Our granduncle Charlie, as an engineer, had designed and supervised the construction of the railway from Galway to Clifden.

Our grandmother had acquired some knowledge of first aid and nursing in her voluntary work for the Red Cross in 1914. She had great sympathy for the sick, as she suffered badly herself from rheumatism. Everyone who came to Milford for treatment within her limits received it freely. Her counsel helped to cure. There was no district nurse, and the nearest doctor in Hollymount charged more than most people could afford. Often I saw Granny at the long deal table in the centre of her kitchen cleaning, applying iodine and bandaging the wounds of a child. Stooped and limping, she looked very frail, even thinner than our mother, but almost as active. Some grateful mothers presented her with a score of eggs or a chicken; another at Christmas gave her a goose, which she asked me to feed. One morning, to my shame, I forgot, and the goose flew back to its original home.

Many years later, at the end of a poetry reading that I gave at St Colman's Secondary School for Boys in Claremorris, I met the principal, Mr Martin Hession, son of our poultry instructor at Rathgranagher. He told me that his brother's life, at the age of twelve, had been saved by my grandmother, and he himself had been treated by her for a lesser injury. 'People went to her at Milford from all over the country,' he said. 'She was known as the Healer.'

Our mother never stopped doing things or getting others to do them, nor did Mary ever cease helping her: writing long letters to our father in Ceylon; designing and making their own clothes; mending ours; baking cakes or making enough jam to last through a two-year siege of Milford; sowing, weeding, picking flowers or soft fruit in the garden and giving instructions to the gardener, John Hughes, who was suffering from TB; taking us all to the woods after lunch to pick primroses and violets in the spring, blackberries and elderberries for jam in the autumn; leading us over the snow in starlight to sing carols outside the thatched cottages of Tavanagh. On Sundays the five of us, with our mother and Mr Tackaberry, would cycle to church, either six miles to Hollymount or eight to Ballinrobe, unless a special service was held for our family alone at Kilmaine. Our grandfather gave Holy Communion to Sally at home.

The five seasons that we spent continuously together, except for our father, at Milford, reached a climax of stress and excitement in the spring and summer of 1941. Sally started to lose her sight and had to leave us in March for treatment in Belfast, but she sent a younger teacher, Barbara Cresswell, from Dublin to take her place; and Sidney Patterson came from Baymount to coach me in maths for two weeks at Easter. I was cramming for the King's School scholarship exam when Trix Hurst, a school friend of Mary, brought measles which, one after another, we caught. I was the last to succumb, only two weeks before the exam, for which the papers were to be sent to Mr Igoe, the National school teacher in Kilmaine.

While I lay itching in a fever sweat, with my eyes shut so as not to go blind, Dr George Maguire of Claremorris having warned us of this danger, my mother sat on the windowsill of my bedroom behind the drawn curtains, reading aloud to me *Alice in Wonderland* from the 1869 edition in French. She and her mother and her mother's mother had each heard this book read to them in childhood. My brain was on fire with her voice forging my will to recover and succeed.

Nine days before the exam, my grandfather noted in his diary, 'Richard much better.' Two days before it he wrote: 'Heard that the German battleship Bismarck has been sunk by the British.' Five days after the exam, Miss Varley brought us from the Cloghans Hill post office a telegram from Dr Fred Shirley awarding me a Milner Scholarship at the King's School at its wartime location in the Carlyon Bay Hotel near St Austell in Cornwall.

For several years we kept in touch with Sally Stokes by mail, but we lost contact with Thomas Tackaberry when he left. Mary saw him last, on the platform at Westland Row Station in Dublin, where he was waiting to meet someone who didn't arrive on the Wexford train.

Life for Mary at Milford was harder than it was for her siblings: she had more responsibility and, though she had passed matric, no hope of going to a university, where she'd have met boys and girls of her age, now that our mother needed her at home. On a visit to Uncle Jack in England shortly before the war, when Mary was sixteen, she had met and liked a subaltern in his regiment, the Royal Artillery, called Toby St George Caulfeild, nineteen years old. An only child, Toby was descended from the Earls of Charlemont in Ireland, and his mother, Roslyn, had been our mother's best friend in Ceylon when Mary was a baby. Our mother had often told Mary that Toby had pushed her pram in Trincomalee, and that his mother had said, 'Wouldn't it be nice if the children were to love each other when they grow up as much as they do now.'

And they fell in love at Milford in the summer of 1941 soon after my Milner Scholarship exam. They had been writing to each other for the previous two years. Toby, who had been badly wounded at Dunkirk, now held the wartime rank of captain. He was under twenty-one and Mary under eighteen. When my mother and I were in Dublin, where I passed another exam for a scholarship at St Columba's College, Mary, who had been left in charge at Milford, received a telegram from Toby saying, 'Propose arriving Hollymount 19.38 hours June 26th.'

She wrote to our mother that she would meet us all at Hollymount Station with the sidecar, and she added, 'Altogether the excitement of you coming home with Toby is getting a bit too much for me, so it is a great cause of thankfulness that I have masses to fit in before you arrive. Please don't run away with the idea that I am working myself to the bone – far from it, but I never am happy if life isn't absolutely brimming full.' She was not yet eighteen, and I in my fourteenth year was almost as excited.

My hero worship of Toby began on the train from Dublin and increased at Milford. He was tall and blue-eyed, with short fair hair and a scarcely noticeable toothbrush moustache. Educated at Wellington College, he put the army above everything else in his life. I wanted to hear how he had fought in France; but he was tight-lipped and laconic, his style a blend of diffidence and hauteur. English officers, he implied, should keep their feelings to themselves.

Wounded in the groin, he had been dragged unconscious aboard one of the little ships that had crossed the channel from Kent to rescue our soldiers from the beaches under fire from German aircraft. He had woken in an ambulance train, wondering why people were waving from windows and cheering from back gardens and clapping from roads under railway bridges as the train moved slowly through towns up the spine of England. Once more he had passed out, and when he woke again, the first thing he saw and smelt, for it was lying on his chest, was a bunch of arum lilies put there by a Hexham hospital visitor who thought he was dead.

We all regarded Toby as a hero and did our utmost to make him feel happily at home with us. There was a heatwave in the west of Ireland at the end of June. On the first of five days, Mary took him on a long walk to Turin, where they climbed the derelict castle for a view of the hills. On the second, Mary, Chris and I cycled with him to Ashford Castle, picnicked by the lake in the grounds, and spent the rest of the day exploring the countryside, its ruins and raths, in one of which Chris discovered a tunnel containing, not gold, but a dead sheep. On the third, we cycled to church in Ballinrobe and later to the shore of Lough Mask.

Each night Granny told Toby's fortune by cards, encouraging a romance. On the fourth day, Chris stayed behind to study for his exam, but our mother and her first cousin, Anne Ormsby, who would have inherited Milford had she been a boy, joined Mary, Toby and me on a thirty-five-mile journey on bikes through Cornamona and Maam to the Leenane Hotel. We were the only guests in the creaky dark pine-panelled interior of a building facing north across the innermost reaches of Killary Bay, with steep gloomy mountains on both sides.

After tea our mother suggested to Mary that she should take Toby up the mountain behind the hotel to watch the sunset, while I went upstairs and lay on a bed with damp woollen blankets, redolent of sheep, wondering what kind of a miracle might be taking place. Downstairs, an hour later, when I saw the joy in Mary's face as she came through the door with Toby, I felt that something like the transfiguration had occurred on the mountain.

After dinner, as the light began to fade in the rose-and-fuchsia garden across the road at the edge of the bay, our mother, in order to have a long talk with Mary and Toby, gave me the task of taking Anne on a slow walk beside the sea. On my return with Anne, the news that Mary and Toby were now engaged to be married gave me feelings I had never had before. When I tried to speak about their engagement or, harder still, their marriage, words stuck in my throat.

Fifty years later, Mary told me at Highfield that when Toby came to stay at Milford, she had been as innocent of sex as our mother had been before her marriage. 'Toby didn't propose to me on the mountain,' she said. 'He gave me a kiss. I took this to mean that he wanted to marry me. Poor Toby! He rejoined his regiment, Daddy cabled his permission from Ceylon, and Toby's mother announced our engagement in the London *Times*. Mr Tackaberry said, "I hope you'll be happy, Miss Mary. Better to remain single than to make a mistake. I made a mistake."'

Mary added, 'I had doubts about it soon afterwards, and from Milford I wrote Toby a long letter breaking off the engagement, which I handed to the postman in the morning. But when I told the family, Grandfather said to me, "You gave him your word that you would marry him, and you ought to keep your word." So I biked over to Cloghans Hill after lunch and asked the girl in the post office to empty the mailbag and give me back my letter. I realised it was my duty to get married.'

'Did you keep the letter?' I asked.

'Oh no,' Mary replied, 'I'm not like you. I burnt it.'

Although we had all agreed at Milford that I should go to St Columba's rather than King's, my father changed my mother's mind by cabling from Colombo that he was 'greatly disappointed'. She sat with me on the stump of a recently felled yew in the Pleasure Ground, persuading me to go with Chris to King's, where I could join the Officers' Training Corps and meet my Choir School friends, such as John Dalrymple. Pictures of the school grounds on Carlyon Bay showed palms and hydrangeas on white cliffs above a beach, where a sports club was available only to the school for the duration of the war. She believed that sheltering from the war by going to St Columba's in neutral Ireland might not be good for my character.

After a summer of active idleness, increasing the profit of my poultry, training Mary's bay mare to jump at the Kilmaine Show, and shooting rabbits, I crossed to England with Chris on an overcrowded boat, praying that it would not be torpedoed, and travelled on a train, with soldiers, sailors and airmen filling every space with their kitbags, to London. We stayed with my godmother, Bunty Spencer, in a house where most of the windows had been boarded up after an air raid. She took us to evensong in St Paul's Cathedral, every seat occupied by people who seemed fearless, calm and proud of carrying on as normal among the ruins of their city. This was an adventure I would not have missed, much as I missed everyone and everything I loved at Milford.

My letters home from Cornwall say nothing about the ordeal of getting to know the boys in my dormitory, house and class; fagging for an ungrateful senior; obeying idiotic rules that were sacred customs; being 'properly dressed' on a Sunday, wearing a starched wing collar that made my chin sore and a black coat with pinstriped trousers and a straw boater; putting on a gas mask during fire drill with alarms ringing in the middle of the night; guarding myself from kicks and indecent grabs during a power cut in the blackout.

Instead, those letters belie my memory, stressing, 'It is grand fun here. The food is not too bad and we have plenty of free time.' My voice had not yet broken and I enjoyed cycling five miles at weekends to rejoin the Choir School boarders who had been evacuated to a house in St Blazey, where Clive Pare remained headmaster. He used to drive us in a bus on Sundays to sing at ancient churches fragrant with incense and dedicated to obscure Cornish saints, as far away as Padstow and Redruth and St Ives. In Truro one day I bought *The Oxford Book of Regency Verse*, and began to enjoy reading Wordsworth, Coleridge and Keats in a handsome edition I revered almost as much as the Bible.

I wrote to Uncle Jack at HQ East Africa Command, because my grandmother had written to say that he had received no letters from Ireland since his embarkation leave at Milford. Ten days later, Chris, looking miserable, took me into the garden, sat me on a green wooden bench beside a clump of dying blue hydrangeas, and, finding it hard to speak without crying, handed me a telegram telling us that Uncle Jack had been killed in action.

Later we learnt what had happened. While commanding the artillery at the Battle of Gondar, Uncle Jack was travelling in a staff car when a biplane, the last Italian fighter left in Abyssinia, began strafing the road. Instead of diving for cover, he got out with a tommy gun and fired at the plane as if it were a game bird and the emperor had invited him to the country for the sport. The pilot returned his fire, wounding him in the groin and his driver in the jaw. Uncle Jack bled to death in eight hours.

In my very short letter of sympathy to my mother and grandparents, I wrote, 'I shall always think how slack I have been in helping to win this war.'

By being at school in Cornwall I missed the great family event of Mary and Toby's wedding in Kilmaine on Monday 16 February 1942. Toby had arrived at Milford four days earlier, and at 2 a.m. on Saturday he and Mary had decided to get married on Monday and spend the two nights left of his leave at Ashford Castle. They woke Mummy to tell her.

Our father was at sea, on his way home from Ceylon before taking up an appointment as colonial secretary of Bermuda. Toby's mother could not come from England at such short notice, and would never forgive my mother or Mary for this. Chris and I received a wire on Saturday, and I spent the next ten days thinking about little else, imagining and longing to know the details.

When at last the story arrived, in two instalments, from our mother, I replied, 'They were the happiest letters you have ever written us … We were thrilled with the wedding and longed to be there.' Unfortunately these letters are lost. A letter from Liz, aged eleven, Mary's bridesmaid, describes Mary wearing our grandmother's wedding dress and our great-great-grandmother's wreath and coming out of the church to be greeted by men with blazing torches of turf sods on hay forks, and the Kilmaine children leaning over their school wall cheering, and Mary cutting the cake with our grandfather's sword.

The day they married was the fourteenth that Mary and Toby had spent in each other's company since their childhood. 'What babes they looked,' wrote a wedding guest the next day. Grandfather, whose bed had been moved down to the drawing room following a stroke, gave them his blessing. He died a month later. His coffin was carried from Milford on a horse cart followed by Edward, aged nine, wearing an Eton collar with his black wedding suit, leading on foot a long cortège of pedestrians but few cars. Our grandfather was buried with his Bowen-Miller ancestors in the churchyard at Kilmaine.

It was nearly three years since I had seen my father when he came to visit us with our mother in Cornwall towards the end of March. They told us that the Colonial Office required her to go to Bermuda, because his job would involve entertaining very important people. We had to make a sacrifice of losing her as part of our war effort.

They had heard bad reports from Mr Pare of homosexuality at King's, so they tackled Dr Shirley about this. He apologised, and assured them that he would do everything in his power to eradicate the problem. They were also worried by reports of lax discipline. So they appointed Mr Pare as one of our guardians and Aunty Kay as another. And Mary, who would have to move her lodgings whenever the army would move Toby around England, would, in our mother's absence, assume her role in my life. Liz would go to Aunty Kay's school at Bowness-upon-Windermere in the Lake District and Edward to the Choir School in Cornwall. Shortly before Easter 1942, our parents brought me to Canterbury, where they said goodbye. It would be two years before we would see each other again.

Canterbury, so far, had escaped the Blitz. I was staying there to sing – for the last time with an unbroken treble voice – at the enthronement of William Temple as the ninety-sixth archbishop. My parents were to listen to the service on the wireless of their ship, the *Nikoya*, sailing out of Tilbury in convoy across the Atlantic. Easter fell that year on the feast of St George, Toby's twenty-first birthday. Joseph Poole, who choreographed the service for filming, told us we were 'to sing the new archbishop in procession to the throne of St Augustine'.

For our safety, in case of an air raid, Mr Pare was lodging us in a house called Beverley outside the Roman city walls. The three Crucifixion hours of Good Friday had come and gone. Sharing my room was another choirboy, a year older, who could play the organ enviably well. Before we went to sleep that night I asked him to teach me how to masturbate because I did not know. As he did what I'd asked, the blaze of pleasure burned away my innocence. During the night I dreamed of running over wet ashes to escape from the smouldering carcass of a cathedral that turned into a skeleton of Milford. Waking, I felt a new anguish of guilt for a deed that could never be undone, and believed that if I were to die in the next air raid, my soul would descend into hell.

But having gained the knowledge, I could not resist kindling the blaze night after night with my left hand. Before leaving Canterbury I bought a prayer book to send to my mother direct from the Cathedral bookshop and a Waterman's fountain pen for myself, using my right hand to compose longer and brighter letters to her, and, a year later, poems.

On returning to Milford for the summer holidays of 1942, I found that my love for my mother, the fountainhead of my happiness, had clung to the place that she had deserted. As I passed through the front gates, warmly greeted by Mrs Davin and her children, before entering the golden-green archway of the limes on the avenue, I had a sense of lost love recovered.

Through grandfather's telescope at Milford, we could pick out trees on the hill above Castlehacket, a small blue mound on the horizon, eight miles as the crow flies across Dalgan Bog and meadows beyond Shrule towards Headford. During our summer holidays with Granny on her own at Milford, Chris received a letter from Lieutenant General Sir Denis K. Bernard KCVO, MC inviting him and me to stay at Castlehacket for two nights, and shoot some rabbits on his thousand-acre estate. This was two months before the Battle of El Alamein. Generals Auchinleck and Ritchie had been dismissed from their North African commands by Churchill, and replaced by Alexander and Montgomery.

I was thrilled, but at the same time scared that we might not know exactly how to behave as the guests of such an important old man, living in a house much larger and grander than Milford. He had recently retired from the governorship of Bermuda, where that same month our father was acting governor, and our mother was busy entertaining important, titled and rich people at Government House.

We cycled to Castlehacket along rutted gravel roads in the rain, and got through lunch the first day without making fools of ourselves, one of us on each side of the general at a long mahogany table in a dining room fit for a banquet, great windows open to the south. Our host was kind and courteous. We were waited upon by his butler, a Protestant loyalist from Northern Ireland. The general spotted a yellow tweed tie that my brother was wearing, and asked where was it bought?

'At Moon's in Galway, sir,' Chris replied.

'I like your Moon's tie, Christopher,' the general said approvingly, much to our relief. After lunch he showed us around the house. It was built, he told us, about fifteen years previously, from Free State government compensation for the burning down by the IRA of an uglier house that had stood on the same site. Why was it burnt? Because in 1921 he had done his bit for Ireland by driving around Cork in an armoured car, shooting at rebels whenever they could be found. The Irish authorities gave him so much that he had £1,000 left over after rebuilding the house, including the cost of bullet-proof shutters.

Our rooms had mahogany washstands with china basins, which we were told would be filled with hot water from a copper kettle before breakfast the next day. I was more interested in the guns, which were kept upstairs in a bow-fronted room at the centre of the house, with windows facing across a park to the wooded hill. From here, he said, if the rebels ever dared again to attack us, he could fire on them as they came up the avenue or crossed the park. His butler had been trained as a loader, so the general could sustain fire from three guns. Or else he could give covering fire, while the butler crawled around on his belly through brushwood to attack them in the flank.

'Rebels can't face cold shot,' he declared, 'they quickly turn and run because they are cowards.'

At dinner all was going well at first. 'Generals are two a penny,' he declared with self-mockery, taking us into his confidence, which we would not have dared to abuse. Churchill, he thought, had made a presumptuous mistake in sacking Sir Claude Auchinleck. As boys whose duty would be to enlist at the age of eighteen, we did our best to agree.

The general was a tall, gaunt man, with ears that stuck out and skin that hung loose on the bones of a face that was hard to look at, especially at our age. It was a mask he had moulded for himself in the army, to freeze up men of inferior rank or warmer heart, but to melt women of the blood that could be traced in *Burke's Landed Gentry of Ireland*. So far so good, we had been treated with honour by our host.

Then he stared at my brother's tie, which Chris had not changed when dressing for dinner, because it was the only tie he had brought. Mine happened to be darker, and not made of tweed, luckily. 'I like your Moon's tie, Christopher. Yes, I told you I liked it at lunch,' and as my brother's face brightened with pleasure, the general snapped: 'But not at dinner! Yellow tweed, yellow tweed! A lovely colour at lunch, Christopher, a good material from a reputable shop, but not a tie to wear at dinner, do you understand?'

Having wounded my brother's pride with this thrust, the general gave us no quarter. If you misplaced a silver salt cellar on the impeccably polished table, he would move it himself, or sign to his butler to do so, making us squirm with embarrassment. If you bravely forced yourself to utter a remark that you thought might please him but which he found impertinent or silly, then a spark would touch the short dry fuse of his temper. He was too intelligent to shout when he was cross: had not the British won their battles by keeping their heads cool, clear and calm under fire in their thin red line? He preferred to attack the pride of his foe with a withering remark, and humble him into unconditional surrender. Then the little purple veins would shine through the sagging skin beneath his cold blue eyes as threateningly as the damascene on the barrels of his shotguns, made to his measure, as he showed us, by Holland and Holland.

On the second day I enjoyed myself thoroughly, because I was mad about shooting, and after tea the general took us out through the park to shoot rabbits. Chris, being older, had the first shot, and was quite upset when he missed a rabbit as it was running into a burrow.

'Oh sir,' he said, 'I'm sure I only missed it by a foot. I almost got it.'

'A foot? You missed it by a foot? Pity about that foot, Christopher!' the general mocked. 'If you'd aimed a foot in front of the rabbit you might have shot it.' It was shameful to waste a cartridge during the Emergency, especially one of the general's, which he might have needed to defend the house. Our final tally was not too bad considering how seldom we shot, but the general kept teasing Christopher, even at dinner, 'Pity you missed that rabbit by a foot! Only a foot? That was quite near, but not near enough!' And again Christopher was reminded that the general did not like to sit with a guest wearing a yellow tweed tie at dinner, even if it had been bought at Moon's, the shop where all the gentry had accounts.

As sons of an acting governor, we got off more lightly from the military lash of his tongue than the workmen did on his estate. Showing us around the yard when the cows were being milked, he insulted a man for not sitting straight on a three-legged milking stool, thereby weakening the legs. Pointing at a similar stool that was lying with a broken leg outside the cowshed, he remarked in a voice sharpened to strike fear into his regiment, and audible to the men who were milking: 'You see, boys! Typical Irish peasants, they have no idea of looking after things that belong to their employer.'

Hearing that horrible remark – peasant was a word my brother and I never used in Ireland, where it was only uttered with contempt – I wondered if the next IRA attack on Castlehacket would occur before we left.

One evening I stood beside our apple tree on the terrace of the Pleasure Ground, holding an old-fashioned moss rose picked from a bush near the well below the pump house, imagining I was in love with Dominica Browne of Breaghwy.

The last time I had seen her was in January, riding to hounds. Aloof from the shabby hunt followers, she had sailed over double limestone walls on her well-bred filly, following Iris, her mother, master of the South Mayo Harriers. I had not been able to keep up with them on Mary's bay pony, jumping wall after limestone wall in the frosty fields around Forde's Cross. Dominica on her high horse had left me far behind.

Encouraged by Granny's belief that a moss rose had the same power as white heather to generate love, I deeply inhaled the scent, and rubbed the velvety green stem. But hard as I tried to generate an image of Dominica to adore, all I could see was the untouchable Dominica I knew: a freckled face shaded by a little black peaked cap, a riding crop tapping her jodhpurs, and her sad eyes turning away, after scowling at me, towards the crowing of cock pheasants in her father's walled demesne.

Back at King's in the autumn, the chaplain, nicknamed The Tank because of his enormous girth, gave me one of his 'sex talks'. He invited me into his study for tea with peanut butter on toast, and got nowhere near the point by asking questions like, 'Did you ever get your clothes wet during the holidays?' Yes, I stood last summer on a rock at Gurteen Bay near Roundstone and let the sea break over me in a storm. This reply made him sigh and shift his huge backside in the chair.

Dressed in a long black leather-belted cassock, The Tank was known to prowl on the cliff with binoculars to spy on and report to Dr Shirley any boys he might have seen pairing off down the path to the beach.

We were warned in vague terms of the dangers of masturbation. I saw a boy carried away in an ambulance with his hands tied to a stretcher because he could not stop for a moment except when he fell asleep. How pale he looked. They said he was running towards the cliff to throw himself over when a rugby player tackled him near a camouflaged army pillbox.

At a crossroads to the station, the sea, the hotel and the woods, I remember the Home Guard at their nightly guard duty; Nissen huts behind hedges; the Cornish Riviera Express steaming and whistling between London and Penzance across the rolling green country of chalk mounds and ancient mine shafts, where we fought each other with blank cartridges on field days.

An older boy in the bed next to mine in our small dormitory attacked me with fists before lights out and seduced me with whispers when five other boys who shared the room had fallen asleep – no moss-rose enchantment in his assaults. Windows blacked out, not a chink of light could get through. He used to get into my bed – at a huge risk of being caught, disgraced and expelled – for the sake of a spasm of manual relief. No thanks he gave me for this, no affection during the day. His eyes were intensely blue and hard, well set apart. He was known as a monitor's 'kick', meaning a boy that the monitor fancied; but any thrill, pleasure or excitement, not necessarily sexual, could in our jargon give one a kick. The guilty kick I got at night made me hunger for purification through history, literature and music during the day.

After passing matric before my fifteenth birthday, and obtaining a bronze medal in lifesaving at the pool on the beach, I had few complaints about King's, where I now had more time to read and write on my own. Dr Phillips, the music master, let me wander into his house and listen to Beethoven, Smetana and Rimsky-Korsakov on his wind-up gramophone. And after finding a livery where horses could be hired, I often went riding with friends.

But I drew many complaints from my housemaster for being cocksure and hanging around with older boys from another house. Reports had reached Bermuda that I had become 'horsy' and was doing no work, with half my class periods 'free', meaning without a teacher, in the lower sixth form. Meanwhile, the correspondence between my parents and Dr Shirley became acrimonious.

The row escalated to the point where my parents decided that I must be removed from King's and sent to Wellington College, where Toby secured a place for me on the strength of his being an old boy. I was so unhappy about the prospect of leaving in mid-career that I consulted Dr Shirley, who helped me to compose a telegram that gave my father and mother a shock far worse than the kick I had given Aunt Bella at the age of three.

MURPHY COLONIAL SECRETARY BERMUDA –
FLATLY DECLINE TO LEAVE STOP IF MOVE TO WELLINGTON
AS BEING ARRANGED ENORMOUS SCHOOL FEES AND NO
POSSIBILITY OF HIGHER CERTIFICATE STOP EDUCATION
HERE EXCELLENT AM VERY HAPPY THIS TERM STOP WORK
PROGRESSING STOP KINGS FIRST CLASS STOP SHIRLEY
WILL COMPLY PLEASE ANSWER TO HUYTON LOVE –
RICHARD MURPHY

My mother copied this into her diary and added, 'Suspect Shirley inspired this cable. Wording completely unlike R. More than ever convinced change to another school is absolutely necessary.'

I was under a false impression that 'decline' would be less offensive than 'refuse', and ever afterwards regretted having allowed the cable to go in my name. Shirley, hoping to prevent the loss of a student who might have brought credit to King's by winning a university scholarship, sent a copy to Major H.W. House, the master of Wellington. My parents forgave me when I apologised, and were willing, on advice from Mr Pare and Aunty Kay, to let me remain at King's. But when Mary rang me up over Christmas at Huyton, where I was staying with Aunty Kay, and told me that Shirley had betrayed me, I changed my mind on the spot and said I would go to Wellington. This pleased my family.

The holidays were times when the possibility of a girl replacing a boy in the bed of my imagination opened briefly. Over Christmas 1942 I stayed with Aunty Kay at Liverpool College for Girls in Huyton, the girls having gone home. Aunty Kay was adept at finding ways to entertain and enlighten the young, but as puritanical as Aunt Bella about intimations of sex. She arranged for me to attend *Twelfth Night* at the Playhouse and *Messiah* with the Philharmonic Orchestra.

On Christmas night, during a dance in the school hall for the Women's Auxiliary Air Force, I took a girl of my age, who was a waitress in the dining hall where we had our meals, into an unlit classroom. We had just begun to kiss when Aunty Kay burst in, switched on the light, and, after telling my partner to go, warned me never to do such a dreadful thing again. At breakfast next morning, when the lovely girl entered the dining room, I dared not meet her eyes.

Stanley House stood apart from the massive red-brick buildings in the style of an eighteenth-century French château, where most of the six hundred boys and their masters at Wellington College were housed and taught. Entering two years after a dozen boys of my age, fifteen, had settled down and made friends, I was doubly excluded for being two years ahead of them in class. Most were following the army curriculum, looking forward to Sandhurst or Woolwich, whereas I had chosen to study on the arts side, in the hope of reaching Oxford or Cambridge. When we walked over to the college for lessons in the morning, they kept together as in a platoon that filled the road, forcing me either to lead and endure their mockery behind me, or to follow, resenting and relishing my isolation.

As an intellectual surrounded by philistines, I got used to the stimulus of opposing and being opposed. They prided themselves on their rugby matches and parades as much as I did on reading *Crime and Punishment* and *For Whom the Bell Tolls* in my cubicle. Each boy in our house had a tiny room with a desk by a window. But the walls were wooden partitions that didn't reach the ceiling, so there was no freedom from noise except during hours of study. Then the silence was occasionally broken by murmurs in the corridor, the trampling of feet down stairs, and the sound of a junior receiving from our brutal head prefect what he called 'a darn good hiding'.

Once he threatened to beat me for going over to college on a Saturday afternoon with my shirt buttoned up to the top, but without a collar or tie. He said, 'It makes you look like a "jallie",' which meant working class, and therefore a disgrace to Stanley House. I defied him to beat me for such a morally unsound reason, and he backed off. We wore no uniform except in the Junior Training Corps – the JTC. A tweed coat and corduroy or grey flannel trousers with a tie were the norm. The war had brought about this relaxation.

To wake us up in the morning, our housemaster, Herbert Wright, a veteran of the trenches, obliged us to strip naked in the bathroom and plunge one after another into three ice-cold baths, submerging our shoulders. Images of thirty-five male bodies in all stages of adolescence were impressed on my mind at an age when I had never seen a girl unclothed.

Games were compulsory in the afternoon, but there was a choice I often took of going for a two-mile run on a rough track through pine woods, or we could do 'land work' to help win the war by double-trenching in the vegetable garden.

Everything we did was done in competition that resulted in winners and losers, the supreme purpose of which was victory. We were weighed, measured, timed, tested and examined. Once a month we filed naked past the doctor who scrutinised our groins for signs of ringworm. Some boys ran competitions as to who could ejaculate most frequently in a day, a month or a year; who could reach the ceiling; or come without using a hand, merely by an act of erotic meditation.

The only bombs that had hit Wellington had killed the master a year before my entry. I suffered nothing worse than the alarm of being woken by the air-raid siren. This required us to go out in pyjamas and dressing gowns, carrying blankets to a nearby underground shelter, where we blew up inflatable mattresses on bunk beds and tried to sleep in a stench of mildew and the sweat of thirty-five boys.

At Wellington I was fortunate in being taught by masters superior to those at King's, among them Raymond Carr and Owen Chadwick, future heads of Oxford and Cambridge colleges. There were only ten of us in our class of potential scholars. Our most inspiring teacher was Robin Gordon-Walker, who wore green corduroy trousers and open-necked colourful shirts without a tie. Short in height but never in temper, with a bald pate surrounded by dark curly hair, a ruddy complexion shadowed by the blue of a shaven beard, he would lie back in his chair with his feet angled on a desk, and read us poems written by men who were still alive – Eliot, Auden, Spender, Day-Lewis and MacNeice. He encouraged me to believe that it would be better to write well in poetry or prose than to rise to the top in any other profession except art or music.

An older boy, Reggie Cliffe, intrigued me with the mystery of his rich Levantine origin, and overawed me with his intellectual arrogance, which I mistook for genius. He told me to read the plays of Eugene O'Neill – 'better than Shakespeare or Sophocles' – and I followed his advice, allowing *Mourning Becomes Electra* and *The Hairy Ape* to darken my mind.

My admiration for Reggie dimmed when he came to visit me in the Lake District during my spring holidays with Aunty Kay. He sneered at the host of golden daffodils on the banks of Windermere because they 'lacked significance in the modern world'. Wordsworth, whose 'Tintern Abbey' I knew by heart, he dismissed with a click of his tongue as 'an irrelevant old fart'.

After he had gone, to get me out into the fresh air and make me do some war work, Aunty Kay found me a job for two weeks on a dairy farm, mucking out the cowsheds before delivering bottled milk from door to door around Bowness-upon-Windermere. The driver used to sip a little cream off two or three bottles, then top them up with milk so that no one would notice.

Mary had taken on more and more of our mother's responsibility for my welfare and progress, housing me for part of the holidays, seeing that I was properly clothed and provided with all necessities down to a face flannel, and encouraging me to make the best of Wellington. In the summer she travelled up to London and queued in a long line to obtain sailing tickets for me to bring Liz and Edward to Milford, where Chris, who was now at Trinity College, Dublin, joined us in mid-August.

When our mother was at home we used to have a dance in Granny's big kitchen on New Year's Eve. Young and old who lived within walking distance were invited. We danced Irish country sets, the *Siege of Ennis* and the *Walls of Limerick*, mingled with waltzes and fast foxtrots, to the tune of the fiddle played by Tom Keville and a melodeon that changed hands throughout the night. Tom was an old man from the mountains behind Tourmakeady, where only Irish was spoken and only Irish music played and sung. The Land Commission had moved him to a better farm across the road from our gate lodge.

Persuading him to play one night in Mummy's drawing room was the first thing I did after we returned to the desolate house; and the second was to cycle around the country begging men and women, boys and girls, at work in the meadows and cornfields, to quit the harvest early and join the dance. We rolled up the carpet, a good crowd turned up, and Delia gave them tea and sandwiches in the dining room during intervals when the musicians needed a rest. Tom Keville alone was refreshed with bottles of Guinness.

In the climax of the sets, where two men and two girls interlock their arms to form a tight ring, the men did their best to raise the girls' feet high in the air while the girls laughed and screamed till the men lost their balance and crashed to the floor. The brothers Jarlath and Francie Cunnane, good-looking as film stars with wavy black hair and blue eyes, were outstanding dancers and floor-crashers among the men.

The dance was in full swing when Chris and I suggested to two girls that we should go out to the Pleasure Ground for 'a bit of a court' with Liz and Jarlath, by whom Liz was dazzled. Innocent fun. The ground being damp with dew, there was nowhere better to sit than the stump of the yew, with room for three boys back to back, each with a girl on his lap. We had no light but the stars and the glow of the summer night sky, but could see the shadowy figures dancing in the house and hear the melodeon muted by the trees.

Chris had a slim pretty girl, but the one who sat on my lap, not the first I had asked, was heavy and five years older. I had to kiss her, because that was why we were there, but her kisses gave me so little pleasure that I felt something must be wrong with me. I got no kick from her mouth and hoped it would not be the same with every girl I might kiss.

Back at Wellington in the autumn, my classmates and I were angry to learn that the master had sacked the chaplain for giving two senior boys sherry in his rooms, and our hero, Gordon-Walker, had resigned in protest. A forlorn poster campaign, led by an old boy, Giles Romilly, from London, urging us to rise up in rebellion to have the master removed, fizzled out. The master stayed, but his best teachers left, one by one.

This was when I put up my own barricade, announcing that I wanted to leave the JTC and devote myself exclusively to the study of English literature. I hoped to become the first Wellingtonian to win a scholarship in that subject, either to Oxford or to Cambridge. The only boy who had ever been allowed to try had failed.

As the hot-tempered head of the English department, Graham Stainforth, 'disliked my attitude' and opposed me, I might have been expelled but for the intervention of T.S. Dorsch, a Shakespeare scholar with a classroom reputation for being as dry as dust. Dorsch didn't know me, but he offered to direct my studies in private tutorials. Under his benign influence I continued to study history and Latin with my form, and to polish my boots for the imbecilic parades and field days, at which Stainforth ran around in a uniform, waving a swagger stick and shouting orders.

Theodore Dorsch, known as Ted, had come to England ten years earlier as a Rhodes Scholar from Australia. He was of German Lutheran descent, his mother having been professor of mathematics at Adelaide University. C.S. Lewis had been his tutor at Oxford, where he had met and married Kathleen, a vicar's daughter and an English graduate.

Dorsch lacked Gordon-Walker's subversive panache and acute modernity, but he had a love of medieval and seventeenth-century English literature, reinforced by a scrupulously accurate, painstaking scholar's mind. He brought me down gently from clouds of illusion, which had built up under the mentoring of Reggie Cliffe, by getting me to read and write coherently about the poetry he loved. He was the only master who invited me to his house, where Kathleen would pour the strictly rationed tea, feeding me homemade scones with honey, while I would pour out my heart. Then Ted would guide me around his shelves, picking out books for me to borrow.

He and Kathleen were like lovers conceived in a book. Not yet did they have children. As a perfect gentle knight, kneeling before the rose of his romance, he waited on her. At home in Australia he had done the washing-up, whereas Kathleen had maids to do the chores in an old English vicarage. He was lean, not as tall as I was; his face parchment-grey, his manner diffident, ironical, anxious and self-deprecatory – almost too polite. Kathleen had rosy cheeks with dimples when she smiled. Accepting his adoration as her due, she gave him all the comfort of her calm rotundity and feline wit.

They lived in a rented cottage called Green Shade in a pine wood up a steep lane on the far side of the village of Crowthorne near the school. On a Hercules bike with two crossbars and no gears, I would arrive in time for tea: a gangly, tall, round-shouldered sixteen-year-old with a white face marred by spots, wartime utility glasses, and a look that my housemaster called 'supercilious'. Escaping from the sound of Frank Sinatra crooning 'You are the one ...' at full volume on the radiogram all of a deadly Sunday afternoon and from the shindy kicked up by boys with not a girl in sight at Stanley House, I would enter with relief a little drawing room where the silence of thought between spoken words was infringed only by the purr of a tabby cat.

Green Shade was walled with poetry of the immortal dead. What did that offer or reveal? Immortality of the well-written word, a verbal English paradise that might replace the Irish one I had lost, and a feeling of redemption. Instead of being cut off from Ireland by the sea, from parents by the ocean, from the hope of peace by the reality of war, from girls I might have loved by boys I had to conquer in work and play, I could be connected to the remote and wonderful past, to lovers of extraordinary passion and beauty, knights of chivalry, the eternal summer of youth that would never fade.

By 1944 Mary had settled in a flat in the holiday resort of Burnham-on-Sea in Somerset, where I stayed with her over Easter. By now Mary was inspiring me to work and win a scholarship to Oxford or Cambridge, so that I could enjoy the privilege of a university education that she had been denied.

On the day when Chris gave up his studies at Trinity College, Dublin, under moral and financial pressure from our parents to enlist as a volunteer in the Royal Ulster Rifles in Omagh, County Tyrone, I went on a long bike ride with a girl of my age, a cousin of Toby's, to the Cheddar Gorge. It was a warm sunny day, with scarcely a vehicle on the road because of the war. We climbed and sat on a grassy bank among primroses and violets where we had a picnic that Mary had packed. In the doldrums of the afternoon, Eileen was reclining among the flowers with her eyes shut. Her eyes and mine had shied away from each other all day. Desire was choking the words I thought I should utter to make sure a kiss or a touch would be acceptable; but the fear that she might not want to be kissed, might scold me and complain to her mother, held me back. I lacked Toby's courage on the mountain at Leenane and cursed myself for being a coward and felt ashamed that my nocturnal habit might have been my hesitation's cause. We cycled back to Burnham as if nothing had happened.

The ambition to write poetry took root in my mind when I was reading Shakespeare's sonnets and the poetry of Donne, Herbert, Marvell, Milton and Wordsworth. By the summer of 1944, the Germans had started to launch their first flying bombs to fall on England, and Wellington was within their range. As long as you could hear the puttering jet engines of these unpiloted 'doodlebugs', which sounded like a motorbike in the sky, you were safe. When the plane ran out of fuel, the engine would cut; the flying bomb was on its way to earth. Then you would wait in an awesome silence, wondering when and where it would explode.

I had fallen in unrequited love with an athlete of my own age, who was destined for the Royal Navy. Scared of bombs, excoriated by my housemaster – a survivor of the Somme – for my Irish lack of British patriotism, I took refuge in the Renaissance conceit that a poem, if well made, could last longer than its maker, giving life after death to himself and his loved ones in the minds of his readers. Rather than in church, I began to seek redemption through poetry. I wrote a sonnet to the athlete whom I could never touch, though twice a day I saw him naked.

On my seventeenth birthday I cycled alone through the Quantock Hills to see the houses where Wordsworth and Coleridge had lived while writing the poems that were published in *Lyrical Ballads*. On that pilgrimage, with much poetry and the lives of poets on my mind, surrounded by the beauty that had inspired some of their best poetry, I dreamed of becoming a poet, expecting a revelation to occur that would make my dream come true. I had misgivings that this might not occur, as no one had ever suggested I was born to be a poet.

Rich red soil under grass, warm summer evening sunlight on sheep and cattle in pastures, oaks and elms in the hedgerows, bells pealing from a church tower in the distance, the war far off but my fear of death coming closer, led to my writing a sonnet to my sister, as Wordsworth had written to his, and another to a solemn sepia-toned photograph of my mother, full of autumn and ashes, clouds of guilt darkening my mind, producing a downpour of remorse and dismal verse.

In the term that I didn't know would be my last, I had a cubicle next to an army boy who was on the college rugby team and obsessed with shining his boots for JTC parades. Occasionally, after lights out, he used to climb over the seven-foot-high timber partition separating our cubicles, wearing only his underpants, holding a small jar of ointment normally applied to bruises for its warming and soothing effect. Then he would get into my bed.

Ejaculation between the thighs, as depicted on ancient Greek vases, occurred without affection. It was like a duel, each taking his turn to fire while holding the other in contempt. The danger of being caught and expelled heightened the spasm of relief but deepened my anxiety, tristesse and guilt. These duels scarred my mind.

Many years after I had left, Harold Nicolson told me an anecdote about Wellington, his old school and mine.

A senior boy walking through the front quad noticed an elderly gentleman standing alone, looking up at one of the dormitory windows, and stopped to ask if he could be of help, thinking the man might need guidance, or perhaps ought not to have been there.

'Oh no, thank you very much,' the man replied. 'I am just looking up at the room where I spent the most unhappy years of my life: I thought of hanging myself out of that window. This is the first time I have had the courage to return.'

'Sir, things must have improved a lot since then.'

'I sincerely hope they have,' the man said, and walked straight out through the porter's lodge, where the boy, following at a discreet distance, saw a soldier jump to attention and salute, then open the door of a Rolls-Royce for the man to step inside.

'Who was that?' the boy asked the porter.

'Didn't you recognise the chap who defeated the communists in the jungles of Malaya after the war? That was Field Marshal Sir Gerald Templer, chief of the Imperial General Staff.'

Five Oxford colleges were offering scholarships in modern subjects, and on Dorsch's advice I put Magdalen as my first choice, because C.S. Lewis taught there and I had seen a picture of Magdalen Tower. English was my main subject, along with history. Dorsch told me to regard the exam in November 1944 as a trial run. He warned that grammar-school boys from Manchester and Birmingham were more likely to succeed because they crammed and wasted less time on sports. I wrote the exam at Wellington and two weeks later my spirits soared when a summons came to attend a viva voce at Oxford.

In a dismal fog I wandered around Oxford, happy to hear more clock-tower bells than since the enthronement of Archbishop Temple at Canterbury. The Luftwaffe had spared Oxford. I followed directions through a maze of high walls, quads, cloisters and stairs to a small dark room, hundreds of years old, where an older boy was sitting on the edge of a table, flicking through pages of notes, a lock of thin yellow hair hanging over one eye.

His shiny beige suit looked new and expensive. I wondered if they would mind my old tweed jacket with leather pads on the elbows and corduroy trousers. His face was spotless; my pimples looked worse after squeezing. He played with his fingers and sniffed like a horse nosing a trough. I swallowed air, had a pain in my stomach, and polished my glasses.

With a Midlands grammar-school accent and a stammer painful to hear and watch, he said, 'I've lost hope.'

'Why?' I asked.

'I wrote too little in the exam.'

'How much did you write?'

'Never more than forty pages.'

A glance at his notes showed a script no larger than mine, twelve pages my maximum.

Called to judgement, I sleepwalked on a wobbly floor in a dream of being examined orally at Oxford to the centre of a room full of middle-aged and elderly dons, and heard a purring voice say, 'Mr Lewis would like to ask you a question.' All eyes turned to the bright jovial face of a short plump man who was sitting on a sofa smoking a pipe. His head reminded me of Shakespeare's in the church at Stratford-upon-Avon last summer.

'Can you tell me, Mr Murphy,' he began, as the sofa started to rise off the floor, 'what is meant by the "divine right of kings", and what importance, if any, is given to belief in that right by characters in Shakespeare's *Richard II*?' While I was answering with fluency beyond my control, quoting passages learnt by heart, the sofa turned upside down in mid-air with the balding top of C.S. Lewis's head a foot above the floor till the end of my answer.

I was told to keep an eye on the noticeboard in the porter's lodge, where the results would be posted under the heading of Demyships. At Magdalen a scholar is called a Demy, with the accent on the second syllable. On my third scanning of notices I found a typewritten sheet that announced the awarding of Demyships, in this order, to:

Tynan, K.P.
Murphy, R.W.L.

At the gateway to paradise, Lewis had let me scrape through.

A few steps from the porter's lodge on a walk up the High Street to the post office to cable my parents, I was stopped by a stranger in a fawn raincoat, carrying an umbrella. He had a scholar's stoop, a sallow complexion, curved nose, dark eyes and a tenor voice. With a sad ironical smile he asked for a light, an excuse for introducing himself, then, 'Are you at Magdalen?' John Simopoulos, son of a former Greek ambassador at the Court of St James's, was the first to congratulate me and give me an older man's advice – four years older – to leave Wellington at once. He had been at Stowe and could imagine that Wellington was worse. Greek philosophy was his subject. He would look me up next term and introduce me to his friends.

What a wonderful place Oxford seemed, where you could meet people on the street who were friendly, intelligent and wise.

My parents yielded to my wish to enjoy Oxford for at least six months before having to join the army on my eighteenth birthday. My housemaster had said I was not mature enough for the university, but C.S. Lewis, who would be my tutor, wrote to my father in Bermuda telling him that schoolmasters always wanted to keep boys at school too long. He believed that the dangers of being at school too old were greater than those of being at college too young. Ken Tynan delayed his entry until the Michaelmas term, making use of the time to spread his prodigious boyhood fame as an actor, director and theatre critic from Birmingham to London.

My first term began in euphoria and ended in shame. One hour a week face to face with Mr Lewis, reading aloud to him my essay on three or four plays of Shakespeare, then discussing those plays, was the only requirement.

Through no fault of his, Lewis continued to sit upside down in a cloud of my awe and admiration. Always affable and courteous, he accepted an invitation to tea in my rooms in Cloisters, but used his affability, bubbling with wit and firing salvoes of quotations, to prevent the conversation from becoming personal, which is what I would have liked it to be. In an argument with a student, he expected the student to oppose him and try to win. I wanted not to argue but believe, not to criticise but adore.

Oxford reminded me of Canterbury at its best. I loved Oxford for saving me from Wellington, as I had loved Canterbury for saving me from Baymount. At that age and time, Oxford was blissful, the war coming to an end, and only sixty students at Magdalen before the influx of three hundred older men from the armed services. Winning a Demyship so young and easily went to my head. Inspired merely by being at Oxford, I felt no need to work hard: work might have spoilt my inspiration. And when, on the second weekend of term, Mary found Oxford as thrilling as I did, my happiness was increased by feeling at home. We were joined by Nanny, back from India looking after twins at Banbury, for a lunch at The George, followed by a tea party for twelve of Mary's and my friends in my rooms at Magdalen.

I had a sitting room and a bedroom to myself upstairs in the Cloisters, a portion of the suite that had once been occupied by Edward, Prince of Wales. Next door lived a brilliant zoologist called J.Z. Young, who knew too much about the brain to believe in the soul. I didn't have to make my own bed or clean the rooms or wash up my tea things; those chores were done by an old man called a scout, who brought hot water in a copper jug to my bedroom to wake me up in time for breakfast in hall. Doors of our dining hall closed against late-comers on the last stroke of nine on the college clock. I seldom got there earlier.

Students were not required to attend the many lectures offered by the university, so I attended few. Tolkien was inaudible except in the front row, where two or three women, who worked much harder than we did, noted every mumbled word. The other rows of seats were empty. When Charles Williams lectured on Milton, the room was packed. Quoting the last line of *Paradise Lost* in a baritone voice on a falling scale of ten equally stressed syllables, he began 'Through E-den took', looking up at the ceiling with his arms outstretched, then leaning forward to cast 'their so-li-tar-y way' into the laps of his disciples, pronouncing 'way' like the River Wye. Before I had a chance of meeting him or hearing him preach about the Holy Ghost, he died.

Soon after term began, John Simopoulos invited me to his large elegant sitting room on the first floor of a house in Beaumont Street, where the people

I met were men of his age and stranger than any I had known. Anthony de Hoghton was the corpulent Catholic heir to one of England's oldest baronetcies, offensively loud-voiced, reeking of decadence. A High Church Anglican lolled in an armchair, twirling an ivory cigarette holder rapidly around in his talkative mouth. Adrian, a tall, urbane postgraduate from Bristol, writing a thesis on Lionel Johnson with encouragement from Harold Nicolson, claimed to have spent a weekend at Sissinghurst without going to bed with either Harold or Vita. Bragging of women who had fallen at his feet and men whose lives he had destroyed because they were communists, he had the evil charm of Iago. John described him as 'metaphysically repulsive in a reptilian way'.

When Adrian heard I was going to London to see Donald Wolfit's famous performance of *King Lear*, he said he would join me. The V2 rockets were falling on London, and the day before our journey I spent an hour among the tombstones in a country churchyard, preparing for death and regretting the poems I had felt inspired to write but had never written. In London Adrian took me by taxi to the Temple, where he introduced me to Mr Nicolson, who gave me a signed copy of *Some People*, containing a good chapter on the Wellington of his youth.

Donald Wolfit was regarded as a great actor because he always acted with a cast of his inferiors and his bombast on stage occurred at a time of real explosions. In the first act he didn't walk on, but entered running backwards to a staggering halt and a burst of applause, some of the audience standing up to cheer. Combined with the thud of rockets hitting other parts of London, his voice, audible whether he roared or whispered, wrought a catharsis. Adrian, to my disgust, walked out in the middle of the play.

John continued opening my eyes and ears, and I enjoyed his friendship. Knowing that I loved music, he gave me an album of Beethoven's *Eroica Symphony*. 'What a strange boy you are,' he said to me on that occasion, and I replied, 'None stranger.' At a sherry party he introduced me to the Anglo-Irish Enid Starkie, an authority on French poetry, and to John Mavrogordato, who had translated the poems of Cavafy. John told me that when he asked Mavrogordato what he thought of Ivy Compton-Burnett's novels, Mavrogordato replied, 'Greek tragedies acted by white mice.' But before the term was over something happened that ended our friendship.

Alone, with the curtains drawn one evening in Beaumont Street, we were talking about the woes of our public schools. John had knocked a few chips off the monument of Lewis in my mind by suggesting that some of Lewis's analogies were false, and others in bad taste. 'How,' he asked me, 'can one take seriously a man who seriously believes that scientists are inspired by Satan?' He thought a great scholar had been lost to English literature when Lewis converted and began writing popular religious tracts. This subversive idea alarmed me.

Meanwhile he played one or two records of Bach chorales, reminding me of Canterbury, and offered me Balkan Sobranie cigarettes and brandy. I was sitting on a sofa and he suggested I might be more comfortable were I to take off my shoes, put up my feet and lie down. He turned out the overhead light, leaving a little red lamp glowing under an icon of Byzantium, and lay down beside me.

I let him unbutton my trousers while he unbuttoned his, but when he guided my hand to his penis, the trembling of his body frightened and revolted me. I jumped up, saying, 'I must go.' He was crying as I left. I had no intention of going back.

But next day I forced myself to return the Beethoven album so that he would have no claim on my affection. Disgusted with myself for what did and did not happen in his rooms, I rejected his appeal for us to remain friends. Contaminated by guilt, needing medicine and prayer to purge it, I took a train to Reading to search for a doctor, who would never know where I came from or who my father was. In a panic I asked him to test me for syphilis – gentle taps of a hammer on my knees – but dared not answer his questions truthfully. Thereafter I went to chapel every day and read the lesson so well that I won an award. Still remorseful, I cycled up to the Cowley Fathers to find an old monk in a brown habit with a white rope knotted around his waist and a tassel dangling to the hem to hear my confession.

Guilt shadowed me everywhere, inclining me to be chaste if only I could have restrained my hands in bed at night. I wanted no contact with that *Yellow Book* set in Beaumont Street for fear of becoming like them. But walking down the High towards Magdalen one afternoon, I came face to face with Adrian, who grinned like the devil at a sinner he was proud of, and said in a voice loud enough for passers-by to hear, 'John tells me that you're not as innocent as you pretend to be.'

In love with Oxford but starved of sex, believing that sex was sinful except in marriage, I drugged myself on the idea of being a poet. Inspiration, I hoped, would descend on me like the Holy Spirit granting the poem in a vision. Janet Muir, the most beautiful girl in Oxford, came to tea in my rooms and promised to come again soon. Like my sisters, she was keen on riding. A week later she was thrown off a horse and killed.

While my brother Chris was soldiering, I wanted to write a poem about St Christopher. No words came while I strolled around Addison's Walk by the River Cherwell, browsed in Blackwell's, or percolated coffee in my rooms. So I cycled alone on empty roads ten miles north of Oxford to a little medieval church where I knelt and sat for an hour meditating on a mural of St Christopher. I prayed that the poem would enter my mind without being soiled by my effort. But the pages of a notebook in my hand remained blank. On the way back, the ecstasy of feeling on the verge of a revelation evaporated into loneliness.

At the end of term I failed my first exam.

When the war in Europe ended, all the bells in all the towers and churches of England were rung and, drunk as we all were, a few of us went up Magdalen Tower and swung on the bell ropes till I pulled a muscle in my chest, which I feared was in my heart. My parents came home from Bermuda and my father was appointed to succeed the Duke of Windsor as governor of the Bahamas, my mother succeeding the duchess as hostess to all the rich and famous who sheltered there from cold winters and high taxes. He was to receive a knighthood and, following Aunt Bella, an honorary degree from Trinity College, Dublin.

At the War Office, where my parents went to obtain permits to travel to the Bahamas, my mother got impatient waiting in a long line and said to my father, who never pushed himself unless she gave him a shove, 'Darling, do go up to the front and tell them who you are.'

As Toby was posted abroad where Mary could not have joined him, she went with her son, John, to help our mother by living at Government House in the Bahamas as social secretary, with responsibility for housekeeping, entertainments, finding out daily who was important among those who signed the visitors' book at the gates, and charming the guests with her liveliness, intelligence and charm.

By then I was so devoted to the Church of England, its ancient cathedrals, chapels, liturgy and choirs, having sung alto at Canterbury over Easter, that I felt no need to go to Ireland during the vacations, not for another year. I could still go 'home' to Aunty Kay in the Lake District, where my brother Edward would spend his holidays from Wellington, or stay in comfort at Magdalen. The first atomic bomb fell on Hiroshima on my eighteenth birthday, bringing the war to an end, and with it my moral obligation to enlist.

We all got drunk and danced around a bonfire misplaced on the site of the burning at the stake of two Anglican bishops in the reign of the Catholic Queen Mary.

My mind was locked, quite willingly, into the Middle Ages. A happy childhood in Ireland and Ceylon and the joy of singing in Canterbury Cathedral inclined me to look back to golden ages that could best be recovered in music and words. Oxford, stronghold of Cavaliers under King Charles I, not only encouraged but compelled me to look back through all of England's literature from *Beowulf* to 1830. Nothing modern was on the syllabus. No student's poetry was taken into consideration in the awarding of a degree, as it was at Cambridge. I seldom read newspapers or listened to news on the wireless. Recent horrors of the concentration camps would seem, filtered by memory, to have affected me less than remote medieval atrocities described by Charles Williams in *Witchcraft* or Shakespeare in his plays. My Oxford was a better preparation for a memoirist than a poet.

For a term I sang alto in New College choir, the best in Oxford, under Dr Ken Andrews. My dream then was to become a country parson with an old rectory, a 'plum living' in the gift of the college, beside a small medieval church with a choir that I would train, writing poetry in the tradition of George Herbert and devotional prose modelled on Jeremy Taylor's *Holy Living* and *Holy Dying*.

But the more religious I became, the more insipidly I wrote, not understanding why. Cutting off the flesh for the spirit didn't help my body or my soul. Recklessly I had decided not to work hard enough to gain a first-class degree, which might have led to a secure life with rooms in an Oxford college, for fear that scholarship would sterilise my imagination. An Oxford don, such as the historian A.L. Rowse, might be able to write verse, in my exalted opinion, but could not be taken seriously as a poet. In theory I wanted to create rather than to criticise. In practice my essays got worse and my embryonic poems were aborted.

I became a recluse, spending more than I could afford on books, next to nothing on clothes, the worst-dressed undergraduate in the college. When Ken Tynan arrived he was wearing a suit made of billiard cloth. I saw him in silhouette, walking from New Buildings to the Cloisters at Magdalen with a stride so like that of John Gielgud as Hamlet, crossing the stage with long delicate steps as if he were a stork, that I called out, 'Ken! You're walking like Gielgud in *Hamlet*.' He looked pleased and strode on.

On another occasion I heard him boast that James Agate, the top theatre critic in London, had invited him, when he was sixteen, to stay in London for a week of play-going. Each morning, on Agate's advice, Ken sat at a typewriter in his room composing original, relevant, funny and provocative remarks.

Agate looked at these remarks before lunch, discarded the failures and showed Ken how the wittiest might be improved. After lunch he sent Ken back to his room to learn them by heart. In the evening they went to the theatre, where in the foyer or the bar, or later at a restaurant or a club, Agate would introduce his prodigious discovery to famous people, giving Ken one cue after another to utter his witticisms as if spontaneously.

Once I went to a meeting where Stephen Spender spoke. If he read his poems I have forgotten. I remember only his big luminous eyes, and my feeling that if those were the eyes of a true poet, I must be an impostor. How could you tell if you were a born poet or not? I had been reading the novels of Charles Williams, metaphysical thrillers in which characters descended into hell or were blessed with beatific vision, lent to me, one by one, by his great friend C.S. Lewis. I was sitting on the floor looking up at Spender, who stood with his back to the fireplace, his eyes, moist with emotion, focused on things above our heads. He looked as I imagined poets to be. Anyone could see by the dimness of my spectacled eyes, as my mother would confirm, that poetry was not my birthright. To me poetry would never come naturally, as a gift. It would have to be made.

My friends at this time were churchgoers who intended to become clergy-men. The much older men returning from the war were determined to make up for lost time by obtaining firsts followed by good jobs. In their company I sometimes felt they were looking down on me as young and foolish with no experience of life.

I broke the ice of the age barrier by going up to a man who resembled my father – the same height, heavy weight and spectacles – to ask him, 'Would you like to be put on the list to read in chapel?' Charles Monteith read the lessons well, as did my father, and we became friends, although Charles was an agnostic. He was brought up and educated in Belfast, where his father, a Presbyterian, owned a drapery shop; his mother was Church of Ireland. Charles had won a Demyship and spent a year reading English with C.S. Lewis as his tutor before joining the Royal Inniskilling Fusiliers and rising to the war rank of major. A mortar bomb in Burma had left him lame, unable to drive a car and, as he said, inclined to give birth to shrapnel. Law was his subject, and everyone who knew how brilliant he was expected him to become a fellow of All Souls and reach the top of his profession as Lord Chancellor. My follies intrigued him, and he indulged me as a child whose absurd behaviour made him laugh.

By the summer term of 1946 I was spending too much time in a punt, poling up and down the River Cherwell with religious friends; browsing in

Blackwell's, where my account went so high that I had to return books to reduce it; pouring devotional feeling into archaic prayers; submitting with too much awe and reverence to the sound of words in a poem or a sacred text; reading them over and over instead of learning what they meant and asking myself if they made sense; sleeping with no one but figments of my imagination; writing poems that nobody read and essays that bored my tutor.

By now Lewis was saying with a chortle, 'Public school knocks the nonsense out of a boy and the university puts it all back.' His favourite quotation, and the one I took to heart, 'Kneel down, kneel down and wonder!' may have done me more harm than good. At the end of term, his report, read out in front of the president and all the fellows of Magdalen seated at their high table in hall, gave me a shock. 'Mr Murphy's work has disappointed me, and unless it improves he will not do well in his finals.' I could not understand how my essays had become so bad under the influence of a teacher so good. Ken Tynan spread it abroad that Lewis had said, 'The university cannot prevent Mr Tynan from getting a first.'

At the end of June 1946 I decided to go back to Milford, suffering from what would now be called depression and treated by tranquillisers. Then I thought of it as melancholia. A similar condition, 'Oxforditis', was said to attack males before the end of their second year. I was drawn back to a place I loved because I had been loved in that place as a child. Going to school and university in England had allowed the west of Ireland, that mournful, impoverished, tempestuous country, to remain in my imagination as the most beautiful place in the world. Ireland would be my cure.

I took a trunk full of heavy books to read and got through hardly any of them. At Milford, Granny was selling off the trees to pay the rates and her chemist's bill. Uncle Jack's widow, Bunty, had returned with her three children from Canada, where they had spent the war. Tom, aged seven, was to come into possession of Milford on his twenty-first birthday.

Happy to be back, I was even happier to be taught to drive by my aunt, and to rediscover Connemara in her car and in the cars of other relations. Through them I found a cottage near Screebe that I could rent for very little. I hired a lorry and brought some furniture, including a zinc bath and a chemical WC, that my mother had left in the East Wing at Milford. In a letter to the Bahamas I said that I was having 'a fruitful time reading and writing and being happy among the hills and rivers, lakes and bogs' at the cottage 'six yards from a salmon river that breaks into noiseless falls under a bridge on the road twenty yards from the door'.

Its rotting thatch had a cover of rusty corrugated iron; the interior was poky, damp and darkened with smoke from a turf fire. The primitive discomfort appealed to my longing to live in the depths of the past. Occasionally I could escape to Screebe Lodge to be wined and dined by rich friends. Yeats had become my favourite poet after Shakespeare, displacing Wordsworth now that I had rediscovered our family's lake district. 'Cold Clare rock and Galway rock and thorn' were to be my touchstones.

As an ambitious theme for a tragedy written in verse, I chose the medieval legend of Lynch, Mayor of Galway, who had hanged his own son for murdering a Spanish guest. No mere Irishman could be found to carry out such an impartial and cruel sentence of Roman as opposed to Brehon law. Long ago my grandmother on a shopping expedition to Galway had pointed out the 'proof' that this had occurred: part of the wall containing the window from which the boy had been hanged. No historical record of the sentence or the hanging has ever been found.

I may have been trying to expiate my guilt in relation to my father, who was still paying for my English education. Now I was becoming exalted by Celtic passion to write poetry, instead of bowing to Graeco-Roman reason in writing essays that would get me a good degree and a decent job.

By the Camus river, with the smell of peat smoke, the sound of rain dashing on tiny windowpanes, and the lyrical harsh voices of my poor landlord's family of ten who spoke almost nothing but Irish, my verse began to flow, even some lines about St Christopher, though I dared not call them poetry. Here I became convinced with religious intensity that the poetry I wanted to write would be written in Connemara.

But the cottage was too close to a road and too far from places I loved, such as Salruck, Letterfrack and Kylemore. Before the long vacation came to an end, I had found a cottage so isolated that no one had ever wanted to live in it. It stood at the base of Ben Choona, a mountain that blocked the sun from striking the windows all winter. The place was called Lecknavarna, meaning 'flagstone of the alders'. Below the cottage was a small peat bog and beyond this Lough Fee, on which Oscar Wilde had fished for salmon during his vacations. Beside the cottage a stream flowed from a great waterfall.

The falls at Lecknavarna were in a cleft where alders, rowans, holly and stunted oaks, remnants of Ireland's indigenous forest, clung to what little nourishment could be drawn from crevices in the sparkling black mica schist rock. A mile-long muddy track across a moor from the nearest house ended at the cottage below this waterfall. No more romantic solitude could be imagined.

Before spending a night at Lecknavarna, but dreaming every night of doing so, I returned to Oxford in October.

Now that ex-servicemen were overcrowding the college, I occupied digs approved by the university in a dingy red-brick house in a lower-middle-class terrace on a quiet street between the Iffley Road and the river. A dank foggy region. My landlady was kind and she tried to cheer me up, but her black cocker spaniel's moulting hairs got into our soup. Cramped, miserable and estranged, without a table or desk in my room, no shelves for books, no chair the right size for the dinner table, the floors covered with ugly purple linoleum, a front and back view of red-brick houses, I could do no work.

Lewis was no longer my tutor. His place had been taken, at least for this term, by another medievalist, J.A.W. Bennett, a shy New Zealander with prematurely grey hair and facial skin like the vellum of a rare old manuscript. Whereas Lewis spoke in clear Johnsonian sentences, Jack Bennett's mind would digress on a tangent of illumination before completing, if he ever did complete, the circle of a sentence. But I gave myself no chance of being illuminated by a scholar who never bullied students with his brilliance.

Feeling excluded by the college, I excluded myself in response, working on my verse play and making up my mind to go and live at Lecknavarna. Week after week I came to Bennett with a confession that I was unable to write an essay on John Donne. It never occurred to me to show him my verse. By midterm I was so depressed by the Iffley fogs and so manic about the play I wanted to write that I told everyone I intended to go down from Oxford at once, giving up the attempt to write literary criticism, and commit myself to writing poetry at Lecknavarna.

'I am more than depressed by Oxford University,' I wrote to Mary in Nassau. 'The criticism and intellectualism of Oxford are for me the inverting walls of a drab and melancholy prison.'

On 17 October I wrote to my parents, saying,

> It may be a shame that I am now disaffected with Oxford, after you have spent so much money to let me come here, but I do not consider the past five terms wasted in the light of my disaffection. I feel urgently that I should begin on my serious work, and give over criticism & scholarship (although I can hardly claim much of either) in the English school, leave Oxford at the end of this term,

and make my own living. This will mean getting work published as soon as any is complete. It is an insecure way of living, and one in which having or not having a degree doesn't matter, but you mustn't consider the insecurity of the existence when the result may be something better. I cannot continue to combine a course in criticism & scholarly study of the English poets, with writing poetry, and I must abandon the less important of the two …

To continue doing Eng. Lit. would be a shameful waste of your money, too much of which you have already freely bestowed in keeping me so comfortably at Oxford. Now I no longer have C.S. Lewis as a tutor, my strongest tie to the English school is out, and even had I Lewis as a tutor, I still think I should leave at the end of this term, and get moving seriously.

Combined with my aversion to the English school is the feeling of depression, of melancholy inactivity, of tired disability, that affects me at Oxford. This is so strong that I have no energy or inclination to work, even to read or to write poetry: so that after 3 months in which I discovered a new energy and new vision, I seem to have returned to a state of incompetent struggling and melancholy, the only difference being that I now know without a doubt where to go and what to do, in order to return to what I have found, and write poetry.

Everyone tried to dissuade me. The president, Sir Henry Tizard, a nuclear physicist, came nowhere near to understanding my predicament when he called me a 'drifter'. A drifter would have drifted through the term and over to Ireland at Christmas. My vocation would not permit me to wait. Lewis lent me a copy of Benjamin Robert Haydon's autobiography as a warning not to embark so young on a life of passionate romanticism, as it might lead to despair and suicide.

Then I sent this telegram:

MURPHY GOVERNMENT HOUSE NASSAU NOV 5 1946
HEALTH AND WORK BREAKING DOWN MUST HAVE YOUR SANCTION
LEAVE OXFORD GO IRELAND IMMEDIATELY
RICHARD

Meanwhile I was arranging by mail and telegraph to buy from a man who lived near Milford a bull-nosed Morris Cowley, seventeen years old. I was running into debt, but the car was needed to get to and from Lecknavarna. It required a roof, which Sonny Joyce, the blacksmith in Kilmaine, built in a few days at my grandmother's request. Her romantic soul and her love of art made her sympathetic to my passion to write poetry within sound and sight of a waterfall in Connemara. The night before my departure on 11 November, Charles Monteith gave a farewell party at which we drank much beer; and Charles, after dimming the lights, chanted 'Byzantium' in a voice of which Yeats might have approved. Charles was as tone deaf as Yeats, but his ear for the cadence of poetry and prose was good. His incantation was as magical as Yeats intended, and now when I read the poem I still hear the 'great cathedral gong' of Charles's voice summoning the 'blood-begotten spirits' to a dance of 'flames that no faggot feeds, nor steel has lit'.

Three students, including Ken Tynan, who encouraged me to continue with the verse play, said they would come and stay as paying guests at my cottage during the Christmas vacation. My solitude would not be absolute. Among those who came to see me off at the railway station the next morning was Peter Wyld, a captain in the Grenadier Guards who had lost a leg in the war.

Shortly after I had gone, C.S. Lewis wrote to my father, saying he could not persuade me to change my mind. He did not think my state of mind was unhealthy, though very foolish. In sympathy with my parents, he suggested that they might feel a little proud of my folly because it was not ignoble.

Connemara looked utterly desolate that winter. Bracken on the foothills had turned rust-red. In pouring rain, with no wiper on the windscreen of the worn-out car, I had to peep through a hole where the glass was broken, my glasses obscured by condensation. I feared that the brakes might not hold on the steep hill down to Salruck, where I collected the keys from my landlord, John 'Bicycle' Coyne, my grand-aunt Violet's caretaker. Night came at four o'clock. The old Hotchkiss engine whined and chugged in low gear, headlights dimming whenever it idled. On the track across the moor to Lecknavarna the rushes were as tall as the bonnet and I had to travel slower than walking to avoid sinking in the bog. How lonely the cottage looked and how cold it felt. No light but a torch and candles. I had to fetch turf from a shed before lighting a fire. The blankets were mouldy and there was no one to share my bed.

Yet all this was a prelude to ecstatic worship of the waterfall, a great white presence and steadfast consolation in the darkness. When it rained heavily, the waterfall thundered and turned red, as if the mountain were bleeding from a wound that stained the water of the lake, and even discoloured, when it got that far, the sea at Lettergesh.

I lived on cornflakes with milk and eggs and homemade bread from a house a mile across the moor, and on baked beans, tea, sugar and mountainy mutton chops from Leenane, six miles away. At the kitchen table, with a fountain pen on lined sheets of quarto paper, my back to the open fire, I wrote many pages of unrhymed iambic verse.

After two weeks on my own, the loneliness was becoming less poetic. I was more worried about my debts, as my parents had cut off my allowance. On Sunday I drove to morning service in Moyard, where we used to be taken as children from Rosleague, and when I came out I was happy to see my grandmother with Dr Maguire from Claremorris sitting in his car.

'You'll have to go back to Oxford,' she told me. 'Your mother and father think you're mad and they sent for Dr Maguire to have you certified if we can't put sense into your head. You may be fed up with Oxford, but it can't be as bad as the asylum in Ballinasloe where you'd never be let out once you were put away.'

She persuaded me to go back.

A humiliating choice, but the humbling brought me down to earth in England. Lewis welcomed me, glad to get back his copy of Haydon, which I had taken and read in Ireland. I lost my Demyship, a blow from Sir Henry Tizard, putting more expense on my father. Charles raised much laughter about my foolish escapade. Aunty Kay invited me to the Lake District, where, not for the first time or the last, she paid my debts and gave me money to raise my morale. The lack of independent means had caused my mission to fail, but henceforth I would go to Lecknavarna for vacations, enjoy visits from friends and family, and work well there, even at the books I had to read for my degree. My poetic ambition, buried in shame, would lie dormant. Meanwhile I had to work all the harder to achieve a not dishonourable second.

In January 1947 I took rooms off the Banbury Road, and cycled back and forth to Magdalen. I was still depressed, but my mania had been quelled. Snow fell and continued to fall and freeze throughout the term, and a pain in my stomach that had troubled me on and off got so bad that I called a doctor.

The last I saw of the snow was through the window of an ambulance taking me to the Acland Nursing Home for the removal of my appendix.

Recovering, I found at my bedside a basket of fruit sent by the Duchess of Marlborough from Blenheim Palace, at my mother's instigation. I had been reading Tolstoy's *Resurrection* and still going to church as a believer. When I came out of the hospital the snow had melted, the grass was green, my mind was clear and I felt reborn, without an appendix or a guilty soul that needed to be saved.

Lack of money had defeated me in Ireland; now I kept wondering how I could make it – fast. Traces of madness remained, in that I ordered three handlooms from an old firm of loom manufacturers in West Yorkshire that had a waiting list of two years. My idea was to produce handwoven tweed in Connemara, where I still wanted to live, for sale in New York through contacts in the Bahamas. I began to mix with students financially much better off than I was.

'Who was that perfumed popinjay you brought to dinner last night?' asked Charles Monteith.

'That was Tony Berry, youngest son of Lord Kemsley who owns the *Sunday Times* and the *Daily Sketch*.' Charles, a supporter of the Labour government, didn't disguise his contempt. Tony had stayed as a guest of my parents in Nassau and was bringing me news of the family. He drove around Oxford in a Jaguar, for which he bought petrol on the black market.

In a reading room at Magdalen frequented by students who lived in digs, I often saw Teddy Goldsmith, and we became friends. He had charm without affectation, a good sense of the absurd, and none of Berry's socialite snobbery and vulgar extravagance. Teddy's father, who had been an MP, owned or had stakes in the Prince George Hotel in Nassau, the Scribe in Paris, the Carlton in Cannes and the Savoy in London.

Teddy invited me to stay at the Scribe for a week in the spring of 1948. After the austerity of college food, with rationing worse than during the war, whale meat alternating with cod for dinner, I was awed by the luxury and opulence. His mother, who distributed surplus food from the kitchen after lunch to people who were starving, took me to a Christian Dior collection.

While I was at the Scribe I heard that my sister Liz was lying unconscious in a hospital in Miami after nearly being killed by Tony Berry's driving while drunk on the way home from a party in Nassau. I would hear later that Tony had escaped prosecution because he was my father's guest; and to celebrate his safe return to England, Lord Kemsley had given him a ball at the Dorchester that cost more than the average price of a house. It would take six months in traction and plaster for Liz to recover.

At night that week in Paris, Teddy and his brother Jimmy, who was sixteen and already famous for winning thousands of pounds on a horse and flooring his housemaster at Eton with a punch, took me out on the town to parties and bars to meet girls. I decided that now was my chance to change my life by having sex with a woman.

Late on my last night I wandered off and was accosted by one of several women I passed, unable to see them clearly in the streetlight. She asked for fifteen hundred francs, and as we walked to her hotel I felt embarrassed and guilty, dared not look her in the face, kept wondering would I be seen by the boys and laughed at, would I be caught, feeling as criminal as if I were committing a crime. Inside her brothel we had to pass a stout elderly madame who recited the rules to me in French.

The woman took me up to a tiny room with a double bed and a washbasin. Too late I realised my mistake: I had picked up a middle-aged woman. She asked for the francs, then told me to wash and put on a condom. I had never done this before, and her frank instruction shrivelled what little desire remained after seeing her rouged haggard face. So she solved this problem with her hands, saying 'Oh la! la! Trop de cognac!' Watching her undressing – horrible black suspenders and rolls of fat – I felt sick. She lay down and waggled her white flabby thighs in the air. Disgusted, I was unable to have an erection. She told me to lie on my back and she straddled me. I kept my eyes shut and lay still while she worked long and efficiently till I came. It would have been better on my own.

The news that I had passed my degree with second-class honours reached me in New York on the eve of my twenty-first birthday. That night Peter Hoguet, a playboy whose parents were friends of mine in Nassau, took me to a party at a nightclub on the roof of the St Regis given by the daughters of Joseph Kennedy. I was on my way to the Bahamas.

My father was so generous and believed so strongly in education that, by the time I left Oxford, he owned neither a house nor the value of a house in shares, but had spent on my education enough to have bought himself a big house like Milford in a walled demesne.

So when he gave me a job, my first after leaving Oxford, as private secretary and later aide-de-camp in charge of the staff, catering and accounts, among other official and social duties, casting an eye occasionally on the prisoners who worked in the garden, all of them coloured, I found the best way of repaying him for a fraction of what my education had cost was to cut the running expenses of Government House. In nine or ten months we saved enough money for my parents to buy the land on which they were to settle and build a house, and later a school for their farm workers' children, in Southern Rhodesia.

His great anxiety was to leave the Bahamas and retire from the colonial service after thirty-nine years without putting a foot wrong. He had never enjoyed succeeding the duke much as it gratified our mother to replace the duchess at the head of society. Most of their income, a tenth of what the Windsors received, was gobbled up entertaining people ten times richer than they were.

Entering the governor's office, adjacent to mine, was an ordeal. He could not allow me, he said, to call him 'Daddy' because he represented the monarch; nor did he want me to call him 'Your Excellency', except on official occasions when my job was to introduce guests, because he was my father. He resolved the dilemma by telling me to call him 'Sir', in the Victorian style of his youth. That put him on a pedestal to be approached with reverence and awe, as with Aunt Bella. Calling him 'Sir' reminded me how little I understood him, and how remote he was. It filled me with stage fright, making me imagine that I was committing a social gaffe that would annoy him and perhaps even cause him to explode. All the males in our family, except his saintly father, had a quick temper.

With little to do in the office, I read *War and Peace* from a book laid open in my desk drawer, which I closed when my father rang his bell or some caller came into the room. Once, by mistake, I happened to leave *Ulysses* on a table in the drawing room, where my father found it. He chastised me indignantly: 'If you must read such filth, at least you should have the decency not to leave it lying around where it might be picked up by your sister.' Liz was eighteen and recovering from her accident. Our father, like other Victorians, had no objection to 'filth' if it were written in Greek or Latin or the English of the King James Bible.

When my brother Chris, on vacation in August 1948, fell in love with a beautiful Bahamian girl, the daughter of a member of the Executive Council, rumoured not to be purely white, our father threatened to deport him unless he broke off the affair. His motives were not simply racist but to avoid a conflict of interest that might have arisen at meetings of a Council notorious for its corruption. He was the first governor to appoint a black Bahamian to that Council. During this crisis, Chris decided to chuck up Trinity, also the dream of a career as a baritone, which our grandmother had encouraged, and take a job with Shell. He was sent to Jamaica, where he fell in love with a Jewish girl, whose parents ironically barred him from their house for six months before accepting him as a son-in-law.

During his national service in the army, which he thought would have done me the world of good by demolishing my ivory-tower illusions, Chris had come to the conclusion that neither Mary's painting nor his music nor my poetry was good enough for us to risk wasting our lives attempting to be artists. We each had a little talent but no genius, therefore it was better to turn to economics and make money. He was offering sensible advice based on his worldly experience and knowledge of our family. The poetry I had written at Oxford and Lecknavarna was so unpromising that I could not argue with his superior judgement. Consequently, the frail spectre of my ambition to be a poet retreated into shadows under royal palms in the compound, or behind shuttered windows of shanties.

One Sunday, after a picnic lunch at the *cabaña* on Cable Beach, which the government had acquired for the pleasure of the Duke and Duchess of Windsor, my mother took me for a walk on the coral sand to talk about my future. Because I stood between her and the sea while she spoke, there was no escaping the maternal force of her attempt to control the direction of my life.

She was afraid that if I were to devote myself to writing poetry, I would certainly be poor and perhaps a failure. My father had already urged me to consider journalism rather than poetry or fiction. 'Even John Buchan,' he stressed, 'who has done very well, says that writing is a good walking stick but a bad crutch.'

My mother was convinced that my birth in the Irish country house of her army-officer relations, who had done their duty, some at the cost of their lives, in the Peninsular War, the Crimea, the Siege of Lucknow, the Gallipoli campaign and Abyssinia, destined me for a life of public duty and high office. In the Bahamas I was doing my duty as the son of a lady admired in high society for her style and her indefatigable support of various charities, especially the Red Cross. Since we had left Milford, she and I had both changed in ways that had pulled us apart.

'I know you,' she argued – and who had a better right than my mother to say this? – 'and I know you were never meant to be a poet.' I could not contradict her. In Nassau I was identified as nobody but the governor's son, the object of flattery from people who wanted their importance recognised by invitations, and this made me feel hollow.

Trapped for ten months, I misspent time, trying to kill it in the hot and humid hours after dinner, having said goodnight to my parents as if I were going to sleep, when I would drive out alone in a borrowed Riley sports car, past a saluting sentry at the gate, to travel around the island of New Providence by its longest route, anticlockwise for fifty miles, encapsulated on a road without traffic that ended where it began.

Driving west along Cable Beach, windows down for a cooling draught and the sha-sha-sha of casuarinas, I would pass the house where Sir Harry Oakes was bludgeoned to death at night in a room next to his estate agent, Harold Christie, who 'never heard a sound', and turn the sharp corner where Liz had been dragged from the wreck of Tony Berry's convertible Buick by suave Prince Stanisław Radziwiłł, who took off his silk shirt and rolled it up as a pillow to put under her head.

Sometimes I would divert for a swim in the nude, followed by a rum and Coca-Cola at the *cabaña*, before driving on through mangrove swamps to Lyford Cay, farmland made out of scarified rock by the silver-and-copper mining magnate Chester Beatty, not another car on the road or cycle or person walking; and around by the leper colony, where our mother would drag us at Christmas to bring presents for the lepers, washing our hands and gargling afterwards. Then crossing the island and back through the coloured quarter, not daring to stop and explore a zone of deprivation and danger that aroused desire, I would return to Government House with a sense of futility – frustrated and bored.

My father was so loyal to the Crown that even when we were dining as a family without guests on the verandah, at the end of the meal he would solemnly raise a toast of port or Madeira to 'the King'. On state occasions, men had to bow to him and women curtsy. He signed warrants for the hanging of murderers. If he had felt qualms, he would never have told me.

Once I made the mistake of sending him off in his regalia, with my mother in evening dress, to dine at the house of an American shoe manufacturer on the wrong night. They walked into a crowd of people in slacks and shirt sleeves around a barbecue, where they put everyone at ease by joining the party. Four years earlier, when he had succeeded the duke, my father was described in a London newspaper as 'warm, human, very friendly and as Irish as they are made'. I didn't see that warmth and friendliness brightening in his face until we were on the plane leaving Nassau for the last time.

Boredom was the worst illness I suffered there, making brittle talk at cocktail parties and dinner dances, enjoying riches that were not mine, bowing to men and women merely because they were rich or titled or famous, showing appreciative awe in the face of their importance, even if this had been achieved by fraud. A Conservative bragged to me of getting massive amounts of money out of Britain without paying tax, and in breach of exchange controls. He felt entitled to cheat the country because Labour was ruining the country for him and his kind. I was not immune to the corruption of wondering whose footsteps I might follow to make a fortune in a few years, so that I could retire at twenty-five or thirty to write poetry in a house like Milford in the west of Ireland.

A Russian princess, Myra, wife of Norman Armour, a rich and famous American ambassador, told me at a beach party that she thought it was very bad for a person of my age to be living in Nassau, enjoying privilege and luxury that he had not earned; it was a place for people who had made their mark in the world. As a child she had escaped from St Petersburg after the Bolshevik revolution, when her mother sat her on the family jewels in a railway carriage, and told the Red Army guards at the frontier that her daughter was suffering from measles. The diplomat she married was one of the grain-elevator Armours of Chicago, not the meat-packers. I knew well that her remark was true, but as I was bound to stay to help my father, her criticism rankled, and seemed unfair coming from a woman who had never experienced life without luxury and privilege.

Meanwhile I tried to do something to redeem the time, and to overcome my ignominious failure two years earlier, when I had left Oxford in midterm to write a verse play at a cottage in Connemara. On the same theme, of a judge who had hanged his own son for murder in medieval Galway because no one else would do the hangman's job, I began to write an historical novel.

As John Marquand had made enough money from his novels and his marriage to spend winters at a house on the harbour in Nassau, with a private anchorage for his boat, I thought he might be a good person to give me advice and access to a publisher, even to emulate. So we invited him and his wife to lunch, and he, being a courteous Bostonian, promised to read my opening chapters. Though I felt that using the privilege of being the governor's son and aide-de-camp, rather than the merit of my writing, was a false way to begin a literary career, my assumption of that identity had inclined me to falsehood.

Though Marquand kept his word, and encouraged me to think that the novel would find a publisher, I soon gave up the writing, because every word I wrote in the Bahamas sounded hollow, and the hollowness infected with disbelief my inner faith that I could write. Such verse as I scribbled on Government House memo pads was obscure and windy rhetoric inspired by passion it did not convey.

Then, under social pressure to which my role and age made me vulnerable, I deceived myself into thinking I might be in love sufficiently to propose to the Honourable Patricia Cavendish, the blonde and blue-eyed daughter of the beautiful, silver-haired Enid, Countess of Kenmare, by the second of four husbands she had buried. Nassau was a place where the countess would have expected her daughter to find a suitable husband, and perhaps my position made me seem eligible, even though I was penniless and without a permanent job. More truly my desire may have been to attach myself to a sensitive, well-read, slightly older woman, because her mother was apparently willing to provide what I wanted most, a big house set in an Irish demesne where I could farm and write poetry. It pleased my mother to think of her son marrying into the aristocracy. Her conviction that I was not born to be a poet mired in poverty seemed confirmed, now that I was more sensibly showing my hand as a fortune hunter.

There was a set of mirrors that could be placed on top of the mahogany dinner table built for the duchess at Government House. It doubled the glitter of jewellery, silver and glass in candlelight. My parents thought it glitzy and vulgar, so it was seldom used. But I set it up to honour the countess, whose beauty and acumen, derived from the Lindeman family of winegrowers in Australia, had won her an independent fortune when she buried her third husband, Viscount Furness, in occupied France during the war and escaped with his will in her favour through Spain and Portugal. After this coup, in order to acquire a better name than the one which the press had defiled with slanderous gossip, Enid married Valentine Castlerosse, Earl of Kenmare, who gave her a nobler, more ancient title. She kept this after he died, which was very soon.

Her beauty, and still more her charm in pretending that she was less intelligent than any man who admired her, had been rewarded by the rich and powerful between and during her marriages. Even old Chester Beatty, though too scared to take off his coat and scarf in our house in case he caught a chill, was wooing Enid that season with gifts of strawberries grown on his scarified rock. She sat on my father's right, saying scarcely a word, but inspiring him to talk more freely than usual, with her almost bare bosom held up by a red velvet dress, and her Carrara marble face poised motionless above the mirror, as if she were sitting for a portrait of herself at the court of Versailles or in Regency Brighton.

No daughter could shine in such a woman's shadow. Pat told me that she had felt miserable as a small child sitting beside her mother, whom she adored, in an immense caravanserai of Rolls-Royces and lesser cars and trucks full of servants and luggage that followed her stepfather, even on safaris in Kenya. She wept for the creatures Lord Furness used to slaughter, formed her own friendships with animals, and trembled with shyness whenever she had to be polite to all the intimidating people they met. She could hardly open her mouth for fear of saying the wrong thing. If I married her, she warned me, I would have to share her bed in her mother's villa at St Jean Cap Ferrat with her porcupine and her silver fox.

It was the legend of her mother that made me want to think I loved Pat enough to propose one afternoon in a borrowed car, which I parked on a deserted road beside a mangrove swamp. I didn't know what to say, and was terrified of making a fool of myself. She was equally scared. Each of us was influenced by our mothers' expectations that I would propose and that she would accept. Until then we had not kissed. Two or three pimples around my lips had deterred me, signs she might detect of a shameful practice that was said in those days to impair a man's virility. All you need to say, I said to myself, and you could say it very quickly, even if you cannot look her in the eyes, is, I love you: will you marry me?

It was as if I were two persons, one goading the other to act a part in an intimate performance that would transform the lives of both, exalting the dual person to join a family that sailed around the world first class on ocean liners, kept a houseboat in Kashmir, and lived in a villa next door to Somerset Maugham in the south of France. The self who was goaded felt sure that the shy girl, who was no fool, would suspect him of wanting to marry her for her money, and say 'No'. But after the goader had forced out the words from my petrified voice, her reply, 'Yes, I'd love to, I was hoping you'd ask,' sounded as if it were offering salvation at the scene of a fatal accident I had miraculously survived. Prolonged kissing rescued us both from having to say more.

Society and custom did the rest. Her mother, by then in France, received the news by cable and cabled back her love and approval. The engagement was announced in *The Times*. During our sex on a couch in the *cabaña*, my anxiety not to fail in the attempt at penetrating the unknown was compounded by her anxiety not to be made pregnant. All too soon we were kissing goodbye at the airport, and I was sending flowers by cable to the *Île de France* on which she sailed from New York to Cherbourg. Love letters came and went, and letters about money. Her mother encouraged me to think that she would buy a big house like Milford in a walled demesne in Ireland, because Pat loved horses and dogs. My sister Mary, who was living with her children at Milford, went with an estate agent to view several old Castle Rackrents with long rutted avenues through rookeries on four or five hundred acres of land that the owners could no longer afford to keep, and nobody wanted to buy.

Then a letter came from Pat, gently breaking off the engagement, giving me a humiliating shock. I replied with frigid anger, showing how false my love had been. Mercifully she accepted my later apology. Her rejection, and my bad response, aggravated a demoralising doubt as to whether I could ever love a woman well enough to marry without deceiving her and myself.

And what became of Pat Cavendish I discovered nearly fifty years later. She had sailed away to Sydney with her mother, and her older half-brother, Roderick Cameron, who was writing a travel book. During the long voyage she had fallen in love with a dental mechanic of Irish descent who was champion of the Australian Olympic swimming team. She married and divorced him, and, after another short marriage, settled down in Kenya, living with lions in her garden and sleeping with a lioness in her bed. No children. Before Enid died, she persuaded Pat to give up the lions in order to breed and train racehorses on a stud farm in the Cape, and to remarry her Australian swimmer.

In March 1997, during my first visit to South Africa, we met again when she invited me to stay at Broadland in Somerset West, where the business of horses seemed a sideline to the interest of her heart – the salvation of wild or neglected creatures, especially chimpanzees and baboons. As soon as I entered her large old Cape Dutch house, at the end of a long avenue through tree-bordered parks grazed by thoroughbreds, I could smell the monkeys and hear their resounding screeches and hoots from a cage adjoining the kitchen. Except for those that were bred by her, each animal had been rescued from death on the highway or cruelty in a zoo or the threat of extinction on account of its violent behaviour.

Fifty or sixty dogs roamed in and out of the house, neither fighting each other nor attacking her guests, though had I been coloured or black I would have feared for my life. Her love of animals seemed capable of pacifying their aggressive instincts, or at least restraining them in the presence of whites. I saw her fearlessly enter the compound of a huge old chimp that could have killed her. He was sitting at the top of the skeleton of a very tall tree he had stripped of leaves and bark. She stood at the trunk while he climbed down to a branch from which he stretched a paw to take a bar of chocolate from a pocket of her coat. He stroked her head before climbing back to the top of his perch.

She was bottle-feeding a baby chimp and changing its nappy, allowing it to sleep in her bed and wake her up to play or be fed at all hours of the night. Before her guests and her husband sat down to dinner in the garden by the pool, she said goodnight to us all and retired to her bedroom with the chimp in her arms.

As to the future, she was planning to set up a trust to keep her animals and their progeny housed and fed for a hundred years. Chimpanzees, she told me, can live to a great age if properly looked after. The work of keeping them alive in zoological luxury and privilege is done at present by coloured and black people, who live more endangered lives in conditions unfit for her animals. Animals have always been her best friends and substitutes for the children she never had.

Before we left the Bahamas at the end of my father's term of office in July 1949, Chester Beatty persuaded him to think about buying a farm in Southern Rhodesia. My father and mother could not face retiring from the colonies, where they had always been warm and had servants, to subsist in the cold wet climate of Ireland, which had just declared itself a republic, on a pension as poor as a curate's stipend. They wanted adventure; he was sixty-two and she was eleven years younger. So they took their Buick by sea to Cape Town and motored up through the Kruger Park to Southern Rhodesia. Near Bromley they bought fifteen hundred acres of virgin land with no house in a farming area unjustly restricted to whites. Aunt Kitty, the last of our mother's Ballinamore aunts, had died and left her some silver and books and enough money to settle and farm.

They sounded happy in letters that came to us in London. When their furniture and books from Ireland arrived with the grand piano that used to accompany our singing at morning prayers in Milford, a Shona carpenter built huts for them out of the packing cases. They lived in these through the first winter, until enough poor black Africans had come from the nearest reserve to build them a house of bricks baked on the site, and to plant their first tobacco and maize crops.

Though tempted, I had decided not to go with them to Africa. My mother's best friend of her youth in Scotland, Beryl Lockerbie, whose brother Bert had been in love with my mother before he was killed in the Great War, had warned me in Nassau that my mother would keep me as a child for ever if I failed to get away soon and stand on my own feet.

So I had come to London to find a job, and joined Mary in sharing a small furnished flat near Harrods with our sister Liz and Mary's two children, John, aged six, and Grania, my god-daughter, aged two. The romance of her hasty wartime marriage to Toby had worn off, and they were soon to be divorced. Mary worked as an advertising rep for the *Queen*, a monthly fashion magazine.

Beryl, in London, saw that I needed a dark-grey three-piece suit, the kind that men had to wear in the city, so she kindly paid for one to be made by her friend Cyril Langley, who was T.S. Eliot's tailor. Mary sent me to Lock's to be fitted for a black bowler hat, and gave me a present of a spotted silver-grey tie and a white shirt with a stiff collar. A black umbrella completed my outfit.

Money was melting away fast. Two months had passed since my twenty-second birthday, and no one had helped in my job hunt except Lord Ennisdale. He and his wife had brought me in their chauffeur-driven Rolls to a Tudor mansion on their vast estate, Baynard's Park in Surrey, for a weekend that included shooting duck. Long before my host obtained a title, he was known as Harry Lyons. He had started work at fourteen as a postboy at Lloyd's, where his poor Irish-born father had been a liveried waiter with the job of ringing the Lutine Bell whenever a ship on the high seas foundered. After fighting in the Boer War, Lyons, at my age in London, became an independent broker, who managed, by impressing J.P. Morgan, to persuade American insurance companies to reinsure their risks at Lloyd's through his company. Commissions accruing from his deals allowed him to retire before the age of thirty to play polo.

I thought, if I were to follow in his footsteps, I might make enough money in a few years to spend the rest of my life writing poetry, if not in a place like Milford, then in a cottage like Bicycle's at Lecknavarna. Lord Ennisdale said he would try to get me placed at C.E. Heath & Co., the largest brokers at Lloyd's. They would start me at the bottom – perhaps on the rung above postboy because of my Oxford degree. The clerks might frustrate me, I'd hate the boring office routine, but on every policy that I could introduce to the company I would receive a commission, and as soon as my commission income became large enough for my needs, I could go off and write poetry anywhere in the world. At dinner in the oak-panelled hall, across the table from a former chief whip of the Conservative Party, it sounded like a doddle.

Anxious for word about Lloyd's, I had been acting for a few days as personal assistant to Harold Christie, who had come to sell Bahamian property from a suite at Claridge's. He had asked me to write a brochure for a paradise island that only the richest of the rich could afford, and he was pleased with the result: a shameful use of style to persuade while deceiving. After a *grande cuisine* lunch, with champagne served in the suite, he tipped me a large white Bank of England five-pound note. These were so rare that people would sometimes sign their names on the back, hoping to recover the note if it were lost or stolen.

That smoky autumnal afternoon, daydreaming on foot through Regent Street, my bowler-hatted head aloof, the umbrella, although there was no sign of rain, correctly on my right arm, I came to Piccadilly Circus and went down the crowded stairway into the Underground below the statue of Eros to take a train back to Knightsbridge, and turned under a blue neon sign into the Gents.

Avoiding a long row of crowded urinals in a large white ceramic-walled chamber that smelt of disinfectant, I walked across to one of a pair of unoccupied stalls. A moment later, an old man in a dirty mackintosh came and stood beside me and exposed an erect but crooked cock, which he began to shake.

Disgusted, I should have walked out, but didn't. Curious and aroused, I covered my cock with my left hand but continued to glance at his through the corner of my left eye, waiting longer than I need have done, hearing the click of penny-in-a-slot brass locks being opened, the cranking of chains to flush water closets, heavy doors thudding shut, the rumble of trains deep in the bowels of London growing louder and fading away. On the way out a notice read NO LOITERING.

With relief, as if I'd safely crossed a street in which a motorist had tried to run me down in a nightmare, I bought a ticket to Knightsbridge and joined the crowd on the escalator going down to the trains on my way home to a family tea at the flat. As I was hurrying along a tubular tunnel with a crowd that flowed in both directions, a man caught up with me, touched my arm and, with a lower middle-class accent, said: 'Keep walking, I'm a police officer and I want to question you.'

Obeying him, I felt as if I were walking upside down on the tunnels roof beside a man in a belted fawn trench coat, his mousy Brylcreemed hair level with the top of my shoulder. I assumed he was a plain-clothes detective, but never dared ask him to show his badge. When we emerged on the westbound platform of the Piccadilly line, he ordered me to 'Step this way' towards an iron bench on which he put a foot, and demanded my name and address and my father's, which he wrote on a slip of paper.

'Do you know how long you spent standing in the toilet?'

'A minute or two. I didn't notice the time, to tell you the truth.'

'Well, Murphy, I know exactly, because I timed you on my watch. You spent six minutes.'

'I'm sure it wasn't as long as that.'

'Don't tell me lies, Murphy, or I'll take you to the station on the spot and have you booked. My colleague has picked up the old man who was standing next to you. He'll go down for two years, because it's not his first time committing a sexual offence. He's a pervert like you, and you both deserve to be punished. Why did you spend so long? It normally takes thirty or forty seconds for a young man like you to pass water.'

'I don't believe I spent much longer than necessary.'

'I'll tell you why you spent six minutes. I could see the hem of your overcoat shaking, so I knew you were engaged in a criminal act of gross indecency in a public place – masturbating.'

'I was doing no such thing, sir,' I replied, my heart thumping, my face a mask of my feelings, my body sinking as if into a lake of pitch. His accusation was false, but what could I say? He was trying to demoralise me, I thought, to make me confess to what I hadn't done, as in Russia – police officers aren't supposed to do this in England. He must have known that I would feel guilty for having stood too long beside the old man in the dirty mackintosh.

'I know your type, Murphy,' he went on, 'and I never make a mistake, because I'm trained to recognise your sort and put a stop to your filthy habits. As soon as you came into the toilet I said to myself, "There goes one of those homosexuals – I'll time him on my watch." You were loitering for six minutes.'

'I'm sure it wasn't that long, sir, and I'm not a homosexual,' I pleaded, not having begun to think that I might be. My heart was thumping as I tried with a look of injured innocence not to let him see that he was delivering the greatest shock of my life. Would he find out about my broken engagement?

'You can't deny it, I recognised you as soon as you came into the Gents with that look on your face, I know you're guilty, it's written in your eyes and in your lips. I'm going to tell you something, so listen to me, Murphy, for your own good. Tonight, when I'm warm in bed with my wife, and I love my wife because I'm a normal bloke, I'll know in my heart I was right, and I'll tell her I had to decide whether to send another young homosexual to prison, which he deserved, or let him off with a caution as a first offender. What am

I to do with you? What would your father say if he saw in the papers that his son had been arrested, or if I wrote to him and told him what I'd seen you doing in the Gents?'

'He'd be deeply upset.'

'I know. This address you've given me, that country, Rhodesia, it's in Africa, isn't it? What's he doing there?'

'He's buying some land to farm in his retirement.'

Now the fear of imprisonment was compounded by the fear that my father and mother would hear about it, and disown me for bringing shame on their whole family. Fleet Street would carry the story with my father's name and rank. Mary might read this in the late-night final edition of the *Evening Standard* before she came back to the flat for our supper.

As one train after another came from Leicester Square and went on to Green Park, I thought of jumping on to the next, just as the doors were closing; but the officer, having names and addresses, could track me down and charge me with a further crime of resisting arrest. I hoped that by talking to my accuser 'ever so nicely' – my mother's words – I could avoid that risk, and otherwise quell the urge to throw myself on the electrified rail.

At last he came round to offering a means of redemption. 'In cases like yours, Murphy, where an officer has been decent enough to let a man off with a warning, the offender usually wants to show his gratitude by making a donation to the Police Widows' and Orphans' Benevolent Fund. If you feel like helping our widows and orphans, you can give me something for that fund. Of course I wouldn't take anything for myself.'

I put my hand into my back pocket and pulled out Harold Christie's white five-pound note. 'Will this be enough, sir? I'm afraid it's all I have.'

'That will do. But let me warn you never to show your face in that toilet again or next time I catch you there you won't get off so lightly.' After pocketing the fiver, he tore up the sheet on which he had made notes, letting the pieces blow away in the funnelled wind of an approaching train, which I boarded.

Not daring to say a word to Mary or Liz, I had to talk to someone. My best friend at Oxford, Charles Monteith, had a fellowship at All Souls and was practising at the London bar. He told me to come round immediately to his rooms in South Kensington. There I relived the ordeal, telling him word for word what had happened.

Before advising me, Charles asked, 'You're not queer, are you, Richard?' When I replied 'No' – because I wished that were the truth – he added, 'I didn't think so.' He told me the detective, if a member of the Metropolitan Police, had done wrong in taking a 'donation', but perhaps he was a conman who preyed on homosexuals and their fear of being imprisoned under the harsh penalties imposed in Britain.

Either way, he reckoned that my mind would never be at ease unless I were to go to the police myself and tell them what I had told him. They would know if a detective like the one I described had been on duty in the Gents. Charles said the police would be more concerned to prosecute a bent copper for extortion, or to catch a blackmailer posing as a detective, than to worry about how long I had spent urinating.

'Go to Scotland Yard,' he said in his commanding voice, 'and ask to speak to a commissioner. Tell the constables at the front desk it's a matter so important that you cannot reveal it to an officer of lower rank. A commissioner will have more interest in rooting out corruption among detectives on the ground, and be more sympathetic.'

On his advice I went next morning to Scotland Yard, using my aide-de-camp experience to be conducted with no delay to an office where a large grey-haired man, wearing a black pinstriped suit dignified enough for a funeral, stood up and shook hands, and asked me to take a seat and tell him what was on my mind. When I had gone through the ordeal again, making one embarrassing revelation after another, to all of which he listened silently, he said, 'You'll have to go to Savile Row Police Station, and sign a statement there. It's not a case for Scotland Yard. Goodbye, Mr Murphy, and good luck!'

I left Scotland Yard even more terrified than I had been when I entered. In Savile Row the detective superintendent who took my statement was indeed sympathetic, and I kept nothing back. He said that the police did have detectives keeping watch on the Gents in Piccadilly Underground, as it's a place frequented by pickpockets, homosexuals and male prostitutes. It would be easy to find out whether the man who accosted me in the Tube was one of their detectives on duty, he said, but would I be willing to give evidence in court if he could be identified? I wasn't willing, I replied, because this could result in my reputation, and my father's name, being tarnished in the newspapers reporting such a banal and squalid case. He went to consult his superior.

Five minutes later he returned with a middle-aged officer of higher rank who demanded to know, 'Why didn't you immediately report the man you saw masturbating to the police?' It never occurred to me to do this. The officer implied that my offence was almost as bad as the one I had witnessed, and my reluctance to appear in court, moral cowardice.

I left the police station feeling guilty rather than redeemed. For years to come I would be afraid of encountering my accuser on the London streets or in the Underground, even of being pursued by him to Connemara. There, the memory of his grilling would strengthen my desire to implant myself and stay away from big cities.

'Not a bad thing,' Charles would say in 1979, justifying his advice, which had doubled my torment by making me endure it twice, talking to the police. At least the incident pulled down my vanity and made me see myself in the worst possible light. Charles might have added, 'Good for a poet.'

Penelope keeps a blue parrot in a cage covered by a silk shawl in her drawing room. 'He's a neurotic bird,' she says, 'and has to be put to sleep before a guest arrives, otherwise he screeches.' She kisses me on the cheek. 'Wonderful to see you again. We had such fun in Paris. When was it?'

'Last year in the spring.'

'That long ago! We lunched at Maxime's. You were at the Hôtel Scribe with those charming wild boys, Teddy and Jimmy Goldsmith.'

'Reresby Sitwell was staying with you. I thought you'd marry him.'

'Whatever made you think that? Reresby was good company, but rather dull. So you've been in the Bahamas. Tell me all about it. You must have met a lot of people I know.'

Penelope fills the room to the high ceiling with an erotic aura of French elegance and English aristocracy. Small as my mother and a little older than Mary, not as beautiful as they are, well read in the novels of Evelyn Waugh and Nancy Mitford, she puts me at my ease as no other woman has done. Her lovely eyes melt to the brink of tears without clinging or crying. After what happened in Piccadilly the day before yesterday, she draws me out of my shame into her gilded corner on the louche side of well-born society.

'Let's have some music,' she says, and out of a black box comes an eerie tune repeated again and again, reminding me of a barrel organ playing outside Grandmother's house in Dublin, when Mary, Chris and I had whooping cough.

'It's a zither,' she corrects me, 'in a film you simply must see, called *The Third Man*. You've missed so much by being away so long.'

The Duke of Westminster is her godfather, and allows her to live rent free in this 'grace and favour' flat on the Grosvenor estate. He likes her coming up from London to visit him in Cheshire. She calls him Bendor, a funny name, how is it spelt? Before the war, she says, Bendor had a special train to take him to the Continent whenever he wished to go. He's still the richest man in England, but now, sadly, the Labour government is grabbing nineteen shillings and six pence out of every pound of his income to pay for Britain's health service.

'I can't give you dinner here, darling, my flat is too small and I hate cooking. Let's go to the Berkeley and you be my guest. It's less grand than the Ritz, but the food is better. There's so much I want to hear about your life.'

Our waiters have cleared the table, brought me a brandy, and Penelope a liqueur. I have told her about my short-lived romance with Patricia Cavendish, and she has told me that I never would have been happy married to a woman with an entourage of animals on the Riviera. I have mentioned Lord Ennisdale, and my hope of making enough in the city in a few years to spend the rest of my life writing poetry. Not a word have I said about the dreadful thing that happened in Piccadilly the day before yesterday, which I want to put behind me so that no one will ever have reason to accuse me of being queer.

Eye to eye across a brandy snifter revolving in my hand, I feel inspired enough to say, 'Let's get married!' and while her astonishment subsides into laughter mixed with tears I drain the glass.

'Oh darling, what an amazing idea! Yes, why don't we get married?'

'Tonight. We could take a taxi to Gretna Green. Isn't that where runaway couples get married on the spot?'

'Gretna Green, darling, is across the Scottish border nearly three hundred miles away, and those instant marriages are a thing of the past.'

'I thought it was near Hampstead.' She laughs at my gaffe. 'Then I'll ring up a clergyman I know and ask him to marry us tomorrow.'

'Oh please do that!'

On a phone in the lobby I speak to Joseph Poole, no longer precentor at Canterbury but now the vicar of Merstham, near London. He saw me last as a choirboy at Temple's enthronement six years ago, thinks I must be crazy if not drunk, and tells me to talk to my local parish priest in the morning.

When our taxi pulls up at midnight outside 62 Eaton Place, Penelope says, after kissing me briefly on the lips, 'Come round, darling, as late as you like in the morning.' I walk on air up Sloane Street to Mary's flat in Brompton Road, saving the taxi fare.

Next day at Penelope's flat we play backgammon and talk about our future, with the solo zither plonking in the background. No sex until we are married, she insists, and we'll never sleep together in her double bed, because she's a light sleeper. I'll have a bed in the box room and a desk for writing my poetry. She has friends she wouldn't want to lose: a famous barrister visits her for a weekend, usually once a month. 'He could be helpful to you.'

Our nearest vicar in Knightsbridge requires us to attend a rehearsal in the church a few days before our wedding. Nervous about being caged like the blue parrot under a silk shawl, I ask Mary to come and support me. She finds Penelope 'strange, but no stranger than you'. The further we run through the marriage service, the sicker I feel with anxiety. While the clergyman is talking to Penelope, I take Mary aside and say, 'Get me out of this, please! I can't go on. It's all a terrible mistake.'

Mary has the tact to break the news gently to Penelope, who neither bursts into tears nor flies into a temper. What cool sophistication she has! On my last visit to her flat she accepts my apology and says, 'We'll remain friends. You're too young to tie yourself down.' Eight years her junior. 'You must go now, because I have to pack and catch a train. Dear Bendor wants me at his place in Cheshire in time for dinner.'

Around this time I read in a newspaper that a man of my age had taken a room on the seventh floor of the Dorchester Hotel, climbed out on to the windowsill and shot himself in the head. I pitied him, whoever he was, as it looked as if he might have got into the kind of trouble with the police or a blackmailer that I had narrowly escaped. Then the name, C.M.C. Lewis, stunned me with the realisation that this was the suicide of a friend who had been in my class at Wellington. A year after I had gone up to Oxford he had gone to Cambridge. He was a sportsman – captain of boxing – as well as an intellectual.

It was not done to use first names at Wellington. During the hot summer of D-Day, he had the courage to tell me about his love for a boy in a more liberal house than either of ours. He adored this boy with red hair, who returned his passion when they kissed under the rhododendrons in the pine woods. Lewis had a warm, sunny complexion and a happy outlook. Our talk encouraged me to declare my love to the athlete from Hong Kong, who made a mockery of me among his hearty friends and never wanted my company in the pine woods. I envied the boxer's good fortune in love.

About a year and a half later, Lewis turned up at the door of my rooms in Magdalen, at an unfortunate time when I was devoting myself to God. I was reading St Augustine and the novels of Charles Williams, trying to be chaste in thought and deed, dreaming of taking holy orders and living in a country parsonage with a small medieval church in which I would train the choir. Lewis was surprised and disappointed to find me so changed. I was scared that he might revive in me the feelings I was trying to repress. As soon as he had gone I regretted not having asked him to stay.

After reading about his death I felt frightened and ashamed.

The clerks at C.E. Heath & Co. at Lloyd's of London saw to it that I would have no future in their midst. Scores of us sat side by side in broad rows of desks, where everyone could keep an eye on his neighbour, and the section manager in a glass booth could keep his eye on everyone. To avoid bad feeling, so it was said, the company had a standard salary structure, known to all the clerks, based on an employee's age and length of service. But an invidious system of secret bonuses, based on the manager's estimate of individual performance, had the opposite effect.

One fifth of my salary of £5 a week as a twenty-two-year-old, with no allowance for my degree, was spent on travelling to and from the city by Underground, and another fifth on smoking twenty Player's a day. Begun at Oxford, this bad habit had worsened when I could help myself to duty-free Benson & Hedges at Government House. My mother had advised me to give them up, because 'with your character, you won't be able to limit yourself to a few, but will want to smoke more and more'.

The clerk assigned to instruct me, which he did amiably, after weeks that stretched into months of my learning to pin the right bits of paper together for posting or filing, decided I was ready to be sent over to the Room at Lloyd's to give one of our brokers, whom I had never seen, particulars of a new risk to be placed with underwriters.

'A simple job,' he said, 'it will give you a break. Lloyd's is on the other side of Leadenhall Street. Go in, and join a queue of clerks at the rostrum in the centre, where you'll see a man in scarlet robes sitting under the Lutine Bell, and say, when your turn comes, "Cuthbert Heath – Pratt". He will then announce those names on the loudspeakers, and you'll see Pratt waving a hand. Give him this document and come straight back.'

I crossed the street and entered a space as awesome as a temple. A monotonous voice was droning inaudible names through a speaker system, no clearer and not much louder than the susurrus of fifteen hundred men conversing in dark-grey, pinstriped black or navy-blue suits. I didn't know Pratt. Someone explained that the names called out were audible only to the person concerned. I was tenth in a queue to the rostrum, and after I reached it and said to the waiter, 'Cuthbert Heath – Pratt', I listened, but could make no sense of names that were jumbled by the building's resonance. Worse still, I saw ten or fifteen hands waving from different points of the compass above a mass of heads, all with short haircuts, neatly parted and smarmed down.

So I queued again, and listened more carefully, and this time detected 'Cuthbert Heath – Pratt', but again, so many distant hands were in the air that I was at a loss to know which was Pratt's. By the time I had asked one or two if he was Mr Pratt of Cuthbert Heath, a different set of hands was waving. I tried a third time, with no more success, and returned to the office in shame.

The clerks rubbed their hands and rubbed it in. They said it was the first time they could remember a clerk coming back from the Room having failed to find a broker from his own company. They never sent me there again. As to making a fortune from commissions, after six months in the job my only client was my father. The chairman turned down my request for a small increase in salary, and offered me what he called friendly advice: 'You can stay with us, Murphy, and by the time you are thirty you will be earning, if you pull your socks up, £10 a week. You might make more money as a schoolmaster.'

What I enjoyed in the city, a real wasteland after the war and before the reconstruction, was following literally in the footsteps of T.S. Eliot. He had worked here in a bank, and was advising young poets to do the same. I could see 'the brown fog of a winter dawn' and the crowd flowing over London Bridge, and could hear, as I reached the office in the rush hour, one surviving church bell 'with a dead sound on the final stroke of nine'. The comparison of city workers in *The Waste Land* to the dead in Dante's *Inferno* chimed with my despair at getting nowhere in my job or in writing poetry or in love. It also underscored my fear of being approached in a crowd by a small man wearing a fawn trench coat and demanding money.

Determined to find an alternative to clerking in the city, I wrote to Harold Nicolson, reminding him of our meeting five years ago, and saying that I had derived great pleasure and instruction in the Bahamas from reading his 'Marginal Comment' in the *Spectator* week after week at Government House – angling, of course, for an invitation, which I soon received: to sherry at six in 10 Neville Terrace, Onslow Gardens, SW7.

His friendliness and wit charmed me. Plump and well dressed, he at once asked me to call him Harold, though he must have been older than my father.

Curly grey locks gave distinction to his partial baldness, and his face with its rosy cheeks and short moustache had a happy, ironical expression, as if his little eyes could always see the funny side of people. Modest and discreet in deploying his fluency in ancient and modern European languages and literature, he struck me as a superb and loveable epicurean who could be trusted never to go further than to bless me with a touch on my head.

For an hour on my first visit, as on many more to come, I listened to risqué anecdotes about Browning, Swinburne, Wilde and Proust evolving in faultless cadences. He never told me the same story twice. My desire to write poetry appealed to his romantic Edwardian sensibility, and after this visit I could always turn to him for encouragement. In the spring of 1950 he wrote a word to the literary editor of the *Spectator*, following which a card came from Derek Hudson inviting me to call at Gower Street.

With my bowler in my hand I begged for a chance to review poetry. Hudson was writing a book on Lewis Carroll, and liked the Mad Hatter contrast between my appearance and my request, so he let me pick a volume off his shelves. After I had proved 'reliable' with five hundred words on *England's Helicon*, a reprint of Elizabethan lyrics, and 'controversial' with a lofty attack on the low quality of the verse in *The Cocktail Party*, T.S. Eliot's most popular play, Hudson gave me all the poetry that came in for review for the next year.

With a prospect of earning three or four guineas a week by reading and writing at home, instead of £5 in the city, I resigned from Lloyd's and gave up smoking – or tried to, since it took three to six months of intermittent success and failure before I finally quit. My mother's advice was clinched by a scientist's proof, announced in 1950, that smoking caused lung cancer. Hudson – we addressed each other by our surnames – let me sell the books I didn't want to keep. Thus I received from the *Spectator* an education in modern poetry that Oxford never gave me: writing reviews of Robert Lowell, Robert Frost, Ezra Pound and W.B. Yeats, to mention the best, within a year.

On my way from London to Connemara in June 1950, I broke my journey in Dublin to stay with Trix Hurst, who remembered our cricket match among the thistles in the Pigeon Park at Milford in 1939 and the measles in 1941. She was now married to the poet and writer Maurice James Craig. They told me it was easy to meet poets in Dublin: go to McDaid's off Grafton Street and you would find Patrick Kavanagh drinking there with his disciples.

I entered McDaid's at lunch hour and introduced myself to Kavanagh, mentioning that I had started to review poetry for the *Spectator*. He looked pleased and began denouncing Dublin as a city with no critical values. I wondered why he continued to live there. He said the country for him was too full of ghosts. At odds with his tweed cap and shabby countryman's clothes were his horn-rimmed spectacles.

He introduced me to Anthony Cronin, a barrister who had little time for the law and much for poetry; to John Ryan, who was editing the monthly magazine *Envoy*; and to Valentin Iremonger, *Envoy's* poetry editor. Val invited me to submit my poems, and thereafter he wrote with good advice regarding my poems, which he was the first to publish in Ireland.

Kavanagh said Cronin was sure to win the Æ Memorial Award next year, as he was the best of the younger poets. That was how I heard of a prize worth £100 given every five years to a poet under the age of thirty. Iremonger had won it in 1946, and *Envoy* was carrying an advertisement asking for submissions before the end of 1950.

When McDaid's closed at 2.30, as the law required, I asked Kavanagh, as we strolled up Grafton Street, where or how I could buy his book *The Great Hunger*, which was out of print. He replied that he would be going round to call on Mrs Yeats that afternoon, and if I would give him ten shillings he would get a copy of the Cuala Press edition from her and give it to me in McDaid's at six o'clock. He took the money and I didn't see him again for five years.

But the following spring I won the Æ Award, another reason to stay in Connemara and keep out of Dublin. And, more than forty years later at lunch in the Shelbourne, Tony Cronin remembered me as 'A tall, lissom Anglo-Irishman who seemed a bit like a lamb that had strayed into a den of wolves'.

My friendship with J.R. Ackerley began with his kindly worded, handwritten rejection of poems that I submitted to the *Listener* at the age of twenty-three. He got to my heart by mixing approval – 'I enjoyed reading "Snow", which has much of interest and feeling in it …' – with fingering of faults – 'but suffers, to my mind, from too many adjectives, especially hyphenated ones. And "pelvised", is there such a word?' – as if he were trying to help the poem, wilfully obscure, to emerge from its raw material.

No reader could have told that it was inspired by a single, solitary act of rolling naked in snow on a patch of level ground outside my cottage in

Connemara, beside a waterfall at the foot of a mountain on the edge of a lake, where I had gone, over Christmas 1950, from reviewing poetry for the *Spectator* in London, to trying to write it myself. I was without a companion, a car, a telephone, or electric light, living a mile across a moor from the nearest house.

What made me decide to strip off my clothes and go out in a bitter cold wind and lie on the snow and turn over and over was a rumour I had heard at the Choir School before the war, that the Red Dean of Canterbury, who always appeared impressively garbed in immaculate white or black or scarlet robes of office, sometimes took off all his clothes and wallowed in snow baths on the lawn of the deanery. In the tingling flow of blood to the top of my head and the tips of my fingers, as I warmed myself at a turf fire after the burning pain of the snow all over my body, a poem began to form in my mind around the image of a boar staining the snow with peaty soil, uprooted by its tusks, as if with the blood of Adonis or Diarmuid.

Fortified by Ackerley's note, I dared to ring him up, never having spoken to him before, and ask him whether he would look at the poem again if I could manage to improve it. He agreed, and I set to work at once.

This was in February 1951, when Mary was giving me the leisure to write while she worked hard at her job on the *Queen*. She let me have a room of my own in a tiny flat, where she slept on a couch in the sitting room while her two children shared the only other room. As our bath was in the kitchen, it was covered by a board when not in use.

Her view from the sitting room was of huge extractor fans in a towering brick side wall of the Royal Cancer Hospital on Fulham Road. To enter or leave our run-down four-storey block, you had to step over a lazy old spaniel lying with its rotting bone on the red tiles.

The few guineas earned by my reviews contributed little to our budget, but I helped by babysitting, decorating the flat, and neither smoking nor drinking. Instead, I craved to see my name in print, especially for the first time, with a poem in one of the London literary weeklies. Opening a BBC envelope addressed by Ackerley, and finding the poem in proof, was a moment of great joy.

This led to our meeting in the basement of a tavern near Victoria Station at the tail end of an evening rush hour. Ackerley's reputation as a misanthrope who lived with a dog had not prepared me for the tall, affable, ageing man who entered, wearing a navy-blue beret and casual clothes without a tie. He looked deliberately déclassé, no slave to his office, in that place and time, carrying a satchel of books and papers on one shoulder. Though his face when he was reflecting could seem grim, it glowed with warmth when he smiled or spoke.

After bringing two pints of bitter to a round table, he sat down facing me, and said, in a voice loud enough for someone near us, who might have been an off-duty policeman, to hear, 'I'm homosexual.' My pulse raced, and I tried not to blush. His candour caught me between not wanting to tell a lie and being too scared to tell the truth. It brought back the horror of being accused of a homosexual offence by the blackmailer who claimed to be a police officer in Piccadilly Underground the previous year. I had never admitted to myself that I was queer, let alone to anybody else, and felt morally bruised by his naked honesty. So I smiled with non-committal complicity, and raised my glass, pretending I was neither frightened nor shocked. Though alarmed, I was glad to meet a man who could freely admit to another that he was queer. But what pleased me more was that a literary editor of his importance was accepting me as a friend. As all his lovers had been working class, and mine never older than myself, our friendship only involved sex as conversation.

Over the next eight years, his fingering of faults in my poems continued to annoy me, and improve my poetry, while giving it an audience that was better than it usually deserved. Sometimes he gave my poems short shrift, while inviting me to dinner, with a note like this in 1953:

> Dear Richard
> No I shan't take these from you & ought not to keep them longer
> in case you can place them elsewhere. I look forward to seeing you
> Thursday: The Shaftesbury again, at 6.45 pm.
> Joe

In the same year he rejected my poem about Wittgenstein at Rosroe, where the philosopher tamed the birds so well that when he left they were eaten by the village cats. Ackerley thought there were 'too many birds in the poem', and 'it looks as though you are blaming the cats, who I'm sure are full of philosophical retorts'. The retort of Isaiah Berlin on reading the poem at All Souls was, 'When the great man is gone, the disciples get gobbled up, gobbled up.'

The most considerate, and honest, of his rejections, dated 29 June 1953, went like this: 'I am sorry, but I simply don't enjoy them: they seem so awkward, the assembly of words and phrases, but without poetic release. I want to like them, because I like you, but I cannot, & so I cannot publish them … Heaven bless & protect you, Joe.' Other poems written after that in Crete he found 'so cerebral & overworked … one simply notices the overload of carefully considered adjectives … something else, and more important slips away while they are being forged … I fancy one should never notice the workmanship of a thing in its various parts; one should get it instantly as a whole.' Another poem was 'far too muscle-bound for my liking. But the New Statesman will like it, no doubt.'

He was more generous to my work than I was to his; and his lessons in style culminated in a detailed critique of 'The Woman of the House', before he published a much improved version in the *Listener,* ahead of its broadcast on the Third Programme in 1959. Looking back, I can see that the clear style and wit of his letters taught me as much as their content.

My affection for him was sharpened by fear of his power as moralist, critic, editor and friend. His belief in the value of friendship was absolute, and extended to the animal kingdom. This meant that I had to allow his Alsatian bitch Queenie to nip my ankles as I entered his flat to dine on the top floor of Star and Garter Mansions overlooking the Thames in Putney. In checking her, his voice gave more encouragement to the dog than correction. He seemed proud of her assault, and greatly amused by my discomfiture. I hated this, and Queenie's continual barking, which he permitted on the very English moral ground of kindness to an animal. It meant that for ten or twelve years he was perversely cruel to his neighbours by allowing her to bark.

Our friendship survived and increased during my marriage, as he accepted Patricia Avis as 'one of us', wrote her many letters, published her poems in the *Listener*, and came to stay with us in Ireland more than once. He was furious with her when she wanted a divorce, but he remained in touch. In June 1966, a year before he died, he stayed at my cottage in Cleggan, County Galway. Feeling isolated by his deafness, he would sit in a deckchair on the tiny lawn, taking ticks out of the ears of a sheepdog called Nero. After giving Nero a worm powder, he followed her around until he could see that she had passed all her worms.

He bought his own gin, and drank rather a lot, but never lost his courtesy, poise and intelligence. John McGahern once remarked that Joe's trouble was that he had spent most of his life dealing with people less intelligent than himself. At the *Listener* he was the servant of writers who were his inferiors, and sexually he chose working-class men for his friends. 'A writer is a servant of the muse,' John added clinchingly.

Late one evening, when the long summer twilight off the ocean continued to filter into my cottage, I returned from the Pier Bar, and thought I heard Joe talking to somebody in his bedroom, with the door ajar. Then I realised he was talking to himself, and this is the gist of what he was saying: 'What a rotten thing to do! To cast the devils out of a wretched human being, and make them drive a herd of poor unfortunate pigs over a cliff to their death. I think Jesus Christ was a most unpleasant person. I am glad we never met, because I would not have liked him.'

I felt guilty about eavesdropping on my guest, so I confessed to Joe in the morning what I had heard. Exonerating me, he replied, 'That's exactly how I feel.'

The Æ Memorial Award acted as nitrogen on the hungry grass of my ambition to be recognised as a poet. I received the news and the cheque at Mary's flat in South Kensington on 4 April 1951. Having won on promise rather than performance, I needed to prove that the five elderly judges in Dublin had made no mistake in identifying me as an Irish poet. Their decision gave me the moral support and means to live in the west of Ireland, with a chance to redeem the failure of my midterm flight from Oxford to write a verse play at Lecknavarna.

When I rang to tell Harold Nicolson, he invited me to dine at the Travellers' Club. While Harold drank pink champagne, I drank water, basking in his benevolence and wit through course after course, until we moved to the smoking room for coffee. There he pointed out an old man with startling white hair and a rubicund face dozing in a leather armchair, and asked, 'Would you like to meet Clive Bell?'

Confronting the provocative, urbane author of *Civilisation*, which our history master, Raymond Carr, had given me a gamma mark for writing about at Wellington, filled me with awe. How would this icon of the Bloomsbury pantheon, brother-in-law of Virginia Woolf, regard my desire to bury myself in Connemara to write a long narrative poem?

'And who is Richard Murphy?' Clive Bell began, leaning back to look me over with a sparkling expectation of being amused by a new young protégé of Harold.

'Richard is a poet,' said Harold, giving me a frisson of pride as he paused after the description; then he added with a benign ironical smile under his trim moustache, 'who doesn't drink, doesn't smoke, and doesn't, as far as we know, do anything else.'

At this, Clive Bell sat up and, in the loud voice of men accustomed to laying down the law of England, causing heads to turn in our direction, declared: 'Then he can't be a poet.'

Trying to look as if I appreciated his wit, I kept silent and resolved more firmly to live in Ireland.

Within a few days I had signed a five-year agreement at £20 a year with Myles Drury, the cathedral architect of Exeter, for his utterly remote cottage, the Quay House at Rosroe near the mouth of the fjord-like Killary. At the dead end of a tortuous lane a mile beyond the gates of Salruck House, Drury's cottage had been built before the Famine to accommodate coastguards on the estate of Lieutenant General Alexander Thomson, my maternal grandmother's grandfather.

Though Mary as a single mother going out to work needed my help at home, she unselfishly encouraged me to depart. She believed that I might be able to write poetry in that beautiful poor country where she herself could have become a painter had she not married Toby at eighteen in the middle of the war and mothered me in my holidays, and now had to rear two children on her own while waiting for a divorce. We celebrated her daughter Grania's fourth birthday on 19 April, and I left at the end of the month.

At Rosroe I washed in water from a beer barrel that the rain kept full in a tiny yard outside the kitchen door. Drinking water I fetched in a bucket from a well reached by climbing over barbed wire on top of a wall and crossing a field in which my boots sank up to the ankles in mud. I cooked on a single paraffin burner. The toilet was a chemical closet in the yard. By continually piling turf on an open fire in the sitting room I managed to keep warm at my typewriter. I went to bed by candlelight and slept on a horsehair mattress on a cast-iron bed under a window three steps from the sea at high tide.

I gloried in being able to live at Rosroe as if in the past. Being poor made me feel virtuous, knowing that I could rely on Mary's help in case of trouble. I suffered the bitter harshness of stormy weather as a penance to achieve the salvation of poetry. For food I had to cycle nine miles over the hill and down along the upper shore of the Killary to a shop at Leenane, where everyone bought on credit, settling accounts once a year after the great autumn sheep fair. The *Spectator* sent me no more poetry to review, and I had cut off the flow of guineas from the BBC for talks on subjects such as 'Narrative Poetry Today'.

For seven or eight hours a day I sat on a kitchen chair at a deal table typing ten or twenty lines of a narrative poem called 'Voyage to an Island' again and again, each time changing a word or two in an effort to match the blustery wind and the slanting rain outside. The modern story was based on an ancient myth.

During the Blitz on London, a pair of young lovers, Diarmuid and Grania, flee from an old tycoon called Finn who wants Grania. They arrive in Connemara, hoping to cross to an island of everlasting youth and salvation in the Atlantic before they are caught. A detective sent by Finn pursues them. He is a paradigm of the boar that killed Diarmuid in the Celtic myth as Adonis was killed in the Greek, and a shadow of the man who had accused me in Piccadilly Circus Underground.

I poured into lines of blank verse the passion I felt while typing, but, when I went back and read them, they sounded wilful and turgid. Each effort to revise produced no better result, yet I continued struggling to revive a narrative form of poetry that many critics believed the modern novel had made obsolete. I had no talent for fiction.

Meanwhile I embraced the solitude that my reading of poetry told me its writing required. The first interruption of the day occurred in the late morning. Smoke was seldom to be seen rising from a chimney in Rosroe before ten o'clock. Tommy Mulkerrins, my landlord's caretaker, used to announce his arrival at my latch gate on the quay by whistling 'Galway Bay' or 'Moonlight in Mayo' out of tune. He was too shy to interrupt my work by knocking on the door. A tall middle-aged bachelor with a sad and lean red face, he complained of an incurable ulcer in his leg. He helped me to dig ridges and sow potatoes, carrots, onions, runner beans and parsley. I wanted to be as self-sufficient as at Milford during the war.

Every afternoon I longed for the postman to arrive on his bicycle from Renvyle, nine miles away. Rain or hailstones would not stop him coming in his yellow oilskin cape and sou'wester, pushing his bicycle loaded with parcels on the steep hills. Sometimes he brought me books from the London Library, or a *London Magazine* rejection slip on which John Lehmann had penned, 'Your poems are too rhetorical for me', spreading gloom like a trough of low pressure over the next few days.

A stone's throw from the Quay House lived the family of George Mortimer, whose father had been steward at Salruck House in the time of my great-grandfather. George and his wife, Nora, had six children. During the Troubles, Nora's father, an active member of the IRA, had spared Salruck when other houses of landlords were being torched. After working and saving money as a labourer in Boston for twenty years, George had come home for a funeral, married Nora and helped in rearing their six children. They welcomed me at their fireside and table. From them I obtained milk, eggs, fish and turf. One by one, all but their youngest boy would emigrate to America or England.

Rosroe was one of the windiest, wettest and poorest places in Ireland, and I admired the Mortimers for keeping discontent at bay with laughter and devotion to their Church. The children had to walk two miles over the Salruck hill to attend a school so small that there were only benches for half the students to be seated. Leaving school at fourteen, they would spend the next four years growing potatoes and oats, minding sheep and catching fish, while waiting for a chance to emigrate. However bad the weather, on Sundays, fasting from midnight, they used to walk or cycle seven miles on the gravel road to Mass in Tully Cross, with no food or drink until they got home. Once a month they would make the same journey on a Saturday to tell their sins to Father Luddon in the confession box.

One of their teenage sons, Georgie, took me on a pilgrimage to Croagh Patrick, which we climbed during the night of the last Saturday in July, the purpose being to hear Mass on the summit at sunrise on Garland Sunday. We put bikes into a currach and rowed across the Killary, then pushed or carried the bikes two miles over rocks, walls and rivers till we reached a road at Tullabawn. From there it took two hours to a pub at Leckanvy, where we quenched our thirst with stout before beginning our climb at midnight.

We took the easy route, preferred by the archbishop who used to ride up on a horse; and we ascended so fast that we reached the top in an hour. Thousands of pilgrims were already reciting the rosary and other prayers as they circulated clockwise in the dark between the chapel and the precipitous edge. A few young priests, monks and poor old women had climbed in bare feet by the long stony pilgrims' path from Murrisk. I remember sparks now and then being struck off the ground by the hobnails of boots. It was far too cold for us to wait four hours for sunrise and the Mass. On our way home we lay under a haystack to rest, where, unable to sleep with the tick-tock metronomic racket kicked up by a corncrake, I watched the stars through wisps of hay.

Tommy Mulkerrins thought I must be lonely living on my own. 'It's a pity you weren't here two years ago,' he said, 'you'd have enjoyed talking to the man who was staying here then, a friend of Con Drury, Myles's brother.'

'Who was that?'

'I have his name written down at home but could never get my tongue around it. He was a German translator of sorts. Con had met him at Cambridge and brought him here for holidays before the war. He told Con to take up medicine, so Con became a psychiatrist in Dublin. The man was here by himself for several months in 1949. He wasn't well.'

'What was he doing at Rosroe?'

'He was writing all the time, like you. After he'd written a whole pile of pages he'd tell me to burn them.'

'Did you?' I asked.

'Of course. What use would they be except to light fires?'

Another day Tommy told me, 'Your man was fond of walking, but he'd not be gone more than a hundred yards up the road before he'd stop and stand for twenty minutes, drawing signs with his walking stick in the gravel.'

One day at lunch in the kitchen Tommy pointed to the table and said, 'I seen a robin coming in and eating off this table. Your man was like St Francis with the birds on his shoulders and his hands. He was so keen to watch seabirds that he asked me to build him a hut on Inishbarna.'

'Did you do this?'

'No, because, you see, if I'd built him a hut on the island, he'd have wanted me to be carrying down the currach on my back to the shore and rowing him out there every day. We might have been caught in a storm. He asked would I let him sleep in my house, but I said no. There was only my bed he could have slept in. He had cases of baked beans sent up on the bus from Lipton's in Galway. A middling poor man, he was, who had once been rich. He told me he'd given all his money away because he didn't want to be wealthy. I'd like to have met him before he gave it away. He wasn't bad, mind you. When he was leaving he gave me some money to buy food for the birds in the garden.'

'Did you do this?'

'Not for long. He had those birds so tame that the cats ate them.'

When I had visitors in August, among them Charles Monteith, I moved out of the Quay House to sleep in the turf shed. Lying in bed, looking up at the rafters supporting rusty corrugated-iron sheets, I noticed a wedge of blue paper folded between a rafter and the iron to stop it rattling. I took down the wedge and found two letters that I showed to Charles, one beginning 'My dear Ludwig' and the other 'Dear Professor Wittgenstein'.

That name, a mystery to me, meant 'everything that is the case' to Charles, who used to dine with philosophers every weekend at All Souls. He informed me that Wittgenstein had published only one book in his life, but notes taken by disciples at his lectures had been passed from hand to hand like gospels. It was only four months since the great man had died of cancer. Tommy must have burnt the worksheets of a book Wittgenstein was trying to finish. Charles quoted, 'Death is not an event in life: it is not lived through.'

Sitting on the edge of the quay with the tide far out and the sun releasing an iodine odour of bladderwrack on the shore, Charles told me, because I had pressed him, how he was wounded in Burma, where he served as an officer with the Royal Inniskilling Fusiliers during the British retreat from the Japanese army. One night in the jungle he had a long drinking session with an army surgeon who shared his love of literature. Charles had two books in his kitbag: Joyce's *Ulysses* and the *Collected Poems* of Yeats.

A day or two later, the Japs advanced, and a mortar bomb exploded at his feet. Dying, he was taken to a tent among thirty or forty badly wounded men. The surgeon, who came to examine the mutilated bodies, recognised Charles, bloodstained and comatose, and gave orders for him to be brought immediately to the operating tent, where he performed a long operation, removing shrapnel, sewing up wounds, saving his limbs and his life.

Poetry didn't make this happen, but it helped. Charles had revealed all this to me only because we were good friends and far away from the city in which he guarded his privacy with a front of jovial good manners and impenetrable reticence, rather like C.S. Lewis, his former tutor and mine. He reminded me so much of my father – in his face, his glasses and his tall broad build, and the way he had of laughing at the end of a funny story he had told – that I kept thinking he *was* my father, and being disturbed by this. Behind us apples were ripening in the garden of the coastguard cottage where Wittgenstein had tamed the birds to eat out of his hand. Across the fjord of the Killary rose the awesome green bald head of Muilrea.

The winter passed with storm after storm, and in the spring, when money was running shorter than ever and my bill in Leenane was becoming too large to settle, Alice Marsh, who had been in Ceylon with her children when we were there, gave me an unskilled job with Georgie. We were to be water bailiffs, guarding the salmon from poachers at night on eight miles of the Erriff river, which Alice was renting from Lord Sligo. Our wages were £4 a week, with the use of a worn-out little car.

Fortunately the highest rainfall in Ireland falls in the valley of the Erriff, and when the river was in flood, Alice permitted us to go wherever we wished, until the river was low enough to allow poachers to cast their nets with ease. From her garden in front of Aasleagh Lodge she could keep an eye on the gauge in the pool below the waterfall.

We lived from April to the end of September 1952 in the Watchers' Cottage at the top of the Killary, nine miles from Rosroe. The Watchers' Cottage was damp; it had lime-washed walls and concrete floors; no furniture other than two iron beds, one kitchen table and two chairs. I loved our view of the estuary, always changing with the weather and the rising and falling of the tides, like a scene in a poem by Dylan Thomas: either a bay from which salmon could enter the river and climb the ladder by the falls, or mudflats with a channel snaking towards the sea. At the back of the cottage, rhododendrons stood taller than the roof. In June their rosy petals at the window were the last thing I would see in a pale glimmer of morning before going to sleep.

Alice was a good employer, and the river was her one and only passion. Her children were reared, and her husband was living on the Duke of Manchester's estate in Kenya. She was small, strong and hardy, with glasses on a round face as brown and weathered from the sun and wind as a hazelnut. Sitting in a car with the engine running to keep myself warm on a cold wet day, I have seen Alice, standing in the river with the water up to her thighs, stitching a prawn on a hook. She hated poachers, unless they were 'decent' enough only to take a fish from the river where it flowed through their land and without making a mess or disturbing the other fish.

An hour before sunset Georgie and I would go up to the lodge, where Alice would give us a three-course dinner with bottled stout on the mahogany table in her dining room. Frank Egginton was her favourite artist; he had paid her with pictures in return for fishing her pools. We would decide at dinner which of the pools we would watch and where we would park our cars. Alice herself could not sleep in her bed at night with her worry of the river being poached. So she would drive up the road and park as near as possible to a pool such as the Cattlepass or the Broken Bridge or the General's Reach, and there she would fall asleep in the car for an hour or two; and then she would move the car to another pool.

Georgie and I would patrol on foot, perhaps the Holly Pool or the Black Banks or, if we felt daring enough, the Dead Man's Pool beyond the oak wood, where a poacher had struck one of the previous watchers on the head with a stone. Every night we took a different route, carrying torches and sticks, but no gun. After we had walked three or four miles, tripping on wire or the stumps of burnt gorse bushes, wading across bogs, rowing with our arms through white-of-egg mists, webs of gossamer tickling our faces as we passed between hawthorn bushes, often alarmed by the screech of a heron or the hooves of a startled sheep, we would doze in the car within sound or sight of a pool. Alice never expected us to catch a poacher: she was happy if our night patrol resulted, as it usually did, in not a sign of the river having been poached.

It was like living in a poem there was no need to write, rich in local memory conserved in the pools' names, which commerce has long since abolished and replaced with numbers. So strong was the river's influence on my senses in the night, and so great the tedium of killing the hours of weariness until dawn, that I never wrote a line that did justice to the river. The *New Statesman* accepted a poem about Georgie's father, after the old man's sudden death while moulding potatoes on his land at Rosroe; but other poems I wrote at Aasleagh were willed and, like the weather, blustery. Ackerley accepted a lyric that emerged from a dream of love to become dreamily obscure.

After a long sleepless wait – I could never sleep in a car – it was redemption for us to see bushes or trees appearing in the darkness as the night began to dissolve in day a little before dawn. Then I could start up the car and turn the headlights for home.

In August 1952 Nanny, having vanished for several years, had come back from India and turned up at Milford, where Granny was becoming senile, aggravated by starvation and loneliness. After watching the river one night until dawn, I drove over to Milford to see them both. The house looked more desolate than ever at the end of the lime-tree avenue.

Alarmingly, in the Leenane pubs Georgie had been bad-mouthed for drinking the Protestant soup of Mrs Marsh, and going out at night to prevent his people from getting a bite to eat from the river that flowed through their land. And some of my people had criticised me for taking a menial job with a Roman Catholic whose grandfather had led a tenant revolt against my great-grandfather in Salruck.

At Milford Nanny stood in the passage at the foot of the stairs leading to the guest room, and looked up in my face, as if she were searching for what it was hiding. She seemed smaller than I remembered, and her hair was snow white. Her little brown eyes in her podgy face bestowed punishment as well as love.

She wanted to give me her black steel trunk, which she said she would not need any more, as she was going to retire. Termite-proof, it would do for my papers wherever I might go. It had travelled back and forth in the hold of ships between Dublin, Liverpool, Karachi, Bombay, Colombo and Madras, labelled NOT WANTED ON VOYAGE, and had survived an earthquake in Quetta.

Also she wanted to give me a good telling-off. 'You ought to have made something of your life by now. What *can* have got into your head to be wasting the money spent by your father on your education, hiding yourself away at the back of beyond? Do continue your writing seriously and get something done. Work hard, Richard darling, and give the lie to everyone who says you are no good. I believe in you and want you to get somewhere. Your granny says people are talking. She thinks some nonsense may have entered your head from reading too many books. Do pull yourself together before it's too late, my lamb!'

Georgie wanted to redeem himself in the eyes of his people for having been a watcher on Lord Sligo's Erriff river, first with me in 1952, then with his older brother John Joe for two more seasons. After this they took out a licence and fished for salmon from a currach with a net on the Killary, several miles downstream from the river's mouth at Aasleagh. But they had no luck.

There was a drought, bringing calm warm weather, and at one o'clock on a fine night, Alice Marsh's handyman was walking with his girlfriend on the road below the Aasleagh Falls when he heard the creaking of oars as a currach came up the estuary at the top of a high spring tide. The sea pool was full of salmon that could not enter the river as it was too low for them to climb the ladder by the falls. Alfie ran up to the lodge and woke Mrs Marsh.

Alice drove down, still wearing pyjamas, and shone her car lights across the brimming pool. She stepped out with a shotgun, fired both barrels into the air, put the gun back in the car, and leaped into the deep cold water. A few breaststrokes short of the currach – hard to see because it was black – she heard a drunk voice murmuring, 'Pull in the nets, John Joe!' That was enough. She swam back to the shore, enraged to think that her honest and reliable watchmen, whom she had treated so well in the past, had proved 'an ungrateful lot'. She woke the guards in Leenane, and the guards drove out to Rosroe, where they caught Georgie and John Joe with salmon scales on their wet trousers.

The story of a gallant little old lady risking her life in Ireland to catch two sturdy poachers was carried on the front page of Lord Beaverbrook's *Daily*

Express. The brothers were convicted and fined the equivalent of three weeks' wages. John Joe left for England, and Georgie for America, never to return.

> *'Islanders are always the kindest people in the world, and I met none anywhere kinder than the good hearts of this place.'*
> Joshua Slocum, *Sailing Alone Around the World*

A writer in *Blackwood's Magazine* in 1899 described the Galway pookaun – in Irish, *púcán* – as 'a small boat with a sort of lateen sail, pretty to look at, but dangerous'. The pookaun I first stepped aboard from the quay of Rosroe on 25 August 1952 was even less safe. She had a bad reputation, having lost her crew of five fishermen in a storm that struck the coast on the night of 28 October 1927. Newspapers called this the Cleggan Disaster, though nine of the drowned were from Inishbofin, and sixteen from a small village near Cleggan called Rossadillisk.

My brother Chris had come on leave from Shell in Kenya, and had hired her, with her owner, Pádraic O'Malley, to sail him from Ballyconneely, passing Slyne Head and up the coast. They had been to Inishbofin and were planning to go to Clare Island, stronghold of the pirate queen Granuaile. Legends have her boarding a Turkish man-of-war with a blunderbuss and capturing it single-handed; visiting Queen Elizabeth in London and throwing into the fire an embroidered handkerchief given to her by the Queen to blow her nose, because Granuaile thought it unclean 'to put her snot into her pocket'; and most famously hanging with her own hands on Cahir Island the murderer of her husband.

Luckily, there was a flood in the Erriff when Chris invited me to join him, so I could go. Mary and the children were staying at the Quay House, and she allowed John to venture forth on a trip that would lead to his spending much of his adult life on yachts. Alice's daughter, Alison, also came. The redness of her brown hair might have alarmed us if we had been superstitious. But a worse anxiety was the condition of the hull and the spars. As poor as everyone else in Ballyconneely, except the priest, the shopkeeper, the guards and the teacher in those days, Pádraic had sealed the rotting planks under the waterline with cement. To make sailing alone easier, he carried a mainsail with a boom. This imperilled our heads as she came about.

We set out in a headwind, making little progress towards Clare. The sea was calm until the tide changed, when wind and sea rose together, forcing us to change course and run for shelter to Inishbofin. It took us nine hours of buffeting over high waves to get there. Not until the boat had passed the Gun Rock and entered the serene calm of Bofin Harbour was I able to empty my bladder into the sea.

As we sailed through a short narrow channel to a little inner harbour, watched by a group of fishermen on the quay, I felt we were arriving among descendants of people long ago marooned on an island where they lived in the fear of God and believed in miracles, travelled on foot or horseback, and lit their houses with oil lamps and candles, as we had done at Milford during the war. A grey-whiskered statuesque captain, known as The Squire, looked down from the quay into our boat and said to Pádraic, 'May the Lord help the poor mother that ever let you put to sea.'

I had been trying for more than a year to reach a mythical island in a poem based on a legend. Now I had really landed on an island where men had turned their seafaring lives into legends they recounted to each other in the island's only pub. A woman seldom entered this dank and gloomy cavern on the quay. The pub never closed at times dictated by the law, but on the whim of its owner, Miko Day, a giant with a painfully strong handshake and a thirst for alcohol.

Late that night he lay supine on the stone floor behind the bar and slept for a couple of hours, trusting his regulars to fill their own glasses and honestly pay for what they drank. Two men I met there in the early hours were to influence my poetry, not only with their legends but their style. Pateen (meaning little Pat) Cloherty was sitting with his legs up on the counter, drinking half a pint of Guinness very slowly because he was poor. In the light of a paraffin lamp with a smoke-blackened globe, he looked like a boy of fifteen, although he was fifty. After ritual goading, refusing and being jibed, he broke into song, a ballad composed by his cousin Patrick Tierney about the loss with all hands of a hooker called the *Maisie* on St John's Day in the year of his birth.

Pateen's traditional Irish voice, imparting the commotion of the sea through the swaying of his shoulders to the rhythm of the words with an atonal melody, silenced the mumblings of half a dozen men who kept putting off going home. Already I had been grasped by the hand of an ancient mariner called Pat Concannon, who had begun to tell me a story that would take years to finish. It was about his ordeal at sea in a rowing boat, battling for eight hours of darkness to save himself and his crew of four in the great storm that had sunk the boat in which we had arrived.

Concannon was a big stout fisherman who hated land work. The mother of his four children was a teacher on the island who had died in childbirth. He spoke fast out of a corner of his mouth close to my ear, with a pipe stuck in the other corner, so as not to be overheard by men nearby, whose eyes were half hidden under the peaks of cloth caps. I almost had to imagine what he was saying. As he began to draw me into his legend, it caught my mind with a drowning man's grip and would not let go. In future I would be drawn back to the island to learn more about legends, seamanship and the art of storytelling, before being able to write a poem in honour of his courage and the island fishermen's dying way of life.

Not long before sunrise I fell asleep in the guest house known as Day's Hotel, where we had been given rooms on arrival, our windows facing the quay a hundred yards from Miko's pub. Whereas Miko treated his regular customers as targets of a despondent sardonic wit, his wife, Margaret, charmed us with her hospitality. The Bofin mailboat landed me at Cleggan on the mainland the next day. In the loneliness of the Quay House at Rosroe the following Sunday, I sat down and wrote a short narrative poem, recording my rite of passage to Inishbofin. After much revision, 'Sailing to an Island' would be published in 1963 as the title poem of my first book with Faber.

In January 1953 I went to London to earn some money by reviewing poetry and teaching at a crammer in Holland Park. This enabled me to meet other poets, which was easy, because the critic and poet G.S. Fraser and his wife, Paddy, regularly welcomed at their flat in Chelsea any poet, known or unknown, good or bad, who brought wine or beer to drink and poems to read aloud for criticism.

There I met William Empson, John Wain, Elizabeth Jennings, Jon Silkin and Constantine Trypanis among many others. John Wain introduced on the BBC my poem about Wittgenstein, and I reviewed some poetry for the *Times Literary Supplement* and the *Spectator*. My star cramming pupil, April Brunner, invited me to her parents' house in Addison Road for a musico-literary soirée at which Cecil Day-Lewis and Jill Balcon read poetry and a pianist played Chopin. April's father drove two vintage Lagondas and her godmother was Queen Mary.

But Louis MacNeice at the BBC rejected for broadcasting the long-winded epic I had been writing at Rosroe. I remember him one day at a pub near the BBC called The Stag: he was wearing a green tweed suit and a bow tie, and kept turning his eyes to the door to see who was entering. He unnerved me by declaring, 'The west of Ireland is finished.'

I returned to Rosroe in May, went by mailboat from Cleggan to Inishbofin, and bought a pookaun from Pat Concannon. We sailed it to Rosroe on a Sunday, taking seven hours to reach the quay. On our journey Pat was teaching me how to sail the pookaun single-handed, and telling me more about his struggle to survive the great storm of 1927 with four other men at sea on a winter's night in a boat the same size as the pookaun. Here, in his own words, arranged for continuity, is Pat Concannon's story, the source of my poem 'The Cleggan Disaster', which would take me another eight years and a much longer visit to the island to write.

> I could be a month telling you what happened on that night, and I wouldn't have a tenth told, not in years if I was to tell all I went through in those eight hours fighting waves. It was pure calm when we went out after dark. The last meal we had about four o'clock. We had no food in the boat. We never brought food in the boat.
>
> I was up in the stem of the boat, my knees under the gunwale, holding the rope, keeping her head up over the wave, facing the storm, now this way, now that. Sometimes the wave would break right on top of me. I had the worst of it. I told the others to row, give them something to do. We could do nothing only keep her head into the storm. They were three young lads. There was one older man, but he was no seaman. We believed we were lost. My hands were skinned with the ropes. When she went down in the trough I had to pull in, and when she went up on the crest I had to give her more rope: otherwise the nets would have pulled the stem under the big wave, or she'd have been turned broadside on to the storm.
>
> They say I'm a good boatsman. What do they mean? They know nothing about boats at all. Now *he* was a good boatsman, Michael O'Toole, my brother-in-law. His skull was broken at Derryinver. And *he* was a good boatsman, Patrick Powell. His boat was upset, and came towards us in the storm, so close that I had to put my foot on the upturned keel to fend it off, and maybe he was trapped inside. When one of the lads heard his own brother crying for help

in the water, he caught him by the hand, but the hand slipped from his grasp and sank under the boat. My cousin who slept in the same bed with me was lost in O'Toole's boat. He was a great swimmer, could lie on the water for hours. The waves smothered him.

I thought of my mother and the girl I was courting at the time. We had known one another a long time. That's all right, that's love. I married her two years after. I thought all the time of God. We were saying our prayers. Acts of contrition. Love God because He is good and for Himself only, and go straight to heaven. You mustn't be afraid of hell. That's no good. Some of them shat in their pants. Frightened? Weren't we all frightened?

That was the hardest test any man could have in his life, what I went through, to hold on to those nets all night and not to give up with the waves breaking in my face and on my chest all the time. The nets saved us because the ebb-tide dragged them against the storm away out far from the shore. I couldn't see at all, blinded with spray. My hands were skinned to the bone holding the rope that held the nets, we call it the guide rope. If she went across on the heave she was lost, I had to keep her bows into it all the time, pulling her this way, then that, to face the storm. No talk at all on the boat, all I said was law, only keep the boat bailed. No oars out. Pull her up to meet the sea, keep working the rope in the stem all the time.

Around Lyon Head, under the light, we were dragged close to Carraigmahog, and a big wave shot up like an arm from the sea to put out the light. But though it has failed us these fifteen years, it kept its flame all that night. We were heading for High Island when the tide turned at the Cuddoo Rocks, and we cut our nets, cut them all away there, at two o'clock, put out the oars and rowed.

We rowed for about an hour, rowing backwards all the time to keep her facing the storm. We crossed a breaker. Then we saw land which Billy Lavelle recognised as Dog Island. We were in the calm then, we knew where we were. We opened the bay of Cleggan and rowed straight to the quay.

There was no one on the quay when we landed, and the five of us in our wet clothes walked straight up the main street to Stephen King's shop. They led me by the hand because the spray had made my eyes swell up and blinded me. It was about three o'clock, and the skin was torn off the palms of my hands. The first person we met in the shop was Stephen's sister, and I said, 'Hullo, Bridget, what's keeping you up so late this night?' and she said, 'Is that you, Pat, God bless you, what brought you to Cleggan?' and I said, 'I had a message to bring over.' With so many lost on the beaches, it was hard to believe we had landed safely.

We rowed into the East End the next day. Everyone came down to the shore meeting us. Michael Schofield [Pat pronounced his name 'Scuffle'] came back from Dawros later. A man from his boat was seen the next day wandering through a field carrying a bailer. In Darcy's boat they bailed all night with their boots.

What can I say of such a hard night now? I'm alive myself. Good men are gone. When a man doesn't know what to do, he does what he can, and he may do wrong. I'm getting old. I wish I had half the strength to use again. Boats are rotting on the beaches around here. The boys won't go out. With their backs to the wall, they scratch themselves like donkeys, but more idle. It's easy for them to manage on the dole. We weren't paid for doing nothing then. We had to fish. Don't mind the weather, it was live on seaweed, or go out. Often it was both, we had so little to eat. That was better than eating too much.

Willie Burke's father could build a pookaun in nine days. Willie took three weeks to build a pookaun himself. His son isn't able to build a pookaun at all. There may be more money now, but I'd sooner be young and have my strength again whatever the hardship. It's worse to be old than hungry. There were more fish in those days and more men to go fishing. Lobsters were half a crown a dozen, and all we got for mackerel was five shillings a hundred. What good is money to a man that drinks it?

It isn't only yourself you have to think of, going out in a boat, if you're lost: there's your mother at home, and you'd be afraid for her sake more than your own. Write nothing about the dead. Their people wouldn't like it. The bodies weren't found.

What is it all anyway but your luck? If your time is up then you'll have to go.

Granny had a habit of nodding off in mid-sentence, sitting on a high-backed chair because it was better for her rheumatism, gradually her head inclining nearer and nearer the heap of muddled papers on the card table she used for everything, until something in her thoughts or in the room would disturb her, and make her sit up straight, and go on with another fragment of a story. Letters would drop near the open fire of logs that many a tree had to be felled to keep blazing.

Under my grandfather's will, his widow had the right to live at Milford for the rest of her life. Then, according to family tradition, her only son's only son, Thomas Miller Ormsby, born in 1939, would inherit the place and all the contents of the house. The boy's two older sisters, Rosemary and Louise, received nothing under the will. My mother had told us that Grandfather had given his word that she had the right to occupy the East Wing as long as she wished, but he had not included this right in his will. She didn't blame her father, as she never wanted to live at Milford after 1942, nor did she want her children to settle in Ireland, where she feared we would degenerate.

Almost eighty years old, Granny was alone too much in the big house, haunted by family members who were dead or abroad, her body wasted by eating only ice-cream wafers dipped in tea, her mind wandering. We would come for short visits and be gone for long periods. She had always taken an interest in things that interested us, encouraged our dreams beyond reason, and given us boundless hospitality and presents.

Now she was in trouble with her daughter-in-law, Bunty, my uncle Jack's widow, for losing money on the farm and selling trees from the woods and silver from the house to pay bills. Her biggest bill was incurred at Ryder's pharmacy in Ballinrobe for medicines, lint and bandages to treat the sick or injured who came to Milford needing her help. A clergyman had taken the Miller–Browne duel papers from the safe, and no one would ever see them again.

And now Delia Madden, who had served my grandmother day and night for fifteen years, had given notice that she would be leaving to get married. Shortly before my mother came back from Southern Rhodesia in May 1953 to decide with Bunty what should be done, Dr Maguire had warned her by telegram that her mother was dying. Delia told me that the doctor, seeing her sitting up in bed, had remarked, 'You're a wonderful woman, Mrs Ormsby. We thought you had gone from us. How did you manage to pull through?' And my grandmother had replied, with a high tinkling laugh, 'I thought of the clay.'

As Delia could not be replaced, my mother and Bunty decided that my grandmother had to be moved out of Milford. They thought she might be happy with some of her own furniture at a cottage belonging to a relation near Salruck, close to her sister Violet, now living at Salruck House. I was at Milford to drive a car my mother had hired when Granny, tiny and frail, started shouting at my mother and my aunt, stamping her foot like a child and cursing them both in a furious temper.

When she turned to me for help, I betrayed her by easily persuading her to come and stay with me at Rosroe, knowing that she would never be brought back to Milford. She cheered up on the journey through scenery she had always encouraged our mother and Mary to paint, and in Leenane ordered a leg of mountainy mutton from a shopkeeper she had known all her life. A few days later she moved with a paid companion into a desolate cottage under the mountains overlooking Lough Muck.

She bore no grudge against me for being the instrument of moving her out of Milford, but she never would forgive my aunt or my mother. Three months later, I left Rosroe for London and then Crete, trying to improve my poetry by moving close to Mount Ida. During my absence, Aunt Violet, fearing that her sister might fall into the fire or the lake, persuaded two doctors to certify her as insane. As the law required, Granny was forcibly removed to a nursing home, which Aunt Violet had arranged, with a police escort.

My ambition to write a modern Irish epic had resulted in a turgid, windy, rhetorical failure that nobody would publish. Harold Nicolson encouraged me to go to Greece, the fountainhead of our civilisation, or to France or Italy. I was almost twenty-six when he supported my application to the British Council for a teaching job in Europe. The Council appointed me as director of the English School in Canea, the capital of Crete. Harold wrote to Francis King, the novelist and friend of J.R. Ackerley, a lecturer at the British Council in Athens, where he entertained me well on my arrival in September 1953 and on subsequent visits.

I travelled on the Simplon-Orient Express, breaking the journey at Venice and Zagreb. The Greeks were then even poorer than the Yugoslavs, having suffered as badly under German occupation, and worse in their subsequent civil war. But as soon as our train crossed into Greece during the night, I was happy to notice that even the frontier guards went about their dull official functions with an expectation that life was meant to be enjoyed. Hearing

Greek spoken by Greeks intensified my feelings. In every second or third face among the crowd on the platform at Salonika, I recognised heroic or godlike features of the ancient world, line of forehead and nose unbroken and straight. When I drew back the curtain of my sleeping berth at a small country station where the train had stopped, I read with awe the Greek letters that spelt Marathon.

Athens astonished and frightened me: the glory of the Parthenon shining above the filth and cacophony of overcrowded streets; good-looking destitute boys, from places with names as redolent of happiness as Arcadia, reduced to offering themselves to foreigners for half a dollar. Warned that Cretans were the most puritanical of Greeks, and inclined to be violent, I sailed from Piraeus to Canea, a crumbling Venetian city of twenty-five thousand people, built around a small harbour of fishing boats. There were no more than nine or ten cars on its dusty gravel roads.

The English School – two classrooms and an office – was attached to a large old house belonging to a lawyer. Classes were held only in the evening after secondary schools and shops and offices had closed. I was paid so little that I had to give private lessons in the afternoon. My sister Mary had given me a bicycle with an engine in the back wheel, so I was able to live outside the town in a pine wood at the top of a honey-coloured hill with a view of the entire city, the sea and the snow-capped White Mountains. There I wrote letters and worked at my poetry.

To get through many hours of teaching, I fortified myself at lunch with a tumbler of strong red wine, and another tumbler at night, after chugging up the long zigzagging road from the city. I ate at home: bread, eggs, spaghetti, olive oil, and sheep's milk feta, sometimes lamb chops or fish. I cooked on paraffin oil. There was one electric bulb in each of four mostly empty rooms and a cold shower. I was lonelier than ever.

In Crete the virginity of girls was valued more highly by their fathers and their brothers than the girls' own happiness or the lives of their lovers, who were likely to be shot if a marriage could not promptly be arranged after a seduction, and sometimes even if it could. One night I took a girl to the cinema, and the next day her brother, wearing a dark business suit and a black overcoat, in which he was carrying a gun, called at my house on the hill. With grave courtesy, he enquired whether my intentions regarding his sister were honourable, and did I wish to marry her, because if not I must never invite her out again, or he would be obliged to shoot me. I had not touched the girl.

At a dance that I gave in the school on New Year's Eve, a short, stocky young man with a black toothbrush moustache asked if I could keep his gun locked up in a drawer in my study for the duration of the dance. He explained that his family had a vendetta with another family, whose turn it was to kill one of his relations, so he had to go armed wherever he went. I expressed the hope that they wouldn't try to kill him at the dance. No question of that, he assured me, they would probably try to get him on the way home. Of course he wasn't afraid, but he had to be careful. I kept the gun, removing the bullets before I locked it in the drawer until ten minutes before the dance ended. He put the bullets into the gun, thanked me for looking after it, and said good night.

Enrolment at the English School, because of its name, dried up after Sir Anthony Eden said 'No' to the Greek government's request for talks with Britain about the independence of Cyprus and its possible union with Greece. The word 'No' in Greek resonated with its famous use by Greece in a forlorn and heroic answer to an ultimatum from Mussolini. I kept most of my students by explaining that as an Irishman I sympathised with the Greek Cypriots. They waited until my departure from Crete before joining the American School. But I felt isolated by the hostile nationalistic anger.

After months of living alone, ironically so on the island where Zeus was born, I fell in love with a proud young shepherd from the White Mountains. He had the ideal wasp waist of an acrobat pictured on a Minoan vase or palace wall somersaulting over a bull, head to head, while gripping its horns. But whereas the eyes of most Cretans were as dark as black olives, his were blue and his hair was red. His name implied descent from an ancient Greek god.

We became friends, conversing in broken English and scraps of Greek, his eyes lighting up when we met, and his hand lingering in mine, long enough for me to deceive myself into thinking that my love would be requited. I was more lonely than I had ever felt in my life, while continually inflamed by the beauty of the landscape, the incense of human, animal and herbal odours arising from the city below my house, the gaunt music of goat and church bells, the taste of earth-red wine drawn from a barrel, and the far too infrequent touch of my friend's hands.

After several meetings, and a meal at a taverna where we put chunks of lamb on our forks into each other's mouths – an old Cretan custom that foreigners are apt to misconstrue – he invited me to meet his family and be their guest for a night. They lived in the one shattered room that remained since the German army of occupation had blown up their house ten years earlier. He invited me to share his bed, where I lay awake in the torment of lying beside someone I loved bodily but dared not embrace.

A few weeks later he came to visit me for a weekend of improving his English and my Greek. When it was time to sleep, I offered him a bed in a separate room, but he preferred to share mine. It was a single cast-iron bed with a horse-hair mattress, so we could not avoid lying close to each other, and it seemed natural that my hand should rest on his thigh as he lay on his back. When I began to stroke him, he didn't push my hand away at first, but suddenly he leaped out of bed, switched on the light and cried that he was going to the kitchen to fetch a knife to sink in my heart and then in his own.

Our lives were in danger. He was burning with a fire I had never lit in anyone before, about to slay himself and me rather than be reviled and ostracised in his village. I stood between him and the door to the kitchen, trying to persuade him to forgive me, blamed myself, promised never to touch him again, but do everything in my power to remain his friend. Gradually my pleading calmed his passion enough to prevent his consummating our friendship with a Cretan catharsis.

We stayed up talking until he felt relaxed enough to go to sleep in the other bedroom. Before he left in the morning he forgave me. He had the power to revenge what he felt was an insult to his manhood as a Cretan, but his pride would not let him take an ignoble revenge. He would rather have killed me in hot blood than expose me to public disgrace. As I had been his friend, his host and his guest, he felt bound not to dishonour me. Killing me would have shown respect. He would not have been imprisoned for such a crime in Crete, not then, or not for more than a few heroic months of expiation. We remained friends until I left the island in June 1954.

Before leaving Greece I went to drink at the fountainhead of poetry: Delphi on the southern slopes of Mount Parnassus, sacred to the Muses and Apollo. After dining alone in a cheap taverna, I walked down the main street looking for a companion. Everyone seemed to have gone to bed, except for a solitary man I caught sight of through the open doors of a restaurant in which he was the last remaining customer. He resembled me in looks, with horn-rimmed spectacles like mine, as he leaned over a book he was reading. Convinced that he was English and might resent an approach without an introduction, I continued down the street; but, meeting no one, turned back, and on my return plucked up courage to enter the restaurant and introduce myself. He closed his guidebook and we chatted amiably about our travels.

His name was Gerald or Gerry Cookson, my senior by two and half years, an immensely tall Northumbrian by birth, and a scientist who had given up science after 'determining the structure of an important biological molecule that builds up in the body of people suffering from porphyria, turning their urine red and disturbing their mental balance'. He had just come from Salisbury, Southern Rhodesia, where all the hotels were full, so he had been obliged to sleep in a dormitory next to a young British Guards officer, Shaun Plunket, who woke him up late every night coming back from a party. On the third night Shaun invited Gerry to join him at a cine-dinner in a rural hotel with a girl called Liz Murphy – my younger sister.

I never expected to see Gerry again, but the following week in Rome, as he would remind me forty-five years later, 'I was in the Vatican Museum looking down at a medieval map of the world showing the Montes Lunae near the supposed source, and when I looked up I saw you standing next to me, so we decided to have lunch together.' Then I gave him my older sister Mary's telephone number, as I was on my way to stay with her in London. On Thursday 17 June, Mary and I went to the theatre to see Terence Rattigan's *Day by the Sea*, and while the bells were ringing just before the curtain went up, 'three huge tall people', according to Mary, 'came into our row and walked all over our feet'. They were Gerry and his sister Margaret and their mother. Gerry gave Mary his telephone number on a scrap of paper, which she put in her bag and could not find the next day or the day after.

Later she was looking for the number of a dentist, thinking she had put it on a scrap of paper in her bag. The person who answered her call was Gerry, who invited her to dinner. From then on they felt drawn to each other by luck that had the force of destiny, and in London on 23 November 1955 they would get married and live together happily until his death, forty-seven years later.

In 1954 Harold Nicolson had passed on to T.S. Eliot a copy I had given him of my long and heavily rhetorical poem 'Voyage to an Island', which Louis MacNeice had rejected. Having spent more than two years writing this unreadable epic in poverty and extreme isolation in the west of Ireland, I wanted to believe that its value as poetry, if this were to be recognised, would redeem a life that otherwise would have been wasted.

A few weeks later, Harold invited me to his rooms in Albany off Piccadilly for a glass of sherry. Tom, he said, unfortunately did not feel that my work was ready for publication by Faber, but he had given Harold a word of advice to pass back to me. 'Tell your friend Murphy that poetry is song.' Harold liked this remark so much that he repeated it like a mantra – 'poetry is song'. To give me an example, he recited one of his favourite lyrics from *A Shropshire Lad*:

> Loveliest of trees, the cherry now
> Is hung with bloom along the bough

Dipping into Housman's poems had never enticed me to read them, but Eliot's remark, transmitted by Nicolson, struck me as a judgement that was irrefutable, determining me to change my style. As a result I endeavoured to write lyric poems. One of these, written when I was in love with Patricia Avis in Paris, was 'Eclogue in the Louvre'. In 1960 I sent it to Eliot, explaining how his message had inspired the poem, and I received a reply from Russell Square, in which he wrote that he had not the slightest recollection of making that particular remark, though he remembered one evening talking about my work with Harold Nicolson. He added that he liked the poem.

Aged twenty-seven in September 1954, I became a student once more, this time in Paris, studying French civilisation at the Sorbonne. My father gave me a small allowance that he could not easily afford from his farm in Southern Rhodesia, and I lived in a room with chocolate-brown furniture in the male section of the Collège Franco-Britannique. Poor, obscure and miserable enough to qualify as a promising poet, I kept my spirits high and low by trying to fulfil two deviously related desires: to write poetry that might be accepted by T.S. Eliot at Faber; and to meet among strangers on the Left Bank a young soldier, sailor or gypsy who would give my poetry the passion and inspiration it lacked.

One day, bent on both forlorn missions, I entered the vast Papeterie de Joseph Gibert in the Boulevard Saint-Michel, looking for a blank notebook to fill the deep pocket of my old Donegal tweed jacket. I wanted it to hold the scraps of verse, elusive images, dreams, desires and revelations that might otherwise be forgotten if they were to cross my mind in bed or on the metro or during a seminar or in a noisy, steamy student restaurant.

Instead, I discovered and bought, from a pile of black, orange and green *cahiers*, a small notebook for mathematicians, the pages lined with little squares, bound in green boards, quite cheap. I imagined that as numbers underlie music, and a score is essential for composition, so the page might hold in its net the music of poetry, and prevent words from swimming into measureless prolixity.

As a symbol of perfection, the mesh of vertical and horizontal lines, which every word written by hand with a fountain pen would overlay, might exert day by day a subtle influence not to lie. So from the start I knew the notebook would have to be kept secret, under guard like a salmon river, in which I alone could fish in the future for poems that might be lured to the surface from the stream of my past.

We met because she had read my poetry in the *Listener*, and had heard someone say, 'He regards women as an unfortunate necessity.' We were living in separate male and female wings in the dismal Collège Franco-Britannique of the Cité Universitaire in Paris. On 26 October 1954 I found a puzzling note in my letter box.

> Same place
> Other side
> No. 37

> It doesn't look as if I'm going to have the nerve to come out with a How d'you do – Mr. Murphy – I've been wanting to meet you for such a long time – just love poetry you know.
>
> But, if you do feel like exchanging a few words in English some time, on matters unconcerned with the cost of living or the world of youth, perhaps you would let me know.
>
> Disqualifications: apart from the obvious one – a passing cold in the head.
>
> Qualifications: not many, I'm afraid. Friend of the Larkin, Amis (Wain) organization. Officially engaged at present on Aspects of Tristan Corbière – man and work.
>
> If all that doesn't dismay you, I might as well add that I don't look anything like
> > George Sand

I obtained her name, Madame Patricia Strang, from the porter by asking him who lived in number 37, and rang her bell. I was astonished by the strange mixture of maturity and childishness when she appeared, sardonically grinning as though she had preconceived every nuance of this meeting, but affecting a little girl's gesture of holding her hands close together just below her breast and waving them, while she stood with her toes pointing inwards.

Yet in spite of this oddness, she was a handsome woman with sad blue eyes and brown wavy hair, strongly built and well dressed, who spoke the language of Oxford sophistication, derisory, allusive, witty, nonchalant and superior, while at the same time revealing through her hands and feet that a vital part of her mind was no more than five years old, pleading with me to be her father. She cooked dinners for me in the college dining room – *Châteaubriand saignants* with Château Lafite 1947 wine – because, she said, I had 'a lean and hungry look'. I tried but failed to stop her chain-smoking.

Gradually she took up more and more of my time. Her conversation amused and flattered me with her interest in my poetry. Lonely and miserable, she appealed for my help to extract her from the spider's web of an entanglement with the historian Lionel Butler at Oxford, where he had been writing her letters in purple ink on All Souls notepaper, dated '2 a.m.'. She was also trying to escape from her marriage to Colin Strang, a lecturer in philosophy at Newcastle University.

With a private income from her father, Meiert Cornelis Avis, known as MCA, a rich businessman in Johannesburg, she was able to bring glamour to the squalor of my life in the Collège Franco-Britannique, suggesting one day we should go to Brittany, or, if I preferred it, to Italy or Greece; to which she added that I was wasting time studying at the Sorbonne, where the teaching was pedantic and stuffy.

A Calvinist of the Dutch Reformed Church, her father had been born in Holland and had emigrated at the age of eighteen to South Africa, where he had fought for the Afrikaners in the Boer War, losing the tops of two fingers. Destitute and single-handed in its aftermath, he had formed a company called African Shipping (established 1903) Limited, which twenty to thirty years later had offices in London, New York, Tokyo and all the major ports of southern Africa. He remained the sole shareholder.

At the age of fifty he had married Patricia Newman, known as Paddy, aged twenty-four, an Irish Catholic receptionist at the Rembrandt Hotel, where he used to stay in London. They were incompatible. Paddy was so frightened of Meiert's bad temper that she encouraged the children to deceive him rather than face his wrath. If he discovered their deceptions, he would become angrier. Patricia told me she had forgotten most of her childhood, except for one horror: 'I used to wake up with wet sheets, and find my father preparing to beat me.'

Her brilliance was scary. At the age of seventeen she had entered Somerville College from South Africa when it was ten times harder for a woman to get into Oxford than for a man. She had chosen to read medicine in order to have an excuse not to return to South Africa for seven years. Her father would always pay for something he approved of, such as education. What he did not want his money to do was to give his children pleasure.

She had an older brother by one year called Keesje, whom she had outshone intellectually in Johannesburg, where she had attended Roedean as a day girl. Keesje, aged nineteen and in his first term at Oxford, had fallen in love with a beautiful green-eyed Irish Australian called Peggy Mulcahy, and had quit the university to marry her and bring her out to South Africa. Without a degree or a trade, he had been obliged to work for his father, who held him in thrall to a violent temper, a paranoid suspicion of being cheated, and great wealth. Keesje and Peggy's two sons, Simon and Meiert, were taught to call their grandfather 'Daddy' in return for payment of their food bills, which Keesje had to submit to 'Daddy' for approval before they were paid. MCA was paying Keesje more than he could have earned elsewhere, but never enough to be free.

Before qualifying in medicine, Patricia had met Colin Strang at Oxford and had married him, she said, to make a new reason for not going home. The wedding had been at the fashionable church of St James's, Spanish Place, to please her mother, who had brought her up as a Catholic, and Lady Strang, who wanted a smart London wedding for her only son. Subsequently Patricia had suffered seven miscarriages.

Through Colin, Patricia had met the poet Philip Larkin, the novelist Kingsley Amis and the composer Bruce Montgomery, who wrote detective novels under the name of Edmund Crispin. From them she had acquired a lofty manner of sending people up with a snort, or putting them down with a sneer. Kingsley's imitations of voices, she said, were cruelly accurate and funny. It was safer in their company to scoff than to admire.

Approving of her marriage to the son of a peer who had reached the top of the British Foreign Service, her father had promised to buy her a house, but never reached the point of signing a cheque for a house she wanted. Instead he wrote by hand every Sunday under a canopy on the *kopje* in his stone-terraced garden, long letters in a style of international business English concerning the kind of property in which he would or would not allow his daughter or her future descendants for seven generations to live. In these letters he still addressed her as 'Dearest Googoo', asserting, 'no one must ever be allowed to come between us'. He kept a carbon copy of every page he wrote.

Patricia took away my loneliness, and could read my thoughts, alarmingly. At Oxford, in a viva for her medical degree, she had read the mind of her examiner when she did not know the answer to his question. 'I looked in his eyes,' she told me, 'and the answer I gave was correct.' The laughter she made out of the misfortunes of her life and mine was infectious. Her mordant wit had been polished in a love affair with Philip Larkin in Belfast, and had saved her from collapse in her affair with Lionel Butler. Enid Starkie at Oxford had given her an introduction to a Parisian scholar who could help her write a book about the Breton poet Corbière; but at their first meeting he had wanted her to go to bed with him as the price of giving her access to manuscript material, and she had refused.

Our first night in bed was a failure: she moved restlessly, counter to every rhythm of mine. I wanted her to be still, and it shamed me to fail to make love to her, besides which I had drunk too much wine. She wanted to help, and I wanted her to help me to be helped. The next day I advised her to find a peasant who would love her well, not an androgynous poet or intellectual who could only make her laugh and cry.

But we persevered, hiring a room in a sordid little hotel with two entrances (each with a different name) after a dinner in a bistro, and she taught me well. Our sex grew into love, though not without difficulty or pain. After I finished recording a talk on Yeats for the BBC, we went to Brittany at her expense and arrived after dark at a little pension in Saint-Guénolé, a fishing village on the southern coast. It was to help her research on Corbière. She hoped I would find in Brittany a resemblance to the Connemara I loved.

The weather was just as bad, cold, windy and wet. The *patronne* wanted to feed us on sparrows caught in traps in the backyard. We met in the bar, where Patricia was the only woman, a bright young fisherman called Vincent, who was about to enter the navy for military service. He approached us wearing breeches the colour of a side of beef. 'Beaucoup de vent ici en Bretagne,' he kept saying like a mantra, and, 'Mademoiselle, sac à la main.' While he was charming me, his eye was on Patricia, who was beginning to despair. Clearly I was unable to give her the wholehearted love she desired.

One stormy dark morning in despair, she handed me the return half of her train ticket as well as mine. She was crying, and when I asked her what was the matter, she said she was so unhappy that she was going to throw herself off the cliff at the Pointe du Raz. I was shocked and felt guilty, refused to accept the tickets, and persuaded her to come with me by bus to Concarneau instead. On the bus I proposed to her, not on my knees like my father, though my head was bowed in shame. I suggested to her that since both of us were miserable, having made a mess of our lives, if we were to join our two miseries together, we might be able to improve our lives, and have children. She agreed.

She said Colin only loved philosophy, which could not be cited as a co-respondent in divorce proceedings. Therefore if we were to get married, she would have to be divorced by him. So we gave evidence of adultery at the pension in Saint-Guénolé and Colin took proceedings. She had drifted away from him because 'He made love with his eyes closed, and at breakfast studied in silence the words on a packet of cornflakes.'

From that day forward, until I received in London three and a half years later a letter from her in Johannesburg asking for a divorce, I felt responsible for keeping her alive and feeling well enough not to want to end her life.

Her mother came to London at Christmas to meet me and, in spite of being a Catholic, gave our future marriage her blessing. While waiting for the divorce to go through, Patricia and I went to Greece. In Athens my wandering eyes and feet brought back her despair; but in Crete, after a long hot walk together across a high plateau covered with anemones in flower, we lay under a pine tree beside a steep path leading down to the river at the bottom of the gorge of Samaria, and there our love was consummated perfectly.

We went from palace to palace, both of us writing poetry. Patricia wrote a poem that Joe Ackerley accepted for the *Listener*, about lepers we met on an island to which they had been exiled. High up at Phaestos, the ancient palace nearest to Zeus and his thunder in the sky, I wrote her a poem called 'The Archaeology of Love', an obscure expression of gratitude for her unearthing and restoration of my heart. She improved my writing with her sensitive criticism. We stayed at several monasteries; one on a mountain where a monk, who had fought as a partisan against the German army during the war, blessed us and gave us a flask of wine.

At Athens, where we were entertained by Francis King, we signed at the British Embassy, as required by her father, an antenuptial contract, drawn up by his lawyers in South Africa, declaring that we would not hold our goods in common nor have a claim on each other's estate.

Colin married a linguist called Barbara a day before our wedding. The divorce had just been granted. Patricia had said, 'Colin would never deceive me.'

Our wedding was at Caxton Hall in Westminster on 3 May 1955. I had sung at weddings in Canterbury Cathedral, crypt and choir, where the bride wore orange roses on her veil. Patricia wanted no ceremony, flowers or crowd, only my sister Mary. I had to go out on the street and beg a passer-by to enter and be a witness. Mary opened a bottle of champagne at her flat in Warwick Square. With an Old English sheepdog called Rocky, which I gave Patricia as a wedding present, we left London on the Irish mail train from Euston the same night.

We drove around the east, south and west coasts of Ireland, looking for a large stone-built house on the sea, surrounded by enough land to give the impression of a demesne, with a small quay or slipway for a boat, beautiful views, the structure not suffering from woodworm or dry rot, and substantial enough to be approved by Patricia's father, who was willing to pay up to £10,000. Two places that would have suited us well, after negotiations wasteful of time, he turned down, or made an offer that he knew would be refused. Our house hunt continued for months.

We based ourselves at the Quay House in Rosroe, from where we sailed to Inishbofin in my pookaun. One day, when Patricia was fishing for pollock on a hand line, trolled at a speed of two knots near a breaker far from the shore, she put the fear of death into me, not for the first time. She wanted me to jibe the pookaun and sail right over a tidal rock that was then submerged, because, she said quite rightly, there'd be a better chance of catching a fish. But she knew it was dangerous, that the force of a pookaun crossing a breaker in a flat calm sea could set up a wave that might sink the boat.

Then she smiled to herself, a mysterious, faraway, almost ecstatic smile, as if she could hear across the sea the singing of Wagner's Rhinemaidens or Richard Strauss's Salome appealing to her, and she begged me to take the risk.

It was a day when we both felt as happy and close as we had been at the palace in Phaestos and in the gorge of Samaria, full of the love we had given each other. But she may have been thinking of my imperfections on that perfect day, with the sun shining on the calm sea, for she seemed to be enticing me with her desire to consummate our love, once and for all, so as never to have to worry about being plunged back into the loneliness and failure of our lives before we had met.

All I needed to do was to jibe the pookaun and cross the breaker. One gigantic plume of water would be thrust up by the sea to swallow us both. But I refused, and disappointed her. Every nerve in my body determined me not to take such a risk.

In the legend that his short life became, the American poet Richard Selig looked like Adonis and behaved like a barracuda. After a marriage lasting fifteen months, his death from Hodgkin's disease drove his widow, the Irish singer and harpist Mary O'Hara, to become a bride of Christ for twelve years in a strictly enclosed convent in England. Introducing his poems posthumously in 1962, Peter Levi SJ wrote, 'He fell on books as he did on life with a violent and exigent hunger, and the history of his talent is also the history of its dissatisfaction.' Theodore Roethke described him to a priest on Inishbofin as 'the most amoral man I ever met'.

I met Selig in August 1955 at lunchtime at Davy Byrne's in Dublin. Among the crowd at the bar I spotted this Jewish dark angel of the Lord standing tall, so good looking that he was bound to be suspicious if I spoke, but wearing a Magdalen College lily tie that gave me an excuse to introduce myself. We talked about C.S. Lewis and Jack Bennett, his tutors and mine. He was as charming as he looked, a little younger than I was, a Rhodes Scholar from Seattle, with poems accepted for *Encounter* by Stephen Spender, whom he must have enchanted. So I boasted that the Dolmen Press had just brought out my first collection, *The Archaeology of Love*, and that the BBC had broadcast this month a programme of new poetry by Philip Larkin, Theodore Roethke and Valentin Iremonger edited and introduced by me. He defeated this by saying Roethke was a poet he knew well, his teacher at the University of Washington. And thus we sparred like friendly gladiators in the literary arena.

'Would you care to meet my wife?' Patricia, sitting in her corner, was reading Pascal's *Pensées* and smoking a cigarette in an ivory holder, with Rocky asleep on the floor. She might have been wondering who I had picked up now. Richard Selig turned the polished innocence of his charm on her. Infatuated with Ireland, he was leaving the following day for the Aran Islands. We were going back the next week to our cottage on the quay at Rosroe, with Charles Monteith from Faber as our guest. Selig wanted to meet that man who worked in an office beside T.S. Eliot in Russell Square, so he said he would visit us at Rosroe when he left Inisheer.

But today, he told us, something wonderful had happened. He had seen a girl once in a coffee shop – his ideal Irish colleen, with golden-red hair – and once on the radio he had heard her sing. He was already in love with her. They had spoken for the first time this morning on the phone, and she had agreed to meet him for dinner that evening across the road at The Bailey. Patricia responded with her sardonic 'we know better' laugh. After dinner they were going to the poet Tom Kinsella's flat in Baggot Street for a late-night party at which Richard now hoped Mary O'Hara would sing. We had already received an invitation from Tom and his wife, Eleanor, so Richard invited us to join him and Mary for coffee after dinner.

By the time we got there, the restaurant upstairs looked empty, and it smelled of cigar smoke. But then, in a niche by an open window, we saw a couple absorbed in each other's radiance. We joined them, talking of this and that, sniffing each other's territory, feeling unwanted except as witnesses of the drama of their blossoming love. When Richard mentioned Hollywood, Mary responded in the voice of an impoverished Abbey actress hoping to enchant a film producer with her Irish feyness. 'Hollywood,' she sighed, 'the land of heartbreak!' This was enough to make Patricia, reaching for her coffee, knock over a wine glass.

In the Kinsella's top-floor flat, Selig sat with legs crossed on the floor, and Francis Barry, whose son Sebastian, of future fame, had just been born, lay supine on a bed like a king on a tomb. As chatter faded into silence, the strings of a harp I couldn't see were plucked very lightly by fingernails, and a faraway voice sang us back through lamentation for the dead of Aughrim to the land of the ever-living young – if only I had known what the Irish words meant.

A week later, at the climax of a correspondence that had taken three months, we acquired as a gift from Patricia's father a large black Humber Hawk that we couldn't afford to run. The old tyrant had written from Johannesburg to say that he would inspect the car when he came to Ireland, and if he found we had not kept it in good condition he would take it away. We met Charles at the airport as planned, and drove at a snail's pace to Rosroe, running in the engine as instructed by MCA in longhand from his *kopje*. When Selig turned up from Aran the next day, Charles revelled with him in witty banter, while Patricia and I gave their act an audience in which they saw their brilliance reflected.

We spent Sunday, warm weather and clear sky, picnicking on the beach at Glassilaun, taking photographs of one another, Patricia reclining on sand in the shade of an umbrella, reading Péguy. We were the only tourists there. The people who had lived all their lives in small cottages of purple stone and oat-straw thatch overlooking the shore had gone to Mass on foot five miles away and not returned. Charles, Richard and I braved the cold sea. Being tossed by Atlantic breakers excited us, and we dried ourselves in a cove between rocks out of sight of Patricia.

This was when you usually wrapped a towel around your loins or turned discreetly away, but Selig put on his white Aran jersey and took off his swimming trunks. Half naked, he stood, revealing to us his stalwart genitals, a cartoon of Irish pudeur undercut by outrage. 'If you took a photograph of me now,' he said 'it could be captioned "What's wrong with this picture?" Answer: "Aran Islanders ain't Jews."' A joke loaded with angst, provocative perhaps, but more disturbing than funny. I decided not to show an interest in the groin of Adonis and trusted Charles to reply, 'A postgraduate student doing research for a doctorate made an amazing discovery that Synge's Aran Islanders fucked in their underwear.'

On the way home I drove with Patricia beside me. If I turned my head I could see Charles, but not Selig, who was telling us about a big strong man of Inisheer rowing him in a currach and saying, 'Boy, if I was a girl, I'd be in love with you.' The banter with Charles increased good-humouredly, as we climbed Salruck Pass in low gear, until it reached a point where Selig was talking about a Jesuit priest who, while trying to convert him, suddenly leaned over and stuck his tongue in his ear. We all laughed, and as the laughter subsided, Charles, to prolong the amusement, asked, 'And did you enjoy it?' Whereupon Selig turned his barracuda teeth on Charles and snapped, 'Are you guys queer?'

The car seemed to slip out of my control in the silence following this attack, as it freewheeled down the steep rutty hill to a hairpin bend where a cyclist had gone head over heels to his death by the spiked iron gates of Salruck, which my great-grandfather had jumped on his horse when he was drunk.

Unable to find a house on the sea, I put an advertisement in the *Irish Times* seeking a big house, or the ruin thereof, on fifty acres of demesne land. The only answer came from Ernest Gébler at Lake Park, Roundwood, County Wicklow. He was willing to sell his elegant, albeit pebble-dashed, Regency fishing lodge, in poor repair, surrounded by one hundred and eighty acres of mountain pasture and woodland, nine hundred feet above sea level, twenty-five miles south of Dublin. The acidity of the soil at this altitude, in a region of high rainfall, produced more bracken and gorse than grass. We liked its beauty, remoteness and challenge.

The house backed on to a square stone-built courtyard of stables and barns. Behind the courtyard, on ground rising to the north, was a beech wood. A walled garden on the west side, growing nothing but weeds, adjoined the 'Lady's Garden', where a few hardy roses had survived around a pond. Beyond these gardens and some pigsties, the ground sloped steeply to a forest of indigenous oak along the shores of Lough Dan, attracting a herd of roe deer from the mountains. On the east was a thicket of rhododendrons that bordered a sycamore avenue with a gate lodge. A pair of large reception rooms, fronted by a verandah, faced south across lawns that sloped into the valley of the Glendalough estate of Robert Barton. The blue hills on the horizon, unlike the jagged Twelve Pins in Connemara, appeared smooth and serene.

Ernie was selling for two reasons: he had run out of money from a historical novel that had sold well in America; and his second wife, Edna O'Brien, though a country girl, preferred to live in a city. Edna had begun to publish articles in the *Irish Press* while Ernie was working on another novel. They were hospitable and charming. We all had to be patient, while Patricia tried to convince her father, in long and grateful letters she hated writing, that the house had no woodworm or dry rot.

Patricia's period pains were insufferable, and drove her to combine double brandies with strong aspirin and codeine tablets. She would writhe on the floor or the ground at the side of the road if we happened to be driving. These were times when she really needed sympathy.

To prevent miscarriage, the gynaecologist at the Rotunda Hospital gave her in July 1955 an oestrogenic hormone called Stilboestrol. She became pregnant in August while we were staying in a large room on the top floor of Buswell's Hotel, where we were allowed to keep Rocky. With wool hanging down over her eyes, the dog used to come everywhere we went. Once in Grafton Street a child cried out as we passed, 'Oh, Mammy, Mammy, look at the blind dog!' Another day, when we entered the Royal Hibernian Hotel, where I had kicked Aunt Bella, Rocky, seeing the sun shining through glass on a carpet as soft as grass, crouched and peed. Patricia, not allowing me to apologise to the waiter, quickly moved an armchair to cover up the puddle.

On the same day as Mary became engaged to Gerry Cookson, 12 November 1955, Patricia became an Irish citizen. After this, all we could do was wait in rented accommodation for her father to proceed with the purchase of Lake Park, which took another two months. We hoped Lake Park would be an antidote to our restlessness. Over Christmas we were invited to stay with Geoffrey and Mary Taylor in Ballinteer.

Geoffrey Taylor had been poetry editor of the *Bell* when that monthly magazine was edited by Seán Ó Faoláin in Dublin during the war. I met him in 1952, thanks to Maurice and Trix Craig, in his south County Dublin rose garden, enclosed by an ivied wall the height of two tall men. On a deckchair under a cedar of Lebanon beside a weedless rockery, he read some of the turgid, effortful narrative verse I had been writing at Rosroe, and gave me more generous encouragement than the work deserved.

At Christmas 1955 Geoffrey and Mary and their two children gave Patricia and me and our dog a warm welcome at their big, dilapidated house fall of books. Now, as poetry editor of the liberal weekly *Time & Tide*, he was writing thoughtful letters to encourage rather than disappoint men and women who submitted poems that he felt obliged to reject. His own verse had earned him little but rejection slips. He exalted my work and blessed our marriage by including in the *Faber Book of Love Poetry*, which he edited with John Betjeman, 'The Archaeology of Love', the lyric I had written for Patricia at the palace of Phaestos in Crete.

I well remember his kindness in giving me his copy of the rare Cuala Press edition of *The Great Hunger* by Patrick Kavanagh, right after I told him how Paddy had defrauded me of ten shillings in McDaid's on a promise of getting me a copy of the book from Mrs Yeats the same afternoon. The gift was symbolic, tending to remove a sting inflicted by a poet of genius on a young one who was unknown, to make good an act of peasant meanness with one of Anglo-Irish generosity, and to recognise the older poet's need to defraud people for money to buy whiskey and stout, and the apprentice's need for books and recognition.

Geoffrey handed it to me with a devil-may-care stab of his deep blue eyes under long dark eyebrows, the right brow drooping in self-mockery over the hollow of a sunken temple, the left brow curving upwards like a miniature kris, worn as an ornament of playful, cut-throat wit. He may have looked 'satanic' to Frank O'Connor, when they worked together at the Carnegie Library in Wicklow during the 1920s, but to us in 1955 he seemed more of a faun than a devil.

I heard him recite, in his gently ironic Anglo-Irish voice, these lines he made up about a cat:

> Sally, having tasted cheese,
> Directs down holes a tainted breeze,
> Enticing thus, with baited breath,
> Nice mice to an untimely death.

Patricia and I were still waiting for her father to send the money for the purchase of Lake Park, where we were to move in January. Geoffrey told us he had changed his surname from Phibbs to Taylor, his mother's family name, after his father, owner of an ancestral estate in Sligo, had disinherited him because he had given breakfast to the rebel leader de Valera when Dev was on the run.

Geoffrey stayed with us at Lake Park for a few days in February, and I remember him warning Patricia with mock seriousness to keep away from the felling of an immensely tall Douglas fir that was shutting the light from our windows, in case the departing spirit of the tree might do her or the child she was carrying an injury. None of us dreamt that a man of his age, only fifty-five, in what seemed like perfect health, would die a few months later of kidney failure, after a medical mix-up between a homoeopath, in whom Geoffrey believed, and a doctor who gave him a dose of mercury for his heart.

He had survived the Great War by being just too young to enlist, and the IRA had not torched his ancestral home, as 'the family had always been good to the tenants'. If he thought meanly of himself for not having been a soldier, in a family whose land was gained by conquest, he had overcome this, as I had after 1945, by trying to conquer the higher moral peaks of poetry.

Why did Patricia imagine, against the real evidence of his domestic happiness, that he was dying of boredom in his rose garden, and longing to escape, even from his library stocked with rare poetry and garden books, bought for half nothing on the Liffey quays during the war, often in John Betjeman's company, unless it was because she dreaded being trapped by me, a distant cousin of Geoffrey on my mother's side, in a family circle of cosy, bickering bondage, after the freedom she had enjoyed in her childless marriage to an academic philosopher?

Our marital agreement required us to be tolerant of each other's affairs, and frank in telling each other the truth. Geoffrey's first marriage, in his twenties to Norah McGuinness, was based on a similar agreement, fashionable among the bright young things of that period. Norah had rebelled against her Protestant family of coal merchants in Derry by becoming an artist. So Geoffrey was intrigued by our present state, and how it might work, as we were about his seriously frivolous past, and how it had failed. With her indiscreet talk, Patricia made him talk indiscreetly, though not within hearing of Mary, Geoffrey's second wife, who was a pious Welsh Quaker.

The high risk we took in our marital agreement seemed, at first, to sharpen and confirm our love. It may have done the same for Geoffrey and Norah, until the day Norah announced that she was leaving Wicklow to live with

David Garnett in England, and would be back in six months. Geoffrey took this in his Anglo-Irish stride, but felt wretched until he received a letter out of the blue from a young American poet called Laura Riding, praising one of his poems that had just appeared in the *New Statesman* and, furthermore inviting him to come and stay with her in London. It was like an invitation from one of the Muses to sport on Mount Helicon.

He found her living with Robert Graves on the third floor of a house close to the river in Hammersmith, both of them writing and publishing poetry under her influence as an avatar of the White Goddess. Robert's wife, Nancy Nicholson, who allowed no one to call her Mrs Graves, was living nearby on a barge on the Thames. Their circle of literary friends included T.E. Lawrence, and Sir Edward Marsh, a top civil servant and editor of the *Georgian Poetry* anthology.

Geoffrey's attraction to Laura was inspired by no worship of an incarnate Muse, but ambition to have his poems published and admired. Hers was inspired by his charm and his arch-devil looks. She required her poets in their pagan priestly role to do the housework, which involved laying the table for meals as if it were an altar. Her sloppy habit of leaning her elbows on the table had been sublimated into a ritual. Mats of a different colour had to be placed where each of her elbows could lean during moments of meditation between dainty mouthfuls of herbal food. If Geoffrey, whether through carelessness or frivolity, reversed the colours for the left and right elbow, Laura would throw a divine tantrum and demand to be appeased.

For penance and self-abnegation she would order him to come with her on a journey, giving him no idea of where they were going or why. They would get on or off a bus, as and when her fancy dictated, the excursion shrouded by her in mystery. The farcical seriousness of this appealed to Geoffrey, who accepted the domination of a woman as an Irish birthright. What he found difficult was making love to Laura, when ordered to do so, turn by turn with Robert Graves in the same bed. He said it impaired his virility. Laura had hung on the wall above her triple bed a sky-blue banner that declared GOD IS A WOMAN. What Robert took seriously, Geoffrey was more inclined to treat as a joke. Laura, superhumanly manipulative, was determined to keep Geoffrey under her spell.

But his diminished potency bothered him, and he tired of their threesome. After one of Laura's frightful scenes, he took a train to the country, where he persuaded his wife to set David aside and join him on a journey of reconciliation to France, telling nobody where they were going. They had reached a small provincial town and spent two nights of their reunion happily in a guest house, when there was a knock on their bedroom door from the concierge announcing the arrival of Monsieur Graves. Laura had sent him to bring Geoffrey back.

He had found out where they were by appealing to Sir Edward Marsh, who was happy to use his influence to advance the cause of minor poets, or relieve their self-inflicted distress. Eddie knew someone who got the police to track them down discreetly.

Geoffrey was vague about why that mission had ended his reconciliation with Norah, and restored him to Laura's bed, and Norah to David's. He said that by going back he hoped to convince Laura to let him go freely, without rancour or cursing or suicide threats. Unable to please or calm her, he fled to Lisheen, his father's walled demesne in County Sligo.

There, after a few weeks of staring all day through golden-rectangular windows at trees in the park, swayed by one storm after another, and at banks of waxy dark-green escallonias drooping in the slanting rain, he was only too glad to see a shadow that turned into a ruffled Robert Graves walking up the avenue, bringing the same message as before, 'Come back to save Laura's life!' Tired of living at Lisheen without a lover or a friend, he succumbed again, and travelled to London, determined this time to use all the charm of his nature to avoid a reunion with Laura and persuade her to let him go without threatening to kill herself.

There followed, in the bedroom on the third floor, a night of intense, hysterical argument, repellent to Geoffrey, whose breeding inclined him to prefer emotional evasiveness to confrontation. Laura was wearing a nightdress, Robert pyjamas, and Geoffrey the Donegal tweeds in which he had arrived. His suitcase remained packed, ready for him to catch an early train to meet his wife at David Garnett's country house.

As he was about to leave, Laura declared that she would go first, and climbed out on to the window ledge. Robert crossed the room, intending to grab her and pull her back, but Geoffrey, who felt sure she was bluffing, argued that they should call her bluff, rather than submit to further threats. As he told it, 'Three times Laura said, "I'm going", and then, by God, she had gone!'

Robert ran down three flights of stairs and jumped out of a window. Geoffrey caught his train to the country. He was sure they had killed themselves, he told me, and he thought there was nothing he could do. He may have panicked, though he spoke as if it were a blackly humorous event, laughing the horror and the pity of it all away.

Of course, the police arrived to interview Geoffrey, treating him as the only suspect in a case of attempted murder. They said Robert had accused him of pushing Laura, and did not tell him that both of them were recovering in hospital. Robert had suffered a broken leg, and Laura's claim to represent the goddess seemed vindicated by the lightness of her injuries and the speed of her recovery.

Up to now, Geoffrey's service to the Muse had been poorly rewarded. Though the Hogarth Press published in 1927 a slim volume called *The Withering of the Fig Leaf* by Geoffrey Phibbs, and the following year *It Was Not Jones* under the pseudonym of R. Fitzurse, these were not well received. On this evidence it looks as if Geoffrey changed his surname to Taylor in order to start a new life after the crisis of Laura's jump on 27 April 1929 brought him no fame but infamy.

Eddie hushed up the police, but the Riding affair got out of his control when Geoffrey 'behaved like a gentleman' in allowing Norah to divorce him in an undefended case. Then the *Daily Mail* splashed on its front page the judge's summing up, with vituperative condemnation of the scandalous immorality of bohemian writers. Feeling abandoned by those he had let down, literally in Laura's case, he turned to Nancy Nicholson, who gave up the barge, and spirited him away to a pastoral setting, where they printed fabrics. This idyllic period ended when Geoffrey met and married Mary Dillwyn.

'Nancy was so upset,' Geoffrey told us, 'that she lay down in a bath full of water, swallowed several aspirins, and would surely have drowned had she not, as her head was going under, pulled the plug with her toe.'

So long as we did what her father told us to do in his Sunday letters – his handwriting doubled in size when he got angry – and so long as Lake Park belonged solely to those who had his blood in their veins, he was prepared to pay for our building and reclamation, but not before every detail of what we had done had been reported to him by his daughter or myself, writing thousands of flattering words about the merits of kiln-dried, tongued-and-grooved native-oak flooring, or why it was necessary for us to refit our six chimneys with louvred anti-downdraught pots.

Though I was never to meet Patricia's father, my brother Chris stayed with him and his wife, Paddy, at Houghton Lodge in Johannesburg in March 1956. Chris described 'old Meiert Avis' in a phone call: 'He was a barking tyrant. He started ordering me around as soon as I walked into the house, and eventually

I said, "No! I am not going to do that!" Afterwards he told his son Keesje, "I like that man. I hope Richard is like that." Keesje took me up in a plane, and gave me the controls. When the plane started to tilt, Keesje said, "I'd better take over, or we might go into a nosedive."'

Patricia and I were sleeping in one of the front rooms of Lake Park while the builders worked on the back. The birth pains began in the night, and I drove her, twenty-five miles, to the Leinster Nursing Home in Dublin. The midwives tried to keep me out of the room, though Patricia wanted me to stay, and the doctor, Alan Browne, the hare of our paper chases at Baymount when we were children, had given instructions that I was to be allowed to be present. Fathers at that time were normally excluded. The midwives failed to phone the doctor in time: there was nearly a crisis, and they kept on telling me, 'You'll have to wait outside for a few minutes, we'll call you.' I defied them by coming back almost at once, Patricia in terrible pain, which the midwives could not alleviate. Their anaesthetic was having no effect. She screamed, then in rushed Alan, calm and quick with the forceps, and a miracle occurred, a birth. He said, 'It's a girl.' She looked blue, and he held her upside down by the ankles, gave her a smack, and her first cry was a loud grip on life, saying I am … I am … I am, while her mother lay exhausted but serenely smiling. 'The happiest moment in my life,' she said, as it was in mine. But when the midwives took the baby upstairs to weigh her – why not in the room? – I got worried and cross in case they might make a mistake and bring back some changeling from another ward.

After travelling from Paris to Saint-Guénolé on the Breton coast, from island to island on the Aegean, from Athens and Phaestos to Rome and Florence, from house to house in England and Ireland; after searching for a place to live within sound and sight of the sea and settling in a Regency hunting lodge on the snow line of the Wicklow Mountains; after sudden lapses of heart, followed by remorseful reconciliations; and having tried again and again to achieve the perfect consummation of our love, we had fathered and mothered our one and only child, Emily. In herself, she was of far more value and importance than all our exotic or devious desires and poetic ambitions and worthless posturing, which somehow had resulted in her birth on 19 May 1956.

We took Emily to Rosroe for her baptism in the Catholic church at Tully Cross. Nora Mortimer, Georgie's mother, was her godmother. Patricia had wanted a Catholic christening. We agreed that it would be better for Emily to be brought up in a Church that most Irish people attended every Sunday, rather than one only full at weddings and funerals. Emily screamed over the font, and Nora said this meant she would have a very long life. My mother felt that I was trying to annoy the family, but was glad that the poor child would at least have *some* religion.

A month after Emily's birth I wrote in a notebook that I was 'as happy as any man has ever been or is likely to become. Blissful to be making love on a deserted afternoon in a shuttered room, the rest of the world remote from us as distant cars on the road across the valley, our child of a former moment such as this asleep under her canopy in the garden.'

We did our nest-building mostly after our child was born, under the pressure of her little mouth opening to be fed. When I should have been writing a poem to celebrate her birth, I gave orders to carpenters, masons and plasterers to begin rebuilding the house by knocking it down. With paternal pride I wanted to remedy all its faults from the ground to the top of the roof, perfecting the house for my family and intending it to last, like Milford, for generations.

So I watched men work for me instead of working, and corrupted myself with power derived from money I had not earned, to satisfy my lust to live in a large, beautiful, old house in perfect condition. I wrote nothing because I was too busy creating separate studies in which my wife and I would in future not disturb each other's writing.

Patricia used to read a book and smoke a Player's cigarette through her ivory holder, with the baby's warm bottle tucked under her chin and the teat in the baby's mouth. Inhaling dust as well as smoke, they had no refuge from the cacophony of club hammers hacking old mortar from stone walls, men whistling 'Danny Boy' again and again. Though I helped with the feeding and changing of nappies, I spent more time away from the screams and the tears, involved in the passions of the building site.

This commotion was not what Patricia wanted, it made her weep. More and more cement, lime and sand would arrive on lorries, rot-proof hemlock for rafters and joists, blue and purple quarry slates for the roof, while our overdraft soared, requiring more letters she hated writing to Daddy for money. We sent him photographs of the wreckage as proof of our plight, knowing he would not want his daughter and granddaughter to live in such a mess.

Week after week would come a fat envelope with fourteen to eighteen pages in nineteenth-century script on foolscap airmail paper; always a wealth of patriarchal advice, Gothic sentimentalities and warnings of destitution if we disobeyed his commands.

Marriage made me greedy to acquire land, made me extravagant with

Patricia's money as well as mine, incurring big overdrafts. Possession of Lake Park, though in my wife's name, made me want more land to pass on to our child and her children. After Mary and Gerry gave me money to buy and farm another forty acres, the duty of an owner to improve his land, making a meadow out of scrub, obsessed me, regardless of the cost. First, I supervised the erection of miles of barbed-wire fences on milled oak stakes; then the ploughing of worn-out pasture that had reverted to gorse; followed by liming, fertilising, harrowing and reseeding the ground with deep-rooting herbs that would draw nutrients from the subsoil and survive a drought.

Faber not only published poetry but books by gentleman farmers who inspired readers to squander money on a fiction of making the world a healthier place. Sir George Stapledon convinced me. His variable lists of deep-rooting herbs to include in seed mixtures – chicory, burnet, cocksfoot, wild white clover, yarrow – restored poetry to farming. Instead of reading or trying to write poetry, I could sink my arms into seeds of all colours and sizes on the barn floor in the spring and watch them growing all summer – or as long as our money would last.

When I tried to write poetry, I found I had nothing to say. Love lyrics of Brittany and Crete died into epic rebuilding of Lake Park. When I felt the lyric dying, I started building on an epic scale. What madness!

In the autumn of 1956, expecting work on our house to be finished by Christmas, we received a telegram from Johannesburg informing us that Peggy had died. In perfect health the previous day, she had stirred in the middle of the night and her stirring had woken Keesje. A few seconds later she died in his arms.

Our immediate response was to invite Keesje and his sons to recover at Lake Park. A few weeks later the three arrive, Simon, aged seven and a half, Meiert, only five. We realised that Keesje was in deep distress, unable to make up his mind what to do. He was a handsome willowy giant, two metres tall, charming in manners, mercurial in temperament, sardonic in humour, with the will of a rebel that his father had crushed. Kind by nature, he hated apartheid and the ill-treatment of blacks. His father, he told me, had once found a night watchman asleep in his garden and had punched him so hard in the face that his hands were covered in blood. The night watchman did not dare to hit back because he feared this might have landed him in prison.

Keesje's mother had hated Peggy, and his father had mistrusted them all.

The autopsy result of mitral stenosis was delayed so long that Keesje came to Ireland with a suspicion on his mind that Peggy had been poisoned.

I advised him to ask his father for an allowance, equivalent to Patricia's, to study for a four-year degree at London University, while also keeping an eye on his father's office and employees in the city.

'Daddy would never agree to that,' Keesje said.

'He will,' I argued, 'if you tell him how grateful you are for all that he has done for you and your children, and how you regret not having completed your degree at Oxford where he was generously supporting you.'

'Then you write the letter. I can't, but I'll sign what you type.' So I did this, and the day MCA received it he cabled his full agreement.

Meanwhile Patricia had helped Keesje to place Simon at Spyway in Dorset, a school that prepared boys for Eton or Winchester; and Meiert at a small nursery school in Devon. MCA agreed to remit funds to Patricia to pay the fees, but not to Keesje. The boys were to spend their holidays at Lake Park, where Keesje was welcome to stay as long as he wished. But he was reluctant to impose his misery on our happiness.

Over Christmas with the children at Lake Park, he produced his will, leaving everything, including the guardianship of his sons, to Patricia.

Both he and Patricia used to drive at suicidal speed from Lake Park to Dublin on those narrow, twisty roads before they were straightened. Arriving home one evening in Patricia's Humber Hawk, Keesje told me he had driven the twenty-five miles in twenty-five minutes. Once Patricia came home badly shaken, but unhurt. At sixty miles an hour on the Bray road, she had seen a car coming around a corner towards her at high speed on the wrong side, and she had immediately crossed to *her* wrong side and passed it, avoiding a head-on collision. I could never have done that.

Patricia took the boys to London to catch their trains back to school towards the end of January, and stayed on a day or two at the Onslow Court Hotel in South Kensington to be near Keesje's digs. On the evening of Tuesday 29 January, I answered the phone in the hall at Lake Park and heard the faint voice of Patricia on a crackly line, telling me that Keesje had hired a plane that afternoon and nosedived into a field near Epping Forest. Instantly killed. I went over to be with Patricia in London. At the inquest on Friday, the coroner, Mr L.F. Beacle, recording a verdict of accidental death, remarked, 'What did happen will never be known.'

On MCA's orders to his London office, the remains of Keesje were shipped by Union Castle from Southampton to Cape Town for burial in Johannesburg. To avoid the risk of mariners refusing to sail on a ship carrying a corpse, the lead-lined coffin was contained in a box marked NATURAL HISTORY SPECIMEN.

Guilt haunted us at Lake Park for having done too little to help and perhaps too much that wrongly allowed Keesje to feel that his children might not need him because Patricia and I would look after them well. Keesje had left in his office a copy of a recent letter he had written to his 'Dearest Mamma' in which he referred to himself as not wanting to be 'strung round Richard's neck like some great rotting albatross'. When this trauma imposed its guilt, Patricia and I were already stressed by the conflict between my love of country life and hers of sophisticated literary conversation.

One of my reactions was to hire half a dozen more craftsmen to complete the reconstruction of the house and courtyard faster, while Patricia despaired that the building would ever be finished. Sometimes she longed to be free of the home in which she felt I was walling her up. I convinced myself that I was building and farming for the good of our family, while she shut herself away in her study upstairs, reading and writing, chain-smoking and sipping wine.

She had taken on the role of writer as keenly as I had the role of parent. She wanted to write poems, and I wanted to have children. The exchange was pulling us apart. She shrugged me off as a farmer, turned away if I asked her to look at a field of my newly seeded grass and herbs. I walked out of the room if she quoted Mauriac, Bernanos or Pascal.

Our hearts had joined in the restoration of the house, which I loved because it was hers. But the role I wanted her to play in the house became repugnant to the writer she wanted to be. She often said she would love me better in ten or twenty years' time. By then I would have understood why she had turned her head away from the fields of rape I wanted her to admire, because I would have read in her own copy of Pascal's *Pensées* in an English translation this passage which gives a clue as to how she felt about my insatiable hunger to acquire and improve more land:

> It is not in space that I must seek my human dignity, but in the ordering of my thought. It will do me no good to own land. Through space the universe grasps me and swallows me up like a speck; through thought I grasp it.

We bought ponies for the boys to ride in their holidays.

As I held her, she seemed to feel that I was not thinking of her, but of someone else holding her thus, changing my body to that of a man I might have wanted, or changing her sex in my arms into mine and mine into hers: and she would always say it was perfect, to please me. I never knew if she was lying, or why she was lying; and if she kissed me suddenly with the light on and the curtains open, I had to withdraw and close them. I did not want to be seen kissing my wife by an open window with the lights on and the curtains open. She rightly resented this.

The Red Bank used to be a restaurant in d'Olier Street with a fish bar at the back, separated from the public bar by a wall of glass. Later it became a Church of Perpetual Adoration, and more recently, across the road from the *Irish Times*, a hostel for students and travellers. I remember eating black sole on a Saturday night in May when Patricia and I played host to a writer she wanted to meet because she was lonely and bored at Lake Park: a not-yet-distinguished author of a book she admired, called *Maria Cross*, about Catholic French novelists. Conor Cruise O'Brien had accepted my invitation on the phone at his office in the Department of External Affairs.

We sat beside the door with our backs to the glass wall that kept out the noise and smoke of the bar crowded with men. Conor sat facing us, often breaking into French to impress Patricia. I thought he was showing off but she was awed by his brilliance.

Raising a glass of wine to her, he quipped *le sang du pauvre*, and his eyes turned up as if inside his head, showing their whites. Then he seemed to recognise and smile at a friend at the far end of the bar. Again and again he did this, usually after a witticism in French. I wondered whether we might ask the friend to join us, another sophisticate who might have amused Patricia. But in a quick glance over my shoulder I caught sight of Conor in a mirror on the far wall of the bar, smiling at himself.

Driving home, I told Patricia, expecting her to snort. She looked away and asked, 'When are we going to see him again?' I invited him to stay at Lake Park for the Whit weekend.

I fetched him from Dublin on the Saturday morning, and when he arrived, Patricia took him to his room and showed him around the house to see things she had designed herself: our Burmese teak dining-room furniture, bedroom walls painted in eggshell lemon, pink, mauve and orange, her strange Scandinavian backstairs, with open treads fixed by wrought-iron rods to a single solid slanting beam, no banisters but ropes as on the gangway of a ship, beautiful but precarious as herself. His tour included my new study with whitewashed walls up a flight of granite steps to the loft of a former barn in the courtyard. Finally, he turned to Patricia and said, 'As Bob Hope remarked, "Everything I like in an apartment: all done over in contrasting shades of money."'

This killed Patricia's enjoyment of the house just when the hammers had at last stopped hammering and the paint had dried on the walls. It reminded us both that the money we had spent on the house, not having been earned by ourselves but prised out of her father in South Africa, was tainted.

A moment in the drawing room at Lake Park after lunch: Rocky's face at the French windows; a bird cherry tree framed in the oval window that Patricia had designed to stop me inserting a golden rectangle; her choice of yellow and white fleur-de-lys wallpaper; mine of an Irish oak floor polished with beeswax; and a log fire burning. I suggested that we should go for a drive to call on Conor's in-laws, a couple who were equally fond of books and mountain pastures. But Conor and Patricia preferred to stay indoors listening to a torrent of French hexameters on two LPs: *La comédie Française joue Phèdre de Racine pour les universités du monde entier*, an album I had asked her to buy in Paris.

Rather than watch them preen themselves in each other's eyes with knowing looks through this great classic, I walked my land to admire the growth of deep-rooting herbs and grasses planted at an unaffordable cost.

At dinner we drank two bottles of Château Léoville-Barton, then drove to the Meeting of the Waters at Avoca to drink until closing time at a pub recommended by Conor. The ceiling and walls were covered with souvenirs, signatures of famous people, a British army balaclava helmet and a copy of the Proclamation of the Irish Republic.

Revived by more claret at lunch on Sunday, Conor surprised me by saying he wanted to be driven home to his house on the summit of Howth in the afternoon. Patricia insisted on driving him, and said to me, as she was leaving Lake Park, 'Don't worry, I'll be back in a couple of hours.' At seven I rang Conor to ask what time she had left. 'We're having a party. She'll be leaving soon,' he replied. Our phone used to be cut off from ten at night until eight the next day. At a quarter to ten I rang again. Patricia herself told me she was sorry for being delayed by the party, but it was almost over and she would soon be coming.

Unable to leave Emily alone in the house, I spent the night fearing Patricia had crashed on the way home. She returned at seven in the morning, exhausted, with an oval bruise on her chin, a purple contusion not quite hidden by powder. 'I went to the bathroom and by mistake picked up another woman's powder compact and caught this nasty infection,' she explained. 'It will go in a few days.' Her medical degree from Oxford made me trust her diagnosis. 'It wasn't safe for me to drive home after drinking more than I wanted at the party.'

About two weeks later, when she returned after a day's shopping in Dublin with another oval bruise on the other side of her chin, she had to admit that it was a painful love bite. To make sure that I would forgive her, she said, 'I prefer it with you.' Justifying myself to myself for seldom having come home late and never having stayed out a whole night, I forgave her in return for her forgiveness.

The third time she returned to Lake Park in a state of shock, though not from a physical injury, she was trembling when she got out of the car and clutched me for support like a child. It was all over, she said. They had been drinking coffee in Robert's on Grafton Street, and she had told him that, because of the love bites, I had found out about their affair. Not her fault but his. Conor's reaction had been swift. In silence he picked up the bill, paid it at the counter, returned to her table, and said, '*C'est tout!*' That's all. Then he had walked out.

I hoped the affair was over, but it lingered as a wound that only one man could have healed, and Conor was no healer.

Things looked well now at Lake Park. We had room to entertain and we both enjoyed entertaining, though our pleasure was polluted by guilt. When her mother came to visit, we drank too much at dinner, they quarrelled and there were tears. My mother-in-law flung in my face that I was living on the Avises. Two girls did our housework and childminding. A gardener worked full-time, and two boys minded the sheep.

Seán and Eileen Ó Faoláin, excellent hosts to writers, artists and architects in Killiney, lunched or dined with us as often as we did with them. Joe Ackerley spent a week at Lake Park, and I asked him to advise Patricia, who would not then have taken such advice from me, to write a novel, instead of trying to write poetry all day.

'Not a bad idea,' Joe said. He rang his friend Elizabeth Bowen, who invited us to lunch at Bowenscourt. We drove across the Wicklow Mountains and the fertile plains and valleys of Carlow, Kilkenny, Tipperary and Cork to a grey gaunt mansion facing a deer park where cattle (not Elizabeth's) were grazing behind an obtrusive barbed-wire fence much too near the front door. Elizabeth walked us through vacant rooms the size of barns with original William Morris wallpaper. When Patricia upset a glass of wine on an antique sofa, Elizabeth comforted her by saying, 'I'm always doing that, it's no harm at all.'

In the car on the way home, Joe advised Patricia, 'Write a novel, dear. Like Elizabeth. You can't spend eight hours a day writing poetry.' Advice that she took to heart. She opened a foolscap ledger with blue-lined pages and wrote the title *Playing the Harlot, or Morning Coffee*. A strong incentive for turning her back on the property that held my attention.

There were twin beds in our marital bedroom at the back of the house. Opening my eyes in the morning I could see the greeny-grey and silver trunks of tall beeches, brightening at the edges of the wood, which darkened with pines here and there as it rose towards the mountain beyond our fences. Emily's nurse, Ann Brady, the daughter of a sheep farmer, brought us breakfast in bed. Eating soft-boiled eggs with toast, reclining on pillows, we watched the sun disgorging gold along the dark aisles of the beech wood that sheltered us from the north wind. The roof over the stables had begun to sag under its ancient burden of blue quarry slates. I had it re-slated.

'I thought I had married a poet but he's turned out to be a farmer,' Patricia had reason to remark to a neighbour. She would have been happier if I had helped her to edit a literary magazine. I could never encourage her writing as much as she had encouraged mine. Now pedigree Wicklow Mountains Cheviot sheep were taking my love in revenge for her love of a man with a brilliant mind. She wanted to get rid of possessions in order to concentrate on ideas that appealed to him. I got ideas by fencing and wiring, planting and reaping, improving the soil of her sloe-hedge field and flushing a flock of ewes on rich grass to make them conceive twin lambs.

My agreement with Professor Earl McCarthy, in the autumn of 1957, was to deliver twelve pregnant ewes to the athletic grounds of University College, Dublin. The Medical Research Council would pay the bill, so I could charge, he said, a fairly high price. By research on the foetus, McCarthy was about to make a discovery that would revolutionise our knowledge of the origins of life.

One or two of his colleagues regarded him as a genius, who might win a Nobel Prize if only he could keep off the drink for the few months it would take to complete his research. They knew he had needed to be so deviously cautious in his behaviour, and so polite in soliciting the support of members of the Catholic hierarchy on the Senate of the National University of Ireland before his appointment, that as soon as he was confirmed in the professorship of physiology for life, he had to relax and enjoy the privilege.

Now he was pulling himself together. A laboratory had been assigned to him, equipped with baths in which the sheep would remain submerged and anaesthetised during the opening up of the womb for his experiments on the living foetus.

My worry was to try not to supply him with ewes that might be barren. The chest of my ram was raddled to mark the rump of each ewe that was tupped. By November I delivered the sheep to the university, and the cheque duly arrived from the Medical Research Council. My flock at Lake Park began to drop their lambs in a foot of snow the following spring, and produced more than two hundred. Had Earl been as lucky? I rang him to ask in July.

'Richard! I've been meaning to ring you myself,' he said at once, 'because I need your advice. My laboratory assistant wants to know if this would be a good time to send our ram lambs to the Dublin market, and what sort of price we should get?'

'About £5 a head,' I suggested.

'And could you give me an idea about the cost of grazing? The Medical Research Council is complaining that the university is charging too much for grazing our sheep. Their numbers have more than doubled. My assistant loves looking after sheep: he's a Tipperary lad. He goes every day to count them, and gives them injections for braxy and pulpy kidney and God knows what. I don't think he feels happy when he's shut up all day in a lab.'

'Earl, do you mind me asking, what about the experiments?'

'We weren't ready in time with the equipment. But we'll do much better next year: we'll have twenty ewes instead of twelve.'

'Is the Medical Research Council happy about this?'

'What can they say? Wasn't I elected to their board last week!'

I saw him only once more, in Dublin six years later, when I happened to enter a pub that was strange to me on Baggot Street, to make a phone call during the evening rush hour. As I was easing through the crowd between the tables and the bar in the gloomy interior, I heard my name called out by someone sitting in a dark, huddled group, and saw a pair of horn-rimmed spectacles with bottle-glass lenses looking up at me appealingly, as if from a circle of despair. 'Do you know who I am?'

'Of course, you're Earl McCarthy.'

'I was afraid you might have forgotten.'

'How could I forget? The sheep, the laughs we had.' His face was on fire with a purple glow from too much whiskey. He put an arm around my shoulder, and made me stoop to hear in confidence what he urgently needed to say.

It was 'something I've been meaning to tell you, dear boy, for a very long time. Do you remember in your house at Lake Park you accused me of going to bed with your wife? No? What I told you then was true. She had come to my room at night and sat on my bed, endlessly smoking and waving her cigarette holder while she talked and talked, drinking more and more wine. For hours I was wondering would she ever leave the room, and give me a chance to go to sleep. I hadn't the courage to tell you then,' he confessed, and his voice became embarrassingly loud, 'but I've got to tell you now. It wasn't your wife that I wanted to sleep with at Lake Park, but you.'

I fooled myself into thinking that the practical business of owning sheep – getting up and going out with a torch on the mountain in the middle of the night if a dog happened to bark in the distance – might in the future enable me to write a pastoral poem. In two years I produced more food from natural sources by natural means than a man could eat in a long life. In spite of our problems, I was as happy as if I had inherited Milford. Patricia had become pregnant again. But at the end of August 1957 she suffered a miscarriage in the middle of the night, and woke me up with a scream as the water and blood started to pour. I feared she was going to die; held the bowl under her, the way she said. She was a doctor, so knew what needed to be done. Then she told me to look in the bowl, and I saw, lying in the blood and water, the body of a male child, perfectly formed, a thumb in his mouth.

I carried the bowl down the backstairs and out to the yard and into a barn to pick up a spade, then out through a wicket in the huge yard gate to climb up a slippery bank into the beech wood.

Larch twigs impede the spade as it slices through leaf mould, a scatter of beechnuts, food for red squirrels, who survive here. As clouds are dimming the moonlight, I shine a torch. He looks like me. Yet also like a figurine moulded from clay and fired thousands of years ago. Having dug deep enough, I tip the body from the bowl, gently, and look at him as he lies in the earth: head with a high forehead, full of intelligence; nose and chin, mouth and ears like mine in a photograph my mother has kept from my infancy; the eyes closed.

After touching my tongue, I inscribe on his forehead with my forefinger the sign of the tree, and recite in the name of the Father and of the Son and of the Holy Ghost, though I do not believe in them. I bless him in his grave as I was blessed in childhood; then bury my unborn son.

Patricia never completely recovered. A month later, in the autumn, she wanted to move to London. Wives were never as happy at Lake Park as their husbands. A hundred years ago a wife had drowned herself in the lake. Gébler's first wife had absconded with their son and sent him divorce papers from Reno.

Together we had been living beyond our means, deluded by windfall wealth and expectations of more to come. So I agreed to go, sell the place if her father would allow, sell it in spite of his threatening edicts if necessary, go with her to London where I could find work, reviewing or teaching, and she could enjoy a more literary life. We found a flat in Kensington, where she worked on her novel. From time to time I returned to Lake Park: to see my grandmother just before she died in January 1958, and to attend to the lambing that occurred in deep snow in March.

In June Patricia flew out to Johannesburg to secure her father's agreement for her to sell Lake Park and buy a house in London, or else increase her allowance to cover the cost of renting a flat and keeping Lake Park as a holiday home for the children. I remained in London to look after Emily. Patricia's first two letters were affectionate, and said she was hoping to come to the point with her father soon. Her third was a volte-face. She wanted a divorce.

My mother, who was in England at the time, was pleased. 'Now you've got a chance to escape.' My father took a sterner line. 'You will have to allow her to divorce you. A gentleman must.' But that would have meant losing custody and control of Emily.

Patricia, when she returned, had no objection to being divorced by me or to my having custody of Emily. In this case I promised that Emily would have two homes and spend time with each of us. I would have to take up residence in England for nearly a year to obtain the divorce. I did not name Conor, as this might have ruined his career in External Affairs. Patricia provided other evidence.

I hated her for wanting a divorce.

Mary and Gerry rescued me financially and gave me money to buy an old house in Muswell Hill, a quiet north London suburb. Once proceedings had begun, Patricia, in another volte-face, moved from Kensington to Dublin, where, for the rest of her life, she would live on the top two floors of a large Georgian house on the corner of Wilton Terrace, overlooking the Grand Canal near Baggot Street bridge.

For the next academic year I taught occasionally for the Workers' Educational Association in the suburbs, and a weekly class in poetry and drama at Morley College. But I would spend only long enough in London to divide the house into a ground-floor flat, which I would sell, and a double-storey maisonette level with treetops in Queen's Park, which I would let, in order to return to the west of Ireland after obtaining a divorce.

Before our marriage, Patricia's touch had given me speech. Afterwards, my possession of her, and her possession of me, reduced the poetry of our love to marital arguments. With separate beds and study apartments, I still wanted to possess her, let nobody else become her crutch. I felt bound to prevent her from having a nervous breakdown as a result of the strain of being married to me. Loving her, I tried to smother all my problems in her body, and to solve them in endless dialogue, concealing nothing that was in my heart, often painful for both of us. I buried the part of myself that wanted to break loose under tons of cement, blue Bangor slates, ground limestone and the hooves of four hundred sheep.

Looking back, Patricia and I agreed that the best of our marriage was Emily.

When the divorce was granted in June 1959, I returned to Inishbofin for the first time in four years, and wrote a poem that I revised and published forty years later, called 'Grounds'.

Grounds

You were not there. I don't know who
That morning lit your cigarette:
But I was there because of you
To take the consequence of deceit
Asking a man in a wig, who'd not
Known or loved you, to interfere
Between us and our daughter.

Four years ago a civil farce
Was paid for, and they dragged in God,
Contracts, champagne, telegrams, cars:
But now needless pomp had dwindled

To needless echoes – 'Yes, m'Lud,'
'No, m'Lud' – and I had lost you,
Lost everything we had gone through.

In white letters on black paper
A judge decreed we were dissolved
From all the good we owed each other,
From all the bad left unresolved.
What we were hangs dead in the air
As dust from a second-hand book
Picked off a shelf and put back.

In a dream you appear to me – sick
And lost in rain on a high cliff
Crying and careless where you walk.
A lighthouse flashes far, far off:
But I cannot, though I try to, speak
To stop the harm in all I've done
Dragging you down and down.

According to Tony White, who watched me arrive at Inishbofin on 17 June 1959 on board The Squire's fifty-foot lugsail-rigged fishing and cargo boat, sixty years old and leaking, I brought a box of books, a carton of orange juice and a case of wine. This put him on his guard, as he felt the owner of that indicative luggage might impair the island culture that he loved. Black-haired, dark-eyed and swarthy, he was almost my height, but stronger and stunningly handsome, dressed in torn darned jeans and a donkey jacket over a white Aran sweater. The buckle of his leather belt bore the eagle and swastika emblem of the German army whose defeat at Cassino in 1944 had cost Tony's older brother, a poet, his life.

A bilingual Londoner with an English father and French mother, after national service as a second lieutenant training soldiers to drive lorries, Tony had studied English under F.R. Leavis at Downing College, Cambridge. He was trying to support himself by lobster fishing from a currach while writing a play. Would he be a rival or would he be a friend? And what kind of a friend would he be?

At first neither of us was glad to meet another Oxford or Cambridge graduate, each of us having 'chucked up everything and just cleared off' from London to write on the same remote island as yet untouched by writers. I had just finished teaching at night for the Workers' Educational Association. Bofin men said to me, 'I love that man: Tony doesn't act like an Englishman at all.' As an Irishman who sounded irredeemably British, I was jealous of this praise. Paul Ferris, radio critic of the *Observer*, had described my voice in a poetry reading on the BBC as 'languid, infuriating and irrelevant'. Tony's voice and looks, as Romeo in a Marlowe Society production of *Romeo and Juliet*, had made him the star of his generation at Cambridge – knowledge that I would gain when his theatre-director friends, Toby Robertson and David Jones, would arrive for a holiday later that summer.

Earlier in 1959 I had met Robert Shaw and Peter O'Toole when those rivals were making their names as stars in *The Long and the Short and the Tall* at the Royal Court Theatre. Tony, playing the part of a fisherman on the island, seemed to have as much talent and charisma as they had, but purged of ambition. Two or three years earlier, he told me, he had torn up his contract with the Old Vic to play leading parts in Shakespeare's plays on a tour of America because he had grown sick of acting and the off-stage lifestyle of actors. He had wanted to see if he could write a play, and had taken a job as a lighter of gas lamps in the streets of the East End of London. But when the weekly magazine *Picture Post* featured 'this audacious, purifying, elemental move' with pages of photographs, Tony had quit, revolted by his own celebrity.

Then he had taken and enjoyed a job as a petrol-pump attendant, until Laurence Olivier, arriving in a Bentley and recognising Tony, started talking to him in a stage voice loud enough for the garage owner to hear. As a result, the owner had promoted Tony to manager, but he had promptly resigned and gone on a walking tour of Ireland, which had brought him eventually to Inishbofin.

'Stand-offish,' Tony later said I had been, until the day I summoned the courage, or suppressed enough jealousy, to walk along the lane on the cliff beside the harbour to the cottage he was renting for five shillings a week. His landlords were three old brothers who seldom emerged from the darkness of a cottage in which they had boarded up the windows. I wanted to see how Tony was living.

His bed was a sleeping bag on the concrete floor with no mattress, and he cooked on the open turf fire with a kettle steaming on a crane. There was one other artefact in the house, decaying on the damp lime-washed stone under a small window facing south across the breakers in the mouth of the harbour. It was a flimsy paperback edition of *Fighting Terms* by Thom Gunn. Inside the flyleaf I saw inscribed: 'To Tony with love from Thom – a book which falls apart on being opened'.

Tony used to rile me by saying that my attitude to him changed from that moment, as if I had checked his credentials and found they were better than I had judged from his working-class clothes. He would remember silly things done or said by his friends, and enjoy deflating our pompous or pretentious absurdities. 'Your mother,' he would say, 'was relieved to find in me a heavily disguised gentleman.'

One evening he came to my room at Day's Hotel, where I had board and lodging, with as much crayfish as I could eat, for less than half the rent I received for my maisonette in London. The room contained a double iron bedstead with brass knobs, covered by coarse woollen blankets stained by mildew on a damp horsehair mattress. The floor was pitch pine without linoleum or carpet. I sat facing him near the window that looked out on the fishing boats lying at the quay or moored in the inner harbour. The glow of sunset was fading and I lit a candle because the hotel dynamo had broken down. I had asked him to read me *The Ancient Mariner*, and at last he agreed.

When he had finished the poem, I was so moved by his presence and his voice that I wanted to kiss him. For one precarious moment I wondered would I dare, and how would he respond, and where would this lead us both? He gave me the answer with his eyes, letting me know, without saying a word, that to touch him would be an unfortunate mistake. Aware of that limit, our friendship would last for his life.

Twelve years later I addressed him in a poem of fifty or sixty lines, which he cut to four, suggesting I call it 'Double Negative':

> You were standing on the quay
> Wondering who was the stranger on the mailboat
> While I was on the mailboat
> Wondering who was the stranger on the quay.

The pookaun I had left in Rosroe in 1955 had fallen apart in my absence and someone had made a henhouse out of the timber. Not to show respect for the remains of a boat that had provided food for a family seemed shameful to Pat

Concannon and other Bofiners. Each boat had her own personality and style the fishermen revered. It was wrong to abuse her, though she could be pressed as hard on the sea as a man might have courage to press her.

My marriage having failed, I had come back to Bofin to learn more from Pat about the sea and gain enough experience of handling an open boat in bad weather to make a poem of his heroic survival. He advised me not to buy a pookaun but a larger boat that I could live aboard and handle alone. A Galway hooker would be seaworthy enough, he said, to cross the Atlantic, and I could buy one from Michael Schofield, another survivor of the Cleggan Disaster.

Her bilges stank but her name was immaculate. The *Ave Maria* was the last of a long line of hookers built for the fishermen of the Claddagh, where, in the early nineteenth century, there had been three hundred that were used for transport, cargo and fishing along the coast between Galway, the Aran Islands, Slyne Head and Achill. Her builder, Seán Cloherty of Inishnee, had died on the job in 1922, having completed no more than her oak frame and spars. His daughter had planed, caulked and tarred the hull, launching her at Long Wall in Galway during the civil war.

For several years the Raineys of the Claddagh had fished the *Ave Maria* on Galway Bay, then a priest had sailed her for pleasure in the Cleggan area before selling her to Schofield. She had a reputation of bringing her owners good luck. At thirty-four feet overall, she was a small hooker of the size and shape known in Irish as a *gleoiteog*, meaning 'something grand'. Single-masted, she carried a lugsail mounted on a larch boom and gaff, a foresail on the front stay, and a jib on a bowsprit that could be taken inboard.

Once I became her owner I lavished all my time and money, as I had done on the restoration of Lake Park, on reviving her former glory as the fastest and best-looking *gleoiteog* on Galway Bay. I travelled to Dublin and London, purchasing from ships' chandlers all that might be needed to put to sea with a four-berth cabin in the centre, a flush toilet in the bows, a Primus stove on gimbals for cooking, a cockpit for steering with a carved oak tiller, and an outboard engine fitted inboard through the sharply raked transom.

Tony, having lost his lobster pots in a storm, worked with energy and panache on her refurbishment, assisting two island men, Jim Cunnane, a boatwright, and Colman Coyne, a sailmaker, whose skills had not been required or practised for many years. Those had been years of stagnation and despondency on the island, with a poor market for fish, seldom a tourist arriving, and most of the young going abroad. Inishark was soon to be evacuated. The death of islands was in the air and on the news. For Tony the job offered variety, risk and privation. For me, while Emily and her Avis cousins, Simon and Meiert, played with the four sons of Margaret and Miko Day, restoring the old hooker was the start of a new life.

That winter my parents gave me an airline ticket to visit them for three months over Christmas 1959 on their Southern Rhodesian farm. There I taught some classes in the school they had established for the children of farm workers, and met, the day he came to lunch, a black poet, lawyer and politician, Herbert Chitepo, who gave me a volume of his poetry in Shona. Chitepo was doomed to die during the future struggle for independence, murdered in Lusaka on the order of a rival black politician. All our table talk at Kiltullagh Farm was about multiracialism, also doomed to extinction.

One morning at a desk in a thatched rondavel, with a view of anthills and fever trees, five hundred miles from the Indian Ocean, I wrote the opening lines of a poem called 'The Last Galway Hooker'.

Back at Inishbofin in February, without Tony, who was employed as a labourer delivering sacks of coal from a lorry on his back to houses in London, I continued to write the poem in my room overlooking the quay where Jim and Colman were rigging the *Ave Maria*. All her spars were larch from the Forest of Cong, shaped by Jim with a handsaw, an adze and a plane. On account of her name, her gunwale was painted blue, her hull remained black, and I chose not to bark her calico sails, which would have made them dark brown, but to keep them white. In two years' time, her sails would be made of tan Terylene.

On Shrove Tuesday, 1 March 1960, we stepped the new mast, and after a blessing of the boat by Father Charles O'Malley, who sprinkled holy water on her deck and spars, Dr Maureen de Valera, a marine biologist and daughter of the president, hoisted the Irish flag. By St Patrick's Day the *Ave Maria* was rigged and ready to sail from a mooring in the harbour on a trial run on the open sea.

That was when I discovered, as the man before the mast, how strong he had to be to hoist the sails and lift the anchor of a hooker by himself. Big Pat Concannon and Pateen Cloherty sat back to back in the cockpit, the tiller between them, arguing as we got under way. All went well until we reached the narrow, choppy mouth between the Gun Rock and the Dog Fish Breaker. As the bows plunged in the troughs and rose on the crests of wave after wave, I felt seasick and thought what a fool I was to have squandered on a boat more than a house would have cost.

Then a shackle bolt that had not been screwed tightly enough worked loose, and the bowsprit sprung free from an iron clasp by which it was held on deck. I had to hold it down while the boat was heaving and my stomach retching until the two Pats had brought the boat back to her harbour moorings. But I didn't give up, and was never overcome by nausea.

To make the boat earn the cost of her upkeep, I chose, rather than enter into competition with the local fishermen, to take tourists out of Cleggan on combined sea angling and day trips to Inishbofin. Sea angling had started in Westport and Kinsale but nowhere on the Connemara coast. Margaret Day was keen to provide lobster lunches on the island, and tourists would book and pay for their passages at the Pier Bar in Cleggan. Matthew O'Malley, a white-haired veteran of Mesopotamia in the First World War, owned the bar and ran it with his daughter, Eileen.

My plan angered Tony and nearly destroyed our friendship. He wrote from London:

> I'm writing in a white heat of fury after seeing your advert in the Spectator. You've bitterly depressed me and I heartily wish I'd never encouraged you to buy the Ave Maria – in fact, I wish you'd sell her now rather than do this grotesque recouping. Do you really want Bofin to turn into an appalling smarty-pants country pub? Obviously you must. I grant you discovered Bofin before me, but your attitude has always been a tourist-landowner one, you've never lived in base cottage there, so I consider I have some proprietary right to sling at your head.
>
> I was aiming to come out next week and start some sailing with you, and spend the month of May lobster-fishing. Now I feel I never want to see the place again.

In reply to this, I argued that Day's Hotel could house at the most a score of visitors:

> I should prefer that some of those people were readers now and then of the Spectator, the Observer and The Times. The Ave Maria has cost so much to perfect, and would cost annually so much to keep afloat, that if I wish to keep her at all I am bound to try and make her pay. This does not strike me as the moral iniquity which you seem to think it is. By working the small amount of capital which my sister gave me, and working it sensibly, I can get months

and months every year of free time for writing, and I don't have to write or publish a line merely for profit's sake. Your suggestion of sailing her out of Bofin to somewhere in England or France struck me as pointless. What should I do with her when we got there, *if we* got there knowing nothing about deep sea navigation the two of us?

More than by this letter, Tony was pacified by the first draft of my poem 'The Last Galway Hooker', and planned to return to Bofin. 'I'm at your service for anything,' he wrote on 7 May, 'providing it's wild and energetic enough.'

To publicise the angling and day trips to Inishbofin, the Irish Tourist Board sent their photographer, Tom Hayde, to take photographs of the *Ave Maria* under sail in the harbour. Tom took his pictures from the shore, while Pat Concannon sailed the boat as close to the shore as I, standing before the mast, could persuade him to go. From the moorings in the harbour, he sailed east through the narrow channel by the quay to the inner harbour, known as 'the hole', and south around an islet called Glassilaun, and north down an even narrower mouth between Glassilaun and a rock, before turning west clear of rocks back to the main harbour. And then Tom wanted us to do the impossible.

The facts were turned into legend night after night in Miko's bar. I kept hearing bits and pieces of what we had been doing on board, as related by Pat to a chorus of fishermen, including a staunch man before the mast known as Johnny the Packet.

What Pat said to Johnny and his mates and what Johnny replied on their behalf I put together as follows:

> Me and Murphy put the new white sails on the *Ave Maria* beyond in the hole. Mainsail, foresail and jib. First tack, down the mouth of Glassilaun. Out by the current.
> *Down the mouth. Out by the current.*
> Murphy before the mast. Change the foresail.
> *Change the foresail.*
> My John went back in the pookaun. Beating her over the harbour he was. First tack across to Porth.
> *Across to Porth.*
> I seen the Dublin man from the Tourist Board running from Dooneen with his camera to the edge of the quay. Putting Inishbofin on the map.

Bofin on the map. Where it never was before.

Murphy'd spent a fortune turning Scuffle's half-rotten hooker into a yacht. Not one bit afraid of drowning himself and his crew. You'd find no holy pictures in *his* engine-room. That man put his faith in a shagging life raft.

A shagging life raft! Must have been idle rich.

Sure he was rotten with money, but what did he know about sailing? Never been out in a storm in his life. Sunshine fisherman. Still, he wanted to take the tiller from me to show the whole world he could sail.

You wouldn't give the tiller to a man like that?

I gave him the tiller. Says I, 'Sail her now, Murphy, if you're able!' I went up before the mast. Across to the corner of the quay from Porth he brought the boat.

Fair enough.

Listen! He takes her over the current and across the hole. God knows how he missed ramming the small boats moored there. Puts her about, catches more wind. Then down the mouth he lets her fly – the jackass! – tiller hard over, going straight for the quay.

Dear God! Straight for the quay. Heaven help you!

Murphy shouted to me, 'What will I do now, Pat?' I was before the mast. 'Do what you like with her now,' says I, 'she's your boat. I thought you told me you knew how to sail.' He couldn't handle her. 'Here!' I shouted, 'come out of that cockpit you mad greenhorn and give me the tiller.' I took the tiller. Blessed myself. Still he wasn't satisfied. Wanted more photographs.

More photographs! Working the head, he was, bringing tourists to Bofin. No better man. Plenty of porter for everyone in Miko's. Good luck to him!

'Pat,' he says in his English voice, real polite, 'please bring her round again by Glassilaun.' Up the mouth this time and into the hole we run, before turning back, beyond the moorings of the Topaz. Then down the mouth again, lying on her side, three sails full. The sea boiling over her deck. Surely the grandest picture a cameraman could find. And do you know what Murphy wanted me to do next?

What more could you do?

Wanted me to take her over the current from the mouth, let down sail, and turn her in sharp for the quay. What no man ever did in his born life!

Heavenly Lord! What did he know about boats except to sink them?

Lacking Roundstone's beauty, the village of Cleggan – four pubs, a shop, nine or ten houses – had never attracted tourists. More famous for its misery, Cleggan looked in 1960 as if the 1927 disaster had just occurred. The angled pier, at which long ago thirty or forty hookers and nobbies had been moored side by side, was now deserted unless a boat from Inishbofin arrived with mail, cattle, sheep, passengers or fish. And nothing, nobody came up or went down the quay without being noticed by Matthew or his daughter, Eileen, through a window in the door of the Pier Bar.

Fishnets hung from the ceiling, baked beans stood on the shelves beside bottled stout. A visitors' book for the *Ave Maria*'s tourists to sign was kept on the counter. The names of Charles Monteith and Rosemary Goad, a senior editor at Faber, appear on the first page, dated Easter Monday 1960. With Pateen as our helmsman ordering me to raise or lower sail, we caught four hundred pound of coalfish and white pollock on two hand lines, drifting at low tide close to Carraigmahog, a dangerous breaker between Inishbofin and Cleggan Head.

Sailing gave me strong, immediate satisfaction. It was easier than imagining in poetry the kind of hero I was not. But as soon as I stepped onto the *Ave Maria* to take charge of her, I discovered to my shame that a person I disliked in myself would take charge of me. In command, my ignorance of seamanship made me fearful, and in a crisis I'd make matters worse by shouting. That's why my friendship with Tony all but foundered on Whit Monday 6 June 1960.

Never had I handled a boat as large as the *Ave Maria* on my own. I admired Tony's verve and love of danger, but preferred to sail within sight of land and upwind from a safe anchorage. Crewing at the mast, he was wearing black jeans and a black T-shirt, with a mutinous red sweatband on his brow. His face and arms were swarthy as a lascar's. My place on board was the cockpit, and to make our tourists feel they were in safe hands, I wore a yachtsman's cap with a shiny black peak, a white plastic cover, and a gold-threaded anchor badge. Though I was an inch taller, Tony was far more robust. He was the master and I the novice of our disguises. Everyone noticed and nobody forgot him, including a Dutch family we took fishing that day, among them a tall girl called Ernie Raab, a jewellery designer.

The weather looked so good in the morning that we sailed to a shoal seldom fished because it was far away and treacherous. Larger pollock than we had ever caught hung themselves on our ten-feathered jigs at a depth that varied between twenty fathoms and five feet. I had no radar and knew of no landmarks to avoid the shallow ground. Once we caught sight of tangleweed growing on rock just under our keel – such was my ignorance. We were light-hearted and lucky, passing the day ankle-deep in dead fish, sinking lead-weighted lines to the bottom and reeling up fast, gulls diving on sprats, blood and fish guts drying on our gunwales, our virgin-blue hull wallowing in hellish dark water, our white calico sails furled.

Until the tide turned. Then the wind rose in a darkening sky, with the sea fermenting into white yeasty waves. So I ordered everyone to reel in quickly and stow the rods. We were six miles from the nearest harbour. Tony was squatting on the foredeck beside Ernie, holding her hand, his head close to her breast. What was he up to? I tugged on the cord of our small outboard engine without raising a spark.

No one seemed aware of the danger I had caused us to be in. This made me all the more worried. One of Ernie's relations said she had a fishhook sunk in the palm of her hand. Everyone up for'ard was focusing on how to remove the hook and ease her pain. Broadside to the waves, we were rocking perilously from side to side, as my voice rose in pitch and volume, ordering Tony to hoist the mainsail. I needed power to steer the boat into and over each wave. Meanwhile I felt impotent, standing in the cockpit with the tiller thrusting feebly against my thigh.

Tony hauled hard on the main halyard, but the jaws of the gaff jammed. A thin cord that laces the sail to the mast had fouled in the cringles. The boat was floundering and falling astern, with the mainsail half set and flogging in the breeze like a cat-o'-nine-tails. One big squall could have capsized her. I tried to show him how to loosen the cords that were binding the sail too tightly to the mast, by demonstrating with my hand circling anticlockwise. He seemed all the more perplexed the more I gesticulated and shouted. I was unaware of myself acting like a furiously impatient officer chastising a con-script, reminding Tony of all the bullshit he had endured for two years in the army after the war. So he drew the sword of his great theatre voice and struck me down with, 'Shut your cakehole!'

The intensity of his anger stunned me into silence. Though I was at fault, I was too proud to apologise, and felt powerless to respond. I had lost control of myself and the boat. With one furious tug, the outboard sparked, and power came slowly back from the engine's vibration through the soles of my feet up my spine to my head. Tony loosened the lacing, the mainsail rose to the hounds filling with air, followed by the foresail, and the hooker gathered speed, dipping her bowsprit and boom into crests of waves as she rose and plunged. Then he returned to comforting the injured girl, as I nursed my injured pride by attending to the boat I loved more than any person except my child in that year after my divorce.

I fixed my eyes through spray-flecked glasses on the sea, the sky and the sails, taking no notice of the people on board, provided they sat still, like a cargo of sheep whose legs have been tied. When we anchored as close to the east end of Bofin as the tide would allow us, Tony said firmly, 'I'm going ashore.' His voice seemed to come from the horizon rather than the deck, and I answered sheepishly, 'Very well', meaning the opposite.

That left me alone with my beloved boat. We'd planned to leave our passengers on the island, and to sail through the long summer twilight across the sea to the Renvyle Hotel, which had made the first booking of full charter of the boat for the following day. I'd not yet sailed a hooker single-handed. Before the backs of Tony and his girl were out of sight on the lane to the pub, I hauled up the anchor, and hoisted the three white sails, catching a light westerly breeze with a tinge of triumph from the setting sun.

Tomorrow I would beg Tony to forgive me on a crackly phone line after long delays in getting through four operators, each winding handles and inserting plugs at little post offices in Lettergesh, Clifden, Cleggan and Inishbofin. He might come back, he'd say, after a few months in London.

For the next fifteen years he would come and go, the best friend of all, wanting to possess or command neither people nor things, and never letting things or people command or possess him. Eventually I would tell innumerable listeners on the air, 'No friend ever helped me more. He could put his finger unerringly on any weak word in a poem, with such tact that in doing so he made it easy for me to see how the fault could be corrected, and my worst lines turned into my best.'

In July 1960 a tall, suave, German tourist, with short, silver-grey hair, booked a day's fishing on the *Ave Maria*, and with four other anglers we sailed in a light breeze to the wild shoals south of Inishark. Having once held the rank of captain in the German navy, he regarded it as his sole right to speak to me all day. Even when I moved from the cockpit to talk to someone else in the bows, he would follow and hog the conversation. I was still prejudiced against Germans because of the war, and resented having to entertain for seven hours a man who was paying me less than he might charge for seven minutes of his professional time in Germany.

'Before the war,' he told me, 'I was lieutenant in cruiser *Emden*. All over the world we sail. Yes, Colombo, we call. Beautiful country, Ceylon,' he said in a tone of imperial envy. The *Emden* was one of Hitler's pocket battleships.

'Did you meet my father, who was Mayor of Colombo in those days?'

'Ach no! I was junior officer then.'

'And later?'

'Later I have command of U-boat.'

'How interesting! So you probably know the sea off the west of Ireland better than I do. You might have caught sight of the *Ave Maria* through your periscope when she was trawling on this coast during the war.'

'Please?' He liked to hear me repeat what I had said so that he could improve his English, before answering. Then he lowered his voice, and declared firmly, as if he were showing me his clean hands: 'During the war I have office job.'

Three different German men piled themselves and their cameras and their picnic lunches onto the *Ave Maria* one morning, as we lay by the slippery steps at the end of the quay in Cleggan, without a word of greeting to me or my mate. As soon as they had grabbed the best positions on the cabin head, the fattest of them uttered these words of command: 'Please! The biggest rod!'

Early one season, when we had no other customers, another German booked a day's fishing for himself and a passage for his wife as a spectator. When I offered her a rod, he refused to allow her to take it, as he knew it would cost more if she did. Instead, he handed her a camera to take photographs of himself catching fish.

He sat on the cabin head a little forward of the engine hatch, in which I was standing, my eyes level with his knees. As we were heading out of Cleggan Bay on the motor, it felt much colder than on shore, and I watched him take out of his bag and put on a long field-grey coat with the buttons and insignia of the German army removed. Then he changed his shoes to a pair of jack-boots, and began to survey the islands through a pair of Zeiss binoculars, as if to show that Germany had not lost the war but won it by different means.

Soon the O'Malleys would begin to frown at locals who asked for pints of stout to be drawn from the wooden barrel and to smile only at tourists who drank bottled beer, wine and spirits. An old salt, who had sailed around the world as a deckhand on a cargo ship under a Geordie skipper, after waiting at the bar fifteen minutes to be served, having travelled from the island on a bad day, said to Eileen, who had been sitting by the fire talking to a tourist, 'If I'm not infringing upon your ease, Miss, will you please draw me a pint of stout.'

When I heard from John Montague that the American poet Theodore Roethke was coming to Ireland, I decided to try to entice him from the literary pub life of Dublin and invite him across to the west coast. Ambition prompted me: aged fifty-two, he was then at the height of his fame. I thought he might help me to find a publisher in America if he were to stay on Inishbofin for a few weeks and sail on my boat. We had never met, but I had introduced and praised three of his poems on the BBC Third Programme in 1955. I wrote on notepaper headed with an address that seemed to link ideas of prostitution and the Virgin Mary:

> Hooker 'Ave Maria'
> Inishbofin nr. Cleggan Co. Galway

His reply came from France, suggesting that he and his 'one wife, aged thirty-four, part Irish' should arrive on 25 July 1960. Phone calls followed, and I sailed the *Ave Maria* alone from Inishbofin to meet them at Cleggan in the late evening.

The sky was dark with a drizzly mist, requiring me often to wipe my spectacles while controlling the tiller with my chest and arm. Preoccupied with lowering sail at precisely the moment that would allow the boat to reach the pier almost without touching it, I saw two glossy blue suitcases designed for American air travel. There was no sign of their owners. The luggage looked surreal, set down beside broken lobster pots, torn fishing nets and empty wooden Guinness barrels.

When a man and a woman emerged from where they were sheltering, I wondered if I'd done wrong in luring them to Inishbofin. There they were: Ted and Beatrice. A touching sadness seemed to connect her fragile elegance to his hunky dishevelment, as they stood at the top of slippery steps, unprotected from the drizzle, waiting to be transported. Her nylon stockings and dainty shoes seemed designed for cocktails at their journey's end, not cups of tea from a metal pot stewing in the ashes of a peat fire. The whiteness of her face glowed like porcelain through a veil of mist. She regarded the roughness of my boat with unconcealed disdain.

Beside her, Roethke was like a defeated old prizefighter, growing bald, groggy and fat, clumsy on his feet, wrapped in silence, which he kept for the hour it took us to reach the island. He wore a grey city suit smart enough for lunch with T.S. Eliot at the Athenaeum, but the ragged poet and his neat clothes were at loggerheads. I helped him climb down into the cabin of the *Ave Maria*, where he sat brooding, his high forehead creased with anxiety, sweating alcohol. He groaned a little now and then, hummed a tune to himself, and grunted in answer to a trivial question, such as 'Are you comfortable?'

They were planning to leave for the Ring of Kerry after one or two days. I argued that they might get to know Ireland better by remaining on the island for longer. More persuasive was the copious hospitality of Margaret Day, who was now the island's district nurse and midwife as well as hotelier and mother of five children. The view of stone and water, grass and rocks, fishing boats and rotting hulks, shore birds, gulls and an occasional heron, in weather that was always getting worse, had the makings of an inspired poem by Roethke. The island was his place before I placed him on the island.

Margaret remembered later, 'It was pitch dark when Richard brought in this great big heavy man, and he had a limp. It took him ten minutes to get upstairs. I wondered what Richard had inflicted on me now, but I persuaded him to stay for a month or two.'

The bedrooms upstairs were divided by narrow partitions that allowed pillow talk to be overheard. Theirs at the end of the corridor, overlooking the inner tidal harbour, was two doors from mine. The hotel was still furnished with the moth- and worm-eaten relics of a Victorian landlord, who had left everything behind, including a grand piano that had not been tuned since his departure in 1922.

A strong attraction for Roethke was Miko's pub. Dark mildewed walls imprisoned in a sense of damnation its entirely male customers, who never took off their caps and overcoats as they sat in a dank odour of stout, tobacco and turf smoke. The poet appeared in their midst as a big-mouthed Yank, flush with dollars and bravado. Silent on the boat, he ranted in the bar. Miko, now a total abstainer, who opened the pub when he pleased and closed it on the minute prescribed by law, found Roethke a godsend in dispelling the boredom of hearing the same old men of the sea repeating their stories night after night.

Meanwhile, the weather being fine and the sea calm, I continued to take tourists from hotels on the mainland sailing and fishing on the *Ave Maria*. Often I landed them on the island for a lobster or crayfish lunch at Margaret's. Some nights I slept on the boat at the quay in Cleggan, to be ready for more tourists the next day. One such night, after two or three pints in the Pier Bar, I was involved in a row that drew an astonishing reaction from Roethke when he heard the story.

A small trawler that fished out of Cleggan that summer was owned by an islander who wanted no crew but his son. He had red hair and a fiery temper. Only his son dared go near him when he was drunk, to try to stop him punching the mast, and to carry him below to bed.

Raising an argument with me, knowing that my Galway hooker and her passengers were fully covered by insurance, he said in a voice that everyone could hear: 'No man would insure a boat, Murphy, unless he meant to sink her!'

He kept provoking me, and when I asked him to stop, he swung back his fists and seemed about to hit me in the face. Foolishly I pulled out a yachting knife, not to attack him but to show I could defend myself. Matthew, the veteran whose back was curved like the bows of a currach upturned on a beach, at once intervened, taking the knife from my hand, mercifully.

When I told Roethke in Miko's at noon the next day that I had been provoked into drawing a knife on a man who was about to strike me, he got wildly excited, and began to tremble with anger on my behalf. There and then he insisted on giving me a lesson about knives he had learnt from a hood in a Chicago speakeasy during Prohibition.

'How did you hold the knife?' he began. 'Show me!'

I took it out, opened the long blade, and held the hilt against my chest.

'No good! He could have killed you if that's how you held it. Let me show you how to fight with a knife! Look!'

He seized the knife, made of stainless steel, and examined it with the disdain of someone who had used better knives in places where his life had hung on their quality. Then he said: 'You gotta have two of these. First, you hold one in your mouth, with the sharp side out, and you clench your teeth on the blade, like this' – he demonstrated, with a savage grunt that rumbled from the pit of his bloated belly – 'while the other,' he said, taking the knife from his mouth and lowering it to his groin, 'you hold down low, low, low like this, and then you rip up and up till his guts are wide open and spill on the ground.'

Once I saw him coming from the pub to our table at the window of the dining room, carrying a pint of Guinness in one unsteady hand and a large notebook in the other. As soon as he sat down he ordered a bottle of wine. Now and then as we spoke, he would make a few notes, disconcerting me. What had we said that was worth recording, and why was I not recording it myself, instead of wasting my energy in action on a boat and unrecorded chatter with tourists and fishermen? I admired his devotion to his craft, even in his cups. It was my first encounter with a poet who made a profession of teaching students to write poetry, in the optimistic American belief that this was possible. He sipped alternately the wine and the stout. When these were finished he took a noggin of Irish from a pocket of his coat, and put it to his lips. I never saw him collapse.

But more than for alcohol he thirsted for praise. He envied the wealth as well as the poetic fame of Wallace Stevens. When I mentioned a poem by Robert Lowell favourably, he banged the counter in the pub with two fists and snarled, 'Why are you always praising Lowell? I'm as mad as he is!' Then he roared with laughter, making me feel that perhaps he was deploying madness, which caused him terrible suffering when he plunged from a manic high into deep depression, as part of a grand strategy to win fame as the greatest poet on earth – America's answer to William Blake. He gave me an offprint of the poem he was proudest of having written about his madness, called 'In a Dark Time'. Insanity was the stinking wound that went with his talent. In *Life Studies* (1959) Lowell had obliquely praised himself as 'nobly mad' and as a drunkard who 'outdrank the Rahvs'. Roethke acted as if the famous lines of Theseus in *A Midsummer Night's Dream*,

> The lunatic, the lover and the poet
> Are of imagination all compact

licensed him to be what his wife once called 'a nut, a drunk and a lecher', because he could write poetry. After keeping her awake half the night with brutal raving, he would redeem himself by writing at dawn a contrite lyric celebrating her beauty and his love. The woman he worshipped as 'My lizard, my lively writher' managed to protect herself from his tirades with the cool detachment she had gained as a model in New York.

Whether his mania drove him to drink or drink aggravated his mania, both got worse after eight of my family from England and Southern Rhodesia arrived to stay in the hotel in mid-August, followed by an ardently republican priest called Máirtín Lang, and the actor John Molloy. Molloy gave what my father described in his diary as 'a brilliant series of impersonations ending with a Picasso and an El Greco', after which Roethke went around collecting for the actor with a hat.

Roethke got on well with the priest, whose recollections I recorded in Galway in 1992: 'He used to come into breakfast each morning, and he'd sit opposite me, and he'd throw a manuscript across the table to me, and he'd say "Gee, Father, you be my Roman Catholic censor," and it was a poem he'd have written the night before under the moon, he was very much in love with this woman, Beatrice. So I'd read the poem, and I'd say, "there's nothing against faith and morals in that."'

Sunday 21 August 1960 was a miserably wet day in the priest's memory. There was an entertainment, followed by a dance in the hall late that night, which my parents and I didn't attend, but my sister Mary and her husband Gerry went to with Mary's two children, John, now sixteen, and Grania, thirteen. When the fiddle and piano accordion struck up for the dance, according to the priest, Roethke 'came in and started dancing around the hall on his own … he was the first on the floor'. Later, Father Lang said a drunk fisherman approached Grania, and demanded that she go dancing, which she refused. Then there was a scuffle, in which Mary thought the man was going to murder Gerry, but instead he fell on the floor on his back, and was carried out by Father Lang and the Bofin priest.

At six o'clock the next morning, my father, in swimming togs and bare feet, stepped out of the hotel to dive off the quay into the harbour, as he and his brother in their teens used to dive off a rock into the sea near Clifden before breakfast at the Rectory. He was not expecting to meet a soul at that hour, when Roethke beckoned to him across the lawn in front of the hotel, and, drawing a half-pint of whiskey from a pocket of his dressing gown, said in a husky conspiratorial whisper, 'Hey! Sir William! Care for a snifter?' My father thanked him, but refused. In his classical opinion, Roethke's trouble came from lack of moderation.

An hour later Margaret saw him sitting on the sea wall in the garden with a glass of wine in his hand. The morning was cool, and she urged him to come into the kitchen and warm up. He followed her inside, and while she was making porridge, he came up behind her, put his right arm around her neck, and held a carving knife with a nine-inch blade pointed at her heart, saying, 'If that man had touched Richard Murphy or any of his relations last night in the hall, I'd have sunk this knife to the heart in him.'

My father wrote in his diary, 'Mr Theodore Roethke the poet in a frenzy today!' And my mother asked Beatrice, 'Don't you think it's time you did something about your husband?' So Beatrice sent for the doctor, who signed a certificate of insanity, committing him as a voluntary patient to the county mental hospital at Ballinasloe, halfway across Ireland. But we were weather-bound on the island. No boat could leave the harbour until the sea calmed down the following day.

When Beatrice was packing, Ted wandered into my room, trembling and hesitant, wanting to borrow some books, carrying a Harvard book bag. Naturally he chose the greatest – Wordsworth, Hardy and Yeats. He had just pulled the cord that closed the bag on their collected poems when Beatrice came in to see what he was doing. She opened the bag, looked inside, and said with the venom of revenge, 'You won't need those where you're going.'

Roethke was in tears as he stumbled down the slippery pebbled shore, past the anchor of an Armada galleon dredged up in a trawl, to the wooden punt that was waiting with a man to row him out to the mailboat on its harbour moorings; a poet on his way to an asylum escorted by a priest. It was the saddest sight of my years at Inishbofin. But Margaret Day remembered 'the extreme peace in Bofin after he'd gone'.

As Roethke had been certified, the law in Ireland required that he be brought to the asylum by the police. But when the boat reached Cleggan, according to Father Lang, Beatrice was worried. 'She said, "He'll go round the bend entirely if the police arrive," and she told me what happened in the Waldorf Astoria Hotel in New York, the time he was presented with his Pulitzer Prize for poetry. He had got a turn, and a policeman was sent for, two policemen arrived, and he took the two of them up, one in either arm, and carried them to the door and threw them out. They had to send for reinforce-ments. So she says, "Have you a car there?" "Well," I said, "I have a small car, a Volkswagen Beetle." "Will you bring us to Ballinasloe?" she asks. "Certainly," I said. I was an awful chancer really, looking back on it, I took a big chance …

'So we put him into the back of my Volkswagen Beetle, sitting across the seat, and his feet were up against the window. He was a tall man, and I was afraid he'd push the window out with his feet, but fortunately the window stood. Beatrice gave him a bottle of wine, red wine, to soothe him. Anyway, as we were pulling out of the quayside, just going up the hill from the quayside, the squad car comes down, and I just wave to the guards and continue on the journey.' Priests in Ireland in 1960 could exercise spiritual – and other – authority over the police.

About six weeks later he returned, without Beatrice. 'He was as quiet as could be,' according to Margaret. All my relations had gone, and my boat was laid up for the winter. Roethke and I were the only visitors on the island, with enough time, space and loneliness to observe, remember and write. He was drinking less and writing more. He praised the treatment at Ballinasloe as better than his previous experience at the most expensive private clinics in America. His psychiatrist had allowed him to wander into the town and drink in a pub frequented by male nurses who kept him out of harm.

His great ambition at this time was to acquire an Irish reputation rivalling Yeats's. I suggested that he should offer his next collection of poems to the Dolmen Press, and I spoke to Liam Miller, who seemed to welcome the idea. Roethke happily agreed, but Miller vacillated and in the end rejected two books that were later published by Doubleday. One of these contained 'nonsense' poems that Roethke performed for the children in Bofin. Margaret told me, 'When he read his poems to the kids in the school, they were like dormice … they were thrilled listening to him.'

Without Beatrice, he needed me to type his new poems for mailing to the *New Yorker* and other magazines. One had only six short lines, five of them quoting 'what they say on the quay'. He was disheartened by my failure to perceive the value of this trinket, and cheered himself up by saying, 'You're a mean grouch, Murphy, but what do I care? The *Ladies' Home Journal* will love it, and pay me ten dollars a line.'

When I had finished typing 'The Shy Man', inspired by Beatrice on Bofin, he asked, 'Don't you think I've got Yeats licked?' I was embarrassed, and withheld the praise he may have needed to avoid depression. Pointing to the line 'And I lie here thinking in bleak Bofin town', I said there was no town in Bofin, and he argued that I was being pedantic. 'Town' had no function in the poem except to rhyme with 'down'.

When I asked him for introductions in America, he gave me addresses of people to whom I could write, mentioning his name. It helped in getting a poem accepted by the *Yale Review* and polite letters of rejection from Howard Moss at the *New Yorker* – always asking to see more, but crushing my ambition. To Yale I sent a Cretan poem that Roethke had redeemed from opaque obscurity with good workshop advice one afternoon. He read the poem aloud, praising passages that he liked, exposing the hollowness of turgid vague sonorities.

As the nights grew longer and darker, with storms cutting off the island for several gloomy days, the longing came upon him to feel celebrated by talking to a celebrity. One evening he asked me to put through a call to Dame Edith Sitwell, finding her number through directory enquiries.

To place a call from Inishbofin you had to lift the receiver off a box on the wall in the lobby of the hotel, where everyone in the building could hear what you were saying, then twist a handle on the box, and wait a few minutes, and twist it again, and wait another few minutes, until an old woman, taking her time, clicked a switch and said 'Number, please!' in a faraway voice that sounded a little vexed at being disturbed out of a fireside reverie. Then you had to hang up and wait an hour or two until the call was connected. Having gone out in the slanting rain to the pub to beg Miko to spare a lot of coins from his till, you had to be ready to insert these in the box when told to do so, and press button A before you could speak, and shout in order to be heard.

At the end of all this we learnt that her number was ex-directory. So he gave me the number of Princess Caetani in Rome, an American married to an Italian prince. She had published many of his poems in *Botteghe Oscure*, and paid him well. Eventually he spoke to the princess, or rather shouted so that she could hear his voice above the maddening interference on the line. At least he was connected to an old friend and admirer.

One evening he showed all of us in the pub a sheaf of Seattle newspaper cuttings about the discovery of a remote Irish island by the Pulitzer Prize-winning poet, Theodore Roethke, who was writing poems there. He had supplied the news himself from what he called the 'Bughouse', the mental hospital, which he had kept out of the story. Treatment had not curbed his mania for self-promotion.

We parted at the end of a journey in a hired van from Cleggan to Galway. I was catching a train to Dublin, and he was going to stay with John Huston's young wife, who was living alone at St Cleran's, the Hustons's big house in East Galway, while her husband was filming abroad. Meeting Ricki Huston was a prize he refused to share. She was to meet him at the Great Southern Hotel next to the railway station. Before I'd even got out of the van, he'd said goodbye, giving me a dismissive hug, to make sure I wouldn't linger in his company and spoil his meeting with Ricki.

Three years after this he died of a heart attack in a swimming pool on an island in Puget Sound in the state of Washington. Robert Lowell concluded that 'Roethke fevered to be the best poet, and perhaps strained for the gift.' Lowell fevered as much, but his gift was greater. Roethke's ambition seemed deplorable because he displayed it so stridently. Without ambition I might never have written poetry, but many years later I came across a sentence by

Henri Michaux that left me chastened and subdued: 'The mere ambition to write a poem is enough to kill it.'

Patricia and I had met Liam Miller and his wife Jo for the first time in the summer of 1955, when Liam had already begun to publish poetry under the imprint of the Dolmen Press. He was typesetting and printing by hand in the garage of his house in a south County Dublin suburb at night-time and weekends. On weekdays he worked as an architect's assistant in Merrion Square.

In those lean years there were no Arts Council subsidies for poetry publishers, but Patricia had subsidised the Dolmen publication of my first collection of poems, *The Archaeology of Love*, in a limited edition of two hundred copies designed by Liam. It was the first Dolmen publication to appear after Liam gave up architectural work in 1955 to devote all his time to the press.

His black hair and beard masked a pale face, with dark-rimmed eyes that usually looked away but would suddenly focus on mine, emitting a spark of burning interest, such as his desire to become Austin Clarke's publisher. He made a good impression on me of charm, evasiveness and a fanatical devotion to publishing Irish poets.

Dolmen's reputation rose high in 1958 when Thomas Kinsella won the Guinness Poetry Prize for a poem in *Another September*, a volume that became a Poetry Book Society Choice in London. Liam subsequently added John Montague to his list and later Austin Clarke. In 1959 he published in vellum and pamphlet form *The Woman of the House*, an elegy of a hundred lines I had written for my grandmother.

By 1960 Liam and Jo had moved with their children to a large old Georgian house in Lower Baggot Street, where I stayed on short visits to Dublin, enjoying their warm hospitality. The Dolmen Press now occupied a basement in Upper Mount Street, where, a few doors away, Jo found two vacant rooms on a third floor that I could rent cheaply. As this was near Patricia's flat, I could see Emily often, while the *Ave Maria* lay on her winter moorings at Inishbofin from October 1960 until the following February.

John Montague and his wife Madeleine, a French countess, who liked to describe John jokingly as 'my handsome Irish peasant husband', were living in a basement flat nearby in Herbert Street. I enjoyed their company, and though John was a rival, he and I became friends. He had trained as a poet at the Writer's Workshop in Iowa, and I learnt from him, while remaining sceptical, that poems did not have to be inspired, but could be crafted.

Tom Kinsella and his wife Eleanor had sailed with me to Inishbofin and caught pollock on the *Ave Maria* during the summer. Tom and I used to send each other poems we were writing and, in Dublin, exchange comments over lunch in the Unicorn Restaurant. I admired his poetry for its intellectual force and lyricism. His critical remarks were helpful because they were severe.

At that time in Dublin, poetry readings were occasionally given by single poets, but only to a handful of friends and relations. So I suggested to Tom and John that the three of us should read together to attract a larger audience. We chose as our venue the ballroom of the Royal Hibernian Hotel. Liam designed and printed cards inviting a hundred and fifty people known to have a literary interest to attend the reading at 8 p.m. on Friday 3 February 1961. He also printed tickets to sell at the door to cover expenses.

The ballroom was packed. Three hundred chairs arranged in semicircular form faced a platform at the centre of one of the long walls. In homage to Peadar O'Donnell, the Donegal rebel and radical writer, who had published our poems in the *Bell*, we had asked him to take the chair.

As it was my first poetry reading in public, I was nervous, but my training as a choirboy pulled me through, even when Patricia, with an empty glass in her hand, stood up in the middle of 'Sailing to an Island' and stumbled towards the exit. Through the doorway I could hear from the lobby the loud rasping cough of Paddy Kavanagh, who had come as far as the ballroom but refused to enter.

Peadar O'Donnell then made a generous offer. When the *Bell* ceased publication, he told us, there was money left over, which was placed in trust with the Irish Academy of Letters. He asked if we would be interested in editing an anthology of hitherto unpublished prose and poetry by young Irish writers. All three of us agreed, and he said the money could subsidise our anthology's publication by the Dolmen Press.

Ten days later I left Dublin to prepare the *Ave Maria* for another tourist season. While I was away, John Montague became editor of the *Dolmen Miscellany*, with Thomas Kinsella as poetry editor. They did the job admirably, presenting a new wave of prose by John McGahern, Aidan Higgins, Brian Moore and James Plunkett, together with poetry by Pearse Hutchinson, Valentin Iremonger, James Liddy and the three of us who had read in the Hibernian. My long contribution was 'The Cleggan Disaster', which I finished in time for the *Miscellany's* publication in 1962. However, being excluded as an editor, and not being mentioned in a review that covered the poets of my generation, confirmed my attachment to the part of Ireland bordered by the

Shannon on one side and the Atlantic on the other. The sea chastened my resentment.

I met Owen Coyne in Cleggan in the spring of 1961, unaware that he had been dreaming since the previous summer of sailing on the hooker, which he used to watch from his mother's meadow on the cliff behind the Pier Bar. Mary Coyne was a Concannon, related to Pat and born on the island. She lived in the last of the old cottages not to lose its thatch for asbestos slates. Her younger son, Seamus, was also longing for his chance to go to sea. Their father had died a few weeks after the birth of 'little Mary', and their mother had reared them alone, with the help of neighbours, on the produce of a few rushy fields, three cows and a small garden in which she grew all kinds of vegetables.

Mary's father, James Concannon, had fished on the *Ave Maria* during the war. He had helped to save the crew of the *Barrister*, a cargo ship wrecked on the Kimeen Rocks off Shark Head in a storm. So we were linked in our love of the boat. She sent word to her father on the island to know if it would be all right to let Owen, who was nineteen years old, sail with a Protestant who sounded British and was divorced. He replied that it would do the boy no harm, since the boat had always been lucky and blessed by a priest. She had never lost a man overboard. I was living at the hotel in Bofin when Owen rang with the good news.

He loved the adventure of working on the boat. It got him away from the land work he hated, such as catching a cow in a field and milking in the rain, while the cow kicked the bucket and swished him with her shitty tail. No longer did he need to walk half a mile for water from a well to make tea for breakfast, or spend the summer on a midge-infested bog saving turf for the open fire on which his mother baked soda bread and cooked while at the same time knitting.

Emily, who was now five, enjoyed the boat and was a good sailor. When we put to sea, Owen would make a nest for her on the deck in front of the cockpit, where she was under my eye. The rougher the passage the sooner she'd fall asleep, never complaining. But when we were fishing she would wake up and want to catch a fish, at once. So Owen used to slip a dead mackerel on to her line when she wasn't looking.

Owen was tall and, like his mother, had the deep-blue eyes and black curly hair of those Connemara people whose looks had given rise to the legend that they were descended from Spanish dons who had swum ashore from the wrecks of Armada galleons in 1588. Some of our younger tourists said he looked like Elvis.

After he began crewing on the *Ave Maria*, he told me that John Ward, the Cleggan blacksmith, was willing to sell his house, which I bought, extended and modernised, calling it the Old Forge. It was on a junction of two lanes separated by a wall with a stile. I had passed it once the previous summer with old Michael Schofield, when he grabbed me by the arm on the quay and took me on a mysterious walk to avoid a fisherman who was raving drunk and raring for a fight. Those lanes were narrow, crooked and rough. Nettles, briars, ragged robin and purple loosestrife overhung in profusion small stones and potholes. The tarred road from the east, all the way from Dublin, ended at the Pier Bar.

On this westerly side towards the ocean, everything seemed to have been fossilised in the year of the Cleggan Disaster, which I was trying to bring to life in a poem. Here I found the past burgeoning out of the ditches, people who seemed traumatised by the malevolence of the sea, the cruelty of the climate, the infertility of the soil, and the general calamity of existence in such a distressful place. Not the beauty of the landscape, which tourists and the gentry were well enough off to appreciate, but the struggle of people to surmount great misfortune, as they all said, 'with the help of God', commanded my agnostic admiration.

In May 1961 M. le Comte de Fauconberge booked full hire of the *Ave Maria* to go fishing. The sky was cloudless, the wind northerly, and there was no take on the fish. He said his wife didn't enjoy our little hooker because she was used to his yacht, which had two drawing rooms. They kept the yacht in Tunis. The second time he fished with us, he lost one of our rods overboard.

The count was using two rods at the time, and when the hooks on one of his lines got fouled in weed on the bottom, he laid the rod down on the deck and told Owen to pick it up. The boat was drifting in a two-knot current near Carraigmahog, a dangerous rock, and, as Owen was reaching to grab the rod, it was plucked overboard. In blaming Owen, the count sank to the bottom of our estimation.

Soon after this, Robert Shaw and Mary Ure, having heard of the *Ave Maria* from their doctor in London, Gerry Slattery, booked a day's hire – my first meeting with Mary and second with Robert, whom I had not seen since we had met at the Royal Court Theatre. On account of bad weather, we were moored in a landlocked bay, and I felt ashamed when we went aground on a sandbar within minutes of getting under way, but we managed to pull through.

Robert sat in the cockpit talking to me. Mary lay on the foredeck with her bare legs over the side, her feet dipping in the sea as we sailed on a fair wind to Cleggan, the sun shining all day. Though still married to John Osborne, she was carrying Robert's child, and Owen heard Robert telling her, 'Be careful the two of you don't fall into the sea.' They were calm, courteous and in love. In the evening we sat in the Pier Bar, recording my poetry in his voice.

Our best customers, who gave little trouble and large tips, came from England. Often we took families with four or five children. We could guarantee that those who paid for fishing would catch a fish. Only on two days in seven years was nothing caught. Many of those who spent the day from noon till five o'clock wandering around the island felt transformed by the experience. There were some near disasters, but the worst injury a visitor suffered was a broken toe. Dubliners and Northern Irish were our next best customers, just as appreciative but inclined to tip less. The French, Spanish, Dutch and Germans were few, but more demanding and harder to please.

Americans seldom paused on their rapid itineraries to spend a day on an old Galway hooker, calling at an island that seemed connected only by unreliable links to the twentieth century. One who did pause was a chemistry professor from St Paul, Minnesota, not far off retirement, who booked a day's fishing for himself on the *Ave Maria* and a passage for his wife to Inishbofin. He was a short, stout, bald and rather solemn gentleman, who had little to say, perhaps because his wife had a lot. When we reached the island under sail at noon, she felt so exhilarated that she changed her mind about spending the day ashore on her own, and said she would stay on board to watch him fishing. He murmured his glum disapproval, but she insisted. Her clothes were more suitable for a shopping mall than for a boat in a rough sea.

Soon we hove to, and were drifting with the tide over a deep rocky shoal between Inishbofin and Inishark. Pollock were easy to catch there, on a six-feathered jig sunk to the seabed by a cone of lead. The professor sat silent in the cockpit, jigging his rod and occasionally reeling up fish that I removed from the hooks. Three other men were fishing in the bows. The professor's wife was sitting on the cabin head, facing broadside waves that were causing the boat to roll, discomforting us all.

Suddenly she stood up and vomited into the sea; and in the sea I saw a brilliant set of gold-mounted false teeth sinking in zigzag curves out of sight to a depth of eight fathoms. She turned to her husband, with a hand covering her mouth, and cried: 'Oh darling, what shall I do? I've lost my teeth! I've lost my teeth! Oh what shall I do?'

The professor replied with Minnesotan logic: 'You'd better keep your mouth shut, honey!'

At the end of the tourist season in September 1961, our takings having more than covered our costs, Owen introduced me to John O'Halloran, tall and stately as his father, The Squire of Inishbofin. John was ten years older than me, a compulsive storyteller who needed a fresh audience every day, and a good sailor who knew every breaker and fishing mark between Slyne Head and Achill. He wanted to save the *Ave Maria* from being sunk, and Owen from being drowned, by taking command of her himself the following year.

Owen was too tactful to put it so bluntly, but he gave me the idea of buying another old hooker in Galway to create jobs on the sea for his brother Seamus and O'Halloran, and for his mother at my house, feeding tourists who would occupy the Old Forge in conjunction with chartering the second boat.

We drove to the Claddagh, where we talked to Martin Oliver, owner of the *True Light* since she had been built shortly before the *Ave Maria* in 1922. Having fished for sixty years since he was ten years old, Martin was ready to retire. The *True Light* appealed to me because Martin and his crew had survived on her by keeping 'well out to sea' on the night of the Cleggan Disaster. We clinched the deal in Maguire's, where he described me with wounding accuracy as a sunshine fisherman.

The *True Light* remained in the Claddagh for the next two days while we waited for the weather to improve. I was in Clifden at lunchtime on 16 September when slates began flying off the roofs, as the west was struck by a hurricane called 'Debbie'. We had left the *Ave Maria* out on her summer moorings in the bay. As soon as Cleggan came into view from the top of a hill, I saw the whole surface of the bay whitened from shore to shore, the broken sea whipped into foam, the foam vaporised into mist, and the mist turning Cleggan Head dark as at nightfall.

Tiny as a toy boat in a bath of soap bubbles, the *Ave Maria* was holding fast, yawing on her chains. When I got out of the car near the dock in comparative shelter, I had to cling to a wall not to be blown down. The *Ave Maria's* bowsprit was now pointing at the sky, then plunging under a wave that rose on a scream of wind to blanch as it crossed the entire bay in seconds. The watchtower built on Cleggan Head, under threat of a French invasion in 1798, was brought to the ground. But the luck of the *Ave Maria* never broke, nor did the *True Light's*.

Three days later Owen and I sailed out of the Claddagh with Martin Oliver at the helm, bound, as I hoped, for Cleggan. The *True Light* had a brown-barked calico sail, so old that Martin had reinforced it in weak spots with tar. She had to be kept bailed because of leaks in a few rotting planks. When we moored for the night at the pier in Spiddal, Martin took a taxi twelve miles back to Galway, saying he could go no further.

We had no engine and no knowledge of the south Connemara coast; but we did have a chart, a small torch, a radio and a life raft. The next day was Sunday, and when Owen returned from Mass we set out in a fair wind until we were almost becalmed in afternoon sunshine between the Aran Islands and Carraroe. Then a breeze sprang up and before the *Six O'Clock News* I heard a good shipping forecast for Shannon and Rockall, which persuaded me to stand 'well out to sea' for the night, rather than risk being wrecked on one of a multitude of rocks and breakers on the south Connemara coast. Being fearless at sea, Owen, whose job at the mast was to keep an eye out for rocks or breakers all through the dark night, could not avoid falling asleep. I stayed at the helm, waking him now and then to bail, and to quell my anxiety, hoping the light of Slyne Head, our only means of navigating, would not disappear in rain or fog. I had never steered a boat on the sea in the dark, and kept imagining how much worse the night at sea had been for Pat Concannon in 1927. He and four men in a much smaller boat had no life raft, torch or food.

At dawn we saw land that we recognised later as High Island; and passing the Cuddoo Rocks we caught two king mackerel for our breakfast. Twenty-four hours after leaving Spiddal, Owen cast our bow rope to John O'Halloran and our stern rope to Seamus, who made the ropes fast to bollards on the quay at Cleggan.

In 1961 Charles Monteith had thought it would be a good idea for a London publisher other than Faber to bring out a volume of my poetry, called *Sailing to an Island*. He felt, because we were such old friends, it would be upsetting for both of us if the book were turned down by T.S. Eliot. If it were accepted, people might think the decision had been swayed by our friendship. In fact, he said firmly, it's Tom who still makes the final decisions about poetry.

He gave me an introduction to Alan Maclean, the poetry editor at Macmillan, and later in the year I sent Alan the manuscript, which he accepted, but apologised for only being able to offer a five-per-cent royalty. What mattered was that the book had been approved by the publishers of Yeats,

Hardy and Tennyson. Charles might no longer have reason to feel embarrassed about my offering the book to Faber. When I mentioned that I was unhappy about the five-per-cent offer, and thinking of refusing it, he encouraged me to send him the manuscript, and said, 'If we take it we'll give you a royalty of ten per cent.'

So I withdrew the book from Macmillan, and sent it with improvements to Faber in the late autumn of 1961. By this time Eliot had gone to the West Indies for his health, and no decision could be made in his absence. Soon after Eliot returned to London in April 1962, Charles sent me the most exciting telegram I had ever received in my life, simply announcing 'Tom says yes.'

On a subsequent visit to London I met Eliot for the first and last time. He didn't take me out to lunch, which would have been the highest honour for a young poet new to the Faber list, but invited me to tea in his office on the top floor of 24 Russell Square, which was nearly the lowest. I felt so awed by his reputation that I found it hard to speak except in a trance, like the one that got me through my first encounter with C.S. Lewis at an oral examination for a scholarship at Oxford when I was seventeen. There was no one in the world I was more anxious for my poetry to impress, and I was scared that after meeting me he might think less of my work.

First I talked to Charles in his office, overcrowded with books. He told me that Tom was next door in the 'eagle's nest'. Charles led the way, and there was the old man, seventy-four, looking like his famous photographs, wearing a very well-tailored dark suit, as he stood up to shake my hand, then motioned me to a chair near the door, which Charles closed as he left us. Not just because I was sitting and Eliot continued to stand, as he prepared our tea, he seemed to exist on a higher plane. He didn't talk down to me, but I could not help talking up to him. He offered me a biscuit from a little silver box, which he said was given to him by a Parsee. I couldn't think of anything intelligent to say about Parsees.

While I was drinking, he asked me, 'What are you writing now?' Nothing, as it happened, because I was exhausted by the business of running the two boats. I could not tell him this, so I hesitated to answer.

Noticing my distress, he relieved it by replying himself, 'I never like being asked that question, so let's talk about something else. I have a friend in America called Robert Lowell who is keen on sailing.' Not a word about the poetry that I had admired since 1950, when I reviewed in the *Spectator* Lowell's first book from Faber; but it was much easier to talk about boats. Mercifully Eliot made no mention of my presumptuous attack in the same journal on the poor poetic quality of his most popular play, *The Cocktail Party*. Had he forgotten or forgiven my juvenile offence? He was so polite I wasn't sure what he was thinking.

At last he talked of Yeats: 'I met him once, when I was young and he was quite old and famous. What impressed me most was his courtesy. Yeats treated me as an equal.' And that was how Eliot was treating me now. Little did I deserve the treatment.

What started me writing 'The Battle of Aughrim' on the morning of the second Sunday in July 1962?

I was alone in Mary Coyne's cottage for an hour while the family were away at Mass. My house, the Old Forge, was let to wealthy British tourists, who were to sail on the *True Light* at eleven, with John O'Halloran as skipper and Owen as crew. Seamus was to crew for me on the *Ave Maria*. Mary and her niece Imelda from Inishbofin were catering for the tourists. The red half-door was open towards the mountains in the east. There was not a sound in the calm but a little squabbling of chickens under a hedge and the lowing of a distant cow. The previous day had ended with me kneeling down in the kitchen with the family while Mary recited the rosary.

Thinking of this, and the fanfare of Orange marches in the North to celebrate victories of 1690 and 1691 that had dispossessed the Irish Catholics, I remembered driving through the village of Aughrim, right in the centre of Ireland, and feeling a sense of desolation in the place. The battle fought there on Sunday 12 July 1691 was the last and bloodiest in a war that established the Protestant ownership of land in Ireland for almost the next two centuries. The Famine of 1845–47, the partitioning of Ireland in 1922, and the long ebb tide of emigration that was, we hoped, about to turn, were remote consequences of the battle. And I recalled that one of my mother's ancestors, Robert Miller, had acquired from a dispossessed Catholic the land and house he called Milford.

A question uppermost in all Irish minds in our agricultural past – Who owns the land? – occurred to me so strongly that I took an envelope from the pocket of my donkey jacket and wrote those words, in case I might forget them during a day of chatting to tourists while trying to navigate safely to and from Inishbofin. One written word led to another, with crossings out, more or less in this rough form:

> Who owns the land where musket balls are buried
> Under whitethorns on the esker, in the drained bogs
> Where flocks of sheep browse and redcoats waded?

From then on, I became curious to learn 'exactly what took place, what it could mean'. I had written enough externally about boats and the sea. Now I wanted to look inward at the divisions and devastations in myself as well as in the country: the conflicts, legends, rituals, myths and histories arising from possession of the land – why we still had borders and bigotries.

At a meeting of the Military History Society at Renmore Barracks in Galway, I met Professor Hayes McCoy and Martin Joyce, the National teacher at Aughrim. Martin presented me with a musket ball from the battlefield, and later invited me to stay at his house so that he could escort me around the battlefield, describing what had happened in the present tense as if it were happening now. He had a museum of objects relating to the battle in his school, and he lived in two time zones, the present and 12 July 1691.

The BBC Third Programme was a good patron of poets in the 1960s, with the novelist P.H. Newby as director, and Douglas Cleverdon able to commission whatever he liked after his success with Dylan Thomas's *Under Milk Wood*. Douglas had recently produced a reading by Denys Hawthorne of 'The Cleggan Disaster' that was well rated by audience research in the BBC, and when I told him my thoughts about Aughrim, he commissioned me to write a poem long enough to fill a programme lasting one hour, of which fifteen minutes could be music. The fee was small – the price of the *Oxford English Dictionary* in its original twelve volumes – but the value of knowing that the poem would have an audience was great. I never thought it would take me over five years to fulfil the contract, or that Douglas would be so patient.

By good fortune I had met Seán Ó Riada a few months earlier, at a poetry reading I gave at the National Book League in London. He had come in a white Aran sweater that matched the one I was wearing, knitted by Mary Coyne. My impression was of a man of immense charm and panache, who enhanced everything he said and did with a touch of comedy and heroism. The moguls of the film industry were trying to hire him as a composer, but his passion to revive Irish folk music in a modern form was keeping him in Ireland, where we both were to travel a few nights later.

We met at Euston Station on the Irish mail train bound for Holyhead.

As I was travelling third class, Seán invited me to join him for a drink in the first-class sleeping car. There he introduced me to what he called 'wedges' – a pint of Guinness followed by a shot of rum or whiskey followed by another pint of Guinness – which was more than I could handle; and he invited me to come to his house in Dublin some night to hear him rehearse a group of traditional musicians who spoke Irish.

His house was on Galloping Green in Stillorgan, and his group was known as Ceoltóirí Chualann. The sound of the *uilleann* pipes, a goatskin drum, a flute, a penny whistle and two fiddles, with the verve that Seán brought out in six Dubliners, most of whom had done a hard day's work in an office or on a bus, enchanted me as if it were coming from the ground out of a hawthorn-ringed rath, bringing the music of the dead to life with renewed vitality.

The music was oral, made up at rehearsals and not written down. Spontaneity was in vogue in the London theatre, a breakthrough from the Old Vic and the rigidities of Shakespearian actors. Joan Littlewood had encouraged her cast at Stratford in east London to improve Brendan Behan's play *The Hostage* by extemporising. Ó Riada's group was at once spontaneous and archaic, wringing from the past a passionate sound that ranged with pathos and humour through all the emotions from grief to joy.

After this rehearsal we talked about my idea of a long poem on the theme of the Battle of Aughrim, and I asked Seán to provide the music. We agreed that his music and my words should not compete for the listener's attention, but be heard separately. On a later occasion I recorded at his house the traditional Irish melodies he had in mind for the subject. He played them on his pianola, and I listened to them again and again in Cleggan over the next few years, to infuse the words I was writing with their spirit. But I wanted the music to evoke the spirit of *both* sides in that conflict. Seán gave me only the tunes of the defeated. So I obtained LP recordings of Henry Purcell's music, with trumpets resounding in Westminster Abbey and a clavichord tinkling in a tower.

Martin Joyce told me what books of the period to read. On the Protestant side I used a 'true blue' eyewitness account by the Reverend George Storey mistitled *An Impartial History of the Wars in Ireland*. Storey expresses what the English conquerors thought about the native Irish: that it would do us good to be subjugated.

From local tradition I learnt that Robert Miller, then at Ballycushen Castle near Milford, had suborned a Spaniard of Irish descent, called O'Donnell of the Red Mouth, by keeping him and his thousand horsemen so drunk that they missed the battle. A Catholic stable boy had galloped off on O'Donnell's horse to warn the army of his treachery, but the horse had taken him astray. Long after the battle, at a gentleman's club established by the Millers in Kilmaine – the one from which John Browne of the Neale was excluded for being the grandson of a papist – there was a toast drunk to the horse that had led the stable boy astray. Other legends I took from the Irish side to form in poetry an equation of the forces bent on each other's destruction on the battlefield.

A little research was to prove that my ancestors, like those of most people of Irish descent, had fought on opposite sides. I learnt that Patrick Sarsfield – who had sailed away in defeat to France, leading ten thousand Irish troops known as the Wild Geese to win victories abroad – was my mother's distant uncle.

My stance was anti-triumphal, anti-militarist. As the horror of colonial warfare in Vietnam increased during the 1960s, the fate of Ireland in the seventeenth century seemed to connect at the Boyne and Aughrim. In each case two great powers made use of foreign troops to fight battles on the soil of a poor distant country in the name of bitterly opposed beliefs. I was trying to come to terms with my own army heritage, and with not having served in the war that was brought to an end by the bomb on Hiroshima on my eighteenth birthday. That heritage accounts for the coolness of tone and the demythologising ironies of the poem.

The poem grew slowly, because organically, from bits and pieces of my life and reading in Ireland between 1962 and 1967, not as a set-piece epic about a battle in the seventeenth century. My underlying wish was to unite my divided self, as a renegade from a family of Protestant imperialists, in our divided country in a sequence faithful to the disunity of both. The poetry was to occupy a no-man's-land between music, myth and history.

My conclusion was that Ireland, united in a new united Europe, would be a happier country for us all. But by the time I had finished the poem in October 1967, the earlier hope inspired by the cross-border meetings of Seán Lemass and Terence O'Neill had been destroyed in the North by the fury of Ian Paisley and his Protestant backlash; while attitudes in the Republic were hardening, as the fiftieth anniversary celebrations of the 1916 Easter Rising culminated in the blowing up of Nelson's Pillar in front of the General Post Office.

In the spring of 1961, when the Dolmen Press published my poem 'The Last Galway Hooker' in a slim volume of that title designed by Liam Miller, the booklet competed on a shelf with Smithwick's beer and Bachelor's baked beans for the custom of tourists drawn to the Pier Bar by my antique sailing boat. We were energised by a new spirit of growth that was beginning to turn the tide of despair and emigration from an Ireland that had seemed without hope of ever progressing. Whereas in the 1940s and 1950s those who tried to work hard to better their lot at home would surely have been told 'You're wasting your time – you'd better go abroad – you'll come to nothing if you stay in Ireland', by the early 1960s there was a new determination to stay at home and make things work.

My sea poems were laments for the losses of the past but inspired by hope. I ended 'The Last Galway Hooker' with these lines:

> Old men my instructors, and with all new gear
> May I handle her well down tomorrow's sea-road.

And I finished 'The Cleggan Disaster' early in 1962 with a young man saying to his mother, who is afraid he may drown if he goes to sea,

> Forget about the disaster,
> We're mounting nets today!

I had entered 'The Cleggan Disaster' for the Guinness Awards at the Cheltenham Festival in the spring of 1962. In accordance with the rules I used a pseudonym, 'Fisherman' – a token disguise. The judges that year were George Hartley, Sylvia Plath and John Press. Before the official verdict came from the festival chairman, I received a letter from Sylvia Plath that surprised and thrilled me. Typed and dated 'Saturday: July 21', from Court Green, North Tawton, Devon, it let me know in advance that 'Years Later', the epilogue of the 'Cleggan Disaster', had won first prize. Sylvia herself, in the previous year, had won that prize for her poem 'Insomniac'.

I had met Sylvia on only two occasions, both of them brief. My first encounter with her and her husband Ted Hughes was at the Mermaid Theatre in London on 17 July 1961. We were taking part in a festival called 'Poetry at the Mermaid', promoted by the Poetry Book Society, with John Wain, the poet and novelist, as director. Twelve poets had been commissioned by the Guinness brewing company to write poems of fifty to two hundred lines

Fig. 1 Aunt Bella (Isabella Mulvany; *second from right, back row*) in 1884 on the day she and eight other women received the first BA degrees awarded to women by the Royal University of Ireland. The *Irish Times* captioned the photo 'The Nine Graces'.

Fig. 2 RM's Uncle Kipher Murphy, of the Oxfordshire and Buckinghamshire Light Infantry, when posted to India in 1913. He would die on his first day in battle at Langemark, Flanders, 21 October 1914.

Fig. 3 Canon Richard Murphy MA (RM's 'saintly' grandfather) with his wife Mary (née Mulvany; Aunt Bella's sister) in the Clifden Rectory garden, *c.* 1912.

Fig. 4 (left–right) Betty Ormsby (RM's future mother) with her Canadian cousin Anthony Ormsby and her mother Lucy at Lusk, Scotland, 1915. Anthony was killed in France during the First World War.

Fig. 5 Lieutenant Colonel T. (Tom) Ormsby DSO (RM's maternal grandfather, known in the family as 'Good Tom') and his wife Lucy (née Thomson) playing with a cat on his shoulder to tease him, *c.* 1919.

Fig. 14 Sir William Murphy, governor of the Bahamas, 1946.

Fig. 15 Betty, Lady Murphy, at Government House, Nassau, Bahamas, *c.* 1946.

Fig. 16 Mary Caulfeild (RM's elder sister) in a donkey car on the Milford avenue, 1948.

Fig. 17 Patricia Avis (RM's wife and Emily's mother) at Lake Park, Count Wicklow, 1957.

Fig. 18 Philip Larkin on the front porch of Lake Park, County Wicklow, where he spent a week as the guest of RM and his wife Patricia in the summer of 1957.

Fig. 19 Tony White (*right*) with Michael Schofield beside
the *Ave Maria* on the quay at Inishbofin, August 1959.

Fig. 20 RM with his daughter
Emily on the *Ave Maria*, 1960.

Fig. 21 Seamus Coyne of Cleggan and
Inishbofin (*standing*; RM's fearless mate)
with RM and anglers on the *Ave Maria*, 1962.

Fig. 22 The *Ave Maria* 'with all new gear' ready to sail in May 1960. Pat (Pateen) Cloherty at the helm, RM at the mast.

Fig. 23 John O'Halloran, son of the Squire of Inishbofin and
grandson of the King of Inishark, at the tiller of the *True Light*, 1962.

Fig. 24 Charles Monteith of Faber and Faber (*left*)
with John O'Halloran on Cleggan pier, 1962.

Fig. 25 My sister Elizabeth's photo of our father on his last of two visits to High Island, 27 September 1964. His first was in 1904, to shoot wild geese with an uncle. The cross was carved by hermits in the tenth century. Our mother kept this photo beside her bed for the next thirty years.

Fig. 26 Lady Murphy (RM's mother), in her garden at Kiltullagh, Bromley, Rhodesia, c. 1963.

Fig. 27 Tony White down a Cornish tin mine, c. 1967. (Photo: Ander Gunn)

Fig. 28 (left–right) RM, Douglas Dunn, Philip Larkin and Ted
Hughes in Lockington churchyard, near Hull, 17 May 1969.

Fig. 29 Tony White in London, *c.* 1970.
(*Photo: Ander Gunn*)

Fig. 30 Emily (RM's daughter)
on High Island, summer 1972.

Fig. 31 Tony White on his
last visit to Inishbofin, 1975.

Fig. 32 Dennis O'Driscoll at
a poetry reading (date unknown).

Fig. 33 Pat Concannon (*left*) with RM at the Inishbofin Arts Festival,
April 1976, after Pat heard RM read 'The Cleggan Disaster' in the school.

Fig. 34 Richard Murphy, 1999.

Fig. 35 Richard Murphy in his garden in Sri Lanka, 2017. *(Photo: Desmond Rodrigo)*

Fig. 36 Richard's granddaughter, Theodora Lee, aged seven, in Durban, *c.* 1997. *(Photo: Jonathan Lee)*

Fig. 37 Richard's grandson, Caspar Lee, aged four, in Durban, *c.* 1997. *(Photo: Jonathan Lee)*

on subjects of their choice for very small fees. The company used this cheap patronage of poets to run a profitable advertising campaign with the slogan 'Thirst Prize'. Eight of the twelve poets had accepted an invitation to read at the Mermaid that evening. We rehearsed in the morning; there was a reading by Ted with Clifford Dyment and Geoffrey Hill at one o'clock; Ted and Sylvia joined me for a meal in the restaurant that afternoon.

Our talk was more about living in the country, fishing and the sea than about poetry. Ted, whose first two volumes I owned and admired, made a strong, silent impression, speaking much less than Sylvia, whose poetry I had never read except for the odd poem in a magazine. They both were interested in my struggle to make a living with an old refurbished hooker on the west coast of Ireland. I met Sylvia again, but not Ted, on 31 October 1961, when she received a Guinness prize at a reception in the Goldsmith's Hall in London. I was a mere spectator. As neither of us knew hardly anyone there, except by name, we sat together before she went up to the rostrum. When I introduced myself to Robert Graves as a friend of the late Geoffrey Taylor, he turned his back on me without a word.

Sylvia's letter of 'Saturday: July 21' went on to plead that she desperately needed a boat and the sea and no squalling babies; and that she thought I would be a lovely person to visit. She added a postscript saying how glad she was about Eliot having accepted my poems at Faber. I replied with a telegram saying, 'Do hope you can come after 8 September stay with me and sail'. By then I expected the tourists to have gone from Connemara, allowing me to reoccupy the Old Forge and entertain them on land and sea.

Sylvia and Ted arrived on Thursday 13 September 1962; they'd travelled by train to Galway and car for the fifty-seven miles to Cleggan. They were planning to stay with me until the following Wednesday. When I asked them to sign the visitors' book of the *Ave Maria* in the Pier Bar that evening, Ted put his address as 'Halifax, Yorkshire', whereas Sylvia wrote 'Court Green, North Tawton, Devon'.

At the Old Forge, a hundred and fifty steps behind and a bit above the Pier Bar, I gave them a room with twin beds made of native elm by an island boatwright. The day after they arrived there was a forecast of rain and south-easterly winds, making a passage to the island undesirable. So I took them to Yeats's Tower at Ballylee and Lady Gregory's Coole Park. I had no car but a seven-horsepower minivan used for selling the fish we had caught. Sylvia sat in front, talking to me about her marriage and mine. In the back, which was too small to contain seats, Ted talked to Seamus about poachers, guns and fishing.

We went first to Coole, where I showed them the copper beech in the Pleasure Ground. Sylvia urged Ted to climb a spiked iron fence that protected the tree, and to carve his initials beside those of Yeats. She said he deserved to be in that company more than some of the Irish writers – J.M. Synge, Æ, George Bernard Shaw – who had made their now almost illegible mark. But the spikes were too sharp for him to climb over.

The Tower at that time was the ruin predicted by Yeats in the poem carved on a stone at Ballylee. People in the neighbourhood had taken everything that could be moved. The Tourist Board had not begun its restoration, and the road was still untarred. A patient ass was rubbing its ears on a gate. Jackdaws fled protesting as we climbed the spiral stairs. From the top Sylvia threw coins into the stream. Then they noticed a moss-coated apple tree, planted in the time of Yeats, bearing a heavy crop of bright red cookers. Ted and Sylvia both insisted that we should steal them. I protested. Ted said they would make good apple pie, enough to keep me through the winter. They put Seamus up the tree to shake the branches, and went to work among the nettles, picking up the apples, gathering more than a hundredweight. My objections were brushed aside. I asked Ted, 'Why are you doing this?' Standing with his back to the grey limestone wall of the Tower, he spoke in a voice of quiet intensity: 'When you come to a place like this you have to violate it.'

From Ballylee we went to Milford. After knocking three or four times on the old hall door, its green paint cracked and peeling, we thought there was no one at home except a barking Labrador, until we heard footsteps, followed by the loud rattling of a huge key in the Victorian lock. Then there was a struggle, which the swollen-headed door gave up reluctantly, opening under the pressure of a strong young girl employed as a maid. In the old way, given up almost everywhere else, she called me 'Master Richard', and left us standing in the hall while she disappeared down a dark corridor saying she would fetch 'the mistress'.

When my Aunt Bunty arrived – Uncle Jack's widow and mother of Tom Ormsby, the new owner – the first person I introduced was Sylvia, who was warmly welcomed. 'Do come into the fire in the drawing room, Sylvia. You must be tired after such a long drive.' Then turning to Seamus, my aunt asked with brusque hauteur: 'And who have we here?'

'This is Seamus Coyne,' I replied. 'He helps me to sail the *Ave Maria*.'

'This way to the kitchen, Seamus,' my aunt commanded, as she nudged him down the corridor. 'I'm sure you'll be much happier there. Rose will give you a cup of tea.'

Taken aback, I wondered would Aunt Bunty pack Ted Hughes off to the kitchen. His voice, with its roots in West Yorkshire, had never acquired the sword edge used by the gentry to cut down the lower classes and let each other know that they have this power and privilege. To play safe I introduced him as Sylvia's husband, so he was graciously received.

Before we left I showed Sylvia the framed prints of Rangoon in 1826, which were, and still are, hanging on the wall of the stairs: pictures of pagodas, temples and some triumphant redcoats with rifles storming a stockade and shooting natives armed with spears. Rangoon prints were to appear in her poem 'The Courage of Shutting Up'.

On the way home, crouched with Ted on the floor in the back of my minivan, Seamus was fuming about an insult from the girl in the kitchen. To impress her he had taken from his pocket two shotgun cartridges. As soon as she saw the cartridges she accused him of stealing them from the master. Rose was the last of the Joyce family that had served ours loyally since before the Famine.

On Friday night I rang Tom Kinsella in Dublin, asking him to come down the next day from Dublin and help me entertain my guests, who were marvellous company but not getting on well together. I wanted to break our triangle into a square. So while Tom was on his way by car to Cleggan, I took Sylvia and Ted out on the *Ave Maria* and landed them on Inishbofin, where they stayed until I picked them up for the return journey at five o'clock. During our passage of six miles across open water with a strong current and an ocean swell, Sylvia lay prone on the foredeck, leaning out over the prow: a triumphal figurehead, inhaling the sea air ecstatically, as if she were challenging the ocean to rise up and claim her. I cannot remember more because I spent the intervening hours on board with Seamus helping other tourists to catch fish, my mind bludgeoned by the heavy boat work followed by two or three pints of assuaging Guinness.

Years later I heard that Sylvia had made a good impression on the islanders and Ted a bad. Margaret Day remembers she had to go out and dig up the roots of an arum lily for Sylvia to take back to Devon. Sylvia told her she loved arum lilies, which Margaret felt was morbid. 'But I thought she was a lovely person. Ted Hughes didn't impress me at all. He was one person you brought to the island whom I didn't like.'

So far Sylvia had managed all the arrangements for their holiday, although Ted appeared to have approved. That was my impression, confirmed by her letters. If I said something to Ted, Sylvia would be quicker to reply. This didn't seem to annoy him. I never heard them quarrel or speak unkindly to each other. In the context of their recent marital difficulties, she told me his lies upset her. He never mentioned any fault of hers in my hearing, either then or subsequently. What he admitted was that after six or seven years that had been marvellously creative for him, the marriage had become destructive, and he thought the best thing to do was to give it a rest by going to Spain for six months. The name of Assia Gutmann, wife of the poet David Wevill, was not mentioned, but her role was implied.

To counter this move of Ted's, Sylvia told me she wanted a legal separation, not a divorce. She could not imagine either Ted or herself truly married to anyone else. Their union had been so complete, on every level, that she felt nothing could really destroy this. She never mentioned suicide as an act she was contemplating herself. I argued with her that a legal separation was a cruel alternative to divorce; but I also urged her not to divorce Ted on account of an affair that might not last. I told her about my experience of marriage and divorce. My wife had threatened suicide, and her brother had ended his life in a solo flying accident. We were left with his two children, and a devastating sense of guilt, of not having done enough to help him after the sudden death of his wife.

One way in which Sylvia apparently needed my help was in finding her a house that she could rent for the period of Ted's visit to Spain. She said she would be writing another novel, a potboiler, which is what she called the *Bell Jar*. She seemed to have fallen in love with Connemara at first sight, and when her enthusiasm reached its peak she even offered to rent my cottage and let me stay in it. This proposal alarmed me, though it didn't worry Ted. I took them to see two or three houses in our neighbourhood, and introduced Sylvia to Kitty Marriott, with whom she made a tenancy agreement beginning on 1 November. Sylvia eulogised Mrs Marriott, and made her plans with astonishing decisiveness.

My alarm increased at dinner that Saturday night in my cottage, a feast cooked as an act of kindness, as all my meals were in those days, by Seamus's mother. Sylvia could not have known that my life in Cleggan, including the sailing of the two Galway hookers and the leasing of my cottage to tourists in the summer, entirely depended upon Mary and her family. They were helping me to look after my daughter Emily whenever she stayed with me in the west rather than with her mother in Dublin. I helped them by providing us all with summer jobs.

While Mary Coyne liked me to invite friends and relations, whom she would gladly feed on lobster or crayfish from the Frenchman's pond, or legs of lamb sweetened on the herbal grasses of Inishbofin or Inishark, she would have drawn the line at my letting a married woman stay with me on her own. Priests had still not lost their power to drive pregnant girls into Magdalene homes to have their babies put up for adoption at birth. They could encourage the boycott of an outsider who violated local standards of behaviour. Sylvia was unaware of this until it was too late.

Tom Kinsella arrived in time for dinner. Ted and Sylvia greatly enjoyed his good nature, strong intelligence and barbed wit. As a civil servant he was one of the driving forces of our new economy, until he decided the following year to go and teach in America so that his wife, Eleanor, might be treated for myasthenia gravis and her life be saved. I admired him most among my Irish contemporaries, and learnt much from him and his poetry.

Sometime during the meal Sylvia gave me a gentle kick under the table. This alarmed me because I didn't want to have an affair with her, or break up her marriage, or be used to make Ted jealous, or upset Mary Coyne.

After dinner the conversation came around, perhaps through Yeats, to the Ouija board, which Ted and Sylvia were willing to demonstrate. After cutting out letters and choosing a suitable wine glass, they began a seance, in which I took no part. Sylvia gave up soon and went to bed, but Ted and Tom continued late into the night. Next morning I found on the table two pages of verse notes that might have been written by either of them: broken lines, fragmentary images, scraps of myth or history.

That Sunday, 16 September, my mother's birthday, I walked down to the pier after breakfast to prepare the boats for sailing. But there was more bad weather on the way, so the sailing was cancelled. By the time I got back to my cottage Sylvia was there alone. She astonished me by saying that Ted had gone to stay with Barrie Cooke, the painter, in County Clare, where he was hoping to do some trout or salmon fishing. She had her return train ticket from Galway to Dublin, and planned to meet Ted on the train on Wednesday.

I wondered why he had left abruptly without a word to me. Sylvia complained that he had walked out on her like this before, but her sign under the dinner table made me suspect she wanted to be alone with me after Ted and Tom had gone. I panicked, asking her to leave the next day by getting a lift to Dublin with Tom. I was happy in Cleggan and didn't want to cause a scandal that might upset my precarious footing as an outsider, a divorced Protestant with a British accent in a village then under the sway of a priest who had no liking for me or for Protestants or for Brits.

Sylvia was enraged. All her warmth and enthusiasm, her gushing excitement that coloured whatever she noticed with hyperbole, changed into strangulated hostility. She scarcely spoke to me, and when she did she put a strained, artificial distance between us. She opened her heart to Mary Coyne, and sowed in her mind seeds of the future myth of her martyrdom. Mary has put on recent record how 'I never saw anyone so miserable. My heart went out to her … If she didn't go then, she wouldn't have gone at all … Anyone who likes women couldn't like Ted Hughes. How could you like someone who couldn't be kind to such a lovely person, who bore him his two children … She was very tearful, very highly strung, poor Sylvia.'

Though Sylvia thanked me politely and said goodbye, under duress of her upbringing and mine, she left me feeling that, after all the effort I had made to entertain them both, I had been mean, and was partly to blame for her misery. Tom wrote from Sandycove in Dublin on 19 September, telling me, 'Sylvia boarded the mailboat at the due hour in fair form, giving the impression (to the casual observer at least) that no fears need be entertained by anyone.'

Sylvia wrote later from Devon, baffling me with thanks and friendliness on the one hand, but on the other accusing me of hypocrisy in showing her houses where I mightn't want her to live, and withdrawing her invitation to me to visit her at Court Green. She gave an excuse that was a mockery of mine for not having her to stay with me alone in Cleggan. She said a little cripple hunchback with a high black boot kept an eye on everybody entering or leaving her house. She ended her letter by urging me to vault the barrier that my understanding had been stuck at when she left, and affirming that she had no desire to see or speak to me or anyone else. After the torrent of utterances during her visit, this sounded false.

I would have loved to have continued the wide-ranging conversation we had enjoyed in the first flush of her visit to Connemara. Both she and Ted had encouraged me to write dramatic monologues, rather than straight narrative, in 'The Battle of Aughrim'. Their company was more of an inspiration than a threat. But I didn't want to be overwhelmed by her genius or to become as deeply responsible for keeping her alive in Connemara as I had been for keeping Patricia alive at Lake Park. Sylvia may have felt I had this capacity but was withholding it from her.

In Cleggan she had jokingly mentioned that she could write *New Yorker* poems about Connemara if she were to live there, but a paragraph in which she tried to reassure me that she had not written a poem for over a year, and would only be writing prose, was hard to believe. I discovered later that it was a lie. She had already written some of her last and soon-to-be famous poems. I disliked the implicit accusation that I was trying to defend my 'literary territory'. Had I not invited them to stay?

So while I was puzzling over what to say in a reply that never got written, I received a letter dated 'Sunday 7 October' in which she said she was getting a divorce, and writing from 4 a.m. until her children woke, 'my real self, long smothered'. She likened this to 'writing in a train tunnel, or Gods intestine'. I thought the best answer to this amazing letter would be to go and see her as soon as she arrived at Mrs Marriott's house near Cleggan. But then she suddenly changed her plans and moved to London instead.

Meanwhile I had gone to England to collect my Guinness Award in the Pump Room at Cheltenham on 6 October, and had travelled from London by train with Eric Walter White, who ran the Poetry Book Society. Eric thought I should read the prize-winning lyric on the platform, but permission had to be obtained from the novelist Elizabeth Jane Howard, who was directing the festival in 1962. Howard rejected the proposal, telling Eric, 'People have come to Cheltenham to enjoy themselves, not to hear poetry', a memorable non sequitur.

Carson McCullers, though dying of cancer, frail in a green silk robe, presented the prizes. I was told she had asked for the winners not to shake her hand but to kiss her. I did. When signing the visitors' book I noticed the large signature of Edna O'Brien, who had given her address as 'Homeless'.

At the end of January 1963 I went to London for the publication by Faber of *Sailing to an Island*, the spring choice of the Poetry Book Society, and Val Iremonger gave a launch party at the Irish embassy. One evening Douglas Cleverdon and his wife, Nest, took me to Jillian and Gerry Becker's house in Islington, where I met Sylvia for the last time.

The Cleverdons had warned that Sylvia was in a very tense state. Her face looked feverish and she seemed ecstatic. Her infant Nick was on her lap and three-year-old Frieda was playing with a toy on the floor. Sylvia said she was happy now, and glad to have got the two-storey upstairs apartment in a house where Yeats had lived, with a plaque on the front wall. She thought this was the best thing to have done, instead of coming to Ireland. There was no trace of ill-feeling towards me. I felt relieved.

On the same visit to London I was invited by Leonie Cohn to take part in a series of BBC talks called *Writers on Themselves*, in which Ted and Sylvia had already participated. Sylvia's piece was called 'Ocean 1212-W', a brilliant celebration of a hurricane she had experienced as a child in Cape Cod, marvelling at the storm's destructive power. To write my talk I went back to Cleggan for a fortnight. When I returned to London on 14 February, I learnt of Sylvia's death, and Ted asked me to meet him at her flat. There he told me what had happened, mentioning the pile of her recent poems that he had found, some of which he had passed to Al Alvarez to publish in the *Observer*. That was just before Ted went to Heptonstall for her funeral in the snow.

A few months after Sylvia's death, Eileen O'Malley surprised me in the Pier Bar by introducing me to Assia and her husband, the poet David Wevill. I assumed they had come to find out what had happened in Cleggan to Ted and Sylvia. The Babylonian beauty of Assia's raven hair, dark eyes and voluptuous bosom astounded me.

For a long time afterwards guilt haunted me for not having given Sylvia the haven she felt she needed in Connemara; and sometimes I felt angry at being made to feel guilty.

I ought to explain why Ted's remark about having to violate the Tower was not included in the brief memoir I gave to Anne Stevenson for her biography of Plath, *Bitter Fame* (1989). In 1987 Olwyn Hughes, his sister and agent, had begged me to put the Plath myth into perspective by writing with authority about Sylvia and Ted's visit to Connemara. I had been reluctant to comply until Ted rang and asked me to give Anne Stevenson a simple record of the facts, saying when they arrived and left: because, he said, there were wild stories circulating in America that he had taken Sylvia to the west of Ireland and abandoned her there with no money while he had gone off to shoot grouse. But as soon as Olwyn had read my draft to him on the phone, Ted had appealed to me in a letter from Court Green on 7 October 1987 to delete his remark. It was, he suggested, a facetious antithetical inversion of the obvious, in a West Yorkshire style of hyperbole, which, if taken out of context could do him harm. He regretted not having spoken about the golden apples of the sun, the silver apples of the moon.

This letter moved me to cut the remark and gloss the gap with the silver and golden apples. To have kept the remark in the text without conveying Ted's idea of its meaning would have been a betrayal of a friend I didn't want to lose for the sake of one sentence. He had not asked me to lie. Only courts make us promise to tell the whole truth, which is impossible either in a court of law or in a book.

But I did feel in 1987 that I was writing under constraint, as if I were addressing a jury in the trial of Ted Hughes. In 1971 Random House had published a poem in a book by Robin Morgan urging Ted's crucifixion and castration. One of my hands was tied by friendship to Ted, who wanted me to scotch rumours far worse than the truth of what he had done in Cleggan; the other by a moral obligation to be fair to Sylvia.

I nearly lost my life at sea by misuse of a knife. It happened on the *True Light* under sail to Cleggan from her winter repairs at Inishbofin, one fine afternoon in the spring of 1963. Seamus Coyne and Paddy Regan were helping to man her. Paddy, a greenhorn on his maiden voyage, stood at the mast. Seamus, who had learnt how to handle a hooker carrying tourists the previous year, was sitting with his arm around the tiller, a beautiful piece of oak, slender and curved, taking its pressure against his bantam chest. A navy-blue peak cap, with the badge of an anchor threaded in gold, laid a weight of authority on the rebel humour that often broke out in his face. Charles – who used to spend a few days every year with me fishing on the *Ave Maria* – thought he resembled James Dean. In a life-threatening storm, I could not have asked for a cooler or braver companion. The boys were sixteen years old.

The *Ave Maria* was a mile behind on the same course, under Captain John O'Halloran, with Seamus's brother Owen as his mate. Because it was the first voyage of the season I had cautiously tied two reefs in the mainsail before casting off from the quay, although the fair south-westerly breeze proved light enough for the hooker to carry a full sail.

When Seamus remarked that the *Ave Maria* was catching up, and might overtake, I stood to untie the reef knots and shake out the reefs. Standing on the edge of the transom behind him, I tried to unfasten the last knot that was keeping the two reefs of the mainsail lashed to the end of the boom. This was impossible. I should have lowered the sail enough to let the boom recline on the transom, but, in a spasm of nautical hubris, didn't want to give John and Owen in the *Ave Maria* a chance of overtaking. So I unsheathed our Japanese saw-edged shark knife, and with my left hand leaning on the boom, in defiance of good seamanship, cut the knot.

At once the boom leapt away to leeward, the full sail unfurled, throwing me off balance. As I felt myself falling into the sea, I jumped right out of the boat far enough to catch the boom and wrap my arms around it. But now the water was up to my thighs, and the drag of the sea on my wellington boots at the rate of knots made me feel as if I were being winched in a life-or-death tug of war between the *True Light* and the sea. I looked down and saw the dark stream rushing past, then noticed that the knife was still in my right hand. I could easily have thrown it back into the boat, but that was out of the question. The sea was about to claim me: *give it the knife instead!*

So I gave the knife to the sea and watched – as if I were a witness of my own execution – the bright steel twist and flash until it disappeared quickly under the turbid waves and was gone for ever to the bottom; and I steeled myself by staring down into the depths where I was on the point of going unless I could use every muscle in my body and brain cell in my head to get back safely into the boat.

If I had let go, Seamus and Paddy would have lost sight of me in the choppy waves long before they could have turned the boat around under sail to pick me up; and the crew of the *Ave Maria* would not have known what had happened until too late. For ten minutes I might have remained alive before dying of exposure, my life brought to an end by my own stupidity.

The mainsheet's four strands of manila rope were like a suspension bridge I could cross from the varnished larch boom to the gold-painted gunwale; but my weight on those ropes made them sag, giving the sea a more deadly grip on my body up to the waist, tearing my arms from my shoulders. Only the fear of drowning gave me strength to reach and grasp the wooden rail and lean on the hooker's black hull, shaped like a pregnant cow, and pull myself up so that the sea could clutch no higher than my groin.

It was all I could do to hold on for a few more seconds. Paddy had no idea how to lower the sails, and Seamus had not yet acquired the skill of bringing the boat to a standstill by heaving to. I asked Paddy to pull me in, but he tried to loosen my grip on the rail, almost releasing me into the sea. I told him to kneel on the deck, for his own safety, and grab me with his two hands by the seat of my trousers, and help me to pull myself up; which is how he managed to hoist me aboard, saving my life.

In the Pier Bar that night, surrounded by a crowd eager to hear about my misadventure, Seamus said: 'When Murphy fell overboard, and clung to the boom, with his legs in the water, Paddy and I were thinking what can the poor man do now if me and Paddy have a smoke?'

Those islanders who were full sure that sooner or later Murphy would sink one of his boats and drown himself and his tourists were not far wrong, as I realised another day when sailing the *True Light* with a boy called Máirtín from Inishark at the mast and a large family from London who had hired the boat with a crew for two weeks. It was a breezy day, but not bad. To please the five children by making sure they would catch fish and the wind would be fair for our return, we sailed upwind to the Leahy Rocks, a good mark for pollock. All was going well as we reached the shoals, but the tide was running against the wind, causing the sea to form short steep waves that were described locally as 'lumps of tide'. The water was so choppy that I realised we could not fish there but would have to continue sailing into the wind until we had circumnavigated the rocks. That was the safe way to proceed. Face into the storm, don't run from it, which was how Pat Concannon had survived seven hours at sea on the night of the Cleggan Disaster.

But at this moment the father, a businessman, asked me to turn the boat and go home at once, as if we were in a car. His wife was weeping in the bows. 'She's terrified,' he said, 'because her father was drowned at sea.' Then why, I wondered, but dared not say to a rich customer, did you not tell me this until now? I tried to explain that it would be much safer to keep heading into the wind so as to sail around the rocks. But this looked to him like going further away from Cleggan. No, no, he insisted, the boat must be turned for home at once, even though we were carrying three sails.

So I loosened out the mainsheet to let the *True Light* wear away with the wind filling her foresail and jib, bringing us closer to the rocks and into shallower, rougher water. The boom was almost at right angles to the boat, and I was doing all I could to prevent her jibing, for that would have been fatal. As she was gathering speed to run before the wind, with her bowsprit pointing towards Cleggan Head, a great wave rose under our stern, lifting it higher and higher till the boat all but turned over, pitching the children helter-skelter off their seats. It looked as if nothing could have prevented them and me from being tossed into the sea but for the boom plunging into the wave and keeping us afloat – a boom carved by hand out of larch from the Forest of Cong, its buoyancy our salvation. So instead of the children floundering in the sea, from which they could never have been rescued, I saw them sprawled on the limestone ballast and picking themselves up, as the angry voice of the Shark lad who was crewing for me, though never again would he dare, hurled his insubordinate accusation from the masthead: 'You put her up on a breaker, Murphy!'

I quickly tried to fill the speechless shock of our passengers with reassuring authority by replying, 'That was no breaker, Máirtín, that was a lump of tide.'

'On my solemn oath it was a bad breaker, Murphy!' he threw back.

As we sailed into calmer waters, running before the wind, I blamed myself for enticing people, by advertisements in the *Sunday Times*, to come from England to the west of Ireland to sail on a Galway hooker at a risk to their lives far greater than my pride had allowed me to imagine until now. After this I resolved to find a way of retiring from a business that so easily might have turned from giving people joy to drowning them.

One evening in May 1963, wearing canary yellow oilskins, I saw a well-dressed English couple looking forlorn on the quay at Cleggan, and I asked them if they wanted to sail on the *Ave Maria*. 'I'm Leonard Russell,' the man replied, 'and this is my wife, Dilys Powell.' She was the famous film critic and he the chief literary editor of the *Sunday Times*. They had heard of my boats and seen copies of *Sailing to an Island* on display under a fishnet in the Pier Bar. After booking a trip to Inishbofin, they invited me to dine at Sweeney's Hotel in Oughterard the following night.

During dinner we talked about Lord Kemsley, their employer for many years. Russell told me that the first he knew about the sale of the *Sunday Times* was when Kemsley called him into his office and showed him a cheque for £3 million lying on his desk, a tactless gesture as Kemsley offered him no share. Russell asked for a photocopy of the cheque, which he pinned up in the lavatory used by guests at his house in London.

I told them that Lord Kemsley's son, Anthony Berry, had maimed and almost killed my younger sister in a motor accident caused by his drunkenness in the Bahamas in 1948, and that my father, out of courtesy to his guest at Government House and in deference to Lord Kemsley, had acted forgivingly and permitted Berry to leave the country and avoid prosecution.

Looking for work in London at the age of twenty-three, I had called on Lord Kemsley and asked to be given a chance to review poetry for the *Sunday Times*. He had told me bluntly to find a job as a reporter on a provincial newspaper and work my way up, but had not offered to introduce me to one of a dozen or more editors whose newspapers he owned. Otherwise, he had said, go and write a book which makes you famous, and then we'll come looking for you to write for us.

Leonard Russell, having listened with sympathy, said that if ever I cared to write a front-page article for the literary section of the *Sunday Times* on a subject that might be of interest to the paper, he would pay £100. I thanked him, but explained that I would much rather write a poem than an article, however long or short. He responded encouragingly and said the serialisation of John Betjeman's *Summoned by Bells* had been a great success: no long poem had ever gained so many readers all at once. From the paper's point of view, he said, it would be a gimmick to commission a poem from a young poet who had recently launched his first book with Faber, but a gimmick he would like to try. The theme would have to be relevant.

A day or two later I showed him a draft of the first four lines of a poem about my father's life in retirement on a Southern Rhodesian farm. By the end of June he had given me a commission to write 'The God Who Eats Corn', stressing the point that it 'will have to be long enough to fill the front page of our weekly review section'. That meant about two hundred lines. The fee that I had requested – a return airline ticket to Rhodesia – would be paid if and when the poem was accepted.

To free myself for this work I had to find a replacement skipper for one of the two hookers and a quiet room in which to write. Graham Tulloch, whose father had been a tea planter in Ceylon, lent me the use of a kitchen table, a hard chair and an iron bed with a horsehair mattress in a vast, vacant drawing room without a carpet on the floor or curtains on the bay windows, in his decaying Victorian house. Graham farmed an inherited estate of mountain land that included High Island, on which he grazed sheep.

In that room I worked for six or seven hours a day, between eleven and six, while the hookers were at sea with tourists. The redolence of colonial power in decline at Shanbolard Hall was conducive to prolonged meditation on my father's life. He had been entertained in that room before he had gained first-class honours in classics at Trinity College, Dublin, and had joined the Ceylon Civil Service in 1910, believing that Britain ruled her colonies for the benefit of the natives and set an example to the world. For this reason he had expected the British Empire to last longer than the Roman.

I had not been to Rhodesia since Christmas 1959. Now I began to study the history and politics of central Africa. Four months later Russell accepted the poem and sent me proofs, followed by a telegram saying, 'You can revise as freely as you wish in proof.' Meanwhile, he had commissioned drawings by Leonard Rosoman based on photographs of the farm and images in the poem. Both my parents had helped with advice on my father's life and the country's political history. By December the galleys had been corrected and page proofs set up ready to print. The poem would fill the front page of the literary section of the *Sunday Times*, and was scheduled to appear on 29 December 1963. It was to mark the demise of the Central African Federation of Rhodesia and Nyasaland and the independence of Zambia and Malawi at the year's end. Faber informed the bookshops.

Before I had arrived in Rhodesia in time for Christmas, publication had been put off until 5 January 1964. But even then it didn't appear. Instead, a letter came from Russell's assistant, telling me, with no apology, that 'January 5 has been overtaken'. I felt crushed.

My parents were polite about the poem in their comments to me by mail, but face to face in the garden at Kiltullagh Farm that Christmas, my father told me what he really thought. He disliked my attitude, which had developed in ways he had never understood or approved, far from the colonies where he had lived for much of his life and nearly all of mine. Our long separations, and the ways in which I had disappointed him, had left scars.

He knew that the Central African Federation had been devised by white Rhodesians, led by Roy Welensky, as a means of transferring the wealth of the Copperbelt from Northern to Southern Rhodesia while supplying the south with docile unskilled labour from Nyasaland. But in 1957 he had been summoned out of retirement to act for three months as governor general when Lord Llewellyn died in office; and his pride in the British colonial service would not allow him to tolerate what he perceived as criticism of its injustice by one of his sons, who owed his good education to that service. In a tone of injury, he said, 'I think the trouble with the poem is that you don't love Africa.'

He was right. I had perceived the poem as a portrait of a good man behaving as well as possible in a bad situation not of his making. Politically he supported Garfield Todd, leader of the only multiracial liberal party in Rhodesian politics. In this my father went against the grain of a massive majority of white settlers in that country, but won the respect of Africans. My poem had been an attempt to come closer to him with more understanding, from a distance of six thousand miles. I replied: 'The poem was written by someone who doesn't love Africa about a person who does, and perhaps the irony of this may increase the interest.'

I was sad to have failed to please my father by writing a poem in his honour. Worse still, I angered him so badly on that visit that he lost his temper one evening at dinner. A barefoot black butler in a white uniform was timidly filling our glasses with South African wine. We were talking about the rapid decolonisation of Africa and what the results might be. My brother Edward had argued me into a corner, and provoked me into quoting the report of a left-wing journalist that only some thirty-eight white settlers were killed by the Mau Mau in Kenya, whereas the British army killed more than ten thousand Kikuyu in trying to suppress the rebellion.

This infuriated my father, who accused me of insulting the colonial service, to which he had devoted his life. He stood up to say this, deeply offended, much to my shame. Why could I not have kept my mouth shut, in spite of my brother's provocation?

Next day, on the verandah by the patio under hibiscus, beside a banana tree heavy with fruit, emerging from seclusion in his thatched rondavel study, where he had been reading Homer, he apologised in the natural way that he in his Church of Ireland rectory youth had been taught, allowing me to feel forgiven and redeemed.

When I got back to London two weeks later, Russell explained that the editor-in-chief had cancelled 'The God Who Eats Corn' because he wanted coverage of a surprise visit by the pope to Jerusalem. Russell added that if there were to be a bloodbath in Rhodesia, the editor-in-chief would want the poem to appear the following Sunday; otherwise he saw no hope of its inclusion in the *Sunday Times*. So he allowed it to be broadcast by the BBC and published by the *Listener* in London and the *Reporter* in New York.

My father could quote more Greek and Latin poetry by heart at seventy-five than I could quote English. While boarding at a grammar school for Protestant boys in Tipperary, he had not needed the threat of corporal punishment to study. He was brought up with the fear of hunger going back to his father's upbringing in a village schoolhouse in Carlow, and his grandfather Christopher Mulvany's memories of the Great Famine.

That was why he and my mother and my brother Edward, their farm manager, built a school on the farm to accommodate two hundred and fifty African children from their own and neighbouring farms, who otherwise would have had no education. One of those children would become general manager of the Zimbabwean railways. Another would be a professor at a college in Texas where he would invite me to read my poetry in 1996.

The excellent skipper, Captain John, whom I was employing for the third consecutive year from April to September to take tourists on either the *Ave Maria* or the *True Light* to Inishbofin or to fish around the islands, while telling them stories they were delighted to hear, had unfortunately been given too much alcohol by some tourists on a few occasions during the month of July 1964.

A German had plied him with whiskey at the start of one trip, and I had to tell him the drinking must stop.

I met him on the quay when he had returned with a party from Bofin, had tied up the boat, and was on his way to rejoin the tourists in the Pier Bar, where they paid for their trip. I gave him his wages for the week, and mentioned that we had agreed there would be no heavy drinking on duty. He screwed the banknotes into a wad, which he flung in my face, drew back his right fist to take a swing at me, and said, 'I've a good mind to put you flying into the dock! No man could listen to you the way you talk.'

I picked up the wages, to give him later, and walked home in distress. The outlay of maintaining two boats all year round, paying wages and insurance, advertising Cleggan and Inishbofin, and buying fishing gear could only be recouped if the boats could be sailed with passengers on every fine day during the peak tourist season of July and August. So I phoned the postmistress of Inishbofin and asked her to send a message to her cousin, Pateen Cloherty, to come to Cleggan on the next boat.

Though he suffered from asthma and was in his mid-sixties, Pateen was happy to hold a tiller in a *gleoiteog* again. Seamus lightened his load, leaving him nothing to do but steer the boat from the cockpit while smoking his pipe and shaking his shoulders, either with laughter or indignation at the carry-on of the liberated girls and boys on board. Once, far out on the fishing grounds in a heavy swell, when he saw Seamus below in the cabin kissing a girl, Pateen blessed himself and called through the hatch, 'Will you come up out of there in God's name quickly, Seamus, before you sink the boat!' But the children of the liberal English families he took sailing – the Beatles generation – enchanted Pateen so much that he said to Seamus's mother at the time, 'You know, Mary, we were born too soon: it's now we should be coming up, when there's a bit of fun in the world.'

Nothing would persuade John O'Halloran to come back that summer. On one occasion when I tried, he rejected me with fervour, invoking his father, a boatman respected for his seamanship from Aran to Broadhaven. This is what John said to me: 'Not if my father was to get up out of the grave and order me to go back to you would I sail your boat again. Tiller of yours I'll never take any more in my hand, Captain Murphy. You'll never find a better man or a more careful seaman on all the coasts of Ireland. I loved the *Ave Maria* more than any man, and more than any boat that stood in the water. But no man can endure these rows. I just walk away. I never had an argument with any man I sailed with until you came to Cleggan. I can work for you all right on the dry land but never again on the sea. You had no right to open your mouth to me when I was skipper of your boat. A captain of a ship cannot be told his business. He knows it, and let no man say a word to him. He's the boss. When she comes and when she goes, it's the captain who decides, not the owner. I know my business. What right had you to come interfering with me when I was skipper of your boat? Did I ever harm her? I loved her better than you did, Captain Murphy, and you'll see, you'll never find as good a man to take my place.'

That was true. We forgave each other during the winter, and he took up his command of the *Ave Maria* the following spring.

One afternoon in July 1964, when the weather was too bad for the *Ave Maria* to go out with tourists from Cleggan, I answered the phone at the Old Forge, and heard a voice with a deep rich sound say, 'O'Grady here!'

This puzzled me, so I asked, 'Who is it?'

'O'Grady here!'

I had read but not met the poet Desmond O'Grady, who lived in Rome, where he wrote in a style less influenced by Philip Larkin than by Dylan Thomas and George Barker. The vatic voice made me guess that the caller was the poet, who then made a portentous announcement: 'I have come three thousand miles to see you.'

'How good of you!' I replied, never having met or spoken to him before. 'Where are you now?'

'In Clifden.'

'If you could wait half an hour I'll drive the seven remaining miles to see you.'

'That's enough!' he answered. 'I can't wait. You don't want to meet me. I'm leaving at once. It doesn't matter.'

'Hold on a minute! Could you come to Cleggan and we'll meet at the Pier Bar?'

'I'll be there,' he said, and I gave directions to a woman who had driven him from Limerick in her car. I searched my shelves and was relieved to find his second volume of poetry, *Reilly*, published three years earlier by the Phoenix Press. Armed with O'Grady's poems, I went down to the Pier Bar to alert Eileen O'Malley, who was serving two or three local customers. A car eventually drew up at the gate, and out of the passenger seat stepped a man aged twenty-nine whose stature seemed magnified by enormous intensity. I thanked him for coming three thousand miles to see me. He brushed that aside, with, 'Where is the sea? I love the sea. I want to drown myself in the ocean!'

'The sea is very close,' I said, pointing; 'Just the other side of that low wall.' He started to walk towards the wall, as there emerged from the back seat a sad, thin old man of austere equanimity, who headed for the bar. The driver was a warm-hearted Limerick woman, Eileen Donovan, trying to help two wayward Limerick poets. She explained that Desmond was depressed about his father, who was dying, and he had talked of killing himself.

I reached the sea wall at the same time as Desmond, who thereupon flung his arms wide as if for the ultimate embrace, and sang, 'The sea and I, O'Grady, here I come!' As the tide was far out, I warned him not to jump from there because he might break a leg on the rocks. 'Where can I reach the sea?'

I gave him instructions that would take him farther away from the deep water at the end of the pier. 'If you keep walking under that cliff, you'll find a better place where you could jump into the sea.' I hoped that fresh air and exercise would calm him down, knowing there was no danger of drowning there for the next three hours of the tide.

Off he went, facing a cold north-westerly breeze from across the bay, calling to the sea, 'I'm coming,' while his companions and I took shelter in the bar.

'He'll be all right in ten minutes,' Mrs Donovan assured me. 'It will do him good to have a walk by himself by the sea.'

The old man sitting beside me said, 'My name is Ryan. I'm a bad poet. May I buy you a drink, Mr Murphy?' As their host, I stood the round, but a few minutes later he uttered the same words in a different order, 'I'm a bad poet, Mr Murphy. May I buy you a drink? My name is Ryan.'

As we were talking, the door burst open, and in staggered O'Grady clutching his forehead, with blood all over his face. Eileen O'Malley screamed, but mercifully conducted him round behind the bar through the door into her house.

'May I buy you a drink, Mr Murphy?' the old man asked, varying his mantra. 'I'm a bad poet. My name is Ryan. I live in Limerick. Do you know Limerick, Mr Murphy?'

'Not well,' I replied, though I had studied its history and had recently written a poem about Sarsfield at the siege. When Eileen returned with O'Grady, having washed his face and stuck a plaster on a little scratch on his forehead, I put the book into his hand, and asked him to read a poem. He stood by the fire, facing the backs of the local fishermen, who craned their necks to watch. Transformed by our attention, he began telling a story, in full control of himself and his audience. 'Ten years ago I fell in love with a classical pianist, my age, and I asked her to marry me. She replied, "I must go to confession." I said again, "Will you marry me? I want you to answer me now." She said she had to go to confession first. On her way to confession, as she was crossing a road to reach the church, a car killed her.'

There was silence in the bar, except for a sigh from O'Grady. Then he read us the poem. His performance was a triumph, so we got on well. When I mentioned that I was planning my first tour of readings in the United States for the autumn semester, he wrote a postcard at the bar introducing me to Professor John Kelleher at Harvard. That was generous. By now I felt safe enough to ask a risky question. 'I heard that you and John Montague read together at the Poetry Center in New York. How did it go?'

'I won,' said O'Grady, 'I won.'

'Did you regard it, then, as a competition?'

'I did. It was. I won.'

As a result of my begging letters to college professors in America from the Old Forge in Cleggan, written on paper bearing my blue logo of a Galway hooker, I had been invited to give forty readings from coast to coast beginning in October. The tour was timed for autumn 1964 to promote publication of *Sailing to an Island* by the Chilmark Press in New York. I had accepted Richard Eberhart's low offer of $75 because Dartmouth College in Hanover, New Hampshire was Ivy League, I could get there by bus from Boston without losing money, and stay at his house. He had paired me with the famous James Dickey, known as Jim – a challenge I could not refuse. The reading was scheduled as the fourth on my tour, soon after my arrival in Boston.

The first three readings were sponsored by three bachelor professors who shared the one elegant, large, old timber-framed house in Cambridge. Each was head of the English department at a different university – Boston, Tufts and Lowell – and each of their names began with the letter *B*. The three *B*s were excellent hosts, giving a dinner party so that I could meet Malcolm Brinnin, author of a recent book about the agony and death of Dylan Thomas during a tour of readings in America. From those three, and from X.J. Kennedy at Tufts, I learnt with trepidation of Dickey's fame as a performing poet on and off the stage, in a college culture admiringly amused by the self-destruction of poets who drank themselves into the madhouse or the grave.

I had arrived in America with little experience of reading in public, but shortly before I left Ireland, Tony White had come from London to Cleggan especially to prepare me with stage directions. What he said, in so many words, amounted to this good advice: 'Learn your poems by heart, so that you can look at the audience: but hold the book open, and turn the pages in case you forget. Keep your hands still except when you intend to make a gesture: the gesture must then be significant and strong. Your body itself should be poised, not fidgety.'

Tony also directed me on where to raise and where to lower my voice, where to pause and where to speed up, taking me through *Sailing to an Island* sentence by sentence, line by line, to the last four words – 'here is a bed' – on which he wanted me to place three firm, slow, and not staccato, stresses.

Richard Eberhart and his wife Betty were warmly welcoming. His love of poetry and her income from a family firm that manufactured polish combined to make his house a haven of civility for visiting poets, however good or bad their work or behaviour might be. I arrived on a bus, and Dickey on a later train, in time for a colloquy with graduate students and faculty, at which we were to answer questions from the floor. On doors and walls of corridors on the way I saw posters announcing a meeting at 3 p.m. with the poet James Dickey, but no mention of my name. I swallowed my pride, and did whatever Dick Eberhart asked me to do, as he was the soul of courtesy and I was his guest.

Jim Dickey took the armchair on the platform, while a smaller chair was found and placed for me. Jim was a big, muscular Georgian, with the danger-ously innocent heart of a boy who plays cowboys and Indians with real bows and arrows. Dickey was fabled for expecting colleges to provide him with a female student for the night. He would make eye contact with a girl in the audience, address her as honey now and then, and by the end of his reading would have secured her as his date. He was admired for having given up a lucrative job copywriting slogans such as 'Things go better with Coke' to concentrate on poetry. He was also reputed to earn a much higher fee than I could command.

Questions were all addressed to him, whose work was well known and whose reputation for bravery as a pilot in nearly a hundred combat missions offset his reputation for effrontery towards women and insulting behaviour towards writers he disliked or suspected of being homosexual. Eberhart put a question to me to prevent my feelings being hurt by lack of attention. I was less nervous listening to Dickey's drawl than having to talk.

When questions and Dickey's answers began to dry up, Eberhart had the bright idea of asking each of us to read a poem as a prelude to further discussion. As we had left our books at the house, Eberhart asked if anyone had a copy of one of Jim's books. Up shot a dozen hands, and Dickey read a famous poem about the beheading of a captured American airman by an Asian enemy swordsman.

Then Eberhart asked for one of my books, but there was an embarrassed silence, broken by a woman who said plaintively, 'I think there may be one in the library.' That would have taken too long to fetch, so Eberhart asked: 'I wonder would Richard like to recite a short poem that he may know by heart?' I had hoped to surprise the much larger audience in the evening by reciting all my poems, long and short, from memory, but now I had to show my hand in presenting 'Epitaph on a Fir-tree', at the end of which Dickey faced me and snarled, 'So you know your stuff by heart!' as if he meant you're carrying an offensive weapon, but wait till you see mine!

Before the reading the Eberharts gave a dinner party, at which I sat next to Betty, and Jim nearer to Dick. I was extremely nervous about the ordeal ahead, knowing that if a commotion were to occur in the hall I might fluff a word or forget the next line completely. Jim had already shown that he regarded our joint reading as a contest he intended to win. Before the dessert Dick asked us to decide on the order in which we would read, and I requested, because I was quite unknown and very nervous, to be allowed to read after Jim, who would be sure to put the audience in a good humour. The Eberharts supported me, saying that American hospitality required them to allow their foreign guest to choose.

Having gained this point, I asked Betty if I might leave the table and go upstairs to prepare for the reading. A few minutes later Dick came into the bedroom, deeply apologetic because Jim had sworn at the table that he was not going to be a curtain-raiser for any goddamn unknown Irish poet. He had claimed as the senior man the right of reading in the place of honour, which was last. Dick pleaded with me to agree, which I did, saying, 'Jim has laid down his terms. May I make mine?'

'Sure!' said Dick.

'I'll be happy to read first if you will allow me to read for an hour.'

'That would be wonderful,' Dick replied, who had the rare interest and generosity to listen to poetry all night. People find it hard to take in more than an hour of recited poetry.

During my reading Dickey sat before me in the front row, crossing and uncrossing his legs, coughing, rustling papers. There was not a sound from the rest of the audience. I read narrative poems as a storyteller would, and survived through the very long chiming of the library clock in the middle of 'The Cleggan Disaster' by remaining silent. At the end an Irish American newspaper proprietor called Gallagher, with snow-white hair, came up to me and, in Dickey's hearing, asked, 'What is your fee, Mr Murphy? I sure would like to have you read your poetry for Governor King at the State House. His father was a lighthouse keeper at Slyne Head, mentioned in one of your poems.'

When Dickey got up on the platform he erred in displaying annoyance. 'I don't know why Murphy kept that book in his hand which he never looked at.' I had done this in case of amnesia brought on by behaviour such as Dickey's. He read well from the book, told stories even better than his poems, and kept the audience laughing so much that I was glad to have read my poems first.

When he was saying goodbye at the train station the next morning he gave me one of his Southern bear hugs.

A month later I felt nervous walking onto the stage of the big auditorium at the Poetry Center in New York when my turn came in a joint reading with Donald Hall. I feared that I might be too hot in the white Aran Island sweater I was wearing to suit my nautical poems and occupation as a fisherman. But my confidence rose as soon as I mentioned Cleggan, whereupon forty pairs of hands in the back row applauded.

After years of good health, my father's fatal illness began on his farm in Southern Rhodesia with a pain in his foot. He thought a mosquito had bitten him while he was sunbathing in the garden beside the pool; nothing to worry about. When he complained of a headache, my mother took his temperature, which had soared. They thought it was a resurgent bout of the malaria he had endured chronically in Ceylon. A doctor said he had a touch of influenza. He wrote in his diary on 18 March 1965: 'Sat up today for the first time and did a bit of Greek.' He could still recite several odes of Horace by heart, and long passages from the *Iliad*, the *Aeneid*, *Paradise Lost* and *The Deserted Village*. His memory, schooled in learning by rote, was better than mine.

When the pain in his foot increased and spread to his leg, he was moved to hospital, where the doctors found a serious problem with his heart and recommended treatment in London. So he and my mother and Edward flew to London, where my father was given a private ward at the Westminster Hospital under the care of Professor Ellis, a heart specialist. My sister Mary rang me to come at once. He and our mother wanted all their children at his bedside. Chris and Liz were already there.

Ellis told my mother the only chance of saving his life would be to amputate the leg, but he might not survive the operation. By now his foot was turning gangrenous. In the corridor old men were learning to propel themselves in wheelchairs, which reminded my parents of their friend Sir Stephen Courtauld, who was miserable as an amputee in a wheelchair on his Rhodesian farm. Ellis wanted our mother to decide without asking our father. In agony, she took the last of many crucial decisions she had taken throughout their lives, and said, 'No operation, please!'

The day before he died he asked me to read aloud from *The Times* – 'but I don't want to hear about the war in Vietnam'. That night Liz heard him say, 'This is the truth, the absolute truth,' followed by some Greek words, perhaps from the New Testament.

With tubes stuck in his veins, with hourly injections, his foot stone cold and black, panting for breath, he was kept barely alive by technology, his head and shoulders propped up by pillows. A nurse, who was worked off her feet, came in and out with pills on a tray and syringes to take more blood samples for analysis. My mother cried, 'Won't they give him peace to die? Have they sent for the clergyman? It will be too late.'

Professor Ellis said she could sleep at the hospital that night, and she made him promise he would keep her husband alive until she woke next day. When I returned in the morning, a clergyman was leaving the room, having just given our father and mother Holy Communion. It was Maundy Thursday in Holy Week, the week in which they had met and fallen in love. Mary, Chris and Liz were holding his hands and his feet, our mother cradling his head. She cried to me, 'Read him a psalm – "The Lord is my shepherd" – which you used to sing.' He was panting hard, his eyes, not seeing us, were staring at what we couldn't see, far out in space or deep within himself, flickering sideways now and then in my mother's direction when she kissed his temple and said, 'I love you.' He seemed to have heard, but made no reply, for he couldn't speak to us any more: he was addressing the world in himself, struggling to mould his mouth to say 'Mother' and 'Kipher' – his brother who was killed in battle – and when by a great effort these names of his youth came out, with the overcoming of a still more terrible obstruction, he whispered, 'Praise'.

That word was the last he spoke before gasping for air. The family urged me to go on reading, though words were sticking in my throat. I found the one hundred and fiftieth psalm, 'O praise God in his holiness: praise him in the firmament of his power.' These words, I feared, sounded absurd, but I had to continue and to avoid breaking down. I asked myself what good is poetry if it cannot help at this moment? What good is it having a voice if you fail to use it well when its most needed? The lute and harp, the cymbals and dances, the strings and pipe of that great psalm resounded with praise in the ward, affirming the life our father had fulfilled.

He died while I was reading. My mother pressed a Bible to his lips. She held and hugged him, saying to us, 'There must be a resurrection!' And when Mary, the best of her children, said, to console her, 'Only his body has died', our mother replied in despair, 'But I loved his body.'

It had not been easy to talk to my father since I was a child. On my second and last visit to Southern Rhodesia at the end of 1963 I remember him sadly reproaching me, more by the look on his face than by what he said, for not upholding his beliefs in God and the empire that he had served, for not submitting my neck to the yoke of an office job as he had done, for living in the Republic of Ireland, for having divorced my wife instead of permitting her to divorce me, which he said would have been the more gentlemanly thing to do, though it might have meant never seeing my child again. I was awed by his frown of moral disdain and his irritable temper if I were to say something he considered disagreeable. When I had asked him on my last visit to his farm why he disliked Sir Edgar Whitehead, the prime minister of Southern Rhodesia, he had replied in a tone of disgust, 'Because he's a queer.'

There was too much between us that was better left unsaid. The journey by Bibby liner, taking twenty-three days between Liverpool and Colombo, had kept us apart. Up to the age of eight I adored him with the fear of God in my heart. Every night I used to say my prayers to him, kneeling to martyr myself with pain on a coconut mat on the verandah of our house in Ward Place, Colombo, where he taught me what fathers in Ceylon were expected to teach their sons, to shoot with an airgun aimed at crows.

The firmament of his power had passed away as I was uttering words of praise more to him than to God the Father. For a long time after he died, whenever I thought or spoke of him I felt a lump in my throat as if I were choking. It made my voice sound subdued to the point of being vanquished, as if all my confidence and strength had been reduced to notes of sorrow and remorse.

He was buried on Saturday 17 April 1965 at 5 p.m. in Clifden, beside the church where his father had been rector. Two Church of Ireland clergy conducted the funeral, which was attended by three Catholic priests. A tall pink granite stone from Omey Island – Clifden being in the parish of Omey, where St Fechin had founded a monastery in the seventh century – would mark the grave. Within five months of his death I began collecting trailer-loads of pink granite from the remnants of seven abandoned cottages near Cleggan so as to build a new house out of the old and replace in stone the lost firmament.

The blending of pink granite houses with the Breton landscape, which I had seen with Patricia in 1954, had given me the idea of building in Connemara a house of the local stone. For two weeks during the summers of 1963 and 1964, James Shearer, a Scottish architect from Dunfermline with a big practice in London, rented the Old Forge, combined with the full charter of the *True Light* and her crew. In return for free holidays and sailing for two more seasons, he drew the plans for a pink granite house with green Cumbrian slates and Irish oak floors. Mary Coyne gave me the site in her meadow next to my garden. By 1965, having sold my maisonette in Muswell Hill, I had the means to fulfil my wish. The house would be known as the New Forge.

Driving around the peninsula of Aughrusmore and Aughrusbeg – names that imply big and little hunger – I had often caught sight of the pink granite gables of derelict cottages whose owners had emigrated, died or moved into modern bungalows. When the evening sun struck these gables, mica in the feldspar sparkled. Decades of rain had washed out the mortar to reveal sharp edges of dressed and closely fitted stones, bringing to mind the stonework of early Celtic monasteries.

Hearing that contractors were buying these ruins for £15 to bury the stone in foundations of new concrete buildings, I paid £20 or more for the shells of seven cottages whose owners needed the money: one, a father sending his daughter to a convent school; another, a widow with a son in hospital; and a third, parents with six children at home on a farm of ten acres. We loaded the stone by hand onto trailers to be tipped on the site. Men warned me that I was wasting money as the last stonemason in the country had been drawing his old-age pension for several years. But a neighbour of mine in Cleggan, John Cosgrove, had built a garden wall for himself and I had admired his gift for placing stones of uneven sizes and shapes to form random patterns that were structurally firm and as pleasing to the eye as a work of art.

John was the youngest of many children of a shoemaker whose family had long ago settled in the village after a landlord had evicted them. All his brothers and sisters had been forced to emigrate to England or America, where his sisters had been hospitable to me in New York. Through financial necessity John had left school at thirteen and worked during the Second World War as a labourer on the construction of airports.

About fifty years old, of medium height, stalwart in body and mind, he was still known as Ginger though he had lost much of his hair by the time I knew him. His head was usually covered by a grey cloth cap, the peak shading his blue eyes. He had a good voice for an old Irish song, but it was hard to persuade him to sing because he was modest and shy. For his family of three sons and two daughters he had built a house of blocks, and a new house for Mary Coyne in 1964, but never a house of stone. When I asked him to build mine, he refused at first as he didn't believe he had the skill; but I convinced him by pointing at his garden walls.

Once he was persuaded, having seen the architect's drawings, we picked a team of four other men who lived nearby: Tommy Coohill, father of six, had the job of selecting from the heap of granite a stone of whatever shape and size John would tell him he required. This was jigsaw-puzzle work, with pieces weighing more than a man could carry on his own, and Tommy combined a knack of finding the right stone with a gift for keeping John entertained in all weathers with his caustic wit. The walls were to be two feet thick, with no mortar visible on the outer edge. Inside there'd be a two-inch cavity for insulation and a four-inch concrete block. While John would build the higher gable with four broad windows on the south side, facing his house on the hill across the road, Tommy King, my next-door neighbour, father of five, was to work with Paul Gordon from Aughrusmore on the north gable, where there was only a small attic window. Owen Coyne, when our boats were laid up for the winter, would lift the heaviest ashlars in his arms, while Tommy Coohill's eldest son, Brendan, would make tea and run errands.

After the foundations were dug in September 1965, I went to America to occupy the Emily Clark Balch chair as visiting writer at the University of Virginia, where my predecessor had been William Faulkner. For the next two months I lived in the Colonnade Club on the Lawn among neo-classical buildings designed by Thomas Jefferson. Inspired by the symmetry around me at Charlottesville, I began writing heroic couplets addressed to Patrick Sarsfield, my mother's uncle seven times great, an elegy I would finish two years later at the New Forge, and place near the end of 'The Battle of Aughrim'.

Before returning to Ireland at Christmas, I gave a reading, paired with James Merrill, at the Poetry Center in New York, and had tea with W.H. Auden at his apartment in St Mark's Place. I remember envying the praise Auden bestowed on Kinsella's poetry, which I later reported to Tom: 'Kinsella has a good ear.' Tom was now teaching at Carbondale, Illinois. After readings at Brown University on the east coast and at Irvine, California, on the west, I flew overnight in time to read at Waco, Texas in the Armstrong Browning Library on Browning's birthday.

That evening a Baptist student drove me from Waco to Dallas to catch a flight to New York on my homeward journey. As we had hours to spare, I asked him to drive past the book depository from which the shots had been fired that had killed John F. Kennedy. The student said he didn't know where it was, he had never seen it, and he would not like to be the person who would ask that question in Dallas.

During the first half of 1966 I often met Ted Hughes and Assia Wevill, who were now living with his children, Frieda and Nick, and their infant, Shura, first near Roundstone and later at a cottage across the bay on Cleggan Head. They were thinking of settling in Ireland, and Ted even offered to sell me Court Green. One week they would dine with me, and I with them the next. Ted was writing his *Wodwo* poems at Cleggan and beginning the series that was to become *Crow*.

In a bitterly cold north wind at the end of January 1966, John Cosgrove worked all day on a scaffold, placing the top stones on the chimney that rose through the centre of the house. I kept indoors, but whenever I stepped out I could hear him singing an Irish song about a seventeenth-century disaster on the Shannon, his trowel ringing on the granite. For the year it took those six men, and later two carpenters, to complete the work, supervised not by me but by John, there were no disputes, as we all took pride in reviving the art of stonework in an ancient Irish style.

I had asked Shearer to face the house inland to catch the morning light and the view across Cleggan Bay to the Diamond Mountain on the horizon, so that the back of the house, with windows on a lower level, would bear the brunt of salt-laden storms off the open sea. The façade would have three windows and a door, to call to mind rather than replicate the cottages whose ruins we had salvaged, while quarry slates and golden-rectangular windows might evoke, with reticence, the fortitude and elegance of Milford.

Tony White came to Cleggan in the summer of 1966, and with Brendan Coohill varnished all the woodwork of the New Forge and painted the interior walls white, talking football and pop stars, listening to the Beatles or Johnny Cash on the radio, and singing, when he didn't know I was listening, 'The Green, Green Grass of Home' in the voice of Tom Jones.

Between 1961 and 1965 Tony had spent much less time in Cleggan than in London, where at first he was reading manuscripts for Hamish Hamilton and translating crime fiction by Georges Simenon, a book on Braque, and another on the music hall by Jacques Damase. We had kept in touch by mail and phone, looking forward over months to the days when he could afford to come back to Connemara. He had also been hard at work and play with Martin Green, of the left-wing publishers Martin Bryan & O'Keeffe, researching a popular *Guide to London Pubs*, which Heinemann would publish in 1965. Martin was a member of the soccer team that Tony organised and captained. Playing on Sundays in Battersea Park, the team included the writers Karl Miller, Brian Glanville and John Moynihan, the poet and publisher James Michie, a steel welder, a carpenter and some unemployed actors.

During 1965 Tony studied law, researched with tape-recorded interviews, and ghosted the life of Alfred Hinds, England's most celebrated jailbreaker. *Contempt of Court* was published by the Bodley Head the following year, with no acknowledgement of Tony. When Alfie had been serving a twelve-year sentence for the robbery of a big store in London, he had twice escaped for long periods, one of which he had spent as a fruit grower in County Wicklow. Eventually, with access to good law books in a prison library, he had won his liberty by successfully suing for wrongful arrest and imprisonment the detective inspector who had secured his conviction. Critics in the Sunday newspapers praised Mr Hinds for having turned himself in prison into a stylist who needed no help from a ghostwriter. Tony could accept that high praise with a good conscience: only his friends would know how well he had done.

Whenever he returned to Cleggan and Inishbofin, he'd express relief and joy, saying little about his life in London, where his theatre friends had rejected his plays, except to tell me that he had been exhausted by hackwork and women. He never divulged their names, but used to say, 'I need a stint of hard manual labour.'

While tourists occupied the Old Forge and Mary Coyne's new house, and I was waiting for the New Forge to be habitable, the Cosgroves accommodated me in the summer of 1966 until my thirty-ninth birthday on 6 August 1966. The following day I drove to visit Emily and Patricia, who were holidaying with Desmond Williams at Lanesborough on the Shannon. I stayed at a hotel in Roscommon, where, late that night, I developed a sore tongue, for which a doctor in the bar gave me an antihistamine tablet that did more harm than good: by morning, I had a rash with fever and severe nausea.

Patricia came, with a bunch of yellow flags and purple loosestrife that Emily had picked by the Shannon, and drove me to the Regional Hospital in Galway, where I was given a private room at no charge. By evening my tongue was on fire, having swollen and turned white; I couldn't swallow without pain and had to force myself to drink to avoid being fed by a tube through my nose; my lips and gums were ulcerated; speaking was so painful that I preferred to write notes; and my skin itched. The senior professor in the Faculty of Medicine at University College, Galway, known as 'Batty' O'Driscoll, had no idea what was wrong with me. All he would say, in a voice that boomed with authority, was, 'Yes, yes … I know … I see … yes, yes.'

A black metal crucifix faced me on a battleship-grey wall. Expecting to die, I regretted not having finished 'The Battle of Aughrim', and from time to time jotted a word or a couple of lines in one of many notebooks Tony had obtained for me from Joseph Gibert in Paris. I couldn't get to sleep, and didn't want to take a sleeping tablet in case I might die under its influence. In the quiet of the ward around midnight, hearing a woman's voice moaning loudly, as if in despair, in the next room, I assumed she was the patient's wife, permitted to make her last visit late at night because he was dying. This encouraged me to think that I was not as close to death as I had imagined, otherwise the nurses would have called back Emily and Patricia. So I took a sleeping tablet; and when the night nurse woke me to take my temperature and pulse at six o'clock, I asked if the man next door was still alive. Laughing, she replied, 'That lad is a doctor, and his girlfriend often visits him at night.'

Anything I wanted to say I had to write down – for the nurses, or the doctors, or for Tony, who recovered my car from Roscommon and would come every day from Cleggan to bring the mail and the village gossip, news of the installation of bookshelves by John Addley and Kieran Coneys, or the painting he and Brendan were doing at the New Forge. Also he would tell me how well Owen and Seamus were faring with Paul Gordon on the *Ave Maria*, entertaining tourists from eleven in the morning until six in the evening, fishing for crayfish and lobsters at dawn and at dusk. One day he reported that the *Ave Maria's* engine had failed, with tourists aboard, near the Cuddoo Rocks, where they were catching so many fish they hadn't noticed, until too late, that the tide had turned. The keel had struck a reef, a woman had dropped her sandwiches into the sea, and a man had fallen and broken a toe. It was our only accident in seven years.

The best news Tony brought was the colour supplement of the London *Observer* dated 14 August, featuring poets photographed by Jane Bown in their habitat, and quoting a poem by each: R.S. Thomas, grim in clerical collar and fawn duffel coat in front of a blurred hill of coal or slag above a Welsh colliery; Philip Larkin, glancing at a white van parked above his poem 'Ambulances'; Thom Gunn, dressed like a lumberjack in a city beside his poem 'Elvis Presley'; Ted Hughes, wearing a black tie and filling a doorway under a vine resembling the serpent in a painting of Adam and Eve – a picture taken in Cleggan – and I, posed on an iron ladder near the *True Light* in the Cleggan dock. A week or two later an anonymous leader in the *Times Literary Supplement* chastised us for being captured and put in a 'poet zoo'.

In Galway the nurses worked harder and were kinder than the doctors. A house surgeon, trying to take a blood sample from a vein in my arm, hit a nerve by mistake, blamed the needle for being blunt, and said he would go and fetch a sharper one. I told him never to come back. A nurse from Tipperary, with arms like a wrestler's, took the sample painlessly.

Professor O'Driscoll, who used to hunt with the Galway Blazers wearing a top hat and tailcoat, would enter the room once a day with a train of junior doctors and nurses, and, hearing me trying to mouth a question, would walk out. On the third morning I held up a note for him to read, asking him to tell me what disease I was suffering from. He replied with lilting pomposity superimposed on a Cork accent: 'I think you have an infestation.' Gesturing to him not to go, I wrote, 'An infestation of *what*?'. Perplexed, he replied, 'An infestation of mites', and walked out.

A few days later he diagnosed Stevens-Johnson syndrome, a rare and sometimes fatal disease. Only once, thirty years earlier, had he treated a case, when a fisherman was brought ashore from a French trawler. Cortisone cured me in another week.

One evening around six o'clock, when I was strong enough to walk, I was surprised to encounter a nurse kneeling in the corridor. She was holding a tray of medicines in one hand, a hypodermic syringe in the other, and she was saying her prayers. Far down at the end of the long echo chamber of the corridor of that male ward, a nun from the Aran Islands was chanting the rosary in Irish, plaintive sea waves breaking through her voice in spasms of sound one might hear on a breezy day from the cliffs of Dun Aengus.

The sunlight hurt my eyes the day I was leaving hospital. Tony drove me home to begin living in the New Forge and to recuperate. As soon as I was strong enough he persuaded me to jog on the beach at Sellerna or the big strand that gave access on foot from Claddaghduff to Omey Island when the tide was out. Jogging before breakfast became a habit that I would maintain, winters and summers, rain or frost, sometimes in the dark before sunrise, until the age of sixty-five. Always when I'd run I'd remember Tony, and still I think of him now when I walk barefoot in the surf on a southern-hemisphere beach as the sun goes down.

Since the summer of 1964 the *True Light* had belonged to one of our best customers, Isabel Geldart, a Maxwell of lairdly origin in Scotland, mother of four children, all of whom enjoyed the sailing and fishing. The chartering of the *True Light* to tourists continued under our joint management. From September 1966 Isabel leased the Old Forge, furnished, for a period of five years. Owen got married that month. Seamus bought the *Ave Maria*, which he would continue to operate for the next three years, attracting more tourists to Cleggan and Inishbofin, leaving me free to finish 'The Battle of Aughrim' in the new house, and to accept offers from universities in Britain and America.

Autumn has often given me a burst of energy or surprised me with a transforming experience. At Milford in the autumn of 1926, I was conceived. In September 1935 my parents placed me in boarding school, and at the end of autumn 1942 I sent my father a defiant telegram from King's in Cornwall. Autumn gave me the energy at Wellington to win an Oxford scholarship in 1944; and I departed from Oxford on 11 November 1946 in midterm, feeling compelled to write a verse play in Connemara. Writing or reading that date reminds me of Armistice Day in Colombo when I was seven: my father in a white uniform laying a poppy wreath at the Cenotaph, then standing to attention during a gun salute and the Last Post and the two-minute silence that ended with the reveille.

At Halloween 1966 Emily came for a half-term break from a convent boarding school in England, and took possession of her room at the New Forge. We gave a house-warming dance party for sixty people from Cleggan and Bofin, the families and friends of those associated with the building and the boats, all except Tony, who had gone back to work in London. The sanded and sealed native-oak floor of the large front room containing my books was impressed that night with the dancers' heels.

Twelve nights later, on 11 November, the Old Forge caught fire. The Geldarts were away and I had been keeping it dry but not warm by lighting a fire in the open hearth now and then. Woken by what sounded like rifle shots, I looked out and saw flames bursting through the roof, sending sparks to the sky that returned them as a golden shower on the garden. I called the Clifden fire brigade, which came within fifteen minutes, put out the fire and completed the building's destruction with water.

The Guardian Assurance Company sent an English fire assessor, who raked among the cinders in my presence and finally picked up a small piece of glass. It had curled into the shape of a broken phial. Studying the glass, he said, 'We can always tell if these fires are started deliberately by the way the glass has melted. This glass tells us …' – and he held it up for me to see – 'that the fire was an accident, because it must have been smouldering for a long time before it broke out. In these old houses, smoke finds its way through the mortar of a stone-built chimney, building up soot that burns when the chimney goes on fire, and through the burning soot the fire reaches the roof beam. Long ago that beam must have been built into the chimney without fire protection. The house is a total loss and should be pulled down.'

This meant more work for John Cosgrove, Tommy Coohill and Tommy King. They cleared the site manually, building garden walls with the stone and landscaping the grounds, which included laying a garden path and a terrace with some small, thick, crudely quarried grey-green slates that I'd acquired on Inishbofin without being aware of their sacred origin. When the path was laid Pat Concannon told me that St Colman's monks had quarried those slates in Cleggan Head for his church on Bofin after the monks came from England thirteen hundred years ago. The slate had been taken from the church to roof a pirate's castle at the entrance to the harbour, and from there to roof a landlord's bailiff's house that became a Royal Irish Constabulary barracks until 1922. By making the history of the uses of the slate known in 'The Battle of Aughrim', I hoped the slate would be preserved and my acquisition redeemed.

Isabel arranged to rent Mary Coyne's new house for holidays, and asked me to buy her a tinkers' caravan with a red door and a green roof shaped like a barrel. I had come to know a family of Travellers called Conroy, whose father, Michael, or one of his five sons, having seen the *Ave Maria* returning from Bofin in the evening with a flock of gulls diving on fish guts in her wake, would be waiting on the Cleggan quay for us to give them a large pollock or a few mackerel. When I went looking for them in November to buy a caravan, they were huddled in wattle tents with barked calico roofs and a bed of wet straw under a hawthorn hedge between a gravel lane and a waterlogged ditch near the small market town of Headford, eight miles from Milford.

Their father was away, but a son who used to save turf for Mary Coyne on her bog in the summer, and another called Tom, said they'd find a caravan and drive it with a piebald pony to Cleggan. Tony returned from London in time to join the purchased caravan when it reached Letterfrack, and to drive it with the lads into Cleggan on Christmas Day 1966.

Tony and I offered to teach Tom to read and write, if he would teach us Shelta, the secret language of Travellers, which they call 'cant', from the Irish word for 'language'. Shelta had been devised centuries ago to outwit the laws of the land and the customs of farmers who ploughed and sowed in fields behind stone walls and thorn hedges. Tom liked to bargain and this was a bargain he liked. He would become the first literate member of his family. But I had no experience of remedial teaching, and the only text I could obtain, the Ladybird series, was imbued with middle-class attitudes, values and assumptions of wealth. Tom found it hard to focus for more than a few seconds on the text. His greeny-grey eyes would always be seeking to escape from the cage of print. My garden walls became oppressive when he wanted not to read but to roam.

As I drove two older sisters of John Cosgrove to Kylemore Abbey to visit the Benedictine nuns, who had taught me the 'Our Father' in Irish when I was seven, they told me stories of their youth before they had emigrated to New York in the Thirties. Two of their stories were about the Lancashire cotton king, Mitchell Henry, for whom Kylemore Castle had been built in 1865. 'Lord Henry built a mausoleum for his wife when she died, and kept her there in a glass coffin, so that people could see her. Every Christmas Day at dinner time, he had the servants wheel the glass coffin on a trolley into the dining room, where it remained by the table while the family ate their turkey and plum pudding. But on one of these occasions the butler got drunk after dinner and the glass got cracked, so they had to bury her afterwards.

'The same Lord Henry had a poor man sent to prison for poaching a salmon out of the Derryinver river in the pool at the bridge. The priest and everyone begged him not to send the man to jail, because he had a wife and a large family. But Lord Henry was a hard man, and he owned the fishing rights, and he sent the poacher away to prison in Galway all the same. Shortly afterwards, Lord Henry's daughter was driving her carriage along the Derryinver road, when the horse bolted and tumbled the carriage into the river, just by the bridge where the poaching was done, and she was drowned.'

A year later I was to learn of John McGahern's success in teaching at a school in the East End of London a boy who was thought incapable of ever learning to read or write. The boy could not recognise the same group of letters if he saw them in a different position. For six months, according to John, he gave the boy special care in class. He threw him a bottle to catch – the bottle fell and broke. John said '*B* for bottle, *B* for break, *B* for bits,' making the boy feel the letters in the broken bits of bottle as he picked them up. Because the pupil never looked at the page but always at the teacher, John made him cut out a cardboard mask, which he put on his own face, and then made the boy stick letters on the mask and read out a word: B A T. After six months the boy read the headlines of the evening paper at home to his father, who came to the school and thanked John with tears in his eyes. The fathers of three of John's pupils were in prison.

At the end of October 1967, after a burst of autumnal energy, I finished 'The Battle of Aughrim' and drove to Coolea to give Seán Ó Riada a copy and talk about the music and the casting for the BBC production. He recommended Niall Tóibín but not Micheál Mac Liammóir. From there, via Rosslare and Fishguard, I drove to Devon to spend a night at Court Green with Ted and his father. Ted had been cooking their food and looking after the children since Assia had left to work in London. He was attracted by a theory that we should not eat at regular hours but, like animals, only when hungry. Our hunger proved to be regular.

There was a meeting of foxhounds in the market of North Tawton at eleven o'clock the next day. It had been raining heavily in the previous hour. Ted and I were standing in a garage doorway, while my car was being fitted with two remould tyres, talking about 'The Battle of Aughrim', which Ted had read since breakfast. Fragments of his remarks made my ears burn: 'It's like iron ... a terrific panorama, original and relevant ... continually interesting to read ... it doesn't take sides and it's not antiquarian ... you can only get through to these things, such as war, through the remoteness of "Aughrim", you can't deal directly with Vietnam horror, it's more effective to set it in the time scale of history.'

We had coffee in an empty shop after the hunt moved away in a downpour as heavy as the one pictured in Kurosawa's film *Rashomon*. When we spoke of Tony, whom we were planning to visit in Cornwall, Ted said he was someone who knew exactly what he was doing, who worked hard and lived cheaply, and was free. Tony did not exhibit his doubts as some of his friends did, and with his friends he made an effort to appear free of doubt, largely out of compassion. Then Ted told me of a theory that animals or men in the paws or jaws of a lion or other predator did not feel pain: they were terrified when hunted, but once they were caught they swooned into a pleasant trance in which they became part of the natural process; they watched an arm being bitten off, or a leg, without feeling pain. The assumption was that if everything is eaten, everything finally is devoured by one mouth.

The next day, Sunday 5 November, I drove with Ted to Exeter, where we met Assia and Shura, now two and a half, at the station, and went on to Cornwall over Dartmoor by Okehampton and Launceston to find Tony. It snowed, the road was icy under the snow, dark winter snow cloud hung over the moor, cars had their lights on. Beyond the moor it was wet but not snowy. We reached St Ives at sunset, waves dashing over the road around the harbour and spraying the painterly tea shops and studios along the Christopher Wood waterfront. Tony was staying down a lane in a row of tin miners' cottages at Boscaswell, a place almost as wild and remote as Slyne Head, and just as windy but with more people about – mostly out-of-work miners.

I gave Tony a copy of the poem and thanked him for his crucial help in showing me how the random, disparate poems I had been writing on themes relating to the battle, its causes and its consequences – the division of Ireland into North and South, Catholic and Protestant, Irish and Anglo-Irish – could form a sequence of four movements: Now, Before, During and After. I compared his advice to John Cosgrove's use of random stone to build a house.

During a meal of Irish stew cooked by Tony, Ted said that when he had something difficult to say he would imagine he was explaining it to a child, and it would become much clearer. Approving my decision not to read a part in the BBC recording of 'Aughrim', Ted agreed to read the sections titled 'Rapparees', 'Wolfhound' and 'Battle Hill Revisited' at the end. We thought Cecil Day-Lewis's voice could well express the triumphant Protestant English viewpoint.

Privately, Assia told me that she had left Court Green to resume work in advertising, but hated being alone, except for her child, in London. She had lost in the conflict waged by Ted's mother from her bed in a Devon hospital, and by his father, who hadn't spoken to her for the past year, though he had lived in the same house and had eaten at the same table the food she had cooked and served. She asked me if I felt the same 'atmosphere' existed today between herself and Ted as the one I had felt between him and Sylvia three months before Sylvia's suicide, and I replied, to give her hope, that it was altogether different.

Since my father's death, my mother had been spending the northern summers with Mary and Gerry at Rougham Chantry, a Queen Anne period house with a large garden, orchards and paddocks near Bury St Edmunds in Suffolk; and she had been going back to Southern Rhodesia for the winters. Now they were to give her a house of her own in the Chantry grounds, with urns on a flint wall enclosing her part of the garden, and peacocks on her bedroom windowsill at night. If the expert resident gardener planted a shrub in a place not selected by her, she'd ask him, politely, to dig it up and move it.

Mary and Gerry never stinted in what they could do to make her happy as a widow, inviting her to dine with them every night. Our mother, who demanded punctuality in others, would usually arrive a little late for dinner, making a regal entry with a gracious apology: 'I hope I haven't kept you all waiting?' She had often asked, 'Haven't you finished "Aughrim" yet? Why is it taking you so long?' and now was saying, 'I hope the next book won't take you five years to write. You'd better hurry up or I'll be dead.' I had heard her utter this warning so often in the previous thirty years that I replied, 'I think you're immortal.'

In Belfast for the arts festival at Queen's University on 24 November I saw much of Charles Monteith, who had decided that Faber would publish 'The Battle of Aughrim' with 'The God Who Eats Corn' as a single volume in September 1968. He showed me around his old school, Royal Belfast Academical Institution, known as 'Inst', and mentioned that when he had to wear spectacles at the age of twelve it made him feel that nobody would ever love him, and since then he could not feel desire for anyone who wore spectacles. He had lived with his parents at their drapery shop in Lisburn, where he sometimes served behind the counter. When he realised he was years ahead of his age group in school he began to think he was peculiar and later discovered he was queer. His only brother, younger than himself, had become a doctor with a practice in County Tyrone. Their father was a Presbyterian and their mother Church of Ireland.

When John McGahern lectured on Herman Melville's 'Bartleby the Scrivener', he made an oral poem out of his love for the story, the style and the vision. The rhythm and sound of his Leitrim voice uttering the refrain 'I'd prefer not to', the clarity of his obscure thought, the trembling of the piece of paper he was holding in his hand, kept me on tenterhooks, not to miss a word, hoping he'd not break down. Of course he didn't, and went on to talk about Proust's *Contre Sainte-Beuve* and to quote Bergson on laughter and Kafka's story *The Metamorphosis* about a man who turned into an insect.

Later – handling hecklers with polite firmness – he read from his own works: the father's boots episode in *The Dark*, the mother's death in *The Barracks*. His abstract statements were a foil to the concrete precision of his prose style. If style is creative memory, as he suggested, may I be forgiven for remembering creatively that John said, 'Art is as mortal as life: whether it lasts one year or a million years, like us it must die. It's a game, the most interesting game there is. It's not religion, but false religion: the writer sets up as God, king and counsellor. A man who takes a pen in his hand has already convicted himself of egotism. Art, like philosophy, merely refines our ignorance. We write to please ourselves: it's amazing that someone should want to publish what we write. That is not our concern, our concern is to write well, to write as well as we can.'

At lunch John introduced me to Madeline Green, who was to become his second wife, now on her first visit to Ireland. She was living in Paris and had grown up in New York in the neighbourhood of John's American publisher, Patrick Gregory, who worked at Knopf. On John's recommendation Patrick was soon to be able to persuade Robert Gottlieb at Knopf to publish 'The Battle of Aughrim' in America. I gave John a copy of the poem and two weeks later he rang from London to tell me what he thought. Because it was written from the outside, it was not the kind of work that had his sympathy, but he felt 'cold admiration'.

Seamus Heaney chaired my reading of 'The Battle of Aughrim' to a small audience, that included Charles Monteith, in the students' union at Queen's University. It was the first reading of the complete poem. Three or four times I was interrupted by a loud Belfast voice on the public-address system telling someone to go to the main entrance as if we were in a railway station. Seamus pleased me in his courteous words at the end by describing the poem as 'relevant'. The trouble in the past that the poem focused upon was about to erupt in the future.

The British Arts Council had awarded Patrick Kavanagh the same amount, £1,200, as I was given. It came when he was dying and, according to Patricia, he had said, 'Too late.' The last time I had met Kavanagh he was talking to a garda sergeant in the sitting room of Patricia's flat overlooking the Grand Canal on the morning after the night in which he had fallen, or been pushed, into the canal. Having dragged himself out at midnight, he had spent the rest of the night at her flat, and she had already gone out and bought him a new suit. At this time she had promised to buy him a bottle of whiskey a day for the rest of his life, knowing that he hadn't long to live. Paddy was making a statement to the sergeant, accusing a man of attempted murder. The sergeant asked if he had seen the man who had pushed him. Paddy replied no, but he knew well who had given him the bum's rush in the dark.

Before this, Emily had told me that once, when her mother was driving Paddy Kavanagh to see his sisters in Monaghan, he was very drunk, kept sighing and saying, 'Oh dear God,' then turned around and asked her, 'What are you?' Emily answered, 'I'm a girl.' 'No, you're not!' said Paddy, 'You're a little beast', which he pronounced 'baysht'. A few minutes later he turned to her and asked again, 'What are you?' 'A little baysht,' said Emily 'No, you're *not!*' said the poet, 'You're a girl', and so on, to her embarrassment. When Paddy's sisters invited Emily to stay in their house, she was too scared to accept.

On my return to Cleggan I received a call from London asking me to write Kavanagh's obituary for *The Times*, and, declining, I recommended Denis Donoghue, who knew the work and the man better than I did. Donoghue wrote, 'Even in print he found it hard to take the high road of thought when the expected route was the low road of temperament.'

With a fraction of my Arts Council tax-free award I bought for £200 a stone-built house that had a quarry-slated roof on a quiet gravel lane in Headford, going nowhere except to a bog. Known as the Old Dispensary, the building had been empty for a couple of years and vandalised, but all it needed were some repairs to make it habitable for the Conroy family of Travellers. I hoped there would be no objections, because the neighbours on each side were more than fifty yards away, with fields in between.

But I was wrong. At the end of November I received a challenge to attend a protest meeting on 6 December in a potato store near the house. The virulence of the crowd astonished me. The Conroys were not accorded the dignity of being mentioned by name. A farmer declared, 'Tinkers will always be tinkers;

they were born the way they are, and they'll never change. Whatever you try to do to improve them, they will always be the same.'

I argued that the Conroys were descended on their father's side from a farmer who had been evicted from his land at Rosmuc in the time of the Famine, and on their mother's from the Wards, who were descended from the bards, whose wandering way of life and poetry had been destroyed by the British occupants of Ireland; and that in my childhood at Milford, eight miles from the small market town of Headford, tinkers who made tin cans had been welcomed and respected by farmers, but the invention of plastic had deprived them of their living. I stressed that the town had raised no objection to the Conroys wintering in squalor on a public road near the Bank of Ireland, but wanted to prevent them living in a house where their children would not be so endangered by disease or traffic.

The young man who chaired the meeting refused to allow me to switch on my tape recorder, argued against me, and finally called for a vote on the question: 'Are we for the tinkers or against them? Those who are for the tinkers having this house raise their hands.' One hand was raised, that of Neil Sharkey, manager of the Royal Tara China Company in Galway, and nearest neighbour to the Old Dispensary. 'Those against.' All except three raised their hands. The chairman said it was unanimous.

Having spoken their minds, the protestors, law-abiding citizens, took no further action. By Christmas the house was repaired and furnished. James Kelly, a priest and teacher at the boys' secondary school, blessed it; the Conroys moved in and their neighbours treated them well. Later Galway County Council purchased the house for what it had cost me, with an agreement that the council would allow the Conroys to live there indefinitely.

Ellen King, who had attended in 1964 my poetry reading in New York, where she had lived for thirty years, told me what had happened to her one day at home when she was a child in Cleggan.

'In a time of hunger after the boats were lost, a tinker woman was walking past the pier. She looked very angry. My father asked her what was the matter. "The little girl in your house gave me nothing, and told me to go away. She swept me out the door with a broom like I was an old hen. I was never so insulted in all my life."

'"Come back to the house with me this minute and I'll teach that lassie of mine some manners," my father replied. But he had a hard time coaxing her to go with him. When they came into the house he made me go down on my knees and beg forgiveness of the woman I had refused. Then I had to boil a kettle on the turf fire and make tea for her, giving her soda bread from the pot-oven, and butter from the churn. "Remember always," my father said, "it's only by the grace of God that you were born in a house and that woman in a tent."

For the first three months of 1968 in London I rented Tony's flat near the Portobello Road. Neither walls nor floors were soundproof. He had tried to hate it less by putting up an almost life-size poster of Marlon Brando in black leather on a motorbike and, facing Brando, footballers in contest for the ball. Tony had a part-time job in a London pub that required him to wash plastic flowers in a bucket of detergent before opening, and he wanted to be 'on the move' – the title of one of his friend Thom Gunn's best poems.

The post of visiting scholar, which required me to do no more than spend a few hours with poetry students one day a week at Reading University, midway between London and Oxford, had been offered to me by Professor D.J. Gordon while he was staying in Connemara the previous summer. The revolution had not yet broken out in the universities. An authority on Oscar Wilde, the *Yellow Book* and the *fin de siècle*, Gordon had been given the professorship at a very young age. He was short, lean and highly intelligent, with a mordant wit, but had published little. Once, when students were waiting for him to come to a classroom on the first floor, he had climbed a ladder, stepped through the window and lectured flawlessly without a word to explain his bizarre entry.

After the main event of my term, a poetry reading that Gordon had arranged, he held a sherry party in his office. 'I couldn't attend your reading, Richard, I'm afraid, because of my back,' he explained, while his left hand applied pressure to the rear of his hip to show where the pain was gripping. 'I never attend lectures because I can't sit down for long, but I gather your reading went rather well. Indeed,' – and he paused to take a long ironical sniff, swinging his shoulders to the right, and throwing back his head to look up into my face at an acute angle – 'it would appear that only Auden ever drew as large a crowd to a poetry reading. They tell me the room was packed. Congratulations, Richard! The students must have thought it was compulsory.'

During the weekend of 17 February, on a visit to Ted in Devon, he and I went for a drink at Burton Hall, a pub owned by Winston Churchill's wartime bodyguard, deserted except for a mynah asleep in a birdcage. We talked about

Ted's version of Seneca's *Oedipus*, which Peter Brook was about to produce at the Old Vic, starring John Gielgud as Oedipus and Irene Worth as Jocasta. The work had appealed to Ted because of its objectivity, the need to write words that actors have to speak. Then he spoke about Sylvia, and I noted some of his remarks soon afterwards.

Sylvia had the power, he said, to see their personal life objectively, to turn it into a myth. The less successful poems in *Ariel* failed only where she had failed to make them completely objective, to see herself as another person, as part of a mythological event. She was really so easy to satisfy, all she wanted was to be told things would be all right. Assia had once rung her up, and this was why she had uprooted the telephone wires from Court Green. He had dreamed of Court Green long before they had bought it: inside was an electric machine that went out of order and turned the house upside down.

Aurelia, Sylvia's mother, advised her to get a divorce, to hit him in his pocket, to remove the children. He thought that Sylvia wanted an alternative for herself in Ireland to balance his plan to spend six months in Spain with Assia. Sylvia had started to write the *Ariel* poems before she came to Ireland, and had already written 'The Moon and the Yew Tree'. She used in her last poems things he had said, and she twisted them with irony. Her poem 'Event' had seemed to him at the time she wrote it a betrayal of their private life, and bit by bit she had betrayed all that life till there was nothing left.

He admitted that his leaving her alone in Cleggan was cruel. Before this he had dreamed of a wolverine drowning itself in shallow water: Sylvia was the wolverine, and she hadn't wanted him to write the poem out of the dream. He saw a snake of immense length uncoiling and turning into a forest. If he had acted more quickly in the last week, when she had asked him to take her away, Ted said, her suicide might have been avoided.

As a new Fellow of the Royal Society of Literature, introduced by Cecil Day-Lewis, I signed a large page with Byron's pen on 29 February. The other fellow to be enrolled that evening, Harold Pinter, didn't appear. Roy Fuller gave a lecture in which he complimented John Lehmann, who was sitting in the front row. A young woman (not a fellow) from Ceylon, wearing a sari, asked me who were the great writers that she ought to meet, and could I tell her, please, who were the poets writing for our time? Clearly one of them was not our chairman, Richard Church, withered and forlorn, who said he was living at Sissinghurst, that Harold Nicolson was gaga, recognised nobody, was not aware of the success his *Diaries* had had, and was cared for by a male nurse. 'He always had a rather shallow mind,' Church opined, 'but Vita's poetry, particularly *The Land*, will survive.'

But for Harold's helping hand, I would not have been listening to Richard Church. Harold often said, 'I've been so lucky in my life, especially being married to Vita.' I remember him with a rolled umbrella hailing a taxi on Piccadilly to take me to dine at the Beefsteak, and pausing to say, 'I'm not afraid to die, but I dread old age.'

Charles entertained me well in London and sometimes for weekends at All Souls. He gave a large lunch party there on Sunday 3 March, attended by Iris Murdoch and John Bayley, Elizabeth Jennings – whose *Collected Poems* had recently been published – and John Wain with his wife, Eirian. The talk turned to whether authors should read reviews of their own books. Wain declared that he never read reviews, and, to make sure, before he looked at a magazine or a newspaper Eirian would cut out any notices of his books that it contained. When I suggested that he might be upset by seeing no gaps on the literary pages, Charles said, 'In that case, Eirian hands John a copy of *Time* magazine with the cover photograph missing.'

At the Portobello studios of Raidió Éireann in Dublin, Seán Ó Riada, wearing dark glasses and smoking thin cigars, directed Ceoltóirí Chualann at a recording of his music for *The Battle of Aughrim* on the last Sunday in May 1968.

Paddy Maloney – 'the greatest piper in Ireland' – complained of fatigue, having played in a pub all the previous night until five in the morning. At first his pipes were too cold, and later they were too hot, so he walked out on to the street, saying he needed to clear from the pipes the smoke of Seán's cigars. The studio manager complained that the harpsichord was emitting a 'string jangle', so he came round from his glass booth and went into action like Buster Keaton in a silent movie, removing the top of the harpsichord and wedging the music stand with books. These preludes ended when Ó Riada charmed the musicians into producing heroic rhythms and sounds beyond the power of words.

Douglas Cleverdon had come over from London to record the music for his BBC production. The words were to be recorded at Broadcasting House with Cyril Cusack, Niall Tóibín, Cecil Day-Lewis, Margaret Robertson and Ted Hughes in London. To open and close the poem, Seán had taken the melody of a song called in English 'After Aughrim's Great Disaster'. He played this as a funeral march, with a goatskin drum suggesting armies. Between the poem's four parts came 'O'Neill's Cavalry March', then 'The White Cockade', with the glorious panache of tragic optimism before the battle. After the battle Seán astonished and moved some of us to tears with 'Limerick's Lamentation', a song he had found in a rare eighteenth-century copy.

The musicians played these great melodies by ear with feeling and dignity. Never mind that the poem's balance of opposing forces was dissolved by the passion of Seán's Irish nationalism. He didn't want his music to reconcile the ancient conflict, but to win.

During one of Emily's summer holidays in Cleggan, perhaps when she was twelve years old in 1968, we received a sudden invitation to dine with Robert Shaw and Mary Ure at the Renvyle House Hotel.

The dining room was crowded with guests who pretended not to be listening but could not help turning to look when the great actor raised his voice. He was talking to me, ignoring Mary and Emily, and during the main course Mary interrupted, in a lyrical voice that could reach every ear in the room without shouting, to ask Emily if she had ever acted in a play at school. With more shame than pride, Emily said she had played Bottom in *A Midsummer Night's Dream*, and Mary replied, 'How wonderful! I had to play that part at school, and everyone teased me about Bottom having the ass' head, but really it's the best part in the play.' Emily was glowing with this encouragement from one of the most beautiful actresses in the world, when Robert roared, 'If I'm not going to be allowed to speak, I'm going upstairs to my room.'

There was dead silence as the manager glided over to our table to enquire if Mr Shaw was enjoying his meal. Then Robert's monologue resumed. After the dessert the manager came to say he had prepared a special place for us to have our coffee and liqueurs where we'd be comfortable and not disturbed by other guests. He led us a long way down to the far end of the basement.

There was a ping-pong table, and Robert in a mellow mood offered to play with Emily. She accepted the challenge, and defeated him by a very narrow margin in two games. I was so sure that he had let her win out of kindness that I thanked him when Emily left the room for a moment. 'Didn't you notice I was playing with my left hand?' he asked abrasively.

Mary intervened: 'Robert can play as well with his left hand as with his right. Before acting in a film that required him to do this, he hired a world champion table-tennis player to teach him.'

On the road to Salruck on Sunday 8 September 1968, my mother told me to 'look at that beautiful view' with so much emphasis that I wanted to close my eyes. She was dressed up in solemn mood to attend the memorial service held annually to commemorate her two first cousins, Colin and Robin Barber, sons of her Aunt Violet, killed in the war. Lord Fisher of Lambeth, formerly archbishop of Canterbury, had accepted Aunt Violet's invitation to preach.

The service was held in the little church that my mother's great-grandfather, Lieutenant General Alexander Thomson CB, colonel of the 74th Highlanders, had built in 1835, hoping to convert his poor Catholic tenants by distributing Protestant Bibles in Irish. The tenants' reluctance to receive the Bibles may be deduced from the large number that remained on the bookshelves in the drawing room at Salruck for the next hundred years. 'Change and decay in all around I see' were apt words to sing in those worm-eaten pews, with my mother scowling at me for mumbling them. Walls weeping with damp carried marble and brass plaques commemorating our dead relations. Lord Fisher in the pulpit played on the faltering organ of his voice, pulling out its richly Anglican, ecclesiastical, officer and gentleman stops.

'The wonderful thing about Ireland,' he intoned, pausing for us to wonder, 'and I've been coming to this country for a very long time,' he continued, with a longer pause for this to sink in, 'is that *nothing* ever changes.' Immured in the Anglican precincts of his mind, the archbishop seemed unaware of the trouble that had broken out in the North, and not to have noticed all the new bungalows with running water and electric light that had replaced the old thatched cottages in the west.

'How should we think of God?' he asked rhetorically, staring up at the roof, and keeping us waiting for his answer. 'I think we should regard the Almighty as the *senior* partner' ... pause ... 'of a firm in which *we*' ... on a higher note followed by a longer pause ... 'are the *junior* partners.' Ten to twelve years after this church was built, a lot of people without a job in God's Anglican firm starved to death in the Famine.

In the drawing room after the service my mother needled me to hand around the cakes, to say something pleasant to Aunt Violet, and to be sure to shake hands with Lord Fisher. She wanted everyone to notice that her son was making a good impression. On our way home she wished I would stop being critical of the senile archbishop.

'I want to die,' she said, 'before I lose my mind like poor Granny. I love Salruck, but oh how sad it makes me feel going back! The house hasn't changed a bit, where Aunt Rosie died when I was a child, during the Great

War, and Granny brought me over from Scotland for the funeral, with black crêpe sewn on my sailor suit. There's even the same smell of old dogs in the hall. Didn't you notice it?'

On the night of Saturday 14 September 1968, Tony introduced me in Dublin for the first time to one of his lovers, an ebullient woman called Pixie Weir, now living in London after having been brought up on a sheep farm in New Zealand. Pixie had come to Dublin as a production assistant for the actor and TV director Richard Marquand, who had been hired to direct an advertisement for the Fianna Fáil party to use in a possible referendum to abolish proportional representation and substitute with first-past-the-post elections. Backing this project designed to keep Fianna Fáil permanently in power was the minister for finance, Charles Haughey.

Pixie and Tony brought me to meet Marquand at the house of Sam Stephenson, well known as the architect of several government buildings in a modern style that had required the destruction of many fine Georgian houses. We entered a split-level, terrazzo-floored living room, with a square sunken area like a shallow splash pool in the centre. Bench seats on three sides of this square were upholstered in brick-red leather. The fourth contained a stone-faced hearth in which a turf fire was burning. Among the prominent people in the room – we were not introduced – was Mr Haughey, who was standing in a group near a glitzy cocktail cabinet on the higher level.

For a while I sat on the lower level talking to Sam's wife, who told me that ten years ago Sam had been earning £6 a week. Since then he had won a few big government contracts. As we were talking, Mr Haughey, with a drink in his hand, instead of walking around the square to the steps beside the fireplace, took a short cut, leaving his footprint on the leather. I didn't meet him until he noticed that we were leaving. When someone told him that a long section from my poem 'The Battle of Aughrim' had appeared that morning in the *Irish Times*, Mr Haughey expressed surprise. 'I thought that was written by an Irishman.' And when someone told him I was an Irishman, living in Connemara, he said, 'We must give you a grant.'

Faber published *The Battle of Aughrim* on 16 September 1968, my mother's seventieth birthday, celebrated by us all in London. Almost at the same time the BBC recording was broadcast on the Third Programme, and a version for television filmed in the summer was broadcast by RTÉ. The TV film, directed by Jack Dowling, took as long as Cleverdon's BBC production, but only used half the text, spoken by Siobhán McKenna, unfortunately not in a Juno but a Joan of Arc mood, and myself, with Seán Ó Riada at the harpsichord. The broadcast earned a good rating from audience research, but the film failed to win the Golden Harp Award, for which it was Ireland's entry.

To mark the occasion in London with Emily, we exchanged gifts of gold-nibbed fountain pens. She needed but could not get a left-handed nib. Her pen was red and mine a black Parker 61, with which I would continue to write in notebooks till the end of the century.

When Douglas Cleverdon's production of *The Battle of Aughrim* was broadcast for the second time on the BBC Third Programme that autumn, my mother was staying in Bray, County Wicklow with her sister-in-law, Bunty Ormsby, mother of my cousin Tom. After moving into Milford, Tom had 'bulldozed three Bronze Age raths' and stripped the slates off our church at Kilmaine to roof a pigsty. I had included in the long poem a short passage that slated my 'kinsman' for abusing an inheritance that I thought should have given him a sense of piety towards the previous occupiers of the soil and the forgotten builders of a well-built church. This passage was read by Ted Hughes, who filled it with his own intense feeling against destroyers of evidence of what in the past had been held sacred.

My mother had heard the first broadcast and was keen for her sister-in-law to hear the second, except for my 'jealous' attack on 'poor Tom who was doing his best to farm Milford profitably'. She told me herself – I wasn't there – that she knew when to expect the words that were likely to offend, after a passage read by the actor Niall Tóibín. As soon as Ted began 'Left a Cromwellian demesne …' my mother stood up, saying, 'I think the wireless needs to be tuned', while she twiddled the knobs, and switched off the power. 'Oh dear!' she said, 'What have I done? I'm so sorry. I seem to have turned it off. How silly of me! I should have left it alone.' By the time Bunty had readjusted the set, Cecil Day-Lewis was reading a poem about my baptism in Kilmaine.

At the Peacock Theatre on Sunday 8 December I directed a reading of 'The Battle of Aughrim' by Eavan Boland, Cyril Cusack, Cecil Day-Lewis, Ted Hughes and Niall Tóibín, with music played on stage by The Chieftains. The actors, poets and musicians generously waived their fees, and tickets were sold at a high price for what was the major event in a week of fundraising by the Dublin Itinerant Settlement Committee. Paddy Maloney later persuaded Garech Browne at Claddagh Records to issue as an LP the BBC recording of the poem, in which Paddy and his players had taken part with Seán Ó Riada.

Before the end of 1968 Cecil Day-Lewis and Philip Larkin had recommended me for the Compton Lectureship in Poetry, which would require me to live at the University of Hull in East Yorkshire for half of three ten-week terms in the calendar year 1969. Larkin was alleged to have taken his appointment as librarian at Hull because in 1954 Hull was a heavily bombed and not yet rebuilt port, smelling of fish, at the end of a branch railway line, where no one would bother to visit him. I was expected to give one poetry reading – no lectures or creative-writing classes – and talk to students who might be interested in writing poetry.

No sooner had I accepted this job by mail from Cleggan than I received a phone call from a stranger called Bruce Berlind at Colgate University in upstate New York inviting me to hold the O'Connor Chair to teach courses in creative writing and modern British and Irish poetry for a term of four months, starting in January, at a far higher salary. Because of my commitment to Hull, I advised Bruce to ring John McGahern, and John accepted. The Colgate English faculty were to admire and appreciate McGahern at Colgate and often invite him to return. Thanks to his recommendation I would hold the same chair for two semesters in 1971.

The attic had become my study at the New Forge, where I still used notebooks lined with small squares from France for the first or the fiftieth draft of a poem before typing it. Routinely I'd begin – after breakfast following a run – by noting a line or a dream that had occurred to me in the night and continuing with notes for a poem that I sometimes destroyed by revising too much. My mother's good advice in my childhood, never to give up a job until it was finished otherwise you'd get used to not finishing jobs, kept me persisting in attempts to redeem failures instead of advancing on new tracks. But before locking my mind into the cage of metre and rhyme, I sometimes let myself go in a passage of prose about my surroundings, as in this paragraph written on 20 March 1969.

> Three pairs of wooden struts form three isosceles triangles in my attic, lit by two golden-rectangular skylights and one window in the gable wall. Behind my black armchair a pink granite chimney breast narrows to the roof. Within arm's reach are the twelve volumes of the *Oxford English Dictionary* and other reference works. An oak workbench, used by the carpenters when they built this house, stands between me and the dictionary on my right; and on my left there's another oak table, made from pieces left over after the new

floors were fitted at Lake Park. From a steel-framed desk, facing a window in the north gable, I can look across a meadow rising to a wall at the top of a cliff. Beyond is the sea, invisible. On a calm day, though days are rarely calm in Cleggan, I can hear the waves. Two skylights give my work the clarity it needs without the distraction of a view of what's happening in the village. At night, rain falling on their panes of thick plate glass sounds as quiet and homely as a clavichord vibrating in the room.

A note written after two lines of verse, that were later discarded from a poem ('Little Hunger') about making 'integral' the granite remnants of ruined houses, shows how the poet as builder wrote himself into a block.

> Did I need stone to build a house
> or a house to build with stone?

Having written those two lines after much effort, I relaxed, expecting to return with renewed vigour, but could not come to grips again, the gathered energy was gone. I could only repeat and repeat and repeat, harking to the sound of words while chipping away their sense. I wandered down the village to ask some post-office workers not to erect a telephone pole in the middle of our public playground. The search for a rhyme stalled me. It reminded me of Tommy Coohill walking round a heap of granite that he had turned over several times already, trying to select the right stone to fit a gap in John Cosgrove's course of random masonry.

The next evening Ted rang with bad news: 'Assia and Shura are dead.' I asked him if there was anything I could do. 'Nothing that anyone can do. Send flowers.' He gave me the address of the Ashton Funeral Parlour in Clapham, and said he would write me a letter. It was difficult to hear on a bad line. I rang Tony, who said he'd have the flowers sent and go to the cremation.

Finding herself in the same situation as Sylvia six years earlier – in a London flat with Ted's child while Ted was in the country with another woman – Assia had ended her life by the same means: poison gas from a cooker. But whereas Sylvia had carefully arranged for her children to be saved, Assia had put Shura, aged five, to sleep on a mattress on the kitchen floor. Then she had drunk whiskey, turned on the gas and lain down.

I was reading Sir Thomas Browne at the time, and copied in my notebook his apt and moving question: 'Who can but pity the merciful intention of those hands that do destroy themselves?' Shortly afterwards, in a low key, I wrote three couplets called 'Lullaby':

> Before you'd given death a name
> Like Bear or Crocodile, death came
>
> To take your mother out one night.
> But when she'd said her last good night
>
> You cried, 'I don't want you to go,'
> So in her arms she took you too.

A year earlier I had last seen Assia in Middlesex Hospital, where she had gone for tests in February 1968 because she feared she had cancer. In fact she was suffering from depression and anxiety, but looked well, reclining on pillows, surrounded by flowers, beautiful as ever.

My first impression of High Island had been formed in 1953 when Pat Concannon was teaching me how to sail a pookaun. Leaving Bofin harbour by the narrow channel between the Gun Rock and the Dog Fish Breaker, he had told me to head for High Island. But he'd never suggested landing there because it was five miles away and landing was impossible unless the sea was exceptionally calm – no pier to tie up at, no smooth sand for beaching a boat and no safe anchorage. Anyone trying to go ashore would have to jump from the boat to the rock and clamber up a cliff.

My first visit to High Island – or Ard Oileán in Irish, sometimes anglicised as Ardilaun – was on my father's last visit, sixty years after his first. With my mother, my sister Liz and Emily, we managed to land on Sunday 27 September 1964. The following Easter my father was buried in Clifden. My mother kept at her bedside until she died, over thirty years later, a photograph, taken by Liz, of my father sitting on the grass beside an ancient carved stone cross that greets pilgrims as they reach the top of the cliff above the landing cove on the south-east side. That was the origin of my interest in the island.

In the Pier Bar in Cleggan, on the night of 30 March 1969, I heard that the owner, Graham Tulloch – who had let me use his vacant drawing room for writing 'The God Who Eats Corn' in 1963 – was planning to sell High Island because grazing sheep there had become unprofitable. I got excited at the thought of buying this inaccessible holy island, restoring the beehive cells and oratory of its derelict hermitage, and preserving the place from destruction either by tourists or by sheep.

I found a description of the island in a book written in 1684 by Roderic O'Flaherty:

> It is unaccessible but in calm settled weather, and so steep that it is hard after landing in it to climb to the top; where there is a well called Brian Boramy (King of Ireland) his well, and a standing water, on the brook whereof was a mill. There is extant a chappel and a large round wall, as also that kind of stone building called Cloghan. Therein yearly an eyrie of hawkes is found. Here St Fechin founded an abbey, as he did at Imay. It is also celebrated for the eremitical retirement of Saint Gormgal, a very spiritual person, and of renouwned sanctity, who dyed the 5th of August, Anno 1017; and was there interred together with divers other holy hermits that lived with him.

The next morning I started negotiations with Graham, who wanted to sell two smaller islands with High Island (eighty statute acres) because all three were on the same title deed. Quickly I found a couple willing to buy Friar and Malthooa, which, between them, had a safe harbour for a small boat in bad weather. Tony rang at 6 p.m. from London to tell me that everyone at the cremation of Assia and Shura was speechless; he hadn't been able to say a word to Ted or Ted to him. Hearing about High Island, he urged me strongly to buy it. So I drove up to Shanbolard Hall and Graham accepted my offer. For little more than Hull University had paid for my first stint I bought High Island, and the following day wrote this note:

> Tuesday 1st April 1969 – Cleggan
> Buying an island, even with the intention of creating a wild life sanctuary, is a predatory act among predators, much easier than writing a book. Once you become the owner, your view of the island alters: you turn possessive and protective. People regard you as a different person – a man who owns an island and therefore must be rich. But I know that High Island can never be possessed because it will always remain in the possession of the sea. Its virtue will grow from its contemplation not its use, from feelings and ideas evoked by its wild life and its end of the world terrain.

St Fechin, I knew, had founded monasteries in the seventh century at Fore in County Westmeath, Cong in County Mayo and on Omey Island (Imay). Now I was to learn that the hermitage on Ard Oileán, his last foundation before he died of the plague, was a cenobitic laura where monks imposed on themselves extraordinary penances, and that Fechin 'used to set his wretched rib on the hard prison without raiment'.

According to John V. Kelleher of Harvard, St Gormgall was a noted *anmchara* ('soul-friend') of the high king Brian Boru, who was killed by a Dane at the Battle of Clontarf on Good Friday 1014. The water in the well near the top of the hill on High Island was said to have turned into blood for ever after the moment when the high king was slain. I'd noticed in 1964 that Brian Boru's well water was still dark red and undrinkable, but by 1969 it had turned black. When Pat Concannon had heard about this, he'd remarked, 'That must be on account of the trouble in the North.' Gormgall's name possibly meant 'dark stranger', but Kelleher thought 'blue valour' or 'blue-eyed foreigner' more likely, and the names of Gormgall's twelve fellow hermits, buried with him on the island, suggested that they had come from Clare, Brian's territory. With a scriptorium attached to the hermitage, High Island had been a literary as well as a religious centre. A poem was written about St Gormgall, but he didn't write poetry, which is what I was hoping the island would inspire.

My second stint at Hull was happier than my first because I rented from the novelist Malcolm Bradbury a cottage situated beside an old church in a village called Lockington, six miles from the university. My post merely required me to sit for a few hours a week in an office in the library where students showed me their work. Most days I had a stand-up lunch of beer and sandwiches with Philip Larkin, who used to drink two pints to my one. At my inaugural reading of 'The Battle of Aughrim' he had switched off his hearing aid, fallen asleep and snored.

On 14 May 1969 Ted Hughes rang to invite me over for the day to see his and the Brontë country, West Yorkshire. His mother had died and he was staying with his father at the Beacon above Heptonstall. Ted showed me a small red-brick end-of-terrace house in Mytholmroyd where he had been born and spent his first eight years before the family had moved to Mexborough. He took me through Hebden Bridge, where his mother and father had been born, telling me his mother had been a Farrar, descended from the family of

Nicholas Ferrar, one of the Little Gidding group in the seventeenth century. And he showed me Haworth.

His father could remember when four hundred men and women were employed at a textile mill in the narrow valley below his house, where nobody was working now. The workers had to walk in clogs ten miles across the moors from Burnley every morning and back at night, for most of the year in the dark. Ted's father used to swim in the warm, dyed effluent of the mill, released promptly at 4.30 p.m. into the river.

After lunch Ted took me on foot down the hill below his father's house to see a place he had intended to buy with Assia six years earlier, called the Manor Farm or Lumb Bank. The large stone house stood on a terrace cut into the hillside among fields walled with sandstone and blackened by the smoke of extinct mills. Sixteen acres of land, Ted said, a house, a flat, two cottages, a barn, a walled garden, several fine beech trees and a folly. The slope felt vertiginous, like some of Ted's bird poems. We could see the rooftops of a town far below us to the east. The hill on the other side of the valley was wooded and equally precipitous.

As we were passing the gate Ted told me that ten years ago a man who fancied this place had gone and knocked on the door and asked the old woman who lived there if she'd like to sell it for £2,000, which she did. Hearing this, I suggested that he should do the same: go and knock on the door and ask the owners if they'd care to sell their house and land. Ted was looking for an alternative to Court Green. So we went together, and the man who answered our knocking said immediately that if anyone offered him £6,000 cash he'd be tempted.

On our walk back to the top of the hill we were caught in a thunderstorm and our clothes were drenched. The lightning seemed to Ted a sign that he should buy the property, which in due course he did. Eventually he would employ Tony to convert it into a centre known as Arvon to accommodate adult students for short courses in creative writing, led by poets and novelists.

From Lumb Bank Ted took me to Heptonstall Church to see Sylvia's grave in a modern annex to the old and overcrowded graveyard. Sylvia's grey headstone, simple and bold, carried a cryptic epigraph from the *Bhagavad Gita*, leaded into the granite: 'EVEN AMIDST FIERCE FLAMES THE GOLDEN LOTUS CAN BE PLANTED.'

Meanwhile, though he had driven with the children all the way from Devon the previous day, he had been working on his new selection of Shakespeare for Faber: scissoring out the passages he liked best, and pasting them into a book. He said that just before Assia's death he had been working on 'Crow' and it had become so horrible he had put it aside. Of Assia herself he said, 'If I'd put a ring on her finger she'd still be alive.'

Two days later Ted paid a return visit to Lockington and stayed overnight. He offered to give some deer to High Island, if they would survive there. On Saturday 17 May Philip Larkin and the young Scottish poet Douglas Dunn came to lunch. Philip wanted to take our photographs standing together in the graveyard, so he placed his camera, which had a time switch, on a flat tombstone and joined the group himself before the camera clicked. While I was cooking our lunch Douglas wanted to know how each of us got going on a poem. Philip replied that it was like knitting: you start with a certain number of stitches on a needle, having chosen a pattern that you have to complete. He also quoted 'the nightingale sings with her breast pressed against a thorn'. Not until many years later did I learn in Sri Lanka that Larkin's apparently flippant metaphor of knitting was rooted, though he may not have known this, in a single Sanskrit word with multiple meanings that included knitting, sewing, or the stitching together of words in poetry.

Being busy in the kitchen I missed Douglas's answer to his own question and Ted's reply. But in Cleggan in 1966 Ted had told me how he sometimes got started on a poem. He'd sit on the edge of a bed and focus his mind on the coccyx, or cuckoo bone, at the base of his spine, blanking out all other thoughts, until he'd start to feel himself falling and falling as if from a great height through the bed and the floor and the ground, deeper and deeper into the underworld, till he'd fall into a wide-awake trance in which he'd assume the body of a bird, a beast, a fish, a tree or a stone. The poem from that depth might take off in ways he could never have consciously conceived. His fault, he said, was sometimes to bombard the poem with technique.

And I remember John McGahern once telling me, 'I look for the pain and when I find the pain I write.'

Needing a boat to reach High Island, I bought from Pete Burke, the son of Willie, the Inishbofin boat wright, the decaying hull of the boat in which Pat Concannon and four others had survived the Cleggan Disaster. She had never been used since 1927, but kept in front of the Burkes's house above the shore of Bofin's East End harbour as a reminder of the great storm. Pete had repaired her over the years to prevent her falling to pieces, never intending to put her again on the sea. When I asked him and Jim Cunnane, who had renovated the *Ave Maria* and built a punt for me in 1959, to build a pookaun on the model of Pete's relic, they agreed. We named the new boat the *Pateen*, after Pat Cloherty, who recently, while sitting by his fire smoking his pipe, had died. The pookaun was to be powered by an outboard engine in addition to a dipping lugsail of tan Terylene fastened to a gaff longer than the mast.

In August my mother and Emily, brother Chris and Marcelle and their four children, Fiona, Anthony, Robert and Oona, with their Spanish nanny, all stayed with me at the New Forge. Instead of buying a holy island that summer, Chris bought a derelict sixteenth-century Norman castle, or tower house, that he would reconstruct and use as a very large holiday home on the eastern shore of Lough Corrib near Headford. To prepare the roofless oratory on High Island for a Mass that we had arranged, Chris and his two sons and I went out in the *Pateen* on Saturday 9 August. A note written two days later gave this account:

> Unscalable cliffs … groundswell resounding like a great deep-noted gong beaten inside the precipitous rock … fouled anchor … haven- less shore … calm coves … slant slits in the mica schist rock … igneous formation … Chris was determined to rebuild the altar, using stones that were lying inside the church … the eastern gable had long ago collapsed into a mound of stones behind the altar … a few large stones had fallen off the top of the western gable, clut- tering the doorway, which we cleared, thereby increasing its height … under the stones we found two stormpetrels' nests, each with a young bird opening its beak to be fed … two empty eggshells … our clearance to find a paved floor had violated the breeding of these shy birds … when a bird built a nest in St Kevin's hand while he was praying, he held the nest in his hand until the chicks had flown.

On 13 August 1969, the sea having calmed enough for us to land on High Island, an eclectic group of Catholics (including my daughter Emily, Mary Coyne and Margaret Day), Protestants (including my mother) and doubters like me came together at the hermitage to hear Mass – whether for summer entertainment, or in varying degrees of reverence for God or the sea or the island and all it contains of the past in the present. With sectar- ian conflict raging in the North, critics might say I had arranged the Mass to counter local objections to the island being bought by a Protestant with

British connections. But I had multiple feelings about the island, and on this occasion felt euphoric.

A young priest, who had come with a boatload of people from Bofin, heard confessions on the grass, and Father Fergus from Claddaghduff agreed to use as much of the old Latin liturgy as he was allowed. Facing the priests at the altar inside the oratory, we knelt on clumps of thrift as soft as hassocks on a mound of stone that covered the hermits' graves. Two candles on the shelterless altar flickered but remained alight as the wind held its breath. Great black-backed seagulls clanged in protest without remission. The declining sun was turning the ocean into a lake of fire. Emily, standing behind the two priests, read from the Wisdom of Solomon about those who have not set their hearts on riches, who could have transgressed but have not transgressed. She held the cadence in the air as gracefully as a bird instinctively timing the beat of its wings. In twos and threes, nine communicants came and knelt on the stones near the altar, and one by one leaned forward so that the hand of the priest could reach their tongues with the host.

> Wednesday 3 September 1969, High Island
> I am alone on Ardilaun for the first time … at the top of the cove, looking down on the landing-place … the pookaun moored, the sea calm, ebb tide, afternoon … now I have two penitential tasks to complete … the purification of the well, and the restoration of the stone incised with a peculiar cross whose arms are like horns, the stone I took from beside the well two years ago and kept in my garden … it was heavy to carry up the cliff on my own today … now I have roped it, and I'll try to drag it up the hill to the well without breaking it …

At the time I wrote that note I could see clearly all the islands and the mainland between Achill Island and Slyne Head. I began my task by dragging the stone cross with a harness of halyards over long coarse grass pitted with rabbit burrows, panting, halting, straining uphill, and along the cliff edge, all the way to the well. First I moved the stones that shepherds had put around the well to prevent sheep drowning there – the skull of a dead sheep lay in the top scraw at the entrance – then shook a handful of lime on the putrid water, bailed it with a bucket, and finally scooped up in my hands a silt of black slime containing the bowl of a clay pipe, a few copper pennies and a silver florin, buttons and a cotton reel. Next I dug an outlet through the bog to keep the water fresh by flowing. For more than a thousand years the peat had risen around the well, causing the water to stagnate.

Four hours I worked, my hands blistering, and had a great reward. Deep in the bog, but only a step from the well, the spade struck a stone, which I dug out carefully. When my nails had scraped off the roots that clung to it, I recognised the broken top of a small cross with roughly weathered arms that stretched as far as the stone would allow the carver to shape them. It was delicately engraved on one side with a Greek cross, jewelled with four embossed circles in the angles of the arms. Probably more than a thousand years old, and buried for much of that time.

I'd been warned in Cleggan not to tamper with Brian Bóruma's well because it was sacred, but now I was proud of my work, feeling that the cross was a reward, a sign that my attempt to purify the water had not violated the well's holiness. At that moment I struck my back against a stone sharply, and cried out with pain. It was then that I first noticed a fog bank looming on the horizon. As it reached and drenched the island in mist, I planted the stone cross firmly in the ground beside the well, my task completed. Aching, parched and exhausted, I walked down to the cliff above the landing, and paused to rest on a clump of thrift among quartz rocks surrounded by sea asters. From there I could see the pookaun securely moored in the mouth of the cove, and drank the last drop of tea from a thermos.

Then I prayed, or almost, at the cross where my father had sat on the turf to be photographed the summer before he died; and climbed down the steep rock to the landing place, launched the Zodiac dinghy, and got my gear aboard. As I was standing in the pookaun, wondering should I wait for the fog to clear or haul up the anchor and risk being wrecked on a submerged rock, capsized by a breaker, or carried out to sea by a two-knot current in the sound between High Island and Friar, I heard a voice that pierced me. It was very clear, high and beautiful, crying and exulting from the darkness of a cove. I presumed it came from a seal, but it sounded like a solo in a requiem or a clarinet in a concerto of the sea. Combining joy with lamentation in a falling atonal cry, it seemed to emanate from the heart of all creatures and go beyond the utmost human grief to reach the music of the spheres. Mermaid, banshee and siren crossed my mind. It left me shaken, enthralled.

As the song ended, a lobster boat, with an aerial in the shape of a cross on the masthead, appeared out of the mist. Salvation? Not at all. She turned, and, without a wave of greeting or goodbye from the crew, headed out of sight like a phantom ship. Then the voice cried out again, and though the fog had thickened, the second song removed my fear, leaving calm of mind – or was it light-headedness? – to face whatever might occur.

I started the engine and put to sea, keeping close to the shore, trying to avoid the cork-buoyed ropes of lobster pots. The fog signal boomed from Slyne Head. When I lost sight of High Island I couldn't see Friar, and when I found Friar I had to change course and steer south around it, then east. The smallest rocky island loomed through the fog as large as a mountain, but the sea was flat calm. With no land in sight, using a small pocket compass to avoid Crow's Rock, I was looking down in the deep water when – too quickly for me to change course – the tip of a rock appeared under the keel as we passed. The song that had lured me to my drowning had helped me to survive.

Just before nightfall I recognised houses near the point of Ganogues, and from there I could keep close to shore all the way to Aughrus. I was met on the pier by a stray dog.

Over the years I heard many versions of the legend that a poor young woman, who lived with her husband in a sod hut at Aughrusmore long ago, had been landed by her husband and his mate on High Island, either to pick carrageen, dillisk and sloke for food, or grass for a cow on the mainland, or to shear sheep for a farmer, while the men went fishing in a currach. Her time was due for giving birth to her first child. A storm blew up from the west and the men were barely able to save their lives when the currach was swept back to Aughrusmore. For three days the woman was left alone on the island without food or shelter except for one *clochán*, or beehive cell, at the hermitage. When the sea calmed, the men rowed out, expecting to have to bring back her remains, and were amazed to see her climbing down the cliff with a baby in her arms.

According to an account from that child's great-grandson, John Joyce of Inishbofin, when he was very old, the woman had taken refuge in the *clochán*, 'And as she started to give birth in the night a lamp was brought by a mysterious hand that gave her all the help she needed, and when the child was born the mysterious hand gave her a little garb to put on the child. People who had sick children used to come from far away to get a portion of the mysterious garb.'

༺༻

Tony White's friends, especially his Cambridge contemporaries, had long been urging him to return to the stage. In October 1969 Jonathan Miller cast him as Edmund in *King Lear* at the Nottingham Playhouse, where, during my third stint at Hull, I watched Tony give a great, restrained performance. But as he no longer liked acting, he decided to let this be his last. Jonathan joined us in the Playhouse bar, where he talked so eloquently about the flora and fauna of offshore islands, such as High Island, that I asked him to recommend a good book on each. He mentioned six titles, which I later ordered from Blackwell's in Oxford. After five books had reached me in Cleggan, Blackwell's wrote to say they could send volume xviii of Fauvel's *Flore de France* and would I care to order all the other volumes?

The island fishermen had a custom of sharing a little of their good fortune with the less fortunate. After landing their catch they used to set aside some fish in a box on the quay for people to help themselves who had no money. The givers neither looked for thanks nor humiliated the receivers by making them beg. One evening in the summer of 1969 I heard a story that someone had taken a whole box of the free fish away in a car to sell at the doors of isolated cottages. The seed of that fiction grew into a thorny shrub of a poem, for which Tony suggested the title 'Largesse'.

> There's a trawler at the quay landing fish.
> Could it be one of the island boats?
> Seldom we see them, but how glad we are.
> They have a generous custom
> Of giving away a box of dabs or fluke,
> For luck, of course, for the unlucky poor.
>
> And this is how it works:
> Three tramps are walking down the docks
> Casually, not hurrying, getting there
> With enough drinking time to spare,
> When a blue car fins along
> And sharks the free fish-box.
>
> Usually at this dusky hour
> That car's owner
> Is kneeling in the parlour with his wife.
> If you go into their shop you hear

> Nine decades of the rosary
> And a prayer for Biafra.

I sent this to the *New Statesman and Nation* in London to avoid offending anyone in Cleggan, where that left-wing literary weekly didn't circulate; and it appeared in November. I made the car in the poem blue, as mine was the only blue car in the village; and because blue, as opposed to red, was a symbol of entrepreneurial capitalism, which had devoured many good country traditions, customs and crafts. But tourism, an avid devourer developed by me with my Galway hookers, had brought a summer visitor to Cleggan who, on his return to England, sent a cutting of the poem to Oliver, the owner of the pub called Oliver's where he had stayed.

When I came home from Hull on 4 December 1969 I walked into trouble. It was almost closing time, and Oliver's was packed. I was trying to edge towards the counter to buy a pint when a young man who had never spoken to me before accused me of attacking the people of Cleggan in a poem. I denied this, and told him he couldn't have read the poem properly.

'Do you think I can't read?' he replied. 'I read between the lines. Go back to John Bull's country where you belong, Murphy. We don't want any of your criticism of us. We love Ireland. We died for our country and we drove you out. Why did you mention tramps? We're not tramps, we can afford to buy our own grub.'

He stepped back to take a swing at me, but his friends, who were also mine, held his arms and bustled him out of the bar into the cold night air. I was almost last to leave the pub, hoping he'd be gone home. But he was waiting for me. He came forward, shook my hand, congratulated me on writing the poem, and urged me to write more. Our mutual friends had wrought this transformation.

That was not the end of the matter. One night in Joyce's, when I edged up through a dark crowd of men to the bar for a pint of stout to be pulled by Bunny or Ulick, a big tall fellow whom I didn't know, wearing a navy-blue belted overcoat, turned his back and pushed me aside. A few minutes later he swung round, drew a clenched fist out of a pocket, raised it up and slammed it down, palm open on the counter. When he took away his hand he pointed to a little heap of glassy worms I recognised as rosary beads, and challenged me to tell him, 'What are those?'

'They look like rosary beads.'

'You insulted them!' he shouted. 'You insulted the rosary in that poem you put on the English paper.'

'The rosary,' I said, 'is a beautiful prayer and I never insulted it. Have you read the poem?'

'No,' he replied, 'but I have heard enough about it to know it was an insult. We love our Church.'

'I'm sorry if you feel your Church was insulted. I did not insult either the Catholic Church or the rosary in the poem. You should read it.'

The trouble passed, but the thought of people reading between the lines of whatever I might publish and attacking me for what they could read there became a curb on my writing, except in my private notebooks.

In January 1970 Ted came for a day and a night, bringing Carol Orchard, aged twenty-one, of North Tawton, formerly a nurse in the hospital where his mother was treated. He said the New Forge was worth building to have a room like my attic for working. Looking out of the skylight, he asked me whether this wasn't where I liked to work. He used to write sitting on a bed; now, he said, he often stands or walks.

He thought too many distracting books and papers were lying around in my house, that I ought to work in a room where nothing would interfere with my concentration, no *Poetry Chicago*, no *Listener* (edited by Tony's friend Karl Miller), no *New York Review of Books*.

When we talked about Edmund Spenser – how I imagined he had been faced at Kilcolman Castle, when the Irish kerns set it on fire, with the choice of saving either his infant son or the last six books of *The Faerie Queene* – Ted told me he had read the whole of *The Faerie Queene* out loud to himself when he was about seventeen, twice. He believed it better to tell lies about Spenser in order to convey something true about oneself than to try to be literally truthful to one's own experience. The trouble with confessional poetry, he said, was that the more direct and literal the account, the less it really revealed.

When Emily, now fourteen, came to Cleggan for her summer holidays, I took her alone to High Island in the pookaun. Her arm was in a sling following an accident caused by diving backwards into the swimming pool at Mayfield, her convent boarding school in Sussex. We were lucky in landing with little swell in the cove, as otherwise she'd have needed the use of both hands. Like Tony, she loved adventure and risk.

Our first job was to climb to the well and clean it. On our way, as we passed close to the edge of the highest cliffs of the largest cove on the south side, a peregrine falcon flew off her nest in the cliff and rose, screeching cacophonously, in a widening spiral of fury. The rising of the water from a spring near the peak had seemed miraculous to pilgrims long ago. During our long absence birds had used the well as a bath, leaving an oily scum on the surface, and the water was undrinkable.

After bailing and whitewashing, I dozed on a grassy bank beside the standing cross while Emily walked westwards down the hill to the hermitage in its green bowl of shelter beside a lake, a place where the hermits believed they were closer to God than anywhere else on earth. Before we left the island we picked carrageen – like soft wet dark purple hair in the palms of our hands – off rocks exposed by a low spring tide for Mary Coyne to make a blackcurrant blancmange that she recommended to prevent colds and flu.

Then Emily wanted to explore in our inflatable dinghy the sea cave out of which perhaps had come in a fog the previous year the song of the seal. We found it at the bottom of the cliff where the peregrines were nesting. Inside the cave the sound of the waves rushing between loose rocks or under low-hanging arches of the dark interior was lifted up and amplified by the cavern to a cathartic fortissimo. Quickly we turned and escaped before the rising tide could trap us. And Emily reminded me of a promise to write her a poem about seals, a happy poem, not a dirge or a requiem.

My next visits to High Island were alone, and there I wrote continuously, sometimes in the dark, with nowhere to sleep except on the ground. A notebook records my experience on three consecutive days and one night.

> 5.30 p.m., 3 August 1970, High Island, at the hermitage
> The Seal Rock and the Gull Rock lie beyond the hermitage in the
> south-west corner of the island … in flood tide the avalanche of
> a wave's downfall is overwhelmed by the rising force of a stronger
> wave surging over the rock … rock pipits perched on the cliff are
> intimately quiet … an isolated cormorant looks backwards over
> his wings, regarding the flood tide's approach, into which it will
> soon be forced to dive … seagulls on a jagged promontory stand
> to attention like sentinels in black and white uniforms, now and
> then shouting at an intruder Sieg Heil.

Perspective of stones … a stone altar seen through the door of the oratory … a sign of order surviving in ruin, of an idea outliving not only the builder but the building by which his idea was expressed … the cross I took from the well, fearing it might have been stolen and never recovered, meant less when I stood it in a flower bed in my garden, where it became an ornament … planted beside the well where it was designed to stand, it joins a metaphysical idea to the ground … showing a circle within a circle on the cross, also a sun and a moon … and on the back, limbs that end in horns, or are they water-diviner's rods or symbols handed down from the Druids?

The sun is breaking through at last, over my shoulder to the west … a glorious evening spreading in from the ocean after a day of heavy low-lying rain clouds … and at once three rabbits run out of their burrows to play … they are not fearless, but less afraid of us here than on the mainland … one rabbit has done more excavating of the abbot's clochan, another is living in the oratory, and several in the souterrain.

Between the crags of a great cliff towering on my right, I can see in the distance Shark Head and the Kimeen Rocks. Below me a bowl of grass, richly fertilised by barnacle geese that graze there in winter, holds the peaty water of a lake used by the hermits as a millpond. Gulls are floating near the rocky verge beside the ruins of the hermitage at the centre of three circles of walls that have collapsed. Rugged outcrops of mica schist sparkle with garnetiferous quartz. Whoever named the sea-rose 'thrift' must not have noticed its improvident wild habits on High Island, its cushioning of sharp stones, and generous provision of comfortable seats. The gulls remain forever awake, watchful and sounding alarms on the bowl's perimeter, silhouetted against the evening sky.

4 August 1970, New Forge

Everything on the island connects, that is its glory, connecting what appears to be disconnected … the only land you can clearly see from the hermitage is Shark Head to the north and Slyne Head to the south, two ultimate fragments broken off the landmass of Europe and almost uninhabitable, the one deserted ten years ago, the other occupied by lighthouse keepers … but on the eastern side of the hill in the centre of the island you can see a panorama of mountains, bays, villages, islands, and rocks that lie between Achill Island and Slyne Head … signs of human activity on the mainland with which you cannot connect can make you yearn to get home, but looking from the hermitage out to sea, you can feel connected to the universe sublimely.

5.20 p.m., 5 August 1970, High Island

I'm sitting on a rock above the blessed well, and a gentle breeze from the north is cooling the day's excessive heat … men are hauling lobster pots in a boat near the Seal's Rock … on landing I tried to cut a foothold in the rock by striking a few blows with a sledgehammer, but the dark rock remained firm … an oystercatcher screeched … fulmar petrels, which resembled on their nests white crockery on the dresser of the cliff, took off and flew silently round and round the cove in figures of eight … as the tide had almost reached low water, I rowed to the cave that Emily and I had not been able to penetrate.

Inside, the vault was embossed with jade, opal, lapis lazuli and carnelian sea squirts, urchins and anemones … I shipped my oars and touched the walls to enter … a cormorant dived into the sea, leaving two young birds on a nest … a swell overtook me, surging into the cave, making me fear I'd be trapped … a wave dashed across the shingle and rumbled deep within the body of the island under its highest point before withdrawing … two seals were lying quite close to me on a rock, one, a spotted white cow was asleep, but the bull watched me eye to eye … suddenly they both dived into the water and swam under the dinghy out into the open sea … when I left the cave the bull followed me to the landing cove, seeing me off.

Tonight I'll keep a vigil in the holy circle of the hermitage to celebrate the feast of St Gormgall and the hatching of stormpetrels in his and his hermits' graves. I feel more affection for everyone when I'm alone on High Island than when I'm among a crowd. Love, the supreme good, the redeeming harmony in every person, in all of nature, needs detachment and space as well as intimacy. Simply by being alone in this place at this time I feel its force.

It's eight o'clock and I'm at the penitential cross above the landing cove, where my father posed for the last photograph we have of him. Light can change the meaning of a stone. Rain and wind of a thousand years have worn down the symbols carved on its face by an unknown hermit more than a thousand years ago. While I'm studying this weathered stone flower, a Greenland Wheatear, the mother of wheatears richly feathered in ripening harvest colours, across her eyes a voluptuous streak of jet, parades her offspring at the entrance to a burrow. If ever there were a communion with the dead it would be here in High Island from nightfall to daybreak. I'll go to the hermitage and watch there till dawn.

Now its 9.15 and the black-backs are muting their catcalls on the higher ground above and beyond the bowl of the hermitage, as the light fades except on the northern horizon. Stormpetrels are beginning to stutter and purr underground, expecting their mates if not their mothers or fathers to come back from sea with food at nightfall, burrowing under mounds of ecclesiastical debris. Their tiny, gurgling voices transmit hope of renewal if not of resurrection, as the hatched birds in the burial ground of their origin cry out for food. Stormpetrels spend most of their lives skimming the surface of oceans from pole to pole, and only come to land to nest underground in remote places, flying over the land only in the dark.

Under the stone on which I'm sitting, a weird sound has begun pulsing, drumming, vibrating, as if the stone itself were coming to life … and a long white caterpillar crawls from under a leaf … now the vibration has turned into mewing and purring with a regular throb … I shine my torch under the leaves between two stones and the purring stops abruptly.

It's too dark now to see what I'm writing, only the page over which my pen continues to flow … the sea is calm … there's shelter here from a light north-easterly breeze … I'm sitting … on a stone bench facing the abbot's clochan … Slyne Head is emitting two flashes every ten seconds away to the south … every now and then I hear a whirr of wings … the gulls have subsided and given up complaining and are almost asleep … a whisper of little wings increases, as they brush close to my head, like a swift breeze … I cannot see them, they are flying at me out of the ground and out of the sky … two black-backs have woken and are making a raucous fuss … a heavy dew has fallen, good for growth.

After midnight … I'm writing by torchlight in St Gormgall's

oratory where the altar sounds like a muted organ or a discord-
ant clavichord ... the stone is humming and mewing, throbbing
and piping, while under the starlight there's a continual vibration
of innumerable wings ... occasionally a voice from underground
utters a piercing cry, followed by a rush of wings around the broken
gable, as one bird after another swoops in and out through the open
doorway, restless, dancing, dancing in random intricate curves ...
souls in purgatory working a severe passage to paradise on wings
... wings brushing close to my head.

Not lonely here, I have the company of thousands of birds
rearing their young ... a life I never knew existed ... as if there were
a resurrection of souls in a paradise of birds ... but subject to pain
and death ... the night itself is short, and the season of warmth, of
rearing young, will soon be over, storms will sweep over the island,
the birds will have gone, I shall be on the other side of the ocean,
and my daughter in another continent.

Yesterday was the feast of St Gormgall, today it is mine ... the
weather favourable for both ... the lobster boats have returned to
the mainland after shooting their pots ... still that music is coming
from under the altar, and the ballet of birds continues in the sky ...
though it really is dark and this church is a ruin, I feel inexpressibly
happy ... the wind in the doorway is playful ... all things as well as
creatures seem to be rejoicing in summer, the high point of life ...
nothing will stop the music of the masonry until those birds come
to the end of their dance and vanish before daybreak ... I shall lie
down and sleep for a while on cushions of thrift between the abbot's
clochan and the lake, while the stormpetrels go on feeding their
young, instructing them in flight and in song ...

By the time I could see the stonework of the hermitage clearly, the storm
petrels had vanished. I hadn't slept, except like Chaucer's birds 'that slepen
all the night with open eye', and my head was wet with dew as I trudged
back over the hill, passing the well, down to my pookaun moored in the
landing cove. Now the more raucous scavengers of the day, oystercatchers and
ravens, were beginning to croak and rattle, shriek and complain with guttural
commands and execrations. Behind my back I thought I heard someone
talking – it was a seagull.

I had prayed at the altar and the birds had answered my prayer. Much later

I'd learn that the male and female storm petrel share the labour of hatching one single egg and rearing the chick, changing places every two or three nights. According to fossil records they have been doing this for millions of years. The bird on the nest only sends out signals the night its mate is due to return from the ocean, and only the Leach's petrel sings in flight.

Tony came to Cleggan in September 1970, having bought from Kieran Coneys a site with a derelict cottage on rocky ground from which he could see herons and swans on Aughrusbeg Lough, mountains to the east and Inishbofin to the west. According to legend the last occupant had been a healer who, for remedies, would go out in the night and consult a rock that lightning had split in half. One night he went out and was never seen again. With shovels, spades, a pickaxe and a sledge, Tony, Tom Conroy and I, stripped to the waist, cleared the site. While Tony would be working in London, where he'd sold his flat, John Cosgrove and Tommy Coohill would reconstruct the cottage in granite.

Among other jobs in London, Tony, as our agent, was arranging poetry readings for Ted Hughes and me in the north-eastern United States to coincide with Harper & Row's publication of *Crow* in New York on 15 March and my first semester of teaching at Colgate University in upstate New York from January to May 1971. Tony himself was to accompany us on our tour. John McGahern and his wife Madeline came to Cleggan in November and stayed with me until they found a house to rent for the following year a mile west of the village. Life was enhanced by conversation with these friends. When I showed John a poem that had been through far too many drafts and still had a weak last line, he said, 'You've given it a rose at the end – I'd give the knife another twist.' He found that in writing fiction he had to tone down reality in order to be believed. But when he spoke of ordinary things, people or events, reality was intensified by his imagination and his style of darkness clarified. At Colgate University in January 1971 I could recognise at a glance the people he had described in Cleggan, but in life they seemed shadows of John's fictions.

At Colgate I had never experienced snow as deep and long lasting as the snow of upstate New York, or air so cold that it hurt to breathe. Every morning at four o'clock two gigantic snowploughs warmed up their diesel motors for half an hour beside the white timber-framed house I was renting in the village of Poolville near the campus. On arrival I had to dig out of a snowdrift a rusty

Plymouth station wagon in which I was to drive Ted and Tony around New England, New York, Philadelphia and Washington on our reading tour. Snow and ice prevented me from jogging, and the danger of being attacked by ferocious guard dogs outside every third or fourth house destroyed the pleasure of walking. 'You need an electric walking stick,' a colleague told me. For every moral or social problem America seemed to have and to prefer a mechanical solution. The most enjoyable aspect of the snow – its silencing effect – was often shattered by another mechanical device, the Japanese snowmobile.

Having to teach required me to re-educate myself and gave me an opportunity to study Shakespeare, Donne, Hardy, Cavafy, Eliot and Lawrence. In a creative-writing course I stressed the value of mastering metre and rhyme before attempting to write free verse. But my theories that the iamb derives from the heartbeat and that the structure of a poem needs a body's or a building's symmetry put me out of key with the time. Metrical rhymed poetry had never come easily to me, nor did I expect it to be easy for students who equated poetry with self-expression. Too often I'd written myself to a standstill going over and over the same lines or stanzas, making no progress.

Five days before meeting Ted and Tony at Dartmouth College, New Hampshire for the first reading of our tour, I succumbed to a severe throat and chest infection. A doctor advised me not to drink alcohol while taking antibiotics for those five days. On Wednesday 10 March I drove between banks of snow on salted roads for several hours and arrived at Dartmouth in the evening. Ted and Tony had flown from London to Boston that morning, drinking champagne on the flight. Tony had never been to America; Ted was returning for the first time since he had lived in New England with Sylvia.

Euphoria induced by the company of my friends caused me to forget the doctor's advice and drink two glasses of wine. After dinner our host sat me down in a low armchair and placed on a coffee table in front of me a bottle of King George IV whiskey. Between studying the unfamiliar label and a blurred moment several hours later when I was pouring out affectionate nonsense in Greek to Tony and throwing my arms around him in the corridor of the inn where we were staying, I could remember nothing until I woke on my knees in acute pain and self-disgust, vomiting into the toilet bowl.

Teasing me at breakfast, Tony said to Ted, 'Don't you wish he'd get drunk more often?' Never would I let myself get so drunk again – for fear of what I might do if I were to lose control.

To fortify himself before his solo reading at Amherst College in Massachusetts the following afternoon, Ted insisted on the three of us drinking two bottles of champagne at lunch. He read with intense power in a small hexagonal room like a chapel, so crowded that people were sitting on the floor, dead quiet, hushed by awe and admiration. At the end of his reading he remained for nearly an hour, talking one by one to those who were waiting in a long line that stretched to the door. Nearly all had come from Smith College to hear him: good-looking, well-brought-up girls, like Sylvia, with long loose hair.

On the drive from Amherst to New York, Ted and Tony challenged each other to a game of placing quotations from Shakespeare, which Ted narrowly won. Tony and I roomed at the YM/YWHA on 92nd Street and Lexington Avenue, where Ted and I were booked to read at the Poetry Center on Monday at 8 p.m. To launch *Crow* before our reading, Ted's editor at Harper & Row, Fran McCullough, hosted a dinner at Pierre's Wine Room, where by good fortune I was placed beside Barbara Epstein, one of the two founding editors of the *New York Review of Books*.

On Wednesday, St Patrick's Day, our reading at night in the replica of Shakespeare's Globe Theatre at the Folger Museum in Washington was followed by a pub crawl in which we drank insipid green beer. On Thursday we read at Boston College, luxuriously hosted by Francis Sweeney, a Jesuit priest and professor of English, who had twice presented readings by T.S. Eliot.

At Colgate, where Ted gave a solo reading on Friday in a large overcrowded room, he got angry with a cameraman who kept moving his camera after Ted had told him to stand still. I sensed hostility to Ted in the audience, and only discovered the cause after he had gone. An associate professor had told his students that an English poet called Ted Hughes would be reading on the campus, and they should bear in mind that he had married an American called Sylvia Plath, who was a far better poet, and that many people thought he was responsible for her suicide. However, Ted made such a good impression that three of the girls at his reading – sophomores – joined our tour to Rochester University a few days later.

Meanwhile, Ted and Tony stayed with me behind a curtain of icicles in Poolville. For lunch on Sunday 21 March Tony prepared what he called a winter salad of tomato and grated carrot, raw broccoli and lettuce, nuts and raisins, chopped apple, garlic and feta cheese. This, with seasonal and local variation, was to become my staple diet, sometimes augmented by cooked and cooled minced beef. During the meal, at which we drank two bottles of a Baron Philippe de Rothschild claret, I mentioned my difficulty in finishing poems that I'd begun to write in metre and rhyme. In three years I'd written only fourteen publishable poems. Having raised the pink granite walls of my garden around the New Forge to demesne-wall height, I'd walled my mind with the idea that a poem could be as solidly built as a house of stone.

After lunch I left Ted and Tony with a third bottle of claret and went upstairs to sleep for a couple of hours. When I came down they told me they had devised a method to break me out of my writer's block, requiring me to submit to certain rules and pay a fine for every breach.

The first rule was 'total secrecy'. I had to subordinate all other activities to this work, studying daily a list of fifteen themes proposed by Ted and another of ten by Tony. Each theme was to be the point of entry, at which I'd start, before 8 a.m., while the door to my dream world was not yet closed by the day's activity, writing three full quarto pages rapidly within one hour. I was to regard metre and rhyme as toys to play with, not binding laws. After the hour I'd be free to continue at a slower pace. The rules didn't allow for the smallness of my script caused by writing in the centimetre squares of my French notebooks. Before going to sleep each night I had to present the next day's theme 'forcibly' to the 'Queen of Inner Operations'. When writing I should never allow the search for a better word, idea or rhyme to hold up the flow, but always remember Beethoven's dictum to his piano pupils, 'Never mind the wrong notes – keep the music going to the end.' Themes set by Ted were playful, fantastic and surreal, designed to force me out of the ruts of literalness and rationality. Tony, having been a student of F.R. Leavis at Downing College, suggested themes that were to encourage me to examine my conscience.

After Ted had flown to San Francisco for a reading there and Tony had followed in a Greyhound bus via New Orleans and Tucson to visit Thom Gunn at his house in Haight-Ashbury, I began the method before leaving Poolville in May and finished at Cleggan in June. Although none of the twenty-five themes resulted in a publishable poem, the method quickened my mind and was to prove helpful evermore when applied to themes set by myself. It reminded me of the golden hands of a clock that my brother Chris, in our childhood, used to imagine as a means of waking early.

The penalty for each failure was a fine of $5 to be paid into a fund to provide champagne for the judges to drink with the contestant – an event we would continually postpone. Our code name for the system was the 'Champagne Method' and for the poems that resulted, 'Champagne Poetry'. The first poem thus to emerge and achieve publication was written at home in July about the problems of a boy, born and reared in a wattle tent on a roadside, learning to read. The last, which I attempted years later, was on the theme of 'How Ireland killed W.B. Yeats', and this emerged in prose, as follows.

> After Yeats had written and published his 'Tower' poems, he and his family never stayed at Thoor Ballylee again. The building was too cold, damp and uncomfortable for a smiling public man of more than sixty years. In heavy rain the river beside it rose and flooded the ground floor. Jackdaws blocked the chimneys with their nests. A local caretaker's wages ceased to be paid. Thatch on the roof of a cottage adjoining the tower, where Mrs Yeats kept the children out of earshot of their father, caved in. It seemed that the family wanted to help his prophecy of ruin to be fulfilled.
>
> A tramp, finding the tower abandoned, with no one in charge, forced open the hall door, and slept in the poet's elm bed, using his chairs for firewood. A farmer, seeing the door unlocked, let his cattle shelter in the ground floor. Since nobody complained about his cattle, when another man needed a strong door for a stable, he knew where to go in the night with his horse and cart. There was a very bad winter during the 'Emergency', 1939–45, when turf was scarce. By this time the furniture had gone, but there were still floorboards. These disappeared, and the more dangerous task of removing the joists followed.
>
> After the war, with nothing left to take from the tower, people noticed that strangers who had no business in the country were coming there with books in their hands, and climbing to the battlements and throwing pennies in the stream. Some of the locals said it was a disgrace to let these foreigners see the old castle in such a mess. If it were cleaned up, it might attract more visitors, and they would spend money if there were souvenirs for them to buy.
>
> So a committee was formed to restore the tower, with permission from Michael Yeats, and funds from the Irish Tourist Board. People who had taken doors and furniture were good enough to accept payment for returning them, so that the place could be made to look as it was when the poet was writing there. Tape-recorded lectures and readings of poems were provided for visitors, who might not otherwise know why they were visiting the place. A

girl was trained as a guide to recite information that tourists were expected to want.

At a gala opening of the tower to the public, attended by all sorts of dignitaries, I felt that the significance of the last two lines of 'To be Carved On a Stone at Thoor Ballylee' had been violated by the restoration. Since the place was no longer a 'ruin', I thought that the lines would make more sense if they were altered to read:

> And may these characters remain
> When all is ruined once again.

The last time I spoke to Ted about the 'Champagne Method', many years later, he told me that he had read a story that had given him the idea of the strategy he and Tony had devised. A clergyman used to write his sermons carefully during the week, and everyone was impressed in church on Sunday. But a week came in which he could think of nothing to write; then on Saturday night he had a dream in which he was delivering a brilliant new sermon. As soon as he woke up he wrote down the sermon from his dream, and everyone said it was the best he'd ever given. He tried to repeat this success, but failed, until he prayed very hard just before he fell asleep on a Saturday night. This worked, and repeatedly thereafter, first thing on a Sunday morning he was able to write the sermon given in his dream as a result of the prayer before he fell asleep.

When I mentioned to Ted that he had advised me, before going to sleep, not to pray to God but to instruct the 'Queen of Inner Operations' to deliver the poem in the morning, he replied, 'You have to pray to the right authority.'

Before the end of my first semester at Colgate I was invited to return in the autumn, and John McGahern was invited the following spring. During my summer in Ireland, Ted brought his children and his wife Carol to Cleggan for a fishing visit that included, on 7 June, High Island, where he caught pollack in the sea and a stickleback in the lake that had been a millpond for the hermits. On the same day John Cosgrove, Tommy Coohill, Tommy's son P.J., Kieran Coneys and three other men began rebuilding one room of a derelict cottage that miners had occupied on the island in 1827. Mary Coyne provided us all with a picnic lunch, after which she sat on a tuft of thrift near the edge of a cliff knitting a gansey and praying for the island not to be violated by Ted Hughes.

The miners had sunk a shaft for copper to redeem the debts of a landlord, Richard Martin of Ballinahinch, alias 'Hairtrigger Dick', who had founded the Royal Society for the Prevention of Cruelty to Animals; but the mine had produced nothing but fool's gold. The Miners' Hut, as I called the room, would enable me to spend up to four or five days and nights alone on the island from time to time, writing poems about the seals and the storm petrels. But two years later, after a retreat of five days in which the sun only shone for twenty minutes, I gave up spending longer than a few hours on High Island, being neither a hermit nor a saint.

During my mother's annual visit in August – 'Darling, will you get some turf from the garden and light the fire, and what are we going to give them for lunch, darling?' – Barbara and her husband, Jason Epstein, arrived. He was on his way to meet the IRA leadership in west Belfast. My mother welcomed them at the New Forge with flowers in all the rooms – a vase of sea holly mauve on the mantelpiece, and in the hall a wicker basket filled with purple loosestrife, angelica, bell heather and royal fern. Barbara picked 'The Reading Lesson' out of a group of several poems to show to her co-editor, Robert Silvers.

During a lull in my teaching at Colgate, almost a month after 'The Reading Lesson' had appeared in the *New York Review of Books*, Barbara Epstein gave me dinner at her apartment in New York on 22 November 1971. The only other guest was W.H. Auden. It was several years since I had met him in Stratford-upon-Avon, where his poetry reading impressed me because he knew his poems by heart. When his memory lapsed in the middle of a longish poem, he didn't fuss and fumble for the book, but closed his eyes and looked up to Heaven as if he were asking God to remind him of what he had wanted to say when writing the poem. Then, recovering his speech, he seemed to be inspired with thoughts he was just now putting into words. It made the poem all the more interesting to hear.

Barbara told me that once, when he was coming to dine, he got out of the elevator on the wrong floor, rang the bell, was admitted by a couple, who did not protest when he came in, and, seating himself in an armchair, asked for a vodka Martini. With this in hand he kept up a monologue that amazed and silenced the couple until his glass was empty. Then noticing the rather strange absence of the Epsteins, Auden asked where they were. 'Barbara and Jason live in the apartment above us,' he was told.

Auden was there when I arrived. He was sixty-four years old, looking rather scruffy and neglected, slouching on a Chesterfield, his hair 'all over the place', his nails dirty, slippers for shoes. Conversation with him was daunting, because he interrupted everything Barbara or I said. He seemed to have made up his brilliant mind about every possible topic, and condensed his conclusions into unanswerable aphorisms. The great crusted oyster of his mouth would open, an artificial pearl of polished thought would pop out, and the mouth would clam shut again. The voice was that of an English prep-school swot who could answer every question, pronouncing the letter *R* with a hint of the sound of a *W*.

While Barbara was cooking the dinner I tried to coax him down off the platform from which he seemed to be addressing an anonymous representative of an audience whom he had no wish to meet socially. So I mentioned J.R. Ackerley, as a friend who had stayed with me in the west of Ireland, knowing that Auden had liked him enough to invite him to stay in Ischia. I plunged into a topic that was very close to Joe's heart, hoping to touch Auden's. I told him that when Joe came back from a visit to Athens in the mid-1950s, where he was a guest of the young novelist Francis King, a charming epicurean host, he told me he was shocked at being given a choice of a sailor, airman or royal guardsman at dinner in a taverna night after night. The promiscuity of his host had seemed immoral. I had suggested to Joe that age had altered his judgement. Hadn't he pursued guardsmen and sailors when he was young enough to enjoy the pursuit? 'You don't seem to understand,' Joe had corrected me, 'I was never promiscuous: I was always looking for an ideal friend.' Then Auden opened his mouth and out popped this pearl: 'All promiscuity is a search for the ideal friend.' During dinner he said, 'I hope God will let me die at seventy. I don't want to live longer than my natural span.' He wanted all his letters burned at his death, as he had burned, without reading, his father's letters when he died; and he wanted his friends to burn his letters to them – he was asking for this in his will. By destroying all his papers he hoped to make it impossible for anyone to write his life. Like the doctors of long ago, whose medical discoveries were kept secret, he expected his secrets to die with him.

In spite of his face's celebrated corrugations of age, he looked strong. He was disturbed by not being able to communicate with the students who attended his seminars at Columbia. They had no knowledge of the past or of form, and no interest in either, which made it impossible for them to understand what poetry, his kind of poetry, was about. Barbara had once told me that she felt he wasn't aware of her as a person, and probably gave his students the same feeling. He had refused to give the Charles Eliot Norton lectures at Harvard, for which he was offered $29,000, on the grounds that he had nothing to say. 'Of course I could have dug something up that I've said before, but that would be bad.' Barbara had told me that he really needed the money.

How did we get on to the subject of witches? 'My mother-in-law was a witch,' he said, referring to the mother of Erika Mann, Thomas Mann's daughter, whom Auden had married in 1935 purely to make her a British subject. Then he said, 'And Louis's first wife is a witch,' referring to MacNeice. 'I'll drink a bottle of champagne the day I hear she's dead.' He was glad that Louis in his last years had found in Mary Wimbush 'the first non-violent woman in his life'. Barbara said she thought my mother was a witch, adding that she liked witches and liked my mother. I agreed that my mother had the power of bewitching people.

Auden also talked of Vietnam, and other politics. He thought 'we' must take over the north of Ireland. Of the carnage in East Pakistan, soon to become Bangladesh, he remarked: 'I ought not to say this, but I'm sure it would never have happened if Britain had still been ruling India. The Greeks,' he continued, 'were better off under the Turks, as they can never govern themselves. They alternate between anarchy and despotism, you've only to read Thucydides.'

Then he denounced the camera as one of the two most abominable inventions – the internal combustion engine was the other – on the grounds that it told lies and reduced human suffering, as in Auschwitz or Hiroshima, to a cheap thrill. At twenty past nine he got up from the table, put on purple shades, and we walked with him to a taxi. On the way he informed us that he always made sure he had $20 to satisfy a mugger and so avoid being murdered. But he had not allowed for inflation since the day he decided, ten or fifteen years earlier, that $20 would be enough to save his life. His opinions, once formed, became rigid.

After he'd gone, Barbara mentioned that his friend Chester Kallman had returned to New York this winter for the first time in many years since he had been arrested by a detective acting as an agent provocateur. Chester invited all his friends to a party at Auden's apartment in Greenwich Village, and at half past eight, when the party was in full swing, Auden went round saying to the guests, 'I'm afraid you'll have to go now because it's my bedtime.'

Barbara said that before I arrived at her apartment she had told Auden that Edmund Wilson, an old friend whom they both admired, was dying at his house on Cape Cod, and had asked about him. Barbara was struck by the stoicism of Auden's answer: 'He should die.'

Not until I returned to Cleggan early in 1972 – Emily having spent Christmas with me in America – did I hear from Tom Kinsella that Seán Ó Riada, his close friend, had died of cirrhosis of the liver on 3 October. Forty years old, Seán had been composing a requiem for the funeral of de Valera, who outlived him, and the unfinished music was played at Seán's funeral. His wife Ruth was left with seven children in Coolea.

On my last visit to discuss his music and my words for *The Battle of Aughrim*, I remember Seán (who wanted no phone in the house) taking me at eleven in the morning to the pub in Ballyvourney, where he booked a call to Dublin on a line with long delays. While waiting for the call I drank a pint and he two 'wedges' – three pints of Guinness split alternately by double brandies. In the afternoon he drove me around the Dingle Peninsula. We passed a meadow where a man mowing rushes with a scythe waved to us, and Seán stopped, climbed a wall and talked to the man for half an hour, in Irish of course. All the people who spoke Irish in that beautiful part of the world were his friends. He led me through his country as if he were its chieftain in a time before England's navy had been built with Irish hearts of oak.

I spent the spring and summer at home working on poems with the help of the 'Queen of Inner Operations' and Tony. His advice redeemed poems that otherwise would have been failures. He helped me to finish 'Seals at High Island' and encouraged me to write poems about my childhood in Ceylon rather than go back to the country that in 1972 became Sri Lanka.

On the phone from London in April, Tony said he was aiming to live in Connemara from 1975 onwards, going to London for short visits, as opposed to living in London and spending holidays at Cleggan. He planned to come in August before my departure to teach at Bard College, a small liberal arts college ninety miles up the Hudson Valley from New York. By then he hoped to have finished a book for Faber on the East End of London, revised his and Martin Green's *Guide to London Pubs*, and done another translation to pay for the building of his cottage. Its completion had been held up for lack of funds.

Three weeks later he injured an eye while playing football – a detached retina – which required him to lie motionless in Moorfields Eye Hospital for two days while waiting for an operation. 'Nelson managed very well with only one eye,' he remarked, 'so I'm not worried.' Doing up a friend's house in the Dordogne the following year he fell through a rotten floor to the ground without serious injury. As he valued the pleasure of taking risks, never would he think of shunning danger.

I was alone in the attic of the New Forge one evening early in June 1972 when I heard my name shouted from the hall below. On opening the door at the top of two flights of stairs I saw Robert Shaw, poised as the star he had become, resplendent in a strawberry-red suit and a white open-necked shirt, with his secretary, whom he called Miss Jay, and an old man whom he described as a reformed alcoholic.

The last time I'd seen Robert had been the previous November in New York, where he was acting with Mary Ure and Rosemary Harris in Harold Pinter's *Old Times* at the Billy Rose Theatre. Mary had told me afterwards that Robert's shouting had nearly blasted her off the stage. Now he had come to tell me that she had been writing poems while under treatment for alcoholism. He read some aloud, and left the rest with me to read: sad, painful accounts of crises in her life rather than poems. At Tourmakeady, on the western shore of Lough Mask, they had bought a big house called Drimbawn in a wooded demesne at the foot of the Partry Mountains.

It took two more years for Shaw's grandiose repairs and extensions to be completed. There I saw Mary Ure for the last time in 1974, and remember her taking me for a walk down to the lake in a wind that made me shiver in an overcoat, while she, in a blue silk gown, acted as if the sun were shining on a summer's day. I was teaching at Princeton the following April when I heard of her death in London from an overdose of alcohol and barbiturates.

During my first term at Bard College my generous and now poor Aunty Kay died at the age of eighty-three in an old people's home in Bray, County Wicklow. I felt ashamed because I hadn't seen her since her sister Eileen had placed her there. Kay had dreamed of being a missionary, and when she retired from teaching in the 1960s had gone to join my parents in Southern Rhodesia. There she drove so many sick black people to hospital that a doctor rang my mother and asked her not to allow Kay to continue these acts of charity as the hospital could not cope with so many non-paying patients.

One morning at the old people's home, Kay heard on the radio that the police were trying to identify the body of a man who had been killed in a motor accident. She went to the morgue and identified the corpse as mine.

After enjoying the company of good people at Bard for the autumn semester of 1972, I spent most of 1973 at home finishing the poems for a collection called *High Island* that Faber was to publish in London and Harper & Row in New York.

At Cleggan on 5 February 1973 I received a call from Lelia Doolin, artistic director of the Abbey Theatre in Dublin, asking for help with an urgent literary problem. The Greek film director Michael Cacoyannis, having agreed to direct Yeats's version of Sophocles's *King Oedipus* to open at the Abbey on 4 April, was complaining that Yeats had failed to translate about one hundred lines by Sophocles. He wanted someone to translate these lines in the style of Yeats but with the sense of Sophocles. Michael would tell me more on the phone from Paris, where he had been living in self-imposed exile since the colonels had set up a military dictatorship in Greece. My role would be defined as literary adviser to the director.

I did what they wanted – invisible mending. Yeats, using a translation by the classical scholar Sir Richard Jebb, had written his version of 1928 mostly in prose with a biblical cadence. Michael objected to Yeats's omission of vital passages, such as Jocasta telling her son Oedipus, who had married her in ignorance of their relationship, that every man dreams of marrying his mother. Cutting political speeches about the House of Labdacus, he had turned the chorus lines into his own style of lyric poetry that suspends action in a web of mood music. During a long discussion with Michael when we were both in Dublin, he argued that every word in the play by Sophocles advances the action to its predetermined end.

While working at home on the seven most painful lines spoken by the chorus – omitted by Yeats – at the sight of Oedipus after he had stabbed his eyes with his mother's gold brooches, I heard on the news that the eyes of a man in Northern Ireland had been gouged out with a crucifix.

When Tony's eye had recovered he teamed up with Johnny and Pete, the sons of Alfie Hinds, whose *Contempt of Court* Tony had ghosted, to take on various jobs refurbishing houses, at which he could make more money with more pleasure than by translating. Yet he still had the energy to read and comment on my poems constructively.

In June Tony arrived in a van with Johnny and Pete to construct the roof of his cottage. Because he enjoyed the anticipation more than the fulfilment of pleasure, he was in no hurry to finish his cottage. Mistrusting gifts that imposed a burden of gratitude on the receiver as an indirect form of coercion, he had asked me not to complete the building in his absence. His publisher James Michie, whose translation of Horace's *Odes* I loved and which I had heard Auden praise, arrived with his family at the same time and stayed at a hotel. On a hot, dry Sunday Tony, James, Pete and I went on a long climb over the Twelve Pins from north to south, from Kylemore to Ballinahinch. James had brought a small bottle of red wine, too little to be shared among four, in a hotel lunch bag, which, in Horatian style, he asked young Pete to carry. Pete let the bottle fall into a gully.

After John Cosgrove and Tommy Coohill had finished the walls of Tony's cottage, they were engaged to work for the actor Peter O'Toole, who had admired their masonry at the New Forge. Peter was building a pink granite house, much larger than mine, high above the sea at Eyrephort, five miles from Cleggan. He had wanted his house located on top of a hill, with more commanding views than those of Robert Shaw in County Mayo, but Galway County Council had insisted on a site some twenty feet lower. So Peter got his builders to erect the house on the lower site and blast away the hilltop.

Unable to reach High Island except by boat on very calm days, I often walked across to Omey Island, where Tony's footballers, when they came to Connemara in 1966, had practised on the beach. Like Holy Island off the coast of Northumbria, Omey can be reached on foot across half a mile of strand when the tide is out. St Fechin's monastery of the seventh century has long been buried under dunes on the north shore. Only the gable of his church and a few bones thrown up by the sea remain. Funerals from the Catholic church in Claddaghduff have to go according to the tide to reach an ancient graveyard still in use above the eastern shore.

Not a stone remains of the Protestant 'soup school' and schoolmaster's house built on Omey by the proselytising Irish Church Missions in the mid-nineteenth century. The father of the poet Louis MacNeice had been born in that house, from which the entire family of ten had to flee one night in 1879. The local Catholic curate had entered the school, demanding the right to teach the Roman catechism, but was struck on the head by a soup ladle. When MacNeice, with his family and his converts from Omey, escorted by two armed Royal Irish Constabulary constables, were walking past the Catholic church on their way to the Protestant church near Cleggan, they were halted and chased by a mob. MacNeice was beaten and kicked. One shot was fired accidentally, wounding a woman, who died many years later. While my grandfather, Canon Richard Murphy, was rector of Clifden in the parish of Omey from 1904 until his death in 1916, he never proselytised or helped the Irish Church Missions to do so; and he kept on good terms with the Catholic parish priest.

Omey, with five hundred acres of land, half of it fertile and smooth, is six times as large as High Island. In 1845 two petty landlords, who lived on Omey in genteel squalor, owned all the land, while five hundred men, women and children occupied sod huts on the margin between the high-water mark and the landlord's fences. Tommy Coohill, born in the 1920s and brought up in a granite cottage thatched with sedge on the exposed south-west shore of Omey, told me he had been so hungry as a child, walking to school in his bare feet, that he used to eat the flowers of water lilies on the lake beside the school.

He said the teacher, Peg Cloherty, was 'wicked cruel to the poorest children'. In those days mothers often made clothes for the family out of old calico flour bags, which they disguised by dyeing the cloth with lichen off the rocks. A widow left with three small children had made a dress for one of them, but had failed to hide the 'Star of the West' brand name of Palmer's Mills in Galway. Peg spotted this when the children were sitting with their slates on their laps, and called out mockingly: 'Stand up there, Miss Palmer, and let's have a look at your dress! I see you're the Star of the West!'

Tommy could remember the last of the Omey squireens, Henry Kearney, as a rich miser too mean to get married. Kearney used to walk to cattle fairs wearing a raincoat belted with a rope of straw and with newspaper stuffed in his boots to save the price of socks. During the 'Emergency' of 1939–45, when news was as scarce as tea and sugar, it was often said in reply to the question 'Where did you hear that?', 'I read it on the paper in Kearney's boots.'

During the spring semester at Bard College in 1974, I acquired in the Bronx from three sisters, who had long since emigrated from Omey, a site on almost the highest ground on the island. One was the girl who had been mocked on account of her dress. Bearing in mind that Peter O'Toole's house from a distance looked like a pink ornament on the green icing of a cake, I designed a hexagonal studio of Omey granite to look as if it had grown out of the rock. While I was at home for the summer of 1974, John Cosgrove and Tommy Coohill, with two islanders, Joeen and his son John MacDonagh, built the Hexagon in seven weeks. On the day it was finished I received a summons for breach of the planning Act and an order from Galway County Council to demolish the building as it 'impaired the visual amenity of the island'. On appeal to the minister for local government, the order was quashed, and at a hearing in Clifden Court the case dismissed.

Meanwhile Tony and his mates had been refurbishing Lumb Bank, which Ted Hughes was to lease to the Arvon Foundation as a centre for creative-writing courses. It went against Tony's grain to help the poet as landlord to evict hippies who were squatting in a garden shed. In July Tony came to Cleggan and stayed in his unfinished cottage. A wren, he told me, had found a way through his unplastered stone walls. He drew his water in a bucket from the lake, cooked on an open turf fire in a pot hanging from a crane, and ate at a table made of driftwood. One of his neighbours, an old man, said to him at his fireside, 'I declare to God, Tony, no one would live in a place like this – only an Englishman such as yourself.'

On Omey, where John MacDonagh was fitting a ceiling of narrow boards hexagonally, Tony made me a bed of broad oak planks from the Forest of Cong. Above the bed he erected a shelf long enough for a hundred books, advising me to reduce my library to that number in order not to burden myself with too much literature. The bed filled one of the six walls opposite a golden-rectangular window facing north with a view across a shallow sound to Aughrusmore. Another big window held in the middle distance the National school, now closed, and the gable of St Fechin's church. Far out on the horizon stood High Island – a brown loaf on a blue tablecloth speckled with white. A half-glazed door faced the church and Sweeney's pub in Claddaghduff. A sink and gas cooker filled the wall under a window looking down across the strand, where, on a rising spring tide, I could watch two arms of the sea join to embrace the island for five hours and part to release it from isolation on the ebb.

In the centre of this 1980s beehive hut, an oak hexagonal pole supported a flat roof. Around that pole was a teak hexagonal table on a stone hexagonal pillar. Whenever I entered, harassed by rain, wind and the anxieties of life on the mainland, the figure of the hexagon, repeated like a musical theme with variations in the walls, the table and the ceiling, calmed me with a sense of concentricity and gave me the centripetal energy I needed to sit down, take out a notebook and pen, and write.

But not always. Because I had acquired with the site eleven acres of land that I could not resist 'improving' – for instance, by hiring a tractor with a trailer and four men to gather a cast of seaweed and spread it on the ground where primroses and violets, harebells, bog orchids and burnet roses had grown without my help. And because the birdlife caught my attention: choughs, red in beak and claw, arguing over perches on a cliff above the lake; and once, five jackdaws nagging a young merlin in the sky to quit the neighbourhood, making feint attacks on a bird that could have killed and eaten any one of them; and later, the sound of a shot fired by a neighbour, killing the merlin.

I had tried and failed to get Tony a job for the autumn semester of 1974 at Bard College, where he would have been more helpful to the bright student poets than I was. One called April Hubinger had detested my assignment to write a sonnet so much that she wrote fourteen lines breaking every rule brilliantly. A few years later she took her own life. Tony had succeeded in helping me obtain an appointment for the academic year 1974–75 in the creative-writing programme at Princeton by speaking well of me to his friend Bob Coover. But it was Edmund (Mike) Keeley, Cavafy's translator, who gave me the job and who, with the novelist George Garrett, made my working life agreeable.

Before leaving Bard in May I had arranged to swap houses and cars with a young professor of geology, but this fell through when he disappeared and his body was discovered in a swamp, with his throat cut by himself. A house was found for me facing a graveyard in a dormitory town fifteen miles from Princeton, its bedrooms decorated with purple, mauve and pink flowery wallpaper, a flight of china ducks glued to the sitting-room wall, every shelf cluttered with supermarket ornaments. My mother, who came for a week and hosted a dinner party for my colleagues, never stopped urging me to ask them for a permanent job so that I could buy a nice old house in the centre of Princeton, where, with my father long ago, she remembered seeing Einstein walking across a lawn.

When the owner of that house, who had been occupying mine in Ireland, had to return to the United States, leaving me houseless for the spring semester, I decided to sleep behind a screen on a mattress on the floor of my office. At Princeton in those days, office carpets had a deep pile. Though informed officially that I was breaking the fire regulations of the building, I preferred – like Bartleby the Scrivener in Melville's short story – not to move; and I stayed, using the windowsill as a refrigerator until the weather got too warm. The janitor, who was black, assumed I was there for kicks, and invited me to a party where he said I could have whatever I wanted. 'Some dudes,' he said, 'dig broads and other dudes dig dudes. Who cares? Come to Trenton, we can drink a few beers and talk a bit of miscellaneous.' I didn't dare go. Instead I reviewed Philip Larkin's *High Windows* for the *New York Review of Books*.

I did go to Stuart Hampshire's Gauss Seminars on Spinoza to stretch my mind beyond its limit, but more often to the home of Julian and Elizabeth Moynahan, delighted by their hospitality and astonished by their brilliance. There I witnessed Liz and Julian talking simultaneously to each other at a speed too fast for me to follow either one or the other while at the same time absorbing the news on television and in his case reading a book or correcting a student's essay. They also were friends of my ex-wife Patricia and of Desmond Williams, professor of modern European history, who lived with Patricia in

Dublin for the last twelve years of her life. The Moynahans had three daughters, Catherine, Bridget and Molly, who entertained Emily when she stayed with them for three weeks in March.

During the summer of 1975 I spent more time at the Hexagon than at the New Forge, except when I had guests, such as Charles Monteith for his regular summer visit. Towards the end of August, Father Francis Sweeney came from Boston College for a few days and travelled with me when I drove across Ireland to give the first in a series of five readings by poets at the Kilkenny Festival. On the way I mentioned Robert Lowell, whom I was apprehensive of meeting. Lowell had a reputation as the greatest poet of his generation, and one who suffered, as Theodore Roethke did, from manic depression. Francis had no desire to meet him again because Lowell had once put him down with the contempt of a Boston Brahmin for someone of South Boston Irish servant-class descent. Francis prided himself on being the only impresario for whom T.S. Eliot had read in America twice.

One of my earliest reviews for the *Spectator* in 1950 was of Lowell's *Poems, 1938–1949*. I found them difficult, but instead of admitting this, handed out praise and blame in a strictly judgemental tone to cover my ignorance. Now I was afraid that if Lowell had read and remembered the review he might be hostile, although his psychiatrist, Dr Merrill Moore, America's champion sonneteer, had written me a letter of approval. Francis said Moore was reputed to have composed a sonnet in his car while waiting at traffic lights for red to turn to green.

At Kilkenny I put Francis on a train for Dublin, and drove thirteen miles through richly cultivated farmland to Jerpoint, where the poets were to stay as guests of the painter Barrie Cooke and his wife, the potter Sonja Landweer. Close to the ruins of an ancient abbey, Jerpoint House was a decently dilapidated Anglo-Irish relic which those artists were restoring with good taste, turning barns into studios. I entered between arrogant stone gateposts and bumped down a pot-holed avenue overarched by beeches as old as the house but in better shape. Tree-lined meadows beyond the buildings sloped down to the gently flowing River Nore.

I thought of Barrie as the man whom Ted Hughes had gone off to fish with in County Clare when Ted suddenly left Sylvia alone with me in Cleggan five months before her death. The Barrie I met at Jerpoint was an artist of English origin with a Harvard degree who had recently returned from a visit to Sarawak, where he had lived in a long house with Dayak headhunters deep in the jungle. There he had persuaded the children to catch butterflies, which he pinned and brought home in half a dozen boxes, along with photographs and sketches of the rain forest. Now he was painting impressive canvases of swirling, tumescent greenery in which the artist seemed to be struggling to overcome the forest's strangulations.

Our festival organisers in Kilkenny had scheduled my reading to begin after eleven o'clock at night. The venue was a room adjacent to a bar in Kyteler's Inn, a restored medieval building. My dislike of having to perform on a platform so late was redeemed, however, by Seamus Heaney's graceful introduction, which included his reading of one of my poems. Ten years earlier Ted Hughes had shown me in Cleggan a proof copy of *Death of a Naturalist*, Heaney's first book with Faber, and had said, 'The charm of the person comes across in the poetry.'

With a book in my hand but my eyes on the audience as I was speaking, I noticed a young couple holding hands in the front row, she with a tape-recorder on her lap. I knew I had better not let their attention distract me or my memory might lapse, better not focus on anyone such as the guy who staggered in late with a half-drunk pint of stout. I remembered Tony's advice not to wave my arms but gesture with my voice.

After my reading, the young man, who came from Thurles in County Tipperary, and his girlfriend, from Chicago, approached and asked me to sign copies of my books. I inscribed them to Dennis O'Driscoll and Julie O'Callaghan. He said he'd like to talk to me about poetry if I could spare the time. His aura of pure aesthetic intensity scared me, but I promised to talk on another night.

The audience drifted down to the cellar bar, which had reopened. There I saw Lowell and Heaney surrounded by poets, artists, journalists, girls from Fordham University, some of whom might have been South Boston Irish, and a priest who had cast off his Roman collar. At the end of a very long day, rather than jostle with this crowd I preferred to take a walk along the path between the river and the towering walls of Kilkenny Castle in the dark.

On Monday morning, in the courtyard of Jerpoint, Seamus Heaney told us he had just received a message that his cousin Colum McCartney had been shot dead the previous night on his way home to the North from the All-Ireland semi-final Gaelic-football match in Dublin. He had been held up by Protestant paramilitaries, probably wearing British army uniforms on a country road just across the border.

Seamus said he might have to leave us to attend the funeral. He kept his feelings to himself. We talked about the politics of funerals in Ireland: Jeremiah O'Donovan Rossa's funeral at Glasnevin; Pádraig Pearse's graveside oration; the final interment of Roger Casement's calcified bones at Glasnevin in 1966, attended by Éamon de Valera as president of Ireland wearing a top hat like John Bull; the power of perpetually renewed desire for revenge which funeral after funeral had generated in the North, even when the relatives begged for no such action to be taken; the thirteen coffins of the Bloody Sunday victims in Derry on 30 January 1972.

We were all glad when Seamus decided to stay, to introduce Norman MacCaig from Edinburgh that night, Derek Mahon on Tuesday, and Robert Lowell on Wednesday. Seamus performed his role as the poet-in-residence with style, bonhomie and playfulness. Off duty he took a craftsman's interest in a Dayak blowpipe at Jerpoint and tried blowing darts from one large room through the door into another, until Derek, unaware of the game, walked into the line of fire and was almost hit. 'Almost' is a word Seamus uses well in his poetry to let himself off some hooks, almost. Years later, in *Station Island*, remembering the blaze of red-hot pokers in the garden at Jerpoint, he wrote, 'I felt like the bottom of a dried-up lake.'

My impressions of Robert Lowell began at Jerpoint with a man wrapped in himself, slumped in a low armchair, surrounded by tribal artefacts and weapons. His grey, ravaged head was bent, as if he had long made a habit of looking down (through books) into his heart. As we talked his arms floated in front of him in a circle like a ring fort with a small gap for words to flow in and out between the fingertips. I was afraid that a thoughtless remark of mine might have been caught in a pincer movement, and held up for trial under pain of execution. His manner was frigid at first but warmed up later.

From another angle his curved arms were antennae that absorbed every vibration in the dialectic air. His hands undulated in very gentle rhythmic emphasis of his words. He talked with quiet intensity, minimising the consonants with aristocratic diffidence, first cousin to a drawl, difficult to understand when other voices were speaking in the room at the same time, but never trivial. Not to miss a word, I leaned towards his fortifications, the bottle and glass of red wine, the cannon puffs of cigarette smoke, to receive whatever emerged with Delphic enlightenment.

A vulnerable openness to new experience or new ideas coexisted with the ramparts he ranged around himself in gesture and look. Sure of his reputation, unlike Theodore Roethke, he didn't bang the table and boast of his madness to put down rivals. He was courteous and diffident, without pomp or pretentiousness. At all hours of the day or night, even after two or three bottles of wine, his mind, if not his voice, kept its clarity and exaltation. When the conversation declined into gossip, as mine often did long before two or three in the morning, he made me feel that I had dropped a precious book which he had stooped to pick up, dust off and quote from, before putting it back on a high shelf in the copious library of his mind.

Impressed by his intellectual seriousness, I asked him how he managed to talk, even at breakfast, on a subject as abstruse as Spinoza. He said it came from being married to three women of the highest intelligence, with whom he had kept up a continual critical dialogue about literature, the arts and philosophy, especially Elizabeth Hardwick.

So his small talk was at odds with that of All Souls, which he told me he had not enjoyed as a visiting fellow. I was not surprised. The Oxford sense of humour – brilliance toying with triviality – would not have appealed to him. He liked living in New York, he said, because you could see your friends there and ignore your neighbours. In the country you knew all your neighbours but seldom saw your friends. New York scared me, I said: no sooner did I arrive than I planned to leave. In Connemara my neighbours used the word friends to mean relations.

On Monday evening at Jerpoint he joined me on a walk (short enough for his shortness of breath) to put the guinea fowl, geese, pheasants and peacocks to roost or to bed in Barrie and Sonja's orchard, before I drove him, with MacCaig, to Kilkenny.

A lean, lively, sixty-five-year-old Scot with a steely wit, Norman MacCaig had managed to combine teaching at a primary school in Edinburgh with the prolific writing of poetry. At a dinner before his reading he astounded me by drinking two tumblers of straight whiskey without a tremor in his hand or a slur in his voice. Meanwhile, he told me that he never revised a poem. If the first draft was good it went into a book, otherwise he threw it away. He said he couldn't bring himself to go back over a line he had written, preferring to progress with something new. I admired his energy, his liver and his thrust. I couldn't endure a hangover or give up revising.

Two hours after midnight I persuaded MacCaig and Lowell to leave their circles of admirers in the cellar and accept a lift in my car to Jerpoint. Fog on the road, bends unmarked by cat's-eyes in the tarmac – all my attention was given to avoiding an accident and not missing a turn. Lowell was lofty as ever in dialogue with the empirical MacCaig.

While swerving to avoid potholes on the Jerpoint avenue, I noticed a grey van stuck in the ditch, with the lights switched off. Breakdown or accident? I stopped, reversed a few yards to light up the van and stepped out to investigate. There was no sign of damage and nobody in the front seats, but from the back came a murmuration of conspirators. Peeping through the window, I could barely see two shapes like lopsided Buddhas leaning towards each other, and recognised the spirituous voices of interior exiles from the Catholic farmyards of Derry and the shipyards of Protestant Belfast. Seamus and Derek were locked in discussion, talking about I don't know what, unaware of being observed, an exemplary image of sorting out our country's troubles in the dead of night.

The hot dry weather continued on Tuesday, when Lowell and I followed Barrie down to the River Nore. Barrie saw a salmon swimming after the fly that he had cast over the shallow water. His black Labrador barked at a herd of Friesian cattle that approached us with snuffling curiosity. We had to climb over two wooden stiles, difficult for Lowell with his quivering unsteadiness of hand and foot.

When we returned to the house, Seamus brought in Helen Vendler, who had come far out of her way from lecturing in Sligo to see Lowell briefly before she returned to teach at Boston University. At once he started praising her new book on George Herbert, quoting precisely a remark on a certain page as if it were printed in his mind. Then he took issue with her argument about a poem that he loved and recited. What greater flattery than this unflattering approach of a poet to a critic?

To me she apologised nicely for not reviewing *High Island* two years ago in the *New York Times,* on the grounds that there were so many books to choose from, and she herself had little or no interest in history, adding also that 'it's a great help if you happen to have met the author'. I wondered would she be attracted or repelled by my poetry after meeting me now?

A young journalist called Elgy Gillespie arrived in the afternoon to continue her interview with Lowell for the *Irish Times,* and they sauntered down to the river for a swim on their own. When they returned he sat down shirtless at a table and poured out more wine. His shoulders were covered with grey hair.

Before Derek Mahon's reading, there was a banquet in Kilkenny, and the poets were invited. I dressed in a room at the Club House Hotel, where I would be staying for my last two nights, then walked up the hill to the castle and turned into a courtyard of warm cut stone that contained the ancient coach houses and stables of the Dukes of Ormonde, magnificently transformed with government funds into the Kilkenny Design Centre.

In the entrance hall, my heart sank at the sight of Conor Cruise O'Brien standing beside the Centre's director, our dapper host, who shook my hand and asked, 'Do you know each other?' Conor turned up the whites of his eyes, as much taken aback to meet me there as I was to encounter him. He was now the Minister for Posts and Telegraphs in the coalition government, and a Labour Party member of the Dáil. I wondered why he was there, since he was not scheduled to speak at the festival.

After sherry and cocktails in the executive suite, we moved to a large conference room with a long table set for a dozen guests. Our host sat in the centre with the poet Máire MacEntee, Conor's wife, on his left. They were facing Conor, who was sandwiched between two handsome married women. The meal was a fugue on a theme of surfeit, funded by the government at a time of high unemployment and a slump in cattle prices. The best wines in the best order, through course after course, culminated in brandy and cigars. At this point, Conor called for silence, riveting our attention. In a voice gilded with nostalgia for the civil rights marches in Washington, he appealed to Lowell to join the Irish Labour Party delegation on their forthcoming visit to Portugal. A glorious revolution of flowers in the muzzles of guns, which had toppled the last of the European fascist dictators in Lisbon, was in danger of being captured by the Communists; and Conor wanted to be there, helping to prevent this, while gaining the limelight of liberal world approval. Lowell gave a noncommittal answer, and told me later that he would like to go to Lisbon, but on his own.

The banquet had not been a blessing for me or for Derek. His voice on the platform in the far-from-quiet room at Kyteler's Inn was inaudible. Derek has suffered more than enough to qualify as a *poète maudit,* which may be why his poetry is so good. What happy person writes good poetry apart from Seamus, and who knows whether he is as happy as he appears? 'What makes you think we are meant to be happy?' the doomed Russian poet Mandelstam, a Heaney favourite, asked his wife not long before his arrest and disappearance on Stalin's order.

On Wednesday I woke ill-tempered with a hangover and a longing to go back to my Hexagon on Omey Island, but I stayed one more night to hear Lowell. He conducted his own reading on a seminar level, treating us all as if we were his equals. At 11.15 p.m. in a stiflingly hot, overcrowded room above the inn, he began, as a matter of protocol, by acknowledging 'Your Excellency', the only public official to attend any of our readings. Brought here by Hubert Butler from Bennetsbridge, the Russian ambassador sat in front of me, a smooth upright elderly man, motionless as a dignitary on a May Day parade in Moscow. He had the shortest haircut in a room among men with hair over their ears and collars like mine.

Lowell on a platform had been described by Norman Mailer as 'that slouch, that personification of ivy climbing a column'. He read not quite well enough for one to accuse him of acting, though his act of occasionally mumbling or stumbling over a word, or asking for a window to be opened to let in some air, was that of a poet who had been persuaded against his inclination to perform. The quietly conversational tone of his voice was hard to hear against the street noise of traffic and revelry.

In a moment of relaxed commentary between two poems, he told us in a voice that seemed to be amplified around the room, 'I hate to say anything good about Russians' – and while he paused you could almost hear the audience missing a heartbeat – 'but I must say they keep their old houses much better than we keep ours.' I was watching the back of the head of the ambassador to see whether he would react. He didn't move or speak, but remained rigid with waxwork dignity. Later we learnt that he was rather deaf and knew little English.

As the crowd enveloped Lowell and drew him down like Don Giovanni into the sulphurous cellar bar, I noticed Dennis and Julie, to whom I had not kept my word. Now was my last chance of talking to them. Then and there we began to talk, and the gap between our ages of twenty-one and forty-eight was bridged as we continued talking for three hours. From this good fortune that I had almost missed, a lifelong conversation would flow.

When I first met Tony on Inishbofin in 1959 he had short hair and was twenty-nine years old. Now, when he arrived in Cleggan soon after I had got back from Kilkenny, he was forty-five and his hair, black as ever, was down to his shoulders, his hirsute torso bronzed from summer construction in Aquitaine and Provence. In a letter dated 19 August 1975 from London he had described himself as 'extremely fit, running 3–4 miles every morning, under 13 stone, ready and willing to undertake anything you require of me'.

What I most required was a bookcase to hold the great *Oxford English Dictionary*. Tony designed and made this at the Hexagon out of thick and broad Parana pine scantlings, with a shelf for the dictionaries at chair level

– no getting up or leaning down to lift them. A lower shelf was available for lighter and less important reference books. The bookcase was panelled so that it could double as a footboard of the bed, and based on castors so that I could move it easily. To use with the bookcase, Tony made stools of the same timber, each large enough to hold a volume lying open.

Then he went to Inishbofin and began converting a small derelict school-house, midway between the hotel and the pub on the quay, into a cottage designed by a Belfast architect for Margaret and Miko Day. But his mother, now in an old people's home, drew him back to London, though he still dreamed of bringing her to live in Connemara. James Michie wrote to me in November, saying, 'Tony is as well as I have ever seen him. I've fixed him up ghosting a book on impotence by an old psychiatrist friend of mine, who was publicity agent for Max Schmeling long ago. What more can you want?' Tony, I thought, was better qualified to write about sexual exhaustion. He wrote on 5 December, 'Everything in London is even more of a mad rush than ever which only confirms that I made the wise choice in deciding to live in Ireland … I miss the cottage terribly and look forward to getting back.'

At Christmas Tony sent me a card with a painting of a field mouse and three brown leaves, with this message:

> Hello, Rick, hope you got my letter OK. Since then life has been eventful. I finally broke my leg playing football (well, it had to come). Some young cowboy scythed me down as if I was an offend-ing thistle and the report echoed across London. Strong men turned pale and we had to wait half-an-hour before an ambulance finally made its way across the steppes of North London. The junior doctors (still on go-slow) X-rayed me and put my leg in plaster, but refused to admit me, so I've been kindly taken in by my old and long-suffering friend John Holmstrom in Hornsey. Come the New Year, before he cracks under the strain of tending a reluctant cripple, I'll probably be moving to Twickenham to stay and work with the shrink. I have to go back to the hospital on January 12 to see how things are progressing and, I hope, to get a lighter plaster cast – the present one weighs a ton. Of course the main problem is to rest the leg, but I haven't done too bad so far (it's a fractured tibia, by the way.) But of course this has put paid to all my imme-diate plans. But I have got over my depression about that and so I hope will you. I'll let you know how I improve as soon as possible.

Everyone has been very sympathetic and I've had lots of visitors. I mean to come to Ireland as soon as I get my discharge papers and stay for a long while. The irony of it all is that this would never have happened if I hadn't been so incredibly fit. Obviously I must have appeared to be a menace … Do write news of Cleggan sometime. I've heard only from Anya, just to say she was coming over, which she hasn't! I long to hear what's been going on. I hope everything's going OK with you, writing, farming, enjoying life. You'll be happily back in the Forge again and Emily will be there over Christmas, I hope. I'll be with you trebly in spirit.
Keep running,
Love,
MacFuite

On Friday 9 January 1976 I drove with Emily from Cleggan to Dublin, where we parted. I was dining with Tom and Eleanor Kinsella at their house on the Grand Canal when Emily rang to tell me that Tony was dead. Her mother had called, having heard from Mary Coyne, who had heard from James Michie in London. The house seemed to turn upside down and I would have fallen if there had not been a chair beside me. When I got through to James, he said that Tony had been working on the book with Carl Lambert in Twickenham when he complained of feeling faint and unable to breathe. His last words were, 'Please call my mother.' He passed out and died in the ambulance, the compound fracture having caused a pulmonary embolism in both lungs.

I joined Emily at once, and returned the next day to Cleggan. Tony had left me in charge of his cottage – the only possession of one who wanted neither to possess nor be possessed. Then I called Anya Barnett, a potter from Belfast. Much loved by her teachers at the Royal College in the late 1960s, Hans Coper and Lucie Rie, Anya had set up a large kiln in the old Protestant schoolhouse where she was living, near the church in Clifden. Tony had not been her lover, she told me later, but her soulmate.

After pages of raw grief I wrote these words: 'All that I ever wrote in these notebooks since I began to use the square-lined page was written with an underlying assumption that Tony would be the one to read with complete understanding all I had written, that he would outlive me, that he would make sense of the confusions in my life … now I must make whatever sense I can … now I must clarify.'

The day before the funeral at Feltham, a western suburb of London, on 20 January, Anya and I went to see Tony's mother, Yvonne White, who had been paralysed by a stroke. Her mind was undamaged though her French-accented speech was impaired, and it was hard for her to make what she wanted to say understood. I remember her saying, 'I've no more tears to shed. I shed all my tears when Alan was killed in the war.' It then occurred to me that Tony's loss of his idealised older brother, a volume of whose poetry, *Garlands and Ash,* was published in 1947 by the Fortune Press, had perhaps inclined him to encourage and improve mine.

My brother Chris drove me with his wife Marcelle and Anya to the crematorium at Feltham, where I met for the first time Tony's great friends from Cambridge days, Jane and her husband, Karl Miller, the actress Sheila Ballantyne, and Sasha Moorsom, BBC producer and novelist. Among those I recognised were Pixie Weir, Isabel Geldart, who had built herself a holiday house with a view of Tony's cottage, the photographer Ander Gunn and, representing Tony's team of workmates and footballers, Peter Docherty and Johnny Hinds. There were other women I didn't know, who obviously must have adored Tony The weather was foul, the ceremony horrible. Some of us repaired to the Duke of York down the road, and later to a favourite spot of Tony's, Becky's Dive in Southwark.

The following morning, I met Tony's older sister, Lois Preston, at the city office of Tony's solicitor, Roger Wellings. Tony had died intestate, leaving only the cottage and some debts; Lois was to inherit his estate and within a year I would buy the cottage to give Emily on her twenty-first birthday. In the afternoon, I collected the ashes from the crematorium, having chosen a mini oak coffin rather than an urn, since Mary Coyne had been talking to the priest about having a burial service in Omey. And the same evening Marcelle came with me to meet Yvonne, who gave me a list of forty-five different kinds of jobs that Tony had undertaken in his forty-five years. I could have added coaching Emily so well for A-levels that she had been admitted by Brendan Kennelly to read English at Trinity College, Dublin.

Emily was with me on the drive from Dublin to Cleggan with the ashes, and when she said, 'I can see the lights of Inishbofin', as we began our descent to the village on the sea, for the first time I did not feel the joy that always used to come at this moment of return after an absence, but that my life had been changed irrevocably and that I must change my life by leaving the west.

On Sunday 25 January, a Catholic burial of the mini coffin had been timed for the afternoon when the Omey strand would be open. In the morning

Emily and I were joined at Tony's cottage by Anya and Tony's friend and co-author Martin Green, and Martin's friend Judith Dainton, for a pagan scattering of some of the ashes. Anya provided one of her light grey pots with two strange lips in the Cycladic style of Hans Coper. The ashes that I spooned into her pot reminded me of bone meal. When we discussed what words to recite at the lake, everyone was pleased by Anya's choice of a three-line Japanese Zen poem.

Then we walked down through rushes and rocks to a place where the lake water narrows into a stream that flows by Rossadillisk into the sea. Not far from this bleak shore is an islet where Tony had noticed swans nesting the previous year. Anya led with the pot, covered, because of the wind, by Tony's scarf. Dark clouds were threatening rain. We hesitated. Then Anya passed the cup to me and Emily told me to hurl it out as far as possible into the lake. The cup emptied its ashes in the sky and they blew away in the time it took for the cup to strike the glittering surface of the peat-brown water. At that sound a heron rose from beyond the islet and slowly climbed in a widening circle till it disappeared in a cloud. Anya and I together recited:

> Coming, going, the waterfowl
> Leaves not a trace,
> Nor does it need a guide.

After lunch we prepared Tony's cottage to receive mourners, and I took Tommy Coohill, who had offered to choose and dig a grave, to Omey. At 4 p.m. Emily, Anya and I, with the mini coffin, led a procession of Tony's friends and neighbours in cars and on foot from Claddaghduff Church across the strand. Tommy had chosen a quiet sandy corner as close as possible to the sea, and Father Austin Fergus spoke the words for burial of a Catholic over the grave of Tony, an agnostic. Finally the priest recited the rosary with more than a hundred people responding.

Mary Coyne, who the previous night in our house had kissed the casket, crying 'Poor Tony!' and saying prayers for his soul, sure that he above all would go to heaven, now knelt on the grave and placed a pot of daffodils, grown by her, to mark the spot. We invited everyone to Tony's cottage afterwards, and as we drove across the strand away from the graveyard Emily pointed to the distant hills with snow on their summit lit up by the sun, whereas all the land close to us looked gloomy under clouds. We burnt candles in the cottage, and kept a turf fire blazing in the open hearth to warm the guests.

Emily told me she had decided not to complain any more, because we had never heard Tony complain. If something annoyed her, instead of complaining, she would think of Tony and smile to herself.

At the New Forge two weeks later, around two o'clock, I heard the doorbell ring, and went to open it, thinking of gunmen ringing doorbells in Belfast. At the top of the steps stood a tall, racked, middle-aged man, with longish dark hair becoming dusty grey, wearing glasses, who simply said, 'O'Toole'. I had to look fast through layers of disguise which time had made up on his features to find the form that reminded me, chiefly in the smile, of the young actor I had met for the first time about eighteen years ago in his dressing room at the Royal Court Theatre after a performance of *The Long and the Short and the Tall*.

Peter had come to talk about Tony and he talked even more about Jimmy Mellor, an actor of their vintage at the Old Vic in the 1950s, for whom Peter and Tony and other friends had been planning a champagne party because Mellor was dying of cancer. But when Peter returned from America in January to give the party, he heard that both Jimmy and Tony were dead. Instead, at a memorial service in the actors' church, St Paul's, Covent Garden, he made a funeral oration culminating with, 'Fear no more the heat of the sun', and when he came to the line, 'Nothing ill come near thee', he had looked hard and scornfully at Peter Hall, who was sitting as near as possible to the coffin. As everyone knew that Hall had thrown Mellor out of a job in the theatre, this had made people laugh.

At his father's cremation, he said, when he went to pick up the ashes, he asked the gloomy official in black who received him mournfully, 'How's business?' It was winter and the man replied, 'At this time of year we're kept busy.' Then, by asking the man how many ovens were kept going and at what temperature, Peter had discovered that the fire leaves the skeleton intact, burning everything else, and then the bones have to be put through a machine that grinds them down to the fineness of coarse sand on a beach. The official told him the ash was excellent for growing crocuses. Peter said his father's ashes had to be divided spoonful by spoonful into different bags going to different places: one to the goalmouth of Sunderland Football Club, one to the graveyard at Ballyconree, another for the crocuses.

He mentioned that Robert Shaw was hard at work filming, while the going was good, and had cut off from most of his friends since Mary's suicide. We talked about getting a headstone carved and erected for Tony on the shore of Aughrusbeg Lough, with the words that I told him we had recited at the scattering. In the end the stone bearing those words under Tony's name and dates, 1930–1976, commissioned by Martin Green, was erected on the grave in Peter's and my absence.

When I asked Peter, who had acted with Tony at the Old Vic, what he thought of Tony's acting, he replied, 'Tony was the only actor whose talent I ever envied.'

Having lost the reader I had borne in mind when writing poetry, I wrote no poems that were publishable for a year and a half after Tony's death. In the autumn of 1976 I began the first of two semesters at the University of Iowa, where, with Anya as my companion in the second, we endured the coldest winter since before Independence in 1776. Anya was invited to use the ceramics department workshops for making pots, but as everyone worked in sight of everyone else, this didn't appeal to her, nor was she keen on making a pot for a kiln that had fired a ceramic model of a motorcar.

The average Iowa graduate student's attitude to the workshop was epitomised in my class by a woman who defended an obscure line written by a friend, 'I think I feel I know what she's trying to say.' My response showed me to be as foreign to these Midwesterners and as out of key as I felt: 'What you have said could be scanned as a line of blank verse with five regular stresses.'

My failure to enjoy Iowa was not exceptional. Mark Strand had ended his first semester of a year's appointment by commuting from New York, and had resigned before the second. A novelist had lost his entire salary by playing poker with the resident poets Marvin Bell and Donald Justice. On leaving he'd said he had no regrets. The workshop seemed like a union headquarters for operators in the field of poetry. When I asked why sixty copies of each student's worksheets were printed and displayed week after week where any passer-by could pick them up, I was told that poets crossing the country would stop by at Iowa to find out what kind of poetry was getting written and accepted in magazines. Poems chosen by Howard Moss for the *New Yorker* were analysed to discover what imagery appealed to him most.

Wanting to find something in the landscape that connected with Ireland, I tried to imagine the brown water of the Iowa River reaching the Mississippi and then the Gulf of Mexico on its way to the Gulf Stream across the Atlantic. But this only made the place seem more remote. When Stephen Spender came to give a lecture, I invited him to join me on a day trip to the Mississippi in a car driven by one of my students. Beforehand I asked Donald Justice where we might get the best view, preferably from a waterside restaurant. Don said he'd never seen the river except from a plane. So did Marvin, who told me to ask Paul Engle, a native Iowan. Engle took out maps and enthused about a spot, a hundred and fifty miles away, where the Mississippi, he said, with cliffs on one side, most nearly resembles the Rhine. 'As to food,' he said, pointing at the map, 'go down the hill in the centre of this town, turn a corner at the bottom, and there you have it on the right-hand side, a restaurant on the water where they serve catfish.' We drove for three hours through rolling corn and hog farms, found the town, the hill and the corner and a shiny steel coach called 'Abe's Diner' with dim red lights inside – beyond this a rail yard. Half a mile across a swamp we glimpsed the Mississippi.

Engle was known for having run the Writer's Workshop well when Lowell, John Berryman and Philip Roth taught there. Before Stephen's lecture he gave us dinner, and I saw on display under glass at the entrance to his living room a large picture of himself as America's most promising young poet, with an adulatory review of his first book in the *New York Times* dated in the early 1930s. Before the meal a radio journalist, summoned by Engle to record an interview with him and Spender, sat them side by side and suggested that they talk about literary life in Germany before the war. When Engle claimed that he had often stepped over dead bodies on the streets of Munich in those days, Stephen replied, 'The only bodies I remember stepping over in Germany were alive and in bed.'

What proved to be my last words with Patricia were spoken on the telephone on 16 August 1977 just after I had drunk my last alcoholic drink – for the next twenty years. She had rung me up at a time when I could tell from her speech that she was mildly intoxicated, and I had urged her to give up booze altogether before it killed her. She replied, 'I don't know what you're talking about,' and hung up.

In July 1972 she had taken Emily and me to Tardets in the Pyrenees and to Lourdes, where all three of us were hoping a reconciliation and a cure for Patricia might be possible. Even Desmond Williams had asked me over lunch at his club on the Green to consider 'taking her back'. I had landed her once on High Island, which she loved although the cliffs had appalled her. In France, where she had refused wine at the table, having promised Emily she wouldn't drink, she had drunk in secret at night. There were awful scenes, and she was unable to walk with Emily and me through the gorge of Kakouetta because the alcohol had made her terrified of heights. I had been unable to help her.

A year later, in 1973, Emily and my sister Mary, who had always been fond of Patricia, had persuaded her to enter a clinic and undergo treatment in London, resulting in a cure that gave Emily what she remembers as 'the best two years of my life with my mother'. Those were the years when Garrett FitzGerald, an economist in charge of Ireland's foreign affairs, sought advice on Europe from Desmond Williams. Once a week Garrett and his wife, Joan, would dine with Patricia, who cooked the meal herself. Desmond, whose addiction to alcohol was as well known in Dublin as Patricia's, had been obliged to give up alcohol when he became diabetic. He had long suffered from osteomyelitis and relied on Patricia to bandage the open wound on his leg every day. Now she had to inject him with insulin; and, being sober, she began to write another novel, called *A Second Adam*.

She had described her novel to me as a thriller concerned with the shipment of a secret cargo by the IRA. When Julian Moynahan asked Patricia what the cargo was, she said she didn't know, and he replied, 'I don't think you can get the book published until you do.' When the novel was rejected, Patricia, who had been taking barbiturates on advice from the clinic, relapsed into drinking alcohol, but combined with sleeping tablets, knowing this would soon result in death. Now she needed a stick for walking. Every third night became a disaster – Wagner or Richard Strauss at full volume, raving and smashing glasses – followed by a day of agonising sickness, then one of perfect clarity, intelligence and charm. Several times I saw Patricia with bruises on her face and a black eye, which she explained as the result of walking into a lamppost.

Two nights after her last phone call, I was missing severely my regular pint of stout in the Pier Bar or Oliver's before dinner at the New Forge and a shot of Jameson in goat's milk afterwards, when I went upstairs and sat on my bed under a skylight and took out a Parisian notebook. Remembering Tony, as I always would remember him every day of my life, I wrote a sentence that extended in half an hour to twenty-four long lines of free verse, not a word crossed out or needing to be changed. Titled 'The Price of Stone', it was published in 1979 by Peter Fallon and Dennis O'Driscoll in *The First Ten Years – Dublin Arts Festival Poetry*. By then Dennis had become my ideal reader whose critical advice would always lead to the improvement of a poem.

My first intention in abstaining had been to save myself from the risk of getting drunk and talking taverna Greek while teaching at Syracuse University, where I was to take up an appointment early in September; but since the Queen of Inner Operations seemed to have blessed my sobriety I had good reason to persist.

On Friday 2 September, three days before I was booked to fly from Dublin to New York, Emily rang in the morning and told me, 'Mummy's dead.' Desmond had seen her at two o'clock before he went to sleep in his bedroom and at ten-thirty he had found her on the floor at the foot of her bed – beside her were bottles of Benedictine and Cointreau, half drunk, and an empty bottle of Nembutal tablets. Emily, who now had a room in Trinity, had gone to Wilton Place to see her mother the day before, and Patricia, in good health, had sent her across the canal with a prescription she had signed for a month's supply of the barbiturates.

The funeral was arranged for Monday morning at the University Church on St Stephen's Green, followed by the burial at Dean's Grange. Emily and I would have preferred Omey. My flight left me no time to go to the cemetery after standing beside Emily at the church door in line with her grandmother, Paddy Avis, her cousins, Simon and Meiert, and Desmond Williams, shaking hands with people as they left. I kissed Emily goodbye as she stepped into the car behind the hearse, followed by other cars, leaving me alone on the pavement waiting for a taxi. Then the two elderly priests, who had conducted the service for someone they had never known, came out of the church, and one of them asked me, 'Where's the hearse?' 'Gone to the graveyard,' I said. He replied, 'What was their hurry? They can't bury her without us.' How Patricia would have laughed!

In Syracuse I rented the garret of a house as old as the century, almost my mother's age. Through diamond panes of glass in the windows I could see the tops of maples stretching higher than the gables and chimneys of neighbouring houses. Next to my garret was a huge attic, full to the ridge with chandeliers and lampshades, which my landlord, David Jenks, collected. Because he warned me that my room had no fire escape, I bought a coil of manila rope forty feet long and half an inch thick, which I kept under my antique bed, tied to one of the round brass legs.

One Christmas, when David Jenks was six years old, his parents had taken him to the pantomime at Loew's Theatre in Syracuse, where he became so entranced by a chandelier hanging in the foyer that he wanted to stay looking up at it in wonder and worship instead of taking his seat and watching the show. Again and again throughout his childhood he had returned to the theatre just to look at the chandelier, which Louis Comfort Tiffany had designed in an Ottoman style of green and white opulence for the mansion of Cornelius Vanderbilt on Fifth Avenue in New York. When that house was demolished to make way for a skyscraper, the chandelier was acquired by Loew for Syracuse: and when David grew up, and Loew's Theatre closed down, he bought the chandelier, which he stored in his attic. He told everyone it was for sale, but whenever a buyer came close to offering him the asking price, he raised it out of reach.

While I slept as a lodger in his garret, walled off by a narrow partition from the vast roof space that held higgledy-piggledy his treasure hoard of old glass lamps, lanterns and chandeliers, I was sometimes woken in the night by David taking a group of friends past my door to admire Tiffany's masterpiece. He talked of lending it to the Metropolitan Museum in New York for five years, as he could not afford to insure it in his highly inflammable old wood-frame house; but nothing came of this because his attachment to the chandelier was like a jealous lovers passion.

I went home for the Christmas vacation, and wrote the following note at what was now Emily's flat in Dublin:

> Sunday, 15 January 1978 – 1 Wilton Place, Dublin 2
> Sunday morning … the softly consoling sound of pigeons coocoo-ing in the loft above this room in the flat where Patricia died four months ago reminds me of the Pleasure Ground at Milford in the summer of 1941 … when I woke up early in a tent under the copper beech and heard their voices … a mother sound … bread in the oven and a smell of yeast … a breath of reconciliation … love of my mother inspiring me to master the skills of harmony to compose an anthem … whatever you dream of doing in your life, let it be good, she said, because what you now dream will one day be fulfilled … that summer she gave me power to fulfil her dream of my winning scholarships both to the King's School Canterbury and to St Columba's … she urged me to go to King's because we were imperialists.

In childhood I had pictured Australia as an outpost of empire to which our father's uncle, Edward Scott-Murphy, had fled as a young man after running away to sea to escape his father's bad temper. There he became a police inspector in the state of Victoria and patriarch of a large, dutiful, churchgoing family of Scott-Murphys, who hyphenated their name to distinguish themselves from Murphys of Catholic, not to mention convict, origin. My Aunt Kay used to tell us that Uncle Edward sang in his local church choir until the Sunday before he died in his ninetieth year.

When I went to Australia in 1978 and gave a poetry reading in Sydney, a big tall man with dark bushy eyebrows who resembled my father approached me afterwards and said, 'I'm Richard Scott-Murphy, your third cousin.' He was a bank manager, having served as a pilot in the Royal Australian Air Force during the Second World War. At his house two days later we talked about the great-grandfather we had in common. We knew that Richard William Murphy had pulled himself up out of the clay of Carlow to become the master of a church school in a village called Nurney. As a result, his family had survived the Great Famine of 1845–52. But the master's wicked temper had caused Edward to flee to Australia and my grandfather, Richard William, to leave home and save enough in fifteen years working as a clerk in Dublin to put himself through Divinity School at Trinity College to become the rector of a parish, first at Ballinlough and finally at Clifden.

Having gathered so much about the Ormsby Bowen-Millers from my mother, I now became interested in assembling bare facts about the Murphys. My father had told us little. I remember his saying, 'My father never talked about his family: he may have felt it wasn't as good as the Mulvanys's.'

Back in Ireland in the summer of 1978 I drove to Nurney and met an old man called Archie Smyth, whose mother had taught in the school. He was living in the modestly grand house that the rector had occupied, built by the Bruens of Oak Park on their estate in the eighteenth century. It stood in one of the angles formed by the crossroads in the centre of the tiny village. But I had come too late to see the schoolhouse. On the site squatted an ochre-washed bungalow, with picture windows glaring at us.

Archie took me to a barn where behind some ancient farm machinery he showed me a crude worm-eaten desk, which he said was my great-grandfather's. At its back, visible to the boys in bare feet and homespun clothes, was a rack for holding the birch rods used for beating them. They were beaten not just for bad behaviour but for every word of Irish they spoke in school. The purpose of this, Archie thought, was to put down rebellion and supply clerks for service in the British Empire.

He described the ritual. In front of the class the offender was lifted off his feet on to the back of a larger boy who held him firmly by his wrists while the master flogged him. After this the boy was required to wear a wooden collar in which a notch was cut each time he was flogged. Almost a hundred years after the master's death, what had kept his name alive was his cruelty.

The school had opened in April 1821, when Richard William was eight years old, the son of a poor Protestant tenant farmer called William. Learning a few verses from the King James Bible every day, he passed through the schools seven grades in reading, writing, arithmetic, geometry and accounts. Then he became a monitor, teaching junior classes for the next ten years. A Quaker educationist of the time criticised the monitorial system as 'allowing the boys who knew a little to teach the boys who knew less'.

To become the master he needed a wife who could teach the girls. At twenty-four he married a woman of a higher class who had a Protestant surname. Fannie Scott was the daughter of a shopkeeper in Bagenalstown, five miles from Nurney. Promotion came within two years. They lived on the top floor of the school, where my grandfather, also named Richard William, was born in 1844. The house had golden-rectangular windows and cut-stone lintels. Downstairs there were two classrooms: one for the boys had an earthen floor, but the other for the girls was boarded.

In 1841 Colonel Henry Bruen MP, through his agent, Captain Cary, paid 'Richd. Murphy Nurney Schoolmaster' a quarterly 'salary' of £7 10s 0d that amounted to £30 in a year. The colonel's butler, groom and gamekeeper each received an annual 'wage' that was £20 more than the schoolmaster's 'salary'. He earned less money but had more prestige.

The school was close to a beautiful church with an elegant spire on top of a tall tower. The master acted as clerk for the vestry and sat prominently with his family, conducting and singing in the choir. His signature as witness to a wedding in 1845 between Thomas Lucas, a servant, and Catharine O'Neill, a farmer's daughter, has the forthright slope and pointed fortitude of my father's. By the 1860s, having reared five children, he had become postmaster of Nurney, with an office attached to the school.

We were never told that our grandfather had two sisters. Eliza Sarah, the schoolmaster's first child, became a teacher like her mother and in 1862 married Thomas Blackbourne, the master of a school at Fenagh, County Carlow. She gave birth to six healthy children in the next six years, by which time she and her husband were teaching at Clara in the King's County, now Offaly. There, on 23 May 1876, she was certified as insane, suffering from 'mania precipitated by pregnancy'. A court order signed the next day by Marcus Goodbody required her to be taken under RIC guard on a long cross-country journey to the Maryboro District Asylum for the Lunatic Poor.

I have seen the large communal room in which for nineteen years this educated Protestant woman slept on straw, with patients described in the register as nuns, cooks and servants. She died on 19 February 1896, having suffered from struma, otherwise scrofula or the King's Evil. Her body was sent to the Royal College of Surgeons instead of receiving Christian burial.

Her sister Frances Mary, youngest of the family, married a police constable called Thomas Dewart a year after his wife had died of consumption. My grandfather was a witness at her wedding, which took place while he was still working as a clerk. Frances had a daughter who died of 'enteric fever' at the age of five, and soon after this she herself died of consumption in 1882.

Families in which there was known to be a 'weakness', meaning TB or, worse still, insanity, were shunned in the marriage market. Perhaps that is why none of us had ever heard of the two pathetic sisters of my grandfather, who was regarded as a saint.

On 7 August 1978 I drove from Cleggan through Leenane and the Partry Mountains to visit Robert Shaw at Drimbawn on Lough Mask. Now he was married to Virginia Jansen, his former secretary, and had returned to Drimbawn to recuperate from the making of bad films and much money in Hollywood after the renown of *Jaws*. I had last seen him on television, bright red in the face and sounding drunk, at the Academy Awards, where he had introduced the prize-winners but won no prize himself. At Drimbawn he was sober and looked well. Avid as ever for fame, wealth and admiration, the antithesis of Tony White, he boasted that he had saved $2 million in a Swiss account, built a separate house for his guests with a squash court and an indoor swimming pool, and fathered his tenth child.

But for the last five years he had failed to finish a novel about alcoholism, old age and death. He wondered would I read it and give him advice? I said I would try. For many years, he told me, he had acted during the day to earn a living, and had written novels and plays during the night because he could not sleep. He admitted that he had drunk heavily all the time, but his constitution had been so strong that drink had never impaired his performance or his writing.

'I gave up drinking nine months ago. How long have you been off?' he asked.

'Two years,' I replied, and he looked annoyed at my surpassing him. He didn't begrudge my being three days older, since he had achieved far more in his fifty-one years.

When his wife, whom he called Jay, came to ask what we would like to drink, I said a soft drink and Robert a pint of beer. This surprised and worried me enough to query, 'Are you starting to drink again?'

'What do you mean?' he asked aggressively 'I don't count three pints of beer a day as *drink*!'

Then, with more pride than pity and more envy than truth, he told me that if Peter O'Toole were to drink so much as one small whiskey it would kill him. Ever since Peter had won the greater fame that Robert had coveted in *The Long and the Short and the Tall* at the Royal Court in 1959, Robert had been denigrating him. Peter, he said, had recently been obliged to accept second-rate parts in films that he, Robert, had refused. On a visit to Drimbawn, wanting to demonstrate how strong he still was, Peter had turned two somersaults in the drawing room and injured his back.

Three weeks later Jay rang with bad news. As she had been driving Robert towards Westport, he had suffered a heart attack and died on the side of the road.

There is a legend, perhaps invented by one of Tony's friends, that an elderly *littérateur* at a party in London was overheard saying: 'It seems that every generation has its own version of the Christ figure, and so, apparently, has ours. People who were at Cambridge in the early 1950s talk about him a good deal. They say he was a brilliant actor being groomed for stardom at the Old Vic, when he gave up acting to take a job as a gas-lamp lighter in the slums. It was the daring thing for a well-educated young man of the time to do – chuck up everything and just clear off. He died rather young, killed in a game of soccer. I believe he was called Tony White.'

In 1974, having sold Rougham Chantry in Suffolk, Mary and Gerry had given our mother a flat in London and had moved to Highfield near Hexham in Northumberland, where Gerry had always felt that he belonged. There they enjoyed the challenge of creating a garden protected by windbreaks on top of a moor; and Mary's painting was inspired by the challenge of her new environment – farms torn up by opencast coal-mining under dark stormy skies.

During the next nineteen years my mother expected me to stay with her if I came to London, and yearly she visited me in Ireland around the time of my birthday in August or hers in September. Shortly before Christmas 1976 I wrote these notes at Cranmer Court in Chelsea:

> In my mother's drawing room I hear the quick tick of an antique clock that loses no time on its way to posterity ... dust is not allowed to settle on the dark shiny surfaces of escritoire or commode ... I have to try to look my best in the cloudy glass of an eighteenth-century mirror ... mementoes adorn the shelves ... a silver boatswain's whistle presented by the captain and the crew of 'HMS Porlock Bay' on 5. 7. 47 inscribed to Sir William and Lady Murphy on the occasion of their silver wedding ... a photograph of her grandson Anthony Murphy, aged fourteen, playing Tom Brown in the BBC television serial of Tom Brown's Schooldays and winning an Emmy Award for best actor in a starring role in 1973 ... presentation copies of my books.
>
> Arriving from Ireland as my mother's guest at Cranmer Court, I feel like a piece of her old furniture from Milford ... examined for faults ... she looks at my shirt, my trousers, my shoes, not noticing my dismay ... 'Wouldn't you like to have a bath before you sit down?' ... do I smell? ... she cooks very good meals, making sure nothing we eat is likely to shorten our lives ... under her influence I have always done the same ... at breakfast she wants me to play a game of passing each other the butter and the marmalade, though for years she has known I prefer to eat breakfast walking round the room ... in the presence of her silver-framed signed photographs of Princess Alice, who stayed with her in the Bahamas, and the Queen Mother, who planted a tree in her garden in Southern Rhodesia, I feel an intruder.

When my first cousin Tom came of age, inherited Milford and married our second cousin, Liz Willoughby, of Salruck – Aunt Violet's granddaughter – he had to modernise the farm to make it pay. I seldom went there, but following a brief visit in 1977 I wrote this note.

> Fifteen years after hurricane Debbie smashed what was left of the Milford woods, the avenue of limes is a bare ruined choir ... gone

is the awe I used to feel when walking up our green cathedral nave
filled on summer evenings with the hum of bees ... the haunted
Black Wood has become a pasture for sheep ... in the Pleasure
Ground my cousin is gradually sawing up two cedars of Lebanon
... he has spared the ancient yew that was our town.

When the life that began in 1959 with our meeting on the Inishbofin quay
ended with Tony's death in 1976, I felt it was time to leave the west of Ireland.
But the difficulty of selling a house in Connemara and buying one in Dublin or
London deterred me, combined as it was with my absence on and off in America
and chronic indecision. It took the 1979 strike of telephone and postal workers,
with neither mail nor phone for three months, aggravated by a petrol shortage,
for me to sell the New Forge, having sold the Hexagon the previous year.

Anya helped me to move to a house I named Knockbrack, facing south
across the Vale of Shanganagh from a hill of grey granite, gorse and heather
in Killiney, ten miles from the centre of Dublin. If not hidden in clouds, the
Sugar Loaf would appear like Mont Sainte-Victoire on the horizon through
a gap between Scots firs and silver birches. The sea off Bray Head was visible
from rocks at the top of the garden. At night from a windy corner behind a
hedge I could see the lights of the city curving around Dublin Bay.

I had not lived in a city since I had left London, fearful of cities, in 1951;
and I missed the west so much that I started to write about it as I had never
done when I was there. Remembering Tony and his advice, I ran every
morning before breakfast to the top of Killiney Hill and back, pausing to
walk three times clockwise around the folly at the summit and look across
the city between the foothills of the Dublin Mountains and the coast from
Bray to Howth Head. During the winter it was always dark, often raining and
sometimes snowing when I ran. A tingling of nerves on my fingertips and the
crown of my head came as I reached the crest.

At Easter 1981, identifying part of myself with the building, I wrote a
sonnet in the persona of the folly and from its point of view as a vandalised
epicene Anglo-Irish relic surrounded by greenery. This led to personifying
other structures, new and old – such as 'Red Bank Restaurant', 'Gym', 'Ice
Rink', 'Baymount' and 'Wellington Testimonial' – that I could connect with
in the Dublin area; and many more structures in the west of Ireland. Each
poem began in the form of random notes examining my life at a particular
time and place, using the second-person singular. Gradually, notes that had

flowed here and there through several pages would be channelled into the form of a sonnet. I regarded the notes as rain falling on a large expanse of moor or mountain, as at Lecknavarna, and the sonnet as a rock that gives shape to a waterfall.

I had a strong motive for self-examination: since Easter 1981 Anya had been carrying my child, having chosen a date that would give her a son born under Aquarius. We had agreed not to get married, lived in separate houses, and usually met for dinner that I cooked at Knockbrack. This suited me but not Anya, and my mother aggravated my sense of guilt by refusing to speak to me for several months. She had not wanted me to marry Anya, but still less did she want a grandchild of hers to be 'illegitimate', a legal concept that Ireland would in 1987 rightly abolish.

With critical encouragement from Dennis O'Driscoll, whose first volume of poetry, *Kist*, appeared in 1982, the sonnets grew into a sequence of fifty. Dennis's perception of faults often led me to improve poems while we were talking. Although he worked for the Revenue Commissioners in Dublin Castle, reviewed for *Hibernia*, and needed time to write his own poetry, he was never too busy to help with advice. The climax, far from the end, came with eight sonnets in January 1982. 'Beehive Cell', about a child's birth on High Island in a *clochán* designed by a man for his own salvation, which required the exclusion of women, was written a few days before Anya gave birth to Richard William on 29 January. The obstetrician at the Rotunda Hospital was my Baymount hero, Alan Browne. Emily and I were present at the birth. The next day I wrote 'Natural Son', the only sonnet written directly in my own voice.

> Natural Son
> Before the spectacled professor snipped
> The cord, I heard your birth-cry flood the ward,
> And felt so wildly happy that I wept.
> The house you'd left would need to be restored.
>
> No worse pain could be borne, to bear the joy
> Of seeing you come in a slow dive from the womb,
> Pushed from your fluid home, pronounced 'a boy'.
> You'll never find so well equipped a room.
>
> No house we build could hope to satisfy
> Every small need, now that you've made this move

> To share our loneliness, much as we try
> Our vocal skill to wall you round with love.
>
> This day you crave so little, we so much
> For you to live, who need our merest touch.

What Anya called my split-level life, our semi-detached relationship, had caused her to suffer because, although I loved her, I could never become her single-minded lover. Now that she had a son her attachment to me dwindled until it died, as she departed across the border into Northern Ireland, later to settle in England.

In 1983, during a visit to the Catholic University of America in Washington, I attended a reading by James Dickey. In the nineteen years between my reading with him at Dartmouth College in 1964 and his solo reading at the Folger Museum, Dickey had become a celebrity whose performance was a frequently copied imitation of himself as a performing poet. In perfecting the ambivalent role of poet and showman, he had learnt a trick from the most famous television chat-show host in the world. As soon as he uttered a phrase or a word that was meant to be witty, he would pause, with his mouth moulded into a Johnny Carson smile, broad as the lips would stretch and full of teeth, signalling the audience to laugh and applaud. Which indeed they did.

But Dickey had not forgotten his primary model for readings that could wring our hearts. He now seemed a replica of the poet Roethke towards the end of Roethke's life – a huge old clumsy bear with a lecherous eye, drunk on liquor and fame, liable to collapse in tears or explode in anger but for the sustenance of our applause.

When he appeared on the Folger's replica of an Elizabethan stage, he was carrying a bundle of his books, showing how many he had published. He put these on a chair, laboriously building a pile angled like the Tower of Pisa. He stepped back and looked at it, his hands folded as if he were praying that the pile would not collapse, though it seemed constructed to do so. This mime evoked a legend about Roethke, who in the middle of reading to a packed house on the big stage of the Poetry Center in New York, where Dylan Thomas had triumphed, let fall a sheaf of poems from the lectern, and crawled like a child on the floor to pick them up, causing some in the audience to weep.

Dickey provoked tears of laughter.

When compiling a list of structures that held significant memories that I wanted to revive in sonnet form, I had excluded the colonies as a possible source for a further sequence. By the autumn of 1984 I had arranged the sonnets with various poems of the past ten years, including four about Tony, in a volume dedicated to Dennis and that he advised me to call *The Price of Stone*. Once Craig Raine, the new poetry editor at Faber, had accepted it, I thought of returning to Sri Lanka, almost fifty years after leaving the island when it was called Ceylon.

Since 1971 I had borne in the back of my mind a sentence of persuasive circularity written by H.A.I. Goonetileke, librarian of the University of Ceylon in Peradeniya: 'The son of your father will be welcome in our still resplendent isle.' But the uprising of a Sinhala village communist movement called the JVP – People's Liberation Front – had deterred me from travelling then. The abortive insurgency had involved the slaying of sixty-five police and military personnel followed by the summary execution of thousands of young men and women after they had emerged from forests and surrendered to the police under an amnesty. News of the horror – bodies floating down the Kelani River under Victoria Bridge on the airport road near Colombo – had brought back a terror of my childhood: dying in Ceylon.

The following year, to erase the bad name Ceylon had acquired abroad and to satisfy the Sinhala majority population imbued since 1956 with cultural chauvinism, Sirimavo Bandaranaike, the first woman in the world to become a democratically elected prime minister, had changed the country's name to Sri Lanka. Astrologers had chosen an auspicious date, 22 May 1972, for a ceremony at Kandy on the balcony of the Octagon at the Temple of the Tooth, from which, at the age of seven, I had watched the perahera of richly caparisoned elephants led and followed around the Milk Ocean Lake by musicians and fire dancers at night. For two and a half thousand years 'Lanka', signifying resplendent, had been the island's Sinhala and Sanskrit name; 'Sri', meaning illustrious or exalted, was an honorific comparable to the 'Great' in 'Great Britain'. The rich sound of 'Sri' was like a sari wrapped around the bones of 'Lanka' to awe its hungry people into worship of Mrs B. while redressing the nation's poverty with archaic verbal silk.

Then in July 1983 I read and heard reports of a three-day massacre of Tamil Hindus and Christians by Sinhala Buddhist mobs, who set fire to shops, houses and cars in Colombo and Kandy, slaying with knives and swords those who tried to escape; they stopped cars to identify Tamil speakers and poured petrol through windows followed by lighted matches. The cause? Sinhalese soldiers in the Northern Province had raped Tamil girls, and the Liberation Tigers of Tamil Eelam, a force of three hundred before the riots and fifteen thousand a month later, had ambushed and shot a number of soldiers whose bodies were brought to Colombo for burial. The riot had erupted thirty-six years after Britain granted independence to Ceylon in 1948 without a shot being fired. At that time Ceylon had the highest literacy rate in Asia and a large surplus of foreign exchange. Yet the Sinhala politicians in the post-1977 government of President J.R. Jayewardene, including a cabinet minister who had masterminded the riot to 'teach Tamils a lesson', blamed Britain for having advanced the Tamil minority in nearly one hundred and fifty years of colonial rule. More killings had occurred in those three days than in fourteen years of the Troubles in Northern Ireland.

I decided to go in November 1984, intending to examine my colonial past in the light of its legacy and to purge my fear. Before flying out of London I was staying with my mother at Cranmer Court when she insisted that I should call upon the Sri Lankan high commissioner, Chandra Monerawela, in Hyde Park Gardens, to obtain introductions to people who might be helpful. I had intended to wander around Colombo, Kandy and Bandarawela, surprising myself with spontaneous recollections evoked by bodies, buildings, sounds and smells. My mother won the argument, and to make sure I got through to the high commissioner, not just a third secretary, came with me. She demonstrated, by her handling of the officials and of me, how much my father had owed to her in his rise to the top of the colonial service.

We were having tea in the drawing room on our return to Cranmer Court when I said, spontaneously, 'You seem more interested in my journey than I am. Why don't you come, too?' She replied, 'You wouldn't want me to.' Swallowing doubts with a biscuit, I said, 'Of course I would.' As soon as we had cleared away the tea things she began to pack. My mother was eighty-six.

On the approach to Colombo airport, as our plane flew over a coral beach lined with coconut palms, my mother remarked, 'That must be Negombo – do look!' A wave of euphoria washed over me, submerging fearful expectations; and as we stepped down on the runway, breathing the hot spicy air of decay, I wanted – absurdly – to kiss the ground. Had I done so it would have burnt my lips. It was old Armistice Day. My mother was wheeled through customs and immigration by two smiling dark girls in red saris, as once she had been borne through the jungle, she told me, in a palanquin on the shoulders of four men.

As a result of our meeting with Chandra we were greeted and garlanded with jasmine by officials of the Ceylon Tourist Board, who drove us to Colombo, stopping at a straw boutique for us to drink the juice of gold king coconuts out of the shell. In spite of the horrendous noise of reckless traffic and the proliferation of bungalows and shanties for a population ten times what it had been when I was on my knees every night praying to escape from Ceylon, I was astonished to feel the estrangement of half a century from a place I had never regarded as home dissolve into love.

The Tourist Board gave us free accommodation for our first night at the Galle Face Hotel overlooking the Indian Ocean: vast rooms furnished with heavy, dark Dutch colonial furniture. Half the hotel had long been closed for repairs; the other half was almost empty because of the July '83 riots. When I mentioned to my mother at breakfast that the pool in which my father had taught me to swim at the age of six had lost its roof, ceramic tiles, teak shoot and underwater lighting, she told me to stop criticising. She was thrilled to see her picture on the front page of the *Daily News* under the headline 'Last British mayor's wife returns'.

I had been thrilled in the middle of the night, when the heat had kept me awake, to go out alone on the Galle Face Green and walk along the unlit beach in fear subverted by insurgent joy.

We moved to the post-colonial opulence of the Oberoi Hotel, where prices were reduced to a third of what they had been before the riots; and we hired an old Peugeot 504, driven by a middle-aged Sinhala Buddhist. Samson Wanaguru said a prayer with a motion of his hands over the steering wheel every time we started a journey, and he stopped to donate a coin at every shrine under a bo tree that we passed. We drove around Colombo, meeting elderly members of the Colombo Ladies' League, friends of the late Cissy Cooray MBE, joint trustee with my mother of the Ceylon Social Service League. Cissy and my mother had organised relief during the malaria epidemic of 1934. Through the joy in my mother's eyes when names of friends long dead were mentioned I could see into her past and connect her memories to mine. We were united more happily than ever since my childhood, our shared memories overcoming our unabated irritation with each other's faults and foibles.

Before we left Colombo for Kandy I had submitted furiously to her insistence on my acting as her ADC and making an appointment to meet J.R. Jayewardene, the seventy-eight-year-old president of the Democratic Socialist Republic of Sri Lanka. On our way through Colombo we passed some high walls, which Samson told us surrounded Welikade Prison. 'That's where more than fifty Tamil detainees were killed during the riots,' I said. 'I wish you'd stop mentioning unpleasant things,' my mother replied, 'you're spoiling the journey.' Samson interrupted: 'One hundred per cent terrorists.'

A year later I was given a tour of the prison by its director, who told me that one of those imprisoned under emergency regulations that allowed the security forces to detain, execute and dispose of bodies without notification of death to the relatives, had been a doctor working at a refugee camp. I saw the woodshed from which the prison guards had allowed Sinhala prisoners to take axes and saws with which they had smashed open the cell doors of the Tamil detainees and butchered them. Passing a gigantic golden statue of the meditating Buddha in the prison yard, the director told me, 'This is where they piled the mutilated bodies.'

Samson made us get out at every batik and curio shop where he had arranged to receive commission on our purchases, a hassle I loathed but my mother allowed because it annoyed me. 'Samson likes us to stop,' she'd say, 'so I think we ought to do this to please him.' He stopped when we passed an elephant carrying a tree, and my mother forced me out of the car to take a photograph, 'to please Liz, who was kind enough to lend you her camera'. Taking notes was impossible in her presence, as she would say, 'I'd like to see what you're writing. I should be writing it all down myself if I wasn't so old.'

Upcountry in beautiful Kandy, surrounded by spice gardens and forested hills, we stayed at the Hôtel Suisse, windows open to the voices of frogs, crows and monkeys, but no noise from the bare feet of room boys bringing us pawpaw and lime for breakfast. The hotel had undergone no alterations that my mother could detect since she had been entertained there as a young bride. It stood across the dull green, unsafe, but utterly sacred water of the Milk Ocean Lake, opposite the Temple of the Tooth, where a relic of the Buddha was housed. My mother's prime wish was to find the bungalow on Brownrigg Street where she had arrived in October 1922, three months after her wedding in Scotland, to join her husband, who had been appointed assistant government agent at Kandy.

Finding the house was no problem, but we had difficulty in persuading the sentries on guard at the gate of the officers' mess of the Sinha Regiment to let us enter. Once inside, Major Nihal Pelpola, adjutant of the regiment, greeted us warmly, his father having fought for Britain on the Western Front in the First World War. My mother's eyes lit up and her voice sounded full of the pleasure of being a young bride as she showed the major exactly where her furniture had been and what shrubs she had made three garden boys plant in what had become a parade ground in which the concrete paving had been split by weeds.

Five years later, in 1989, I visited Pelpola, by then a colonel, lying motionless in the intensive care unit of Colombo General Hospital, where he had been rushed from the Galle Face green after a knife had been plunged into his back while he was jogging at 6 a.m. with a brigadier. His assailant was not a Tamil Tiger but a young member of the Sinhala Buddhist nationalist JVP, revived by its leader Rohana Wijeweera seventeen years after that movement's extinction in 1971.

From Kandy we drove, though advised not to take the risk, across the island via Dambulla to Trincomalee, my first visit and my mother's first since 1925. Two of the happiest years of her life, she said, had been spent in the Residency on a prominent bluff overlooking the long coral curve of Dutchman's Bay, ending in the distance at Fort Frederick. 'We must go there at once. They won't mind, if we explain who we are and why we've come back.' Several army checkpoints had stopped us on our way, but these seemed more like illusions than reality in the vivid world of my mother's memories. 'Did you notice,' I asked, 'that we've just passed a long line of prisoners chained together, led and followed by policemen?' Before she could reply, Samson interrupted, 'Honest workers, no chains.' My mother preferred to believe Samson, and she thought the Tamil wife of the Anglican church rector was exaggerating to get our sympathy when she told us that young Tamil boys were being taken by the police and castrated.

On our way up the drive to the Residency my mother remembered that a bowser drawn by a bullock used to arrive daily with fresh water, and because the previous assistant government agent's wife had died of cholera, endemic in Trinco, she had put a teaspoonful of permanganate of potash into the water, turning it pink, before having it boiled. Then it went through a filter and finally, before a drop was drunk, she added Milton as a purifier. 'It tasted horrible,' she said, 'but we survived.' When we parked near the house, quite new, though presently unoccupied, she showed me a bo tree that had rooted from its branches in wider and wider circles. The bo tree, *Ficus religiosa*, is revered in Sri Lanka as the tree under which the Buddha achieved enlightenment. Under the specimen in Trinco my father had shot a leopard. 'I had gone upcountry with my mother to have my first baby, that was Mary, in a creeper's bungalow on a tea estate, to avoid infection, and Daddy had bought a cow with a calf to provide us with milk on my return. But a leopard killed the calf one night, and the next night, with the dead calf acting as bait under the bo tree, Daddy shot the leopard. My mother took the skin home to have it cured and to cover a workbox, which I still use.'

My mother was suffering acute pain from arthritis of the hip as she stood on the site of the old Residency, pointing with her stick to where screens had been placed to divide a house that had no internal walls into rooms. 'Down that steep cliff there's a winding path which the Ayah took with Mary every morning to the beach. And over the other side there's another smaller bay, even more beautiful, but very dangerous for swimming. Someone was drowned there. We had wonderful parties here with my friends, Admiral Richmond's daughters and the officers of the *Hood*. I was terribly sad when she was sunk by the *Bismarck* during the war.'

The Seven Islands Hotel where we stayed had once been the naval officers' mess. Here at night, during a monsoon downpour and a power cut, I heard, as often in my childhood, the orchestral sounds that heavy rain can make: dropping on palm and banana leaves, on tiles and tin roofs, in eaves and gutter shoots, in china bowls and metal buckets, and on the slippery smooth-polished concrete floor of my room. This music spread through my restless body a feeling akin to *ānanda,* one of the four cardinal virtues of Buddhism, variously interpreted as 'bliss' and 'universal love'. In Sanskrit *ānanda* may also mean 'sensual desire'.

We returned from Trincomalee to Colombo on 21 November to spend two nights and a day confined to the Oberoi, much of the time with no electricity, during a curfew. The staff entertained us well, working around the clock, never losing patience or their charming smiles. Before our meeting with the president at 8.30 a.m., when the curfew was lifted on the eve of my mother's departure, she got so excited that she wanted to arrive half an hour early. 'We'll be late,' she kept saying.

The president was living in his wife's old colonial bungalow on Ward Place, a few gardens away from where we had lived. Inside we were ushered from the hall into a small dark room by an elderly man, his long-serving secretary, who greeted the president every morning by kneeling down and kissing his feet, and was known to have described him as a 'God among men'.

After a few minutes the president entered, wearing 'national costume', a white cotton robe that reached to his sandalled feet. He looked as if he had not slept during the curfew, with dark-yellow pouches under foxy eyes. My mother rose and curtsied, as if he had been a king. When seated she told him, 'We were barbarians when you had a great civilisation at Anuradhapura.' Jayewardene replied, 'Yes, but a long time ago you overtook us.'

Emily flew out on the plane on which my mother flew home, and we went in Samson's car, paid for by my mother, on a tour of the south coast. At a village in the jungle near Galle one night we attended a ritual performance by devil dancers trying to heal a very sick man, a dancer's fire and sword revolving close to the faces of the villagers whose company was part of the healing process. At midnight the invalid had to rise from the ground where he lay groaning, place a live cock in a basket on his head, and lead a procession through an unlit rubber plantation to the grave of his grandparents. There – but by then we had gone home – his cure would have occurred, or might not, as he bit the neck and drank the blood of the dying cock.

On we drove to Hambantota, where my father, in the years following his brother Kipher's death in battle, had relieved his loneliness as assistant government agent by reading the official diaries of Leonard Woolf. At the Yala Safari Beach Hotel we sat on a rock at sunset by a lagoon in which there were boulders that looked like elephants and elephants that looked like boulders moving across the water. But Emily was terrified in the middle of the night when a security guard kept tapping on her beach door, saying 'Whist! Madam!' hoping she would let him in. After returning through Bandarawela and Kandy in the central highlands, Emily was keen to get back to London, where the following July she married Jonathan Lee, a film editor with whom she was working in Soho. They would continue to live in England, working as television producers, until they emigrated to the new South Africa with their two children, Theodora and Caspar, in 1996.

Alone in Colombo in December 1984 I moved to a cheap guest house near Slave Island and started exploring Colombo on foot. Again and again I was approached by impoverished young men and boys, who addressed me with a rapid sequence of elided questions: 'Which country you from? Where you going? Are you rich? When are you leaving Sri Lanka?' and finally, after telling me they had 'No mama, no papa', asking the impossible, 'Will you take me to your country?' No, I replied, but it made me think that perhaps I might if I were to meet and become guardian to a fatherless youth who was never on the street approaching foreigners with questions redolent of misery, but who was leaving high school with a talent no one would recognise if he were to remain in Sri Lanka, handicapped by being an outcast in a still caste-conscious isle.

One stiflingly hot afternoon I was walking past a hedge beside a municipal playground when a man sprang out and said, as I passed him, looking away to avoid being hassled, 'I'm not going to ask you for money. May I help you?' So courteous and well spoken he sounded that I turned and talked to him. Stephen Anthony was a Tamil in his thirties, reduced by the July '83 riots, during which his workshop with all his tools had been destroyed by fire and looting, to selling illicit arrack from a plastic container hidden in a gully under the hedge, and to drinking himself into a stupor. His employer was a Sinhalese thug who had promised him protection. He worked a day shift with an employee of the municipal council, who gave his supervisor one third of his monthly salary to allow him to do no work other than moonlighting under the municipal hedge. I imagined what my father would have thought of this.

Stephen became my guide for a day through the shanties, showing me what the government had not done to help the people while enriching the middle classes and giving United National Party supporters free sites in good areas. Some of these sites had belonged to Tamil lawyers, doctors, accountants and businessmen who had fled abroad after the burning and looting of their houses. Then he brought me in a trishaw to a Methodist orphanage where he had been raised.

The buildings were a hundred years old and falling down. The boys, victims of caste, violence, poverty and civil war, looked sad and hungry. The warden, Victor Atapattu, was a retired teacher and preacher who immediately appealed to me to adopt 'an honest deserving intelligent boy' of seventeen, liked by everybody, called Nimal Jayasinghe. The boy had to leave the orphanage after Christmas as he had finished school and had nowhere to go. His poor mother was living in a shanty with a man who had once hit Nimal on the head with a hatchet. I could save him from joining the army and perhaps getting killed in Jaffna, as was to happen to one of his friends. After introducing me to Nimal, who came smiling and in bare feet carrying a cup of tea to the verandah, the warden said, '"Nimal" means "nothing bad" and there's nothing I could tell you about Nimal that is bad.'

Having lost touch with my natural son since his mother had taken him to live in rural England, I gained the legal guardianship of Nimal, the natural son of a Sinhala Buddhist mother. She gave her consent at the Mount Lavinia District Court on Friday 18 January 1985. A Tamil lawyer, Mervyn CanagaRetna, recommended for his integrity by the British High Commission, gave his services free. Nine days later, with British and American visas stamped on Nimal's new passport, we flew to London. My mother was shocked when she saw his dark handsome face at her door in Cranmer Court. 'What will the other tenants think and say?' she worried. 'They don't like people bringing Asians or Blacks into England.' But she was courteous to him and bought him a present, after telling me she had been keen on helping the beggars in Ceylon. I had to swallow her advice to 'give him plenty to do and keep him in his place'. She showed me what she meant by asking him to polish her silver.

A day or two later we flew to Tacoma, Washington, where Nimal was given free tuition at the Intensive English Language Institute and I took up a post as visiting poet at the Pacific Lutheran University, which housed us in a pinewood on the shore of Dumas Bay in Puget Sound. We had to stoke a boiler with logs to keep warm, but Nimal enjoyed the novelty of feeling cold. His instructors told me he was learning better than rich students from Kuwait, Saudi Arabia, Mexico and Japan.

When we arrived in Ireland in May, Nimal became an Irish citizen and embarked on courses of study that would eventually lead, via catering, landscape gardening and photography, to operating his own fabric business, making curtains and loose covers for big houses in south Dublin and County Kildare, well enough off to buy his mother a house in Sri Lanka. But meanwhile he was young and we both could benefit from his acting as my guide and interpreter when we returned to Sri Lanka for three to five months in each of the next two years. As a guide he was good at fending off importuners, who were skilful at making someone of my colonial background feel guilty for their plight. As interpreter, Nimal could improve his knowledge of English and of the world.

Four miles from Kandy and two from Peradeniya we rented a house in the village of Dangolla on a hillside of lush growth – mango, pawpaw, coconut, areca and kithul palm – with flowering shrubs enlivened by black-headed golden orioles and Indian paradise flycatchers, which the Sinhalese, inspired by the long white tails of the cock in its undulating flight, call 'handkerchief thieves'. Opposite my bedroom was a small temple – young *bikkhus* in orange or saffron robes poured buckets of water over their heads every morning. The only drawbacks were the chanting of Buddhist prayers in Pali, amplified from the temple roof, all night on the nights of full moon; and the frantic barking of a dog in the yard of a professor of botany's house during the day.

I could not afford a car, but Nimal relieved me of the sweat of shopping in Kandy market, and in the evening he cooked our rice and curry. He soon made friends with a neighbour called Arosha Dharmasena, who used to play cricket with three or four other boys on the dusty laterite temple road, and Arosha soon started helping Nimal to shop and meet his friends in Kandy.

Arosha's name, meaning 'free from anger', suited him well, as he never appeared to get cross. He had an enquiring practical mind and took delight in tackling tasks that he knew nothing about, such as repairing a watch or a Walkman, in order to learn. Youngest of three sons of a beauty queen of Kandy and a journalist who had died young, Arosha was a Buddhist attending the local secondary school. He lived with his stepfather's extended family of fifteen in one large tin-roofed room divided by a curtain. His mother and stepfather were working in the Middle East to pay for the building of a house. The family had lost their previous house and all their possessions, including a brass workshop, in a great flood of the Mahaweli River.

Nimal began receiving letters from girls in Sinhala, containing lines of spontaneous poetry, the overflow of powerful feelings, metre and rhyme coming naturally to minds formed by the Sinhala language. One of its features is a wealth of ambiguity – two, three or four words of similar sound but different meaning in Sanskrit expressed by one in Sinhala – allowing politicians to promise everything under the sun but under the moon to deliver nothing. The Sinhala script at a glance seems all curves and curlicues, poles apart from the straight-lined script of Tamil.

The horror stories I read and heard never made me fear for my own safety in Sri Lanka, where no one robbed, mugged or threatened me or told me to go back to Britain where I belonged. At that time I felt safer in Kandy or Colombo than in Dublin, protected by my guide and Sri Lankans' genuine courtesy to foreigners. King coconut juice, buffalo curd and all the fruits, vegetables and spices of the Kandyan hills, cooler than Colombo or Jaffna at night, kept me in good health. After running two or three miles up and downhill before breakfast, I used to stay indoors to avoid the sun, reading the history and literature of Ceylon and translations of the chronicles and poetry of ancient Lanka. At times I felt as if long ago I had been banished from a paradise such as this and now my banishment had been revoked.

By good fortune, on my first visit to Sri Lanka I had met Ashley Halpé, poet, painter and professor of English at the University of Sri Lanka (formerly Ceylon) at Peradeniya. I have never seen a more beautiful modern campus, set near the Botanical Gardens in the evergreen valley of the Mahaweli River. Ashley had interviewed me on television in Colombo at a Dutch colonial bungalow that resembled Tilton and had found me the house in Dangolla, lent me books and told me what others to buy. My mentor in matters concerning the literature, history, customs, politics and problems of Sri Lanka,

Ashley, with his wife Bridget, a talented pianist, made me always welcome to join them and their two daughters for a family meal.

From him I learnt that in Sinhala the idiomatic word for the English language is *kaduwa*, meaning 'sword', a weapon used to cut down defenceless people or to carve out a fortune; a commanding, oppressive, fearsome tongue. The four hundred upper-class Sinhala families had continued after independence to speak English to each other and Sinhalese to their servants, and to take turns in ruling the country as 'democratic socialists'. My mother recalled that long before the war, when S.W.R.D. Bandaranaike, scion of a rich and ancient dynasty, returned to Colombo from Oxford, where he had been president of the Oxford Union, he had apologised to the Sinhala people who welcomed him on the jetty for not being able to address them in their native language. In 1956 he gained power on an electoral slogan to abolish English as the unifying language of the ethnically divided island: 'Sinhala only in twenty-four hours.' Within a year the first anti-Tamil riots in the country's history had broken out.

Ashley's translations of thirty ancient Sinhala poems, scratched with a stylus on the highly polished plaster of the Mirror Wall at Sigiriya, gave me my first insight into Sinhala poetry and the idea of trying my hand at less accurate versions. In February 1986, when Mary and Gerry flew out with my mother, they took Nimal and me in air-conditioned comfort to the 'cultural triangle', staying overnight at Anuradhapura, Polonaruwa and Sigiriya. Mary filled several sketchbooks with drawings, the source of many watercolours that she painted at home.

For me the climax of our tour was the vision of Sigiriya, a great natural rock rising almost two hundred metres out of the jungle, paddy fields and tanks in the centre of the island: dark-reddish brown, glistening in the radiant heat, a gigantic national lingam more than a monument, site of the greatest water garden of Asia in the fifth century, fortress of a usurper called Kassapa, who ruled there from a palace on the summit for eighteen years. Built into the rock with bricks more than halfway up was the head of a roaring lion, symbol of the Sinhala race, out of whose mouth water had poured at festivals. My mother had climbed the long flights of marble steps up the vertical side of the rock with my father soon after their marriage. 'Don't miss the frescoes above the Mirror Wall, but mind the hornets.'

Kassapa may have chosen the rock to liken himself to the three-legged Hindu god of wealth, reigning on Mount Meru in the Himalayas, surrounded by hundreds of cloud nymphs. The diverse lyrics, written by pilgrims on the parapet wall that protected them on a path of ninety metres between precipitous flights of steps, address the women in the frescoes as cloud nymphs, wives or concubines of the king, dancers or prostitutes. Lifelike in spite of being stylised in their beauty, these women's faces radiate *ānanda* and *maitri*, the cardinal virtue of 'loving kindness'. The mystery of their origin, purpose and significance has intrigued visitors from the eighth century to the present. Bearing flowers in their hands as if on their way to a nearby temple, eighteen of them have survived in a dark inaccessible grotto, where the undulations of the rock on which they are painted resemble the motions of a water snake that I saw in a pond at our hotel. The king's engineers had cut drip channels in the overhanging rock to save the frescoes from destruction by water.

The brief syllabic wall poems, written by at least fifteen hundred visitors in Old Sinhala between the eighth and tenth centuries, add to their mystery by trying to solve it. Some are inscribed by monks to condemn the women as prostitutes or unfaithful wives. Others revere them as goddesses or dwell with hyperbole on their waistlines, too slender to bear the opulent burdens of their breasts. A few signed by women are almost feminist, attacking foolish men for offering poems to women who would prefer to be given rum and molasses.

One theory is that the 'golden women with dark blue eyes like water lilies' were positioned on the rock to inspire the gods of the clouds to discharge their semen on the earth as rain. The culture depended upon rice and reservoirs in a region of low rainfall. Truly the frescoes inspired a growth of songs from people who were not poets, yet whose impromptu poetry has lasted for more than a thousand years. Starting on my return with Nimal to Dangolla in November 1986, I became absorbed by the graffiti.

Every day, shirtless and wearing a batik sarong, sitting cross-legged on a cushion on a concrete floor in a room with no furniture, three heavy tomes and a notebook on a low table in front of me, I began inventing graffiti poems sparked by variant meanings in the wonderful transcripts and literal translations, with a glossary by the palaeographer and archaeologist Senarat Paranavitana. The glossary, backed up by the Sanskrit dictionary of Monier-Williams, gave me shocks and surprises. In Old Sinhala the word for a girl was derived from the word for a creeper; and the word for a wife had the root meaning 'property of her lord'; but a single word could express both heart and mind, as if the mind would always have a heart.

On 11 January 1987 I set out with Nimal and Arosha to Sigiriya, which we climbed in a deluge. From the shelter of the grotto of the frescoes I saw through a curtain of rain, lowered from a drip channel, the whole country, purged of demons and terrorists, transformed into a mural of paradise.

When I returned to Ireland with Nimal in April, my work on the Mirror Wall poems slowed down, but quickened when I came back to Sri Lanka in October 1987, alone because Nimal had begun to train as a chef. This time I obtained a flat on a hill above the lake in Kandy, where Arosha and a friend of his from Dangolla called Anura Wickremasinghe, both aged seventeen, guided, interpreted, shopped and cooked for me – rice and curry – when Arosha was not at school studying for his O-level exams.

Nimal had told me, 'Anura is a Buddhist boy you can absolutely trust: his name means "causing happiness".' Anura's father had died when he was an infant, and his mother with her extended family had been evicted from the shanty they had occupied for fifteen years on university land. Their possessions were thrown on the street the day the shanty was bulldozed – a ghoulish reminder of Ireland in the nineteenth century. Tension was rising in the country, with the Indian army, after Jayewardene's accord with Rajiv Gandhi, occupying the northern and eastern provinces, its soldiers raping Tamil girls and being shot in revenge by Tamil Tigers. The JVP had been secretly gathering thousands of recruits on a wave of anti-Indian, anti-government anger, bombing government buildings, and shooting public officials and supporters of Jayewardene's United National Party or anyone who disobeyed what they politely called 'requests' to close their shops or go on strike.

Fortunately April Brunner, my former star pupil at Holland Park in 1953, had arrived as the wife of Britain's recently appointed high commissioner, David Gladstone. From then on, for the next two or three years, the Gladstones entertained me as a guest at Westminster House, where, on visits to Colombo, I met many of their friends, notably Arthur C. Clarke. Arthur, aged seventy, seemed to have the exuberant mind and heart of a fifteen-year-old genius the night he took April, David and me onto his roof to view Jupiter's four Galilean moons through his powerful telescope. 'Sit down there,' he said to me when my turn came, 'it will blow your mind!' And on 24 March 1988, at a gala reception for two hundred guests, including my mother, who was staying at Westminster House, the Gladstones hosted a reading of my Mirror Wall poems. An overture, interlude and finale, arranged by Lalanath de Silva, was played on traditional instruments by seven Sri Lankan musicians.

That was my mother's last visit, as she was now eighty-eight. Asked in a television interview how she had felt as the wife of the Mayor of Colombo in the 1930s, she replied without hesitation: 'Wonderful but sad. Married to someone in the colonial service in those days you were always saying goodbye, either to your husband or to your children.'

Nimal and I had remained in touch with the orphanage, which badly needed help, particularly with the health and education of brighter boys, who might, if given a chance, have benefited from a university education. The local school had such poor standards, or treated the orphanage boys so dismissively, that hardly any of them had passed O levels. The principal was a Buddhist monk who moonlighted as a gem dealer on school premises, investing his profits in trishaws. By 1988 I had decided to help two other boys who were recommended for their intelligence and honesty by Victor Atapattu and his wife Girlie, who was also a teacher.

Darrell Varney's race, according to his birth certificate, was 'Burgher', meaning of mixed Dutch or Eurasian descent. Most of the Burghers had left Ceylon and gone to Australia after independence; the remnant was a depressed and tiny minority. Darrell, whose mother was a Weldon of Irish origin, had a more fair than dark complexion. I had met him when he was doing homework while babysitting in the warden's house, where I happened to arrive when Victor and Girlie were out. He impressed me by standing up and speaking his native Ceylon English with perfect manners. His mother, an Anglican, had placed him in the Methodist orphanage when he was seven, having divorced his father when Darrell was a year old. To support two younger twins, Diana and Judith, after their father's sudden death, she had put them in another orphanage and gone to work in Saudi Arabia, hoping to earn enough money to buy a small house. But she had almost died of ill-treatment, working as a housemaid for employers less well educated than herself. Darrell wanted to be an airline pilot.

His best friend, whom he introduced to me, was a Tamil boy called Sathiya Ramakrishnan. The name Sathiya means 'truth', and the warden had found him so truthful that he had appointed him storekeeper. By birth Sathiya was a stateless Indian Tamil of Hindu religion, the son of stateless Indian Tamils whose parents had left India as untouchables to seek a better life in Ceylon, but there they had been classed as coolies. Within a year of independence, under a racist Act of Parliament, half a million Tamils of Indian origin over the previous century were deprived of citizenship and rendered stateless.

Sathiya had entered the orphanage at the age of seven when his mother, having earlier divorced his father, remarried. The boy had nearly died of rheumatic fever, and knew little or no Sinhala, the language of the orphanage and the school. During the riots of July '83 his mother and family had gone into hiding. Sathiya was as reticent as Darrell was outgoing, as dark as he was fair, as capable of working patiently at boring subjects as Darrell was of streaking ahead in those that caught his interest. I urged Sathiya not to neglect his mother tongue but to speak it whenever possible. One reason for the high performance of Tamils in Sri Lanka has been the necessity for them to speak and read three languages from an early age.

With their mothers' approval and the warden's, I arranged in March 1988 for them to be taught at Wesley College instead of the local school, while still residing at the orphanage. In April I brought Arosha to Ireland – where he had Nimal as a friend – for a course in electronics, and he returned with me to Sri Lanka in November. Soon after arriving at the walled sanctuary of Westminster House, I noted: 'Last week the government advised tourists to leave the country, as the JVP had "asked" hotel workers and public employees, especially train and bus drivers and conductors, not to report for duty. Several of those who continued to work had been shot.' David told me his office was inundated with pleas for British visas from people, including cabinet ministers, who feared the JVP had infiltrated the army and might soon take over the country in a bloody revolution, as in Cambodia.

The schools had been closed by orders of both the government and the JVP. Only in Jaffna did they remain open, the Jaffna Tamils having always grasped education as the best way to overcome the hardship of their dry sandy soil, where nothing would grow without irrigation. 'My country before my education' was a Sinhala nationalist JVP slogan at the time. In these anarchic circumstances, with their parents' consent, the warden applied for me to be appointed guardian of Darrell and Sathiya by the Mount Lavinia District Court. The court had just been reopened after a closure of three months, when, with the boys and their mothers, we attended for a hearing on Friday 2 December 1988, and obtained guardianship certificates the following week, shortly before the court was destroyed by a bomb. Then I discovered that Sathiya, being born stateless, was not entitled to a passport; instead, he was issued with an identity document allowing him to leave the country and not come back.

I took the boys to Kandy and rented an apartment at the Institute of Fundamental Studies (IFS), situated in what had been a three-star modern hotel high up on a hill at Hantana overlooking the entire city. Every night we heard gunfire, and sometimes during the day. As the schools were closed I easily found two teachers, one to teach the boys English from eight to eleven in the morning, and another to teach them mathematics from three to six. In between we walked on our way to their swimming lessons at the Hôtel Suisse in burning heat down a long steep hill, passing the hospital, the mortuary – frequented by people whose relatives were missing – and the prison, where once the superintendent allowed me to talk for half an hour to Tamil detainees. The prison guards had always treated them well, the detainees told me, but the police had been brutal. One described being hung upside down by his ankles, beaten on the soles of his feet and having his nails torn out with pliers. An old man, formerly the manager of a bank, said he was being detained because they could not find his son.

The presidential election on 19 December that secured a victory for Ranasinghe Premadasa over Sirimavo Bandaranaike was conducted with massive fraud in areas no foreign observers could reach, where voters were intimidated by a JVP 'request' not to go to the polls, by numerous killings in the previous days, and an awesome show of army and police.

On that day, which I spent indoors, Arosha, who had already made friends with Darrell and Sathiya, came from Dangolla with Anura and Anura's friend Lal to meet us at the IFS and to give me some JVP leaflets, printed in red ink, that I had asked him to obtain. I had not realised, then, that if he had been caught with these he would have 'disappeared'. Anura told us he had gone to the polls and put an *X* against all three candidates, thus spoiling his vote, being disgusted by politicians and their false promises. The boys brought me the news that an uncle of our hairdresser, Wasantha, whose name meant 'spring', had been hacked to death in Dangolla by the JVP, near the Ladyhill Hotel, now closed, where my mother and Mary and Gerry had stayed on their last visit to Kandy. On 21 December I made this note:

> The family of Wasantha's uncle were told in a letter from the JVP how the funeral was to be conducted. There must be no hearse. The coffin must be carried, not on the shoulders of four men, but only by two men carrying it in their hands, one man at each end of the coffin. Only ten people were to go to the funeral. No lights, no radios, no televisions were to be switched on in Dangolla from six that evening until six the next morning. The grave had to be shallow, level with the ground, and no earth piled upon it. As it happened, the army came and forced the people to switch on their lights.

This made me so concerned for Arosha's safety – Arosha had attended three funerals of victims – that I rang up a friend in Dublin, Patricia Morrison, founder of a ceramic tile business called Mosaic Assemblers, and asked her to sponsor his immediate return to Ireland, which she kindly did. Luckily his visa for education in Ireland had not yet expired, and he reached Dublin in time for Christmas. Later he applied for asylum, worked on a dairy farm in return for his keep, studied electronics and waited six years to become an Irish citizen – without ever getting angry. Equanimity is one of the four virtues of Buddhism.

There was no such chance of protecting Anura. I had paid a year's rent for him and his family to be housed, but by now he had built a new shanty on what he thought was state-owned land. His intrusion was unwelcome, except to Lal and a few other poor friends in the village of Elagola, a mile from Dangolla, on another heavily wooded hill, where bungalows and shanties were not mixing well. I was unaware that his life might be in danger, as he had always seemed a quiet, harmless and sincere Buddhist. I gave him enough money to open a small boutique built of straw at the side of the road.

On Sunday 22 January 1989 the boys were swimming and I was watching when people started running from the Hôtel Suisse down to the shore, some climbing a tree to get a better view. I wrote next day about the incident:

> People are so inured to reports and rumours of killings that when the dead body of an old man floated up to the surface of the mud-water near the shore of the Kandy lake, in front of the Hôtel Suisse, at about 3.30 p.m. yesterday afternoon, the telephone operator at the front desk had difficulty in trying to persuade the Kandy police to take note of the fact. She was told to try another number, a number that was engaged. When she eventually got through, she was given a different number to ring. The man who answered her wanted to know *her* number and reason for calling. She was afraid that if she said the wrong thing, or said too much, the police might come and take her in for questioning and keep her in the station for hours or even days.

The police paid no attention until I spoke on the phone to the deputy inspector general, who was lunching at home.

> It took another half-hour for the police to arrive. Seven men in uniform got out of a dark green van and a big car with a rolled-up flag on the bonnet. Three of these were carrying automatic handguns, which they pointed carelessly at their own or each other's legs or stomachs, depending on how they turned their bodies or twiddled the guns. One, I noticed, had his index finger on the

trigger all the time. I assumed that the safety catch was on. None of the three kept watch on the road, in case a vanload of subversives were to appear from around the corners on either side of the little promontory. They were all keeping their eyes on the floating corpse. Why bring such weaponry on a mission to remove a dead body from a temple lake in a sacred area, a lake in which it is prohibited to catch fish? Because the police are afraid of being shot at by subversives wherever they happen to go.

The body was removed from the lake, not by the seven policemen, but by a couple of low-caste labourers. The most pathetic aspect of the corpse was the rigid position of the forearms, stretching out in a pleading gesture, with the fine-boned fingers curling inwards as if at the moment of death he was trying, with his elbows bound tightly to his waist, to reach out and embrace someone he loved, who might have saved his life.

> I had read that in 1805 the last King of Kandy, summoning hundreds of peasants to supply their labour freely, had created the Milk Ocean Lake by digging away the whole valley which had previously grown rice. When more than a hundred men went on strike to protest what they regarded as a waste of good land, the king ordered them to be impaled alive on the bed of the lake. He watched them die from the balcony of the Octagon of the Temple of the Tooth, where, on 2 January three weeks ago, I saw from far off Ranasinghe Premadasa take the oath of office as President. Warned by astrologers of a danger in his horoscope, he made his wife, whose horoscope was better, stand beside him and touch the document as he was signing.
>
> From the same balcony with my family in August 1933, I watched a hundred or more richly caparisoned elephants, the richest bearing the sacred Tooth of the Buddha inside a gold casket in a gem-encrusted howdah, led and followed by Kandyan drummers and fire dancers and men on stilts dressed in paddy straw, go by in the ancient Buddhist festival of the sacred Tooth, known as the Perahera.

In April 1989, having obtained visas, I took Darrell and Sathiya to Ireland, where they were granted Irish citizenship and accepted at St Andrew's College, Dublin, from which in due course they passed into universities. Sathiya eventually obtained a first-class honours degree in hotel and catering management. Darrell moved more swiftly into electronics, following Arosha at Intel, until he was invited to join a growing private electronics company.

My *New Selected Poems,* published by Faber, was launched in May 1989 at the Groucho Club, not by Faber but by David Donoghue, acting for the Irish embassy; and two days later my mother, having sent out over one hundred invitations herself, gave a party at the Ceylon Tea Centre to launch *The Mirror Wall.* Along with six pages of colour photographs of the cloud nymphs by the Sri Lankan photographer Nihal Fernando, half of the poems I had written had been chosen and edited by Dillon Johnston at Wake Forest University Press. The book was designed by Neil Astley and published by Bloodaxe in Britain, the Wolfhound Press in Ireland and Wake Forest in America. Rejected by Faber, it won a Poetry Book Society Translation Award.

After being writer in residence, part-time, in my native County Mayo, I returned to Colombo on 29 November, and stayed in a flat adjoining the house and photographic studio of Nihal Fernando and his wife Dodo, whose grandmother, Lady Peiris, had befriended me as a child in Ceylon. While I was away the JVP crisis had come to a head, the movement having overreached itself. All the hospitals had been closed by a JVP 'request' for a strike by doctors and nurses. Fifty cancer patients had died without medical or nursing assistance. The army, Dodo informed me, had gone into the hospital merely to remove the dead. Dodo had taken rice packets every day and handed them to a very old nun, the only person allowed by the JVP to help the sick and dying, whose families had not been able to bring them home. When the hospitals reopened a child's body was found stuck to a bed.

Having got what he wanted from the hospital strike – terror – Rohana Wijeweera had sent out from his hiding place a 'request' to all servicemen to desert. The punishment for those who failed to desert was rumoured to be the killing of their families. There were a few desertions and three or four families were slaughtered. Protected by emergency regulations, the army and police began to annihilate the JVP, abducting anyone suspected of having contact with the movement and executing without trial those who were reckoned to have been involved, even if involvement had merely meant possession of a JVP leaflet. On a single day, Sathiya's uncle told me, he had counted three hundred bodies floating down the Kelani River through Colombo. People who could afford to buy it had stopped eating fish.

Fearing for Anura, I went to Kandy, and with difficulty persuaded the driver who had driven me to Sigiriya with Nimal and Arosha in 1987 to drive me in his Delica van to Elagola. He was terrified of being identified and reported to the police, if not caught by one of the death squads that were roaming the country under various pseudonyms, abducting and slaying 'suspects'. I walked on a rough path between trees and small houses that seemed deserted to Anura's two-room shanty, where he told me he was all right, though every young male in the village had either gone into hiding, like his friend Lal, or been taken for questioning. I gave him some money and he walked with me back to the van. That was on 6 December.

From Rohan Guneratna at the IFS, who was writing a book about the JVP, I heard more about what had happened and was happening. He reckoned that fifty or sixty thousand JVP 'suspects', mostly young men, had been taken by special units of the army and the police, and slain. Nearly every morning, Rohan said, he passed bodies that had been burnt on tyres at the side of the road leading down from Heerassigala, a village next to Elagola. By lunchtime most corpses were cleared away, never to be seen again. The JVP leader, Wijeweera, had been tracked to a planter's house near Kandy, where he was living in bourgeois comfort. No documents were found, as the records of this organisational genius, who had masterminded the slaying of thousands, were kept only in his memory. His request for peace talks with Premadasa was refused. Instead, intelligence officers questioned him before video recorders for seventy-two hours, of which only a few edited minutes were broadcast to the world. Then he was taken to the crematorium near the golf course in Colombo, where shootings were heard every night, and thrown into the oven, alive. The village people who had supported the JVP were now supporting the army.

Back at the Fernandos's flat on Skelton Road in Colombo, Gamini Perera, formerly Nimal's best friend at the orphanage and a foster brother to Darrell and Sathiya, came to tell me what was being reported on the streets. He was working as an office messenger, known in Sri Lanka as a *peon*, for the managing director of a Mercedes dealership, and was hoping that I might take him to join the others, whom he greatly missed, in Ireland. His ability to work long hours at a boring job, in oppressive heat, in order to overcome worse hardship and help his mother impressed me, and I was moved by the gravity of her misfortune.

He told me she was called Samaleen, a Sinhala Buddhist who had lost both her parents when she was six. She remembered her brother taking her from their jungle village to Colombo, where he had told her he was leaving her to play with some children of her age. The children never played with her after her brother had gone. She was kept as a kitchen maid, unpaid for the work she did, slapped by her mistress if she was idle or broke anything, and made to sleep on a coconut mat on the kitchen floor, where cockroaches fed off traces of rice on her lips, causing sores. Her Sinhalese master held a post at a major university, but she was not allowed to go to school. In an age-old Sri Lankan tradition, she had been 'adopted as a servant'.

At thirteen she ran away and got a sequence of poorly paid domestic jobs, still without schooling. When she became pregnant in her teens the villager responsible took her for a walk in the forest, and she realised, because he drew a knife, that he meant to kill her, so she fled. Gamini was born in Kandy General Hospital and given his name by a nurse, who offered his mother, knowing how poor she was, a sewing machine in exchange for her baby. She refused, though to rear him she had to pay a poor family in Peradeniya to look after him while she took a job as a resident kitchen maid. The child had to work for those who were paid to look after him.

A few years later Samaleen suffered a spinal injury in a motor accident when she was travelling in the back of her employer's van. She was left with a severe and painful stoop, lost her job, and received no compensation. Gamini got only a year's schooling when he stayed with a relation of his mother in a village called Pilligala, ten miles from Kandy, before he was placed at the age of ten in the Methodist orphanage by his mother's employer. The warden had appointed Nimal to protect him, though Gamini was a year older than Nimal. That's how I came to meet Gamini.

In Colombo a Toyota dealer told me everyone – meaning every middle-class family that supported the government of Premadasa – could now relax and enjoy Christmas. Firecrackers that sounded like gunshots had replaced after dark the gunshots that had sounded like firecrackers. On the other hand, a journalist called Nihal Ratnayake, who wrote for the liberal *Lanka Guardian*, told me ironically there was no censorship in Sri Lanka because self-censorship operated more effectively. If a journalist stepped over the line he put his own life in jeopardy. 'What does stepping over the line mean?' I asked. He answered, 'Telling the truth!'

The Gladstones entertained me on Christmas Day at Westminster House, and among their guests was Asoka Ratwatte. A cousin of Sirimavo Bandaranaike, Asoka belonged to a powerful family of Kandyan chieftains, wore his black hair in a bun on top of his head, nineteenth-century Sinhala style, and lived in a *walawa* – the equivalent of an Irish demesne house – near Peradeniya. He was convinced that the army was killing innocent people who had no connection with the movement. Swathed in a long white robe at a candlelit dinner party in the garden, he told us: 'Now they are decorating trees in my village with chopped-off hands and feet, taking the hands of one young man and tying them on a tree with the feet of another. I can't stand that! It's got to stop. There are some things we can't put up with.' And he added, 'I love absurdity.'

My notes remind me of what happened the day after Christmas. An aunt of Arosha arrived from Kandy and told me that soldiers dressed in civilian trousers with dark blue T-shirts had come to her sister's house where she was staying in Heerassigala. They had stood in front of the house, propping up a tall man who seemed inclined to fall and stumble because they had been kicking his legs with their army boots. He was wearing trousers but no shirt. When she saw him first, his head and shoulders were covered with a gunnybag, an old type of sack made of jute, still used in the villages as it was cheap. When a soldier removed the gunnybag she immediately recognised Anura. He was blindfolded with the sleeve torn off a shirt. A soldier removed the blindfold. His face was bloated and bruised, his eyes closed by the swollen flesh around them. The soldiers kept asking, 'Do you know this man?' and 'Is this Anura?' She and her sister kept replying, 'I don't know.' And they kept telling Anura to open his eyes so that she could recognise him, and he kept replying in Sinhala, painfully and defectively because his teeth had been smashed, 'I can't, I can't.' She told me his chest and his back were covered with bruises and wounds, one big gash on a shoulder blade, bleeding. The soldiers accused him of being one of the JVP men who had burnt the Mulgampola post office and the Heerassigala bus. He was taken like this, she said, from house to house in Heerassigala and everyone, including two small children she saw and heard, was asked if this was Anura. Then they drove off with him in their vehicles. He has never been seen alive since that day. His mother collapsed and spent three days in Kandy Hospital.

Anura's loyalty to his friends, his reticence, natural to him, would have angered his inquisitors and condemned him in their ignorant judgement as a hard-core terrorist. I rang Rohan Guneratna at the IFS to ask him to make enquiries about Anura, in case there was a possibility of saving him. He rang back to say he had heard from a friend of his in army intelligence that Anura had been shot. The army knew that Anura had visited me at the IFS, but they did not suspect me of involvement in the JVP. They suspected Anura and his friend Lal, who had gone into hiding. Rohan ended by saying, 'Richard, I believe an innocent man has been killed.'

With little hope I went to Kandy the next day to make enquiries and find out what had happened to Anura.

> Came to Kandy on a second-class coach, overcrowded. A young porter jumped on to the train as it entered Fort Station to grab me a seat, fighting off passengers who tried to push him out of the way. Horrible journey. The beauty of the mountains was an irrelevance, an aesthetic joy for which there seemed no justification in our circumstances.

Anura's sister's husband, Cyril Pilapitiya – a man who had come down in the world from a supervisory job on a tea estate – gave me a more detailed account at the shanty in Elagola. 'Our neighbours,' he assured me, 'know that Anura was innocent.' He had been reading a newspaper on his bed at the time when the smoke of the burning bus had darkened the sky. All the other young men had run away from the area; only Anura had stayed.

The next morning Pilapitiya and Anura's mother, Seelawathie, came to talk to me at the IFS. Pilapitiya interpreted for Seelawathie, telling me what they had heard from Anura's older brother, Upali, who had survived. The village people, they said, had written letters to the army accusing Anura. One man had owed him money for goods bought from the boutique. While the brothers were walking past the Bowela police station on their way to Kandy, Anura had been recognised by a 'gonebille'. The word 'gonebille' – 'bogeyman' of Sinhala myth – was applied to someone captured by the security forces and compelled, with torture if necessary, to identify supporters of the JVP on the public roads. The informer had to wear a gunnybag – derived from 'gone' – with eyeholes as a hood. As the brothers were reaching the main Colombo to Kandy road, three men in dark-blue T-shirts caught and blindfolded them and dragged them on board a bus. Upali had heard Anura saying that I could vouch for him that he was not in the JVP. One of their abductors had replied, 'Your friends can't help you now.' The army had released Upali, with a caution not to make any enquiries, or 'we might shoot you'. Pilapitiya continued, according to my notes:

> Nobody gave us any news. What we heard from others, Anura was brought to Dangolla wearing only trousers, and with a gunnybag

pulled down over his head. Near the public cemetery there are some houses, so he was taken there by men in civil clothes carrying rifles, seven in number, and they have shown him to the people in those houses close by the cemetery.

He was very thirsty and asked for some water to drink, so the house people have brought water in a glass. Then these fellows have shouted, 'Why should we give water in a glass, get us a coconut shell.' Now Anura's hands are tied, no? And this army fellow has poured the whole coconut shell into Anura's mouth, and a cough has come and some drops of water have fallen on this army man's clothes. Then this man has got angry and beaten Anura in a very bad manner.

They have taken him to five villages, all over, same day: Dangolla, Udabowela, Elagola, Heerassigala, and at last to Bowela. Walking all the way, they have been beating him from behind. Some have seen blood oozing from his heels. In certain places they have taken off the gunnybag and shown him to the people and they have seen his face swollen and bleeding. The soldiers have been saying, 'This is the man who set fire to the Heerassigala bus and the Mulgampola post office,' and then hitting him in front of the people.

Tissa Wijeyeratne, a former Sri Lankan ambassador to France and son of Ceylon's ambassador to Britain after independence, told me in his office near the temple on the same day, 29 December:

> In Colombo the municipal crematorium works all night long. In Ireland the government abhors the violence, here the government is sanctioning what is happening. Ninety-nine per cent of the people in the rural areas approve the beating and killing of JVP suspects. I saw three corpses hung from an electric transformer, multiple injuries, holes in the head. My first reaction was immediate fear, that this could happen to me, not moral horror. A niece of the Prime Minister, a twenty-five-year-old girl, had a heart attack and died on seeing a decapitated body on the road to Kegalla. Four corpses were found hanging from the bridge at Peradeniya, one underneath the other on the same rope.

That night at a dinner party given by Leela Bibile, widow of a university professor, and attended by the Gladstones, I heard a friend of ours, known as Dissa – Professor S.B. Dissanayaka – telling us that the skin of the temple elephant Rajah, who used to carry the Sacred Tooth Relic in the Perahera, had been stuffed by a taxidermist and put in a special room of the Temple of the Tooth, to be worshipped by the people as a bodhisattva on the path close to enlightenment.

Dissa said that he was on a bus coming from Colombo at 6.30 in the morning a few months ago. The driver had slowed down to let the people see a whole lot of bodies of young men and women, recently killed as rigor mortis hadn't set in – they looked fresh and beautiful – he felt he would like to get out and lift them up and embrace them. They were all stripped to the waist, girls as well as boys, and they looked intelligent; he thought they may have been university students; there were no signs of mutilation on their bodies. Women in the bus held up small children so that they could see the dead bodies. No one said a word. There was absolute silence in the bus. 'I wish someone had screamed,' he said. 'Why were they so absolutely silent?'

This reminded me of Ashley Halpé's remark that most writers were struck dumb by what was happening in Sri Lanka. When Dissa went to Lankatilleke, famous for its combined Buddhist and Hindu temple, he saw dismembered bodies lying under a tree on whose branches were hanging arms and hands and legs; and he heard from some boys at a boutique selling gold king coconuts that a dog was eating a human leg behind the boutique. 'Dogs eat the flesh that isn't burnt by the tyres set alight under the corpses that are strewn along the roads at night.'

Major Asoka Amunugama of Amunugama Wallawa received me in the officers' mess of the Sinha Regiment in the bungalow where my father and mother had first lived together after they were married. He was very well bred, and appreciated my saying that the Sinha Regiment was officered by gentlemen. I had begun by enquiring after the health of Colonel Nihal Pelpola, which he told me was improving, and I had inscribed for Amunugama a copy of *The Mirror Wall*. He said he had no information from the army about any killings at Heerassigala, but had indeed heard people around the area all saying that the men involved in the burning of the Mulgampola post office and the Heerassigala bus were dead.

'If you came to me right after he was taken, I might have been able to help, but now I'm afraid it's too late. The best thing to do is to ask his nearest relations to come and see me here tomorrow, or bring them to see me, I'll see them any time, and I'll give them a letter which they can take around the camps like St Sylvester's and Pallekella enquiring about their missing person.

The army isn't doing these killings, it's the vigilante groups, we don't know who they are. The army does kill known JVP men, but not in that way, leaving bodies on the road. In the Sinha Regiment we have our own way of dealing with them under the emergency regulations.'

I wondered if he meant the crematorium? The more horrendous the details of our discussion became, the more the major smiled. He admitted that five to ten per cent of the people who were being killed by the services and the vigilante groups were innocent. 'You can't help that in war,' he said with a very big smile and a laugh, inviting my agreement.

He admitted that he thought a military victory could never solve the political problem of poverty and frustrated youth, and he implied that the government was fully behind the vigilante groups and might have a big problem in getting them under control in the end. He wanted to be helpful, but was restrained by fear of stepping out of line, and warned me of the danger to myself if I tried to interfere. 'An accident might be made to occur,' I suggested, and he agreed with several short laughs and much smiling. My friends, too, could be put in danger, he warned, smiling. 'You'll always get sadistic men in the army and the police.'

I don't think Amunugama smiled because he was amused by the horror, but in order to charm it away from himself. Sri Lankans have developed the most radiant smiles in the world by living in paradise with their demons for more than two millennia. Ashley Halpé told me that smiling at horror is a way people have of saying, 'Isn't it awful, I wish I hadn't to tell you this,' and while they are saying these terrible things they smile to take away the hurt. He said he often caught himself smiling when talking of the atrocities, and felt he ought not to be.

Anuradha Seneviratna, professor of Sinhala at Peradeniya, to whom I was indebted for scholarly advice on my versions of the Mirror Wall poems, thought that things were much better in Sri Lanka than they had been a year before. A minute or two later he told me that his younger son, about fifteen or sixteen years old, had not been able to eat for two days after seeing a dead body burning on a tyre by the road, and could not sleep in a room on his own; but after seeing a number of dead bodies he had became used to them and no longer got upset. A number of Anuradha's students had been taken by the army. 'The parents came to see me, wanting me to help, but what could I do? If I tried to save them or get them out, I might put myself and my own family in danger.'

Gamini came to Kandy and stayed with me at the cheap Olde Empire

Hotel near the Temple of the Tooth over the New Year holiday, during which the precincts of the temple were lit up with as many coloured electric lights as I remember seeing in Colombo to welcome the Duke of Gloucester when he brought the throne of the last king of Kandy back to the country in 1934.

> Monday, 1st January 1990 – Olde Empire Hotel, Kandy
> Today the President of the Social Democratic Republic of Sri Lanka is taking a step on the way to becoming a god-king, marking the first anniversary of his rule by exposing himself to the masses on the balcony of the Octagon, built for the last king of Kandy to watch the procession of elephants in the Perahera.

I met Gamini's mother at the house where she was working in another woman's kitchen near Pilligala. She never stopped smiling. Gamini told her that I would try to obtain a visa for him to come to Ireland so that he could send her enough money for her to live without a job.

On our way through Peradeniya, as the Delica van we had hired was turning a corner where drivers would normally stop to let tourists take pictures of the university across the valley of the Mahaweli, I saw a skeleton blackened by the smoke of the tyre on which the body had been burnt. Our driver said it had been lying there for two or three days. The sun of resplendent Sri Lanka shone through the ribcage, which crows and dogs had picked clean.

Not long before, on the other side of the river, a young man acting on orders of the JVP, before it was crushed, had shot dead the bursar of the university as he was walking from his office to his car. The killer rode away on a bicycle and was never caught. That night a squad of army men 'went on the rampage' through the nearby village of Rajawatte, seizing a large number of boys who were not quick enough to escape. Among these were schoolmates of Arosha and Anura.

The next morning people coming to work at the university saw fourteen severed heads, with faces smashed to make them unrecognisable, arranged on the parapet wall surrounding the lotus pond – emblem of the Buddha's teaching – at a crossroads in the centre of this beautiful campus. Fourteen naked torsos were found in a secluded part of the campus where they had been butchered. Clothes of the victims had been reduced to a heap of ashes to prevent identification. The execution squad had spread a rumour that one of the victims had been forced to do the butchering before he himself was shot and beheaded.

A few hours after I had pressed Rohan Guneratna to try to obtain more information about the fate of Anura, he replied that a major in military intelligence had instructed him, 'Tell your friend Murphy that Anura is non-existent.'

On my last, short visit to Sri Lanka in December 1991 I was disheartened by the absence of the Gladstones. Premadasa had ordered David to leave the country because he had witnessed and complained of cheating by the president's supporters in a local election. And I felt that the country I loved was being changed for the worse by a president who had ordered his staff and the media he controlled to modify the country's name. The English spelling of the honorific 'Sri', which some foreigners, especially Americans, tend to pronounce as 'Siri', a word that means 'beautiful', had changed in the *Daily News* to 'Shri', as in 'shriek'. I was told that 'sh' in English is written in Sinhala as a different form of the letter *S*. Premadasa had acted on the advice of an astrologer who had advised that the aspirated letter was more auspicious.

In Ireland in 1993 I read a report that a boy on a bicycle at a May Day parade in Colombo had ridden wobbling out of the crowd behind the cavalcade and had blown himself up with a mighty bomb, killing the president and many of his entourage. Soon after this, at home and abroad, a beautiful sound was restored to the country's name.

Gamini had been granted an Irish visa for life on the strength of his character, his brotherly links with Nimal, Arosha, Darrell and Sathiya, and the danger of his being abducted. With a change of government in Sri Lanka, human rights were less abused, and my wards were able to improve the lives of their mothers and siblings, buying or building them houses, visiting them from time to time. Darrell, with the help of his wife Ethna, from Cahirciveen in Kerry, redeemed his twin sisters, Diana and Judith, from an orphanage in Colombo and placed them as day girls at a private school in Dublin. None of the five that I brought to Ireland encountered racist hostility until the end of the millennium, by which time our country had become multiracial with an economy powered by multinationals.

My mother came to Ireland in July 1992 to attend the wedding of her brother Jack's granddaughter, Lucy Ormsby, at Cong, followed by a reception with dancing until late at night in a marquee on the front lawn at Milford. The wedding took her mind off her plans for her own funeral, except to remind everyone that she wanted, after her brain had been examined, a burial in Clifden and a party at the castle that Chris had restored on the shore of Lough Corrib: 'I want you all to enjoy yourselves at the party.'

She was almost ninety-four, and though she addressed me in an order of words that never began with my name but a variable combination of 'Ted–Mary–Liz–Chris–I mean Rick – you know how forgetful I am', her memory of the remote past revived with clarity when she recognised places. The next day we drove to Salruck – relations, family history and dogs – and from there to Rosroe. As we paused on the quay in front of the house I had occupied in 1951, now enlarged into a youth hostel, my mother asked: 'Do you remember, you put a candle lighting in the window of your cottage, and I said "Why are you putting a candle there?" You said "We might need a light to guide us back to the quay in the pookaun." I was so surprised because it was broad daylight when we went out, but by the time we got home, after a terrifying ordeal tacking against the wind and tide in the pitch darkness of the Killary under the mountains, the only light to guide us was the candle.'

Before returning with Mary and Gerry to Highfield in Northumberland, where they had given her a cottage in their garden for the rest of her life, my mother said, 'You wouldn't write a diary of our visit for the wedding at Milford, would you, and send me a copy? I'll never remember all the things that have happened.'

The following April 1993, on her last visit to Ireland, we had a row at my house in Dublin and I lost my temper – impossible to remember what it was about. My mother was chipping with her voice all day at the foundation of my patience till the walls of good manners and reason collapsed, letting in and out a storm of anger. At supper we made it up. When I went to kiss her goodnight, she came to the door in her nightie, and confessed, in a wistful tone of admiration and disappointment: 'Do you know, Daddy never lost his temper with me, he never got cross. I was very angry with him once, and he didn't get angry whatever I said, so I threw a glass of water in his face, and do you know, even that didn't make him lose his temper.'

The family legend that Aunt Bella had cut me out of her will because I had kicked her at the Royal Hibernian Hotel was proved false when I found among my mother's papers at Highfield in July 1993 the last codicil to Bella's will. Leaving £100 each to Mary, Christopher and our cousins on the Mulvany side, Betty and Dick, it was signed and dated three weeks before I was born.

On 22 July, after telling me to pour out the tea in her sunroom, my mother was rambling through the garden calling 'Sooty, Sooty, Sooty' for her cat, which had strayed because she insisted on leaving all the doors open for Sooty to come and go. The cat killed at least one blue tit and a mouse every day, but this serial killing was excused on the grounds that there were a lot of murderers in the world, and poor Sooty had a very unhappy time, she was nearly starved. 'Sooty doesn't like you,' she said, 'Sooty doesn't like men.'

My present for my mother's ninety-fifth birthday, on 16 September 1993, was an A3-sized album containing family photographs – her childhood and wedding in Scotland, our days in Ceylon and at Milford – greatly enlarged. This helped her to revive memories and share them with me on my short visits to Highfield, or more frequently on the phone. I was in Ireland when Grania, her granddaughter, and Grania's husband, Hugh Cavendish, gave her a party at Holker Hall at Morecambe Bay between Cartmel Priory and Furness Abbey. This was attended, together with their eight spouses, by four of our mother's five children, her seven grandchildren and at least five great-grandchildren.

In the McFarlin Library at Tulsa University, where I held a post as visiting poet in 1994, manuscripts of the novel that Patricia had begun to write at Lake Park in 1957 caught the interest of George Gilpin and Hermione de Almeida, who edited and wrote an introduction to *Playing the Harlot, or Mostly Coffee*. This *roman-à-clef*, containing recognisable likenesses of Conor Cruise O'Brien, Philip Larkin and me, was published by Virago in 1996, with a launch that Emily and I attended at the Shelbourne Hotel. The book received good reviews and sold more than three thousand copies.

On 13 February 1994 at Tulsa I noted:

> Early this morning I met Paddy Kavanagh in a dream. He was sitting alone at a bar, although it was crowded, and he seemed to be in a mood of meditative benevolence. He didn't scowl at me but smiled. I had encountered his good nature in his poetry more than in meeting him on a few occasions in bars. Here, now, I felt in the dream, is the Kavanagh who inspired devotion in his disciples at McDaid's; and I wished I had brought a copy of his *Collected Poems* for him to inscribe for Emily. I remembered how he had frightened her in the car driven by her mother from Dublin to Inishkeen, when she was six years old, by calling her 'a little baysht', but I had forgiven him. On our first meeting forty-four years ago he

had defrauded me of ten shillings. But now I bore no grudge, and gladly agreed when he asked me to give him a lift to the west coast of Ireland, where we were soon climbing a penitential cliff on our hands and knees. Long ago, when he complained to me that Dublin was a wretched place where he was ruining his life, I had urged him to leave the city and live on his farm in the country.

'I know I should do that, get away from here altogether. This rotten place is killing me, and I love the country, but there are too many ghosts in my village, and I'm afraid of them. I can't live with all the ghosts that would haunt me in Monaghan.' He must have mentioned this conversation to Patricia, who told me that Paddy had said, 'It's all right for Murphy to live in Cleggan, because he's a Protestant, so they can't get at him the way they could get at me if I went back to Inishkeen.' On another occasion he had told her, 'Murphy has technique, but that's all, and it's not enough.'

Now in this morning's dream, as I was waking up, Paddy was in a sublime mood, free of rancour, inspired by the country we had reached at the end of our journey: but he couldn't wait, because he had to get back to Dublin, where he would be meeting Patricia among the dead.

When I spoke on the phone to Eilís Dillon, poet, novelist and friend, at a hospital in Dublin and told her that I had dreamed last night of meeting Paddy Kavanagh in a benign mood, free of rancour, she replied in a faraway voice that still had the strength to carry her wit, 'That can't be right.' Then she asked, 'What are you writing?' 'Memoirs.' With generous conviction she replied, 'Good!'

Thanks to Eilís I had met Darcy O'Brien, the novelist son of two Hollywood stars, George O'Brien and Marguerite Churchill; Darcy had brought me to Tulsa. The friendship, wit and hospitality of Darcy and his wife Suzanne sustained me on long visits to the university, where they urged me to write memoirs. Every friend of theirs, and all Darcy's former students, were shocked when he died suddenly in March 1998, aged fifty-eight, shortly before his book, *The Hidden Pope*, about John Paul's lifelong friendship with a Polish Jew, was published. And thanks to Darcy, Suzanne and Sidney Huttner, curator of the Special Collections at the McFarlin Library, not only were Patricia's and my papers housed there but the library agreed in 1994 to acquire my mother's archive. When I rang my mother from Tulsa to let her know that a reception would soon be held at the library to mark the acquisition of her documents, she said, 'Tell them I'd like to come to the reception and die at it.'

Back in Dublin in August 1994 I heard that a carved stone cross on High Island had disappeared from above the south-east landing place. A photograph of my father sitting beside that cross in 1964 had been kept by my mother at her bedside since he had died. When I told her of the theft over the phone on my sixty-seventh birthday, she replied, 'Nothing is safe. What are you doing about it?'

'The gardaí and Interpol and the FBI will all be informed by the National Museum of Ireland, and a publicity campaign in Europe and America organised to recover it.'

'Who does it belong to?'

'The state, under the Ancient Monuments Act, since before you were born. The stone may be worth £100,000 on the international art market, but as it has been photographed and drawn by archaeologists it can be identified if put up for sale. If a tourist has stolen it for his garden it may never be found.'

I had been disheartened by its loss, making phone calls, talking too much, not writing a word. The stone had kept its Celtic Christianised phallic rectitude for more than one thousand years, preserved by the adoration of women and men, or at least by their respect. Three different signs of the cross – Greek, Celtic and Lorraine – were carved upon three of its weatherworn faces. It could only have been taken by a man.

A few days later Feicín Mulkerrin, who had loved and lived within sight of High Island all his life, ferried and guided a search party of gardaí that discovered the cross. It had been hidden above a cove from which it could have been lowered into a boat. Feicín was to succeed me in 1998 as the island's guardian owner.

Tim Robinson, the polymath author of *Stones of Aran*, had drawn the cross and was glad to hear of its recovery undamaged. He said he had come, with reluctance, to the conclusion that replicas will have to replace the stones on sites that are open to visitors, even though the value of the original is lost as soon as it is removed from the place where it had stood since it was carved. I told him that Michael Herity, the archaeologist, had consoled himself, on a phone line from Glencolumcille, by saying 'Well, the cross has been documented.' Tim said archaeologists believe 'their documentation becomes all the more interesting if the thing they have documented no longer exists'.

In *Space, Time and Connemara*, Tim described High Island in words that express my farewell feelings: 'The sea-sanctuary best suited to more turbulent spirits.'

On the phone at Christmas my mother had asked me her age, and when I said ninety-six, she replied, 'Too old to be alive. I'd like to be killed – it's not much fun dying slowly. Do you remember those lovely days when we went to church at Easter?'

'Yes, at Canterbury.'

'No, in Dublin.' Then I realised she was mistaking me for my father, who had died nearly thirty years ago. 'At St Patrick's where we heard Bach's *St Matthew Passion*, and that lovely church, what was it called?'

'St Ann's?'

'St Ann's, where we heard the *Messiah*.'

It was hard for her to die as she never wanted to lose control – of the family or herself; seldom could she relax her hyperactive attention. One nurse after another came and went, worn out by her demands. A nurse reported to Mary, 'After Lady Murphy had made me pull up thirty-four flowering dandelions on a short walk through the wood, because they were weeds, I knew what it must have felt like to have been a native servant in Rhodesia or Ceylon.'

Every evening at six o'clock Mary arranged for her to drink a glass of champagne. On one of these occasions she had said, 'Sooty is the only friend I have.' But on another she had said to Mary, 'I feel you've done everything for me, and Gerry has been a saint.'

The last time I saw my mother was between Christmas and New Year, when Emily came with me to Highfield. My mother remembered to ask Emily, whom she loved, about Theodora and Caspar. Now, when she walked from her bedroom to her high chair by the fire in the drawing room, trying not to need the arms of her nurses, Shirley Nicholson and Anne Benboe, she looked like a weathered leaning statue. She had lost neither mind nor willpower, which the nurses said was all that was keeping her alive. Her prevailing mood had become benign, as if she had decided not to be cross about dying and to make a good impression. She still wanted her children gathered around her, keeping her alive by remaining under her control. But mercifully that control had become as gentle as it was in the happiest moments of our childhood.

Each morning our cousin Anne Ormsby, now a deaconess aged eighty-two, read prayers in my mother's bedroom and Liz read her a psalm. On the quilt lay another stray adopted cat, a tabby she had called Tigger, while Sooty slept on her pillow. I thanked her for giving me the family papers that she had kept in perfect order, enabling me to write memoirs in which she would be a dominant presence. Her quick reply was, 'I wish you would hurry up and finish them before I die. I'd like to read what you're going to write.' This brought back one of her frequent sayings at Milford – 'You should always finish something you have started: otherwise you might get into a bad habit of starting things that you never finish' – a directive that has helped me to finish this book.

At champagne time on New Year's Eve she was holding my left hand in her right, not wanting to let go, her hand much warmer than mine. 'Let me warm your hand in mine,' she gently commanded, and for half an hour rubbed my palm with her thumb, her eyes almost closed with weariness, the bones visible under blotched and shrivelled skin. When Mary came to show her a bowl of hyacinths bursting out of a bed of primroses and said, 'Look at the hyacinths, Mummy, flowering before New Year's Day!' our mother poked a finger into the clay and replied, 'They look lovely, darling, but give them a little water or else they'll die.'

As my mother continued to wake up each morning and prove the nurses wrong in their nightly prediction that she was 'slipping away and cannot last more than a few hours', I went home to Dublin, keeping in touch by phone.

'Where are you? Are you coming to see me?' Her voice came slowly and painfully. 'Yes,' I told her, for I knew she would like to have all five of her children holding her hands and her feet as she uttered her last words, remembering how our father had died in our presence.

'Come soon!'

'I'll do my best,' I replied, but Gerry advised me not to attempt it, with gales in Ireland and snow on the moors in Northumberland. 'Come soon,' she repeated, using the imperative, her favourite mood, for the last time in my hearing.

On Saturday 28 January 1995 Shirley informed me that my mother had sunk into a deep sleep late the previous night, having told the nurses she could see a bright light in the room and hear her mother and her brother Jack and her husband calling from outside. She had asked the nurses to come with her on the journey, and Shirley had replied, 'I'm sorry, Lady Murphy, but it's not our time to go.' With her last recorded words my mother had tried to persuade them: 'Well, its dark outside. Can't you come part of the way?' And Shirley had replied, 'We'll come part of the way, but you'll have to take the last steps on your own.'

That night Mary rang at 10.25 to tell me that she had died while Chris, Liz and Edward were in her room and the two cats were lying, the black at her head and the tabby at her feet. Over the next few days I made arrangements for the funeral at Clifden on Saturday 4 February. The church where my grandfather, Canon Richard Murphy, had preached, had been reduced to half its size in 1961 after the slates were ripped off its roof by 'Hurricane Debbie'.

The finest day of the whole winter was the day of my mother's funeral, when the sun shone and the wind held its breath. Even the ocean fell calm. By the time I got to Clifden with Dennis O'Driscoll and Julie O'Callaghan, the evening before the funeral, my sisters had filled the church with flowers. There I met the gravediggers, who had placed the coffin on a bier of trestles so high in the church that it seemed ready to take off for Heaven, or for a flaming brand to set it on fire. When I queried this bizarre elevation, they fetched a trolley from the hospital, which, at the crux of the funeral, Chris, Edward and I were able to draw down the aisle behind the four clergymen who officiated. As the coffin was passing Mary Coyne she stretched out her hand and touched it.

One hundred and fifty people filled the little church: family and friends from Milford and Salruck, from Highfield and Holker, from Kilmaine, Oughterard, Roundstone, Cleggan, Inishbofin, Kylemore, Goleen and Killala, from Galway, Dublin, London, Harare, Colombo and Kandy. At the climax, instead of Chopin's *Marche funèbre*, which 'Mummy hated', a Kodály Quartet recording of the *poco adagio, cantabile* movement from Haydn's 'Emperor' Quartet filled the church with music that was the source of the tune for 'Glorious Things of Thee Are Spoken', sung at our parents' wedding and their funerals and at the voice trial in 1937 for Canterbury Cathedral choir.

At the door of the church grandsons and great-grandsons lifted the coffin off the trolley and carried it on their shoulders. My father's grave, twenty yards from the door of his father's church, had been reopened and we stayed until the grave was filled. I was holding Theodora in my arms, a three-year-old with my mother's commanding and lively temperament. She watched in absolute stillness and silence. That afternoon, on the beach at Omey, Theodora, who liked her dolls to perform in plays that she made up, re-enacted the burial, digging a grave with a rod of kelp to show her younger cousin Isabella what had happened to Great-granny. Emily overheard her saying, 'Aren't we lucky, Isabella, that we're not old: it'll be a long time before we have to die.'

After the funeral, one hundred and forty of the mourners came to lunch at the Abbeyglen Castle Hotel, a building that had once been an orphanage for Protestant girls. Our mother adored parties and had told us she wanted her funeral to be a celebration. It was.

On returning to Dublin I received a fax from a bookseller in Dalkey informing me, 'Richard – *Afterlife* by Updike now in stock.'

Charles Monteith, my friend for forty-nine years, died on 9 May 1995 in his Maida Vale flat in London of a massive heart attack. A woman who was cleaning the flat that afternoon heard him fall and, panicking, ran out for help, but forgot to bring a key and couldn't get in again; then she asked someone to call the police, who broke in the door. It was too late to resuscitate him. Rosemary Goad, an old friend and director of Faber, said on the phone that he would not have wanted to be resuscitated to a life in which he could have done none of the things he enjoyed. And Charles did enjoy his life.

Digging on High Island in 1997 Georgina Scally and other archaeologists found the graves of seven hermits and removed a skeleton to Queen's University, Belfast for a day of judgement by scientists. The man had injured his neck by carrying heavy weights, probably stones, on his head. According to the annals, Gormgall, the last Galway saint, died on the island in 1018. A few young men on the mainland tried to stop the digging on the grounds that it was violating the dead. In defence of the diggers I argued that they showed respect by discovering those graves under the debris of centuries, thereby gaining knowledge of the hermits' lives. The bones were to be buried again in their carved stone coffins with the blessing of a priest. But a spokesman for the protestors replied, 'They should not have dug up those graves without permission from the families.'

More than twenty years after Patricia's death, Mary said, 'I very much liked her, although she was impossible. I would sooner call Patricia back to life and have a bottle of wine with her than almost anyone else.'

I met Ted Hughes in London for the last time on Thursday 17 September 1998. He had said on the phone from Devon that he would be at the Connaught Hotel in London at three o'clock, and there he was, sitting in the left-hand corner of the lounge on the left of the lobby, facing the entrance, when I arrived a few minutes late.

We had met only twice since he had been appointed Poet Laureate in 1984. As I approached he put away a copy of his translation of Racine's *Phèdre* in which he had been altering words that he had revised since its publication. Nearly three hours later, when we were leaving, he inscribed it with his 'Love as ever' and a cryptic Yorkshire proverb that still puzzles me: 'bout's bare, but it's easy'. I was going to see the play that night.

Ted looked haggard but undefeated, and quite unspoilt by the huge celebrity of *Tales from Ovid* and *Birthday Letters*. He complained of a chronic resurgence of shingles in the aftermath of a serious illness, affecting, indeed almost blinding, his right, dominant eye, with severe irritation in the eyelid, and resulting in itching all over his scalp and sores on his forehead. I had not noticed the sores because he was sitting with his back to a window, from which the glare made his face at times almost invisible.

He talked fast and at great length, with warm ebullience, ranging over many topics, such as the benefit of wine to keep the hearts of people our age ticking. I told him that after twenty years of total abstinence I had begun drinking a glass of red wine at dinner last year, when I reached seventy. 'Two glasses,' he said, 'is the amount one should drink.'

Then he surprised me by saying he had spoken about my notebooks to Faber, and he urged me to stay with the house that had published five volumes of my poetry between 1963 and 1989. But since the retirement of Charles Monteith, the interest at Faber in either my poetry or my memoirs had been marginal. When I asked Ted whether I should let Bloodaxe publish my *Collected Poems*, he said: 'Going to Bloodaxe from Faber would be like leaving the Brigade of Guards to join a Territorial Regiment.'

So I asked, 'What about the Oxford University Press?'

Ted paused before he replied: 'Salvation Army.'

It wasn't until we were leaving that he let me know why he had chosen for us to meet at the Connaught Hotel.

'I sat in this chair in this corner on my thirty-second birthday.'

'Was that in August 1962?'

'August 17th. Sylvia was sitting where you are, with her mother next to her, and a woman who was a mentor of Sylvia's on the other side. This woman sensed there was something troubling us, and said, to brush it aside, "None of us will remember that we were sitting here in this corner of the Connaught Hotel in thirty years' time."'

That gathering had occurred three weeks before Ted and Sylvia arrived together to stay with me in Cleggan.

Six weeks after he and I embraced at the door of a black taxi that would take him from the Connaught to the train for Devon – my last words to him were 'Stay alive!' – I heard on the lunchtime news in Ireland that he had died.

One afternoon, when I was walking around the side of Emily's house in South Africa, I heard Caspar, my three-year-old grandson, yelling at his sister Theodora, who was six; and, because I thought he was disturbing the neighbours, as I turned the corner to come face to face with him I put a finger to my lips and said, 'Sh!'

Proving he had no feebler spirit than mine when I kicked my awesome Aunt Bella at his age, he replied on the spot, 'I don't like having you as my grandfather.'

When my sister Mary and I were talking on the phone about the title of this memoir, shortly before it was finished, Mary said, 'You should call it "A Conventional Rebel" because that's what you've always been. But I don't want to read about your past.'

About the Author

Born at Milford House near Kilmaine, County Mayo in 1927, Richard Murphy spent five of his early childhood years in Ceylon, now Sri Lanka. Educated from the age of eight at boarding schools in Ireland and England, including the Canterbury Cathedral Choir School, the King's School, Canterbury and Wellington College, he gained a scholarship to Oxford at the age of seventeen and studied English under C.S. Lewis. Between 1951, when he won the Æ Memorial Award, and 1980, when he moved to Dublin, he lived mostly in Connemara, but with long interludes in London, Crete, Paris and Roundwood, County Wicklow. During the 1960s he sailed a Galway hooker ferrying tourists on fishing trips between Cleggan and Inishbofin. On and off since 1971 he has been a visiting poet at nine American universities.

His poetry collections published by Faber include *Sailing to an Island* (1963; Poetry Book Society Choice), *The Battle of Aughrim* (1968), *High Island* (1974) and *The Price of Stone* (1985; Poetry Book Society recommendation). *The Mirror Wall* (Bloodaxe, Wolfhound and Wake Forest, 1989), versions of ancient Sinhala songs from Sri Lanka, won the Poetry Book Society Translation Award in Britain. His *Collected Poems* was published by the Gallery Press in 2000. His memoir *The Kick* (Granta Books, 2002, hardback; 2003, paperback, entitled *The Kick: a life among writers*) was acclaimed by John Montague and Declan Kiberd in the *Irish Times*, by John Banville in the *New York Review of Books*, by Ciaran Carson in the *Guardian*, by Karl Miller in the *Spectator*, and by Ruth Padell in the *Literary Review*. All his books have appeared in the US, from publishers including Knopf, Harper & Row, Granta and Wake Forest University Press. In 1997 he moved to South Africa to live near his daughter Emily and her children.

Since 2007 Richard Murphy has been living in a remote rural area of the Kandy district of Sri Lanka, where he completed work on his collection *The Pleasure Ground: poems, 1952–2012*. This volume, written with support from the Arts Council of Ireland and published jointly by the Lilliput Press in Ireland and Bloodaxe Books in England, received the summer 2013 Special Commendation of the Poetry Book Society. His most recent book, combining prose and verse, is called *In Search of Poetry*, and was published by the Clutag Press in May 2017.

Index